Whitehall and the Jews is the most comprehensive study to date of the British response to the plight of European Jewry under Nazism. It contains the definitive account of immigration controls on the admission of refugee Jews to the United Kingdom, and reveals the doubts and dissent that lay behind British policy.

British self-interest consistently limited humanitarian aid to Jews. Refuge was severely restricted during the Holocaust, and little attempt made to save lives. Louise London nonetheless brings out the compassionate side of Whitehall, and the real concerns of individual mandarins. Certain officials and ministers within the government were responsive to arguments for more generous policies towards the Jews, and the government did permit some admissions on a purely humanitarian basis. After the war, the British government delayed announcing whether refugees would obtain permanent residence, reflecting the government's aim of avoiding long-term responsibility for large numbers of homeless Jews. The balance of state self-interest against humanitarian concern in refugee policy is an abiding theme of *Whitehall and the Jews*, one of the most important contributions to the understanding of the Holocaust and Britain yet published.

LOUISE LONDON is uniquely qualified to write this book. Herself the daughter of Jewish refugees, she combines historical knowledge with considerable legal experience as a solicitor specialising in immigration law. She has published and lectured widely on British immigration controls and refugees, and has taught at Royal Holloway and University College London. *Whitehall and the Jews* is her first book.

Whitehall and the Jews, 1933–1948

British immigration policy, Jewish refugees and the Holocaust

Louise London

To Jonny
with love
Connie
11/3/03.

CAMBRIDGE
UNIVERSITY PRESS

PUBLISHED BY THE PRESS SYNDICATE OF THE UNIVERSITY OF CAMBRIDGE
The Pitt Building, Trumpington Street, Cambridge, United Kingdom

CAMBRIDGE UNIVERSITY PRESS
The Edinburgh Building, Cambridge CB2 2RU, UK
40 West 20th Street, New York NY 10011–4211, USA
477 Williamstown Road, Port Melbourne, VIC 3207, Australia
Ruiz de Alarcón 13, 28014 Madrid, Spain
Dock House, The Waterfront, Cape Town 8001, South Africa

http://www.cambridge.org

First published 2000
Reprinted 2001 (twice), 2002
First paperback edition 2003

Typeset in Plantin 10/12pt [CE]

A catalogue record for this book is available from the British Library

Library of Congress cataloguing in publication data
London, Louise.
Whitehall and the Jews, 1933–1948: British immigration policy, Jewish refugees and the Holocaust / Louise London.
p. cm.
Includes bibliographical references.
ISBN 0 521 63187 4 (hb)
1. Refugees, Jewish – Great Britain. 2. Refugees, Jewish – Government policy – Great Britain. 3. Holocaust, Jewish (1939–1945) – Foreign public opinion, British. 4. Public opinion – Great Britain. 5. Great Britain – Emigration and immigration.
I. Title.
DS135.J67 1999E5L66 1999
325.41′089′924–dc21 99–24282 CIP

ISBN 0 521 63187 4 hardback
ISBN 0 521 53449 6 paperback

Transferred to digital printing 2003

To my mother and father

Lucie London (née Meissner)
born Vienna, 1918

and Heinz London
born Bonn, 1907, died Oxford, 1970

Contents

Illustrations

Preface

My parents came to England as Jewish refugees. My father delayed his departure from Nazi Germany only to complete his Breslau Ph.D degree. He arrived in Oxford in early 1934 to join the group of refugee low temperature physicists led by Franz Simon at the University's Clarendon Laboratory. My mother came from Vienna in March 1939 to start a job as a domestic servant in a private home in Bedford. They first met in Birmingham at a party celebrating VE Day and married the following year. They went to live at Harwell in Berkshire, near the government research establishment where my father worked, while my mother brought up their four children. I grew up hardly aware of my parents' past hardships. They explained that they had been persecuted by the Nazis because they were Jews. I heard about some of the less pleasant aspects of their experience as refugees in England. But neither of my parents harboured resentment over the decision to intern them in 1940. I heard them express only gratitude to the British government. I assumed that the government had welcomed Jewish refugees with open arms and that their acceptance as permanent residents had been automatic. It was only in 1985, when the British government introduced a visa requirement to stem the flow of Tamil asylum seekers from Sri Lanka, that I first became interested in how the government had responded to my parents' generation of refugees. By then I was a solicitor specialising in immigration cases. I learned that in 1938 the Home Office had introduced visa requirements to exclude refugee Jews. My curiosity increased. Further reading made me realise that key aspects of British policy towards European Jews in the Nazi period had yet to be explored. The decision to write this book was the result.

I gratefully acknowledge financial assistance for my research from a number of sources. My doctoral studies were funded by Queen Mary and Westfield College of the University of London, the Economic and Social Research Council, the Central Research Fund of the University of London and the Memorial Foundation for Jewish Culture in New York. The project of writing this book received funding from the Oxford

Centre for Postgraduate Hebrew Studies, the Harold Hyam Wingate Foundation and the British Academy.

I thank for their assistance the institutions and staff of the BBC Written Archives Centre, Birmingham University Library, the Board of Deputies of British Jews, the Bodleian Library, the British Library, Cambridge University Library, the Foreign Office Library, the Imperial War Museum, the Institute of Historical Research, the Institute of Jewish Affairs, the Library of the Religious Society of Friends, Liverpool University Library, the National Sound Archive, the Parkes Library of the University of Southampton, the Rothschild Archive, the Wiener Library, the library of University College London, the Archives Nationales in France and, in the United States, the American Jewish Joint Distribution Committee, Columbia University Library, the Franklin D. Roosevelt Library, the Leo Baeck Institute, the Library of Congress, the New York Public Library, the US Holocaust Memorial Museum, the US National Archives and the YIVO Institute of Jewish Research.

I am particularly indebted to the staff of the Public Record Office at Kew for their kindness and assistance. I received valuable advice from Pat Andrews and Richard Ponman of the Cabinet Office Historical Section. I thank the Home Office Departmental Records Officer for granting access to certain closed records. I never managed to gain access to closed records on policy concerning refugee immigration. Many of these were eventually transferred to the Public Record Office, but too late, so far as this book is concerned, for it to be possible to do more than include a few additional references.

Crown copyright material in the Public Record Office (PRO) is reproduced by permission of Her Majesty's Stationery Office. The Neville Chamberlain papers are quoted by permission of Birmingham University Library; the Rothschild Archives by permission of Sir Evelyn de Rothschild; papers in the possession of the Home Office by permission of the Home Office Departmental Records Officer.

My special thanks go to the many former refugees, refugee workers, civil servants and others who kindly spared the time to answer my questions and share their experiences with me. Their names appear in the list of interviews at the end of the book.

For the correct identification of illustration 4 (p. 120) I am most grateful to Mr Michael Wellman, who was himself on this transport and knew three of the older boys in the photo.

I wish to express my gratitude to certain people who have given me particular assistance in taking this project forward. My supervisors, David Cesarani, George Peden, Ken Young and Graham Zellick, gave support and guidance. Tony Kushner offered encouragement and advice. Vernon Bogdanor, Eva Hoffman and Peter Prince kindly commented on an early draft of the book. My friend Sara Bershtel generously spared the time to offer detailed comments on the typescript, for which I am deeply grateful. I also wish to thank a large number of my friends and members of my family for much kind help and encouragement.

My most heartfelt thanks go to Andrew McDonald, my husband. This book would not have been finished without Andrew's endlessly patient support and his commitment to its completion. I am especially grateful for his forthright and searching comments on draft chapters. I am also greatly indebted to him for giving me time to write, especially in the final stages of working on the typescript, when our daughter Juliet was absorbing much of my attention. Lastly, thank you to Juliet, the sweetest little girl there ever was.

Abbreviations

AAC	Academic Assistance Council
ADAC	Aliens Deportation Advisory Committee
AJDC	American Jewish Joint Distribution Committee
ANJSC	Aliens and Nationality Joint Standing Committee
BCRC	British Committee for Refugees from Czechoslovakia
Bermuda Report	'Report to the Governments of the United States and the United Kingdom from their delegates to the Conference on the Refugee Problem held at Bermuda, April 19–29, 1943', 29 April 1943, PRO FO 371/36725, W6711/6711/48
CAW	Sub-committee on the Treatment of Aliens in Time of War
CBF	Central British Fund for the Relief of German Jewry
CCJR	Central Council for Jewish Refugees
CGJ	Council for German Jewry
CID	Committee of Imperial Defence
CO	Colonial Office
COM	Committee on Overseas Manpower
CRTF	Czech Refugee Trust Fund
DO	Dominions Office
FO	Foreign Office
GEC	Germany Emergency Committee (of the Religious Society of Friends)
GJAC	German Jewish Aid Committee
HO	Home Office
IGC	Intergovernmental Committee on Refugees
IRO	International Refugee Organisation
JFC	Joint Foreign Committee (of the Board of Deputies and the Anglo-Jewish Association)
JRC	Jewish Refugees Committee
JTS	Jews' Temporary Shelter
LCC	London County Council

Long	Breckinridge Long papers, Manuscripts Division, Library of Congress, Washington, DC
MCCG	Movement for the Care of Children from Germany
MEW	Ministry of Economic Warfare
Meynell	Sir Francis Meynell papers, Cambridge University Library
MOLANS	Ministry of Labour and National Service
MP	Member of Parliament
NC	Neville Chamberlain papers
NCRNT	National Committee for Rescue from Nazi Terror
NJCSR	National Joint Committee for Spanish Relief
Noel-Baker	Lord Noel-Baker papers, Churchill Archives Centre, Churchill College, University of Cambridge
PCD	Passport Control Department
PCO	Passport Control Officer
PRO	Public Record Office
RA	Rothschild Archive, London
SOF	Religious Society of Friends (Quakers)
SPSL	Society for the Protection of Science and Learning
TUC	Trades Union Congress
UNRRA	United Nations Relief and Rehabilitation Administration
USNA	United States National Archives
WJC	World Jewish Congress
WRB	War Refugee Board

For explanation of references in the notes to documents in the Public Record Office, see the list of archives consulted in the bibliography.

1 Introduction

Nazi persecution of European Jews confronted the world with an unprecedented humanitarian challenge. The extraordinary circumstances of the plight of the Jews called for a response that was also out of the ordinary. But countries around the globe resisted the pressure to take special measures to relieve Jewish suffering. The United Kingdom was no exception. It opted for caution and pragmatism, subordinating humanitarianism to Britain's national interest. Nor, when the crisis of the Jews became yet more grave, did the British approach change fundamentally. During the Holocaust, Britain's policy – much of it made in conjunction with the United States government – continued to put self-interest first, leaving minimal scope for humanitarian action.

The rationale for such policies is now seen as highly questionable. Even at the time, however, many believed that greater generosity was possible in British and American policy. Within the United States government, the aspiration that policy should have a humanitarian dimension received its most resolute expression in mid-December 1943, when a select group of senior US Treasury officials met to formulate demands that American refugee policy be taken out of the hands of the State Department, which was hostile to rescue. The Treasury group officials wanted rescue efforts to be given top priority. In the course of their discussions the Treasury group analysed a recent message from the British government, objecting to the recent authorisation by the US Treasury of licences for the remission of funds in connection with a large-scale rescue project. The funds had been raised by American Jewish organisations. Their intended use was to rescue some 70,000 Romanian Jewish deportees in Transnistria, a part of the Soviet Union then occupied by Romania. The fundamental British objection was explained as 'the difficulties of disposing of any considerable number of Jews should they be rescued from enemy-occupied territory'.[1] The

[1] Quoted in J. G. Winant (London) to US State Department, 15 Dec. 1943, USNA 840.51 Frozen Credits 12144, cited in Bernard Wasserstein, *Britain and the Jews of Europe, 1939–1945* (Oxford, 1979), p. 247.

group of Americans felt they were at last seeing the true face of British policy. One US Treasury official, Josiah DuBois, exclaimed, 'Their position is, "What could we do with them if we got them out?" Amazing, most amazing position.' Minutes later, DuBois returned to the British telegram, saying, 'For instance, take the complaint, "What are we going to do with the Jews?" – we let them die because we don't know what to do with them.'[2] The shock Dubois voiced is still palpable. His characterisation of British policy was melodramatic and oversimplified. But his comments pinpoint a key element in the rationale of the British government's approach to Jewish suffering, namely that the problem of what to do with the Jews took precedence over saving them, whether from Nazi persecution or mass murder.

The necessity for such an order of priorities was apparent to the politicians who decided British policy and the officials who upheld it. To make sense of it, at this distance, we must investigate the process which produced British policy. A balanced account needs to track its development in response to each new twist in the predicament of the Jews. It must examine the policy process and the officials and ministers who were responsible for it. It must also give due weight to the context and underlying rationale of British policy towards persecuted Jews.

This book investigates British refugee policy towards European Jewry from 1933 to 1948. During this fifteen-year period, British policy passed through several phases. But, though its emphasis changed as did the details, the principles and preoccupations that guided it remained remarkably constant. The government assessed the question of helping Jews primarily in terms of British self-interest. Humanitarian aid to the Jews was assigned much lower priority than, for example, the maintenance of severe restrictions on alien immigration to the United Kingdom. It was such concerns that created the context for decisions concerning the Jews. Thus, while the particulars of refugee policy varied according to the ever-changing circumstances of the Jews, its limits were defined by self-interest. It follows that the central question for this investigation of British policy-making is this: how did ministers and officials in Whitehall balance their perceptions of national interest against humanitarian considerations?

This study aims to show what Britain's policies towards Jews attempted and what they achieved. It assumes that the British response to the plight of Europe's Jews cannot be understood without an appreciation of the frame of reference within which this issue was perceived. It

[2] Record of meeting on 18 Dec. 1943, Morgenthau Diaries, Franklin D. Roosevelt Presidential Library, Hyde Park, New York, vol. 688II, pp. 84–5.

finds that the plight of the Jews ranked low on the British government's scale of priorities.

The leading scholarly monographs concentrate on the content of British policy towards the Jews, to the comparative neglect of both the context of that policy and its administration. They give insufficient emphasis to the British government's perception of the Jewish problem. They place it at the heart of their studies but neglect to explain that it was not a central preoccupation of the British government. At times, British policy comes across as a series of inexplicable interventions in the fate of the Jews by a succession of indistinguishable bureaucrats and politicians.

The first monograph on British refugee policy was A. J. Sherman's *Island Refuge: Britain and Refugees from the Third Reich, 1933–1939*, which appeared in 1973. Sherman charts the development of policy before the war, devoting most space to the depressing tale of British involvement in international discussions of the refugee problem. Sherman also brings out the important role of Anglo-Jewish leaders in shaping the policy and operation of controls on refugee immigration to the United Kingdom.[3] Bernard Wasserstein's *Britain and the Jews of Europe, 1939–1945*, published in 1979, the leading study of British policy during the Second World War, recounts, in devastating detail, a succession of episodes which demonstrate the ungenerosity of British policy towards the Jews. Much of the book is concerned with the continuing contest over the entry of refugees to Palestine during the war.[4] Martin Gilbert's *Auschwitz and the Allies*, published in 1981, discusses Allied inaction in response to the Holocaust, putting particular emphasis on incomplete comprehension of the true nature of Auschwitz.[5]

By the time these first accounts of British policy were published, the study of refugee policy in the United States was well under way. In 1967 *While Six Million Died* by Arthur Morse appeared, followed in 1968 by David Wyman's *Paper Walls*, the first monograph by a historian. Wyman covered American refugee policy between 1939 and 1941 and demonstrated how the State Department tightened its visa procedures to deny refuge to Jews.[6] Henry Feingold's *Politics of Rescue*, which was published

[3] A. J. Sherman, *Island Refuge: Britain and Refugees from the Third Reich, 1933–1939* (London, 1973).

[4] Wasserstein, *Britain and Jews*; see also Wasserstein, 'The British Government and the German Emigration, 1933–1945', in Gerhard Hirschfeld (ed.), *Exile in Great Britain: Refugees from Hitler's Germany* (London, 1984), pp. 63–81.

[5] Martin Gilbert, *Auschwitz and the Allies* (London, 1981).

[6] Arthur D. Morse, *While Six Million Died: A Chronicle of American Apathy* (New York, 1967); David Wyman, *Paper Walls: America and the Refugee Crisis, 1938–1941* (Amherst, 1968).

in 1970, offered a balanced analysis of the Roosevelt administration's failure to do more to rescue the Jews of Europe. Feingold's study remains important and has been supplemented by further reflections since the first edition.[7] In 1984 Wyman produced a second major book, *The Abandonment of the Jews: America and the Holocaust, 1941–1945*, which documents the making of American policy in exhaustive detail and offers a highly critical assessment of the US government's failure to take more substantial and more urgent action to rescue Jews.[8] In 1987 the most complete study to date of the policy of the US government appeared, Richard Breitman and Alan Kraut's *American Refugee Policy and European Jewry, 1933–1945*.[9] All of these works are valuable for understanding British policy, because the two governments often confronted many of the same questions and in close conjunction with one another.

The approach of this book places it squarely within an emerging tendency in the study of refugee policy: the belief that for a balanced account of the responses of bystanders it is vital to distinguish the centrality of the Jewish experience for Jews themselves from its relative unimportance for the rest of humanity and to locate the response to refugees within its political and institutional context. Breitman and Kraut's study is an outstanding example of this approach.[10] And Feingold's articles on why American Jewry did not put more pressure on President Roosevelt's administration to rescue Europe's Jews show the value of such an approach in the analysis of Jewish responses.[11]

Feingold concludes his book with the suggestion that, by the inter-war period, it was incorrect to assume that nation-states would be prepared to act on the basis of humanitarian concern.[12] British immigration restrictions on refugees reflected not only economic considerations and the concern to control numbers, but also the established policy that the United Kingdom was not a country of immigration. The British position formed part of an international pattern of immigration restriction which

[7] Henry L. Feingold, *The Politics of Rescue: The Roosevelt Administration and the Holocaust 1938–1945* (New Brunswick, NJ, 1970; paperback edn, New York, 1980).

[8] Wyman, *The Abandonment of the Jews: America and the Holocaust, 1941–1945* (New York, 1984).

[9] Richard Breitman and Alan Kraut, *American Refugee Policy and European Jewry, 1933–1945* (Bloomington, 1987).

[10] *Ibid.*; see esp. Introduction, pp. 1–10.

[11] Henry L. Feingold, 'Courage First and Intelligence Second: The American Jewish Secular Elite, Roosevelt and the Failure to Rescue', *American Jewish History* 72 (June 1983), 424–60; Feingold, 'Was There Communal Failure? Some Thoughts on the American Jewish Response to the Holocaust', *American Jewish History* 81 (Autumn 1993), 60–80.

[12] Feingold, *Politics of Rescue*, pp. 329–30.

was already in place before this wave of persecution of the Jews began. Herbert Strauss, in two long essays, has provided a commanding overview of this climate of restriction and its impact on prospective Jewish emigrants from Nazi Germany.[13] Britain resembled other western European countries, such as France, the Netherlands and Belgium, in its determination to operate principally as a country of temporary refuge, not settlement.[14] These countries offered refugees only a conditional welcome. In contrast, other countries, such as the United States, Palestine and the dominions, still saw themselves as countries of immigration and, to the extent that they accepted Jewish refugees, did so on a permanent basis. Notwithstanding this difference, there are suggestive comparisons with the British experience in Wyman's study of the restrictive operation of US visa policy.[15] The record of the Canadian government, which has been documented by Irving Abella and Harold Troper, stands out as particularly ungenerous.[16] But all the democratic countries where Jews sought refuge found ways of manipulating immigration procedures to exclude them. It is all too obvious why Michael Marrus's sweeping survey of twentieth-century responses to refugees is entitled *The Unwanted*.[17]

The international organisations concerned with refugees largely reflected the policies of the governments that controlled them. Tommie Sjöberg's examination of the record of the Intergovernmental Committee on Refugees (IGC) shows how the British and United States governments manipulated the IGC largely for their own ends, especially to deflect humanitarian pressure away from themselves.[18] Claudena M. Skran uses an international relations perspective to evaluate the refugee work of both the League of Nations and the IGC. Skran investigates the connections between the failure of these agencies to do more for refugees and nation-states' intolerance of minorities and ethnic diversity, raising important issues to which we shall return at the end of this book.[19]

[13] Herbert A. Strauss, 'Jewish Emigration from Germany: Nazi Policies and Jewish Responses', (I) and (II), *Leo Baeck Institute Year Book* 25 and 26 (1980 and 1981), 313–61 and 343–409.

[14] Louise London, 'British Immigration Control Procedures and Jewish Refugees, 1933–1939', in Werner E. Mosse (ed.), *Second Chance: Two Centuries of German-Speaking Jews in the United Kingdom* (Tübingen, 1991), pp. 485–518.

[15] Wyman, *Paper Walls*.

[16] Irving Abella and Harold Troper, *None Is Too Many: Canada and the Jews of Europe, 1933–1948* (Toronto, 1983).

[17] Michael Marrus, *The Unwanted: European Refugees in the Twentieth Century* (Oxford, 1985).

[18] Tommie Sjöberg, *The Powers and the Persecuted: The Refugee Problem and the Intergovernmental Committee on Refugees* (Lund, 1991).

[19] Claudena M. Skran, *Refugees in Inter-War Europe: The Emergence of a Regime* (Oxford, 1995).

To escape from the Nazis, resourcefulness and money and support from family, friends and strangers were necessary, but rarely sufficient. Jewish organisations played the major part in organising emigration, raising funds and persuading governments to expand the possibilities of asylum. The organisation that was most active in aiding Europe's Jews, the American Jewish Joint Distribution Committee, has been the subject of two authoritative studies by Yehuda Bauer.[20] In Britain, Anglo-Jewry played the key role in underwriting and facilitating the pre-war admission of Jews.[21] But, as the Nazi trap closed around the Jews, the limited ability of the leaders of Britain's small Jewish community to influence government policy became plain, as Bernard Wasserstein has emphasised.[22] Richard Bolchover's highly critical verdict on Anglo-Jewry's attempts to influence government policy is unsatisfactory, since it does not take sufficient account either of the constraints under which they operated or of their achievements.[23]

The leaders of British Jewry were inhibited from doing more to aid endangered Jews abroad by their own fear of anti-semitism. The fear of stimulating anti-semitism was also a factor in the government's refugee policy. As the leading studies note, both before and during the war home secretaries cited the need to contain the growth of political anti-semitism as a self-evident argument for constraint on the admission of Jewish refugees. Wasserstein notes the tendency of policy to bend with the wind of hostility to refugees, but concludes that 'conscious anti-Semitism should not be regarded as an adequate explanation of official behaviour'.[24] He thus allows that conscious anti-semitism may provide a partial explanation, but he considers other, political factors to be the crucial determinants of British policy.[25]

In British society anti-Jewish hostility typically manifested itself in forms which fell short of political extremism. Indeed, British anti-semitism could coexist with liberal convictions. Tony Kushner, the leading scholar of British anti-semitism, emphasised the ambivalence of British attitudes to Jews and pointed to this ambivalence as the root of Britain's contradictory responses to refugees and the Holocaust.[26]

[20] Yehuda Bauer, *My Brother's Keeper: A History of the American Jewish Joint Distribution Committee 1929–1939* (Philadelphia, 1974); Bauer, *American Jewry and the Holocaust: The American Jewish Joint Distribution Committee 1939–1945* (Detroit, 1981).

[21] London, 'Jewish Refugees, Anglo-Jewry and British Government Policy', in D. Cesarani (ed.), *The Making of Modern Anglo-Jewry* (Oxford, 1990), pp. 163–90.

[22] Bernard Wasserstein, 'Patterns of Jewish Leadership in Great Britain during the Nazi Era', in Randolph L. Braham (ed.), *Jewish Leadership During the Nazi Era: Patterns of Behaviour in the Free World* (New York, 1985), pp. 29–43.

[23] Richard Bolchover, *British Jewry and the Holocaust* (Cambridge, 1993).

[24] Wasserstein, *Britain and Jews*, pp. 351–2. [25] *Ibid.*, p. 353.

[26] Tony Kushner, *The Persistence of Prejudice: Antisemitism in British Society During the*

Scholarship in this field suffers from relative isolation from the mainstream of British history. Perhaps this partly explains the silence surrounding the publication in 1985 of Michael Cohen's *Churchill and the Jews*, which challenges established views of Churchill, arguing that in practice he was far less concerned to aid the Jews than other authors, notably Martin Gilbert, have been prepared to acknowledge.[27] Growing interest in the Holocaust is reflected in the greater attention paid to William D. Rubinstein's *The Myth of Rescue*, published in 1997, which poses pertinent questions, but fails – partly because the argument is not always underpinned by archival evidence – to prove its hypothesis that the democracies could not have saved more Jews.[28]

The conviction on which *Whitehall and the Jews* is based is that the study of British refugee policy needs to take a more comprehensive approach than that adopted in the existing literature. Too often, discussion is confined to the level of counterblasts between those who condemn the alleged inhumanity of British policy and those who seek to defend it and apologise for it. This is partly the outcome of a narrow focus on the detail of policy towards the Jews and a corresponding neglect of the circumstances in which it was made. The belief in the necessity of transcending these limitations is fundamental to this book. It argues that to understand how a nation acted in a time of catastrophe we must take adequate account of the context in which those actions occurred.

Whitehall and the Jews is the fullest exploration of British refugee policy to date. It examines British policy towards the Jews from 1933 to 1948. It places much greater emphasis on the context of policy than previous studies have done. It seeks to investigate the government's position and actions in more depth. Its scope embraces a wider range of departments and it places greater emphasis on the policy process.

Throughout, the book concentrates on the detailed workings of British government and on the small group of individuals who left their mark on British policy. It explores how particular departments, officials

Second World War (Manchester, 1989); Kushner, 'The Paradox of Prejudice: The Impact of Organised Antisemitism in Britain During an Anti-Nazi War', in T. Kushner and K. Lunn (eds.), *Traditions of Intolerance: Historical Perspectives on Fascism and Race Discourse in Britain* (Manchester, 1989), pp. 72–90; Kushner, 'The Impact of British Anti-Semitism, 1939–1945', in Cesarani, *Making Anglo-Jewry*, pp. 191–208; Kushner, *The Holocaust and the Liberal Imagination* (Oxford, 1994); Kushner, 'The Meaning of Auschwitz: Anglo-American Responses to the Hungarian Jewish Tragedy', in D. Cesarani (ed.), *Genocide and Rescue: The Holocaust in Hungary 1944* (Oxford, 1997), pp. 159–78.

27 Michael J. Cohen, *Churchill and the Jews* (London, 1985).

28 William D. Rubinstein, *The Myth of Rescue: Why the Democracies Could Not Have Saved More Jews from the Nazis* (London, 1997).

and ministers responded to the Jews' plight. Often these reactions were triggered by the interventions of Jewish leaders, especially over the operation of immigration controls.

This study deals with refugee policy towards Jews, but does so in a period when Britain had no refugee laws and in which the government was reluctant to formulate specific policies on refugees in general, and unwilling to concede the need for special policies to aid Jews to find refuge.[29] Consequently, an important element in this story is the government's efforts to ensure that the Jewish refugee problem did not compromise concerns to which it attached higher priority.

Chapter 2 outlines the legal and administrative framework of British policy. By the 1930s the United Kingdom's tradition of granting asylum to refugees had been relegated to the background. Still the source of much national pride, the humanitarian tradition had little impact on practice and had been largely superseded. The inter-war system of immigration control contained no trace of any legal obligation to admit refugees. In fact, government policy stringently ruled out the entry of aliens for permanent settlement. Thus, in the period covered by this book, to gain entry alien refugees needed to qualify for entry under the existing immigration law and practice. Failing this, their only hope was that the government would exercise its discretion to treat their case as exceptional.

As far as refugees were concerned, the government consciously avoided articulating clear and comprehensive policies. Intent on preserving sovereignty and freedom of manoeuvre on all aspects of the refugee issue, it operated on the principle that the more policy the United Kingdom had on this problem, the more it would be pushed into responsibility for solving it. Minimising policy on refugees was seen as a way to minimise British involvement in action on refugees. The government was nervous about international action. As late as the year 1938 it hoped that the refugee problem would be disposed of through the efforts and funds of private organisations. The British government never considered trying to solve the Jewish refugee problem nor did it believe that to do so would be in the interests of the United Kingdom.

Jews seeking a haven in the United Kingdom found that persecution alone was no passport to refuge. As the pressure for refuge grew, increasing significance was attached to the refugee's identity, profession

[29] In the years examined here, the term 'potential refugees' denoted persons who remained in territory where they faced Nazi persecution. It was used with particular frequency by British policy-makers to refer to Jews in enemy and enemy-occupied territory. In this book, the term 'refugee policy' is used in a broad, non-legalistic sense, to cover not only policy towards 'actual' refugees, who had already fled abroad, but 'potential' refugees as well.

and ultimate destination. Throughout, obtaining refuge depended on the availability of resources to maintain the applicant. Since the number of refugees in Britain was not allowed to exceed the available financial support, only a fraction of all candidates succeeded in gaining admission.

Britain's policy of operating predominantly as a country of transit for Jewish refugees meant that entrants needed to have prospects of re-emigration. However, the settlement opportunities overseas were limited. Governments outside Europe showed little disposition to accept refugee Jews for settlement. The one exception, the USA, initially admitted many more refugee Jews than Britain. Over the period 1933 to 1945, it allowed in perhaps three times as many. Britain made repeated efforts to persuade the USA to increase its admission of refugees from the United Kingdom. But the Americans would admit Jews for settlement only on their own terms and at their own pace. As for the empire, Whitehall did not envisage doing battle with the dominions or colonies over their reluctance to offer settlement opportunities for refugee Jews. Only in Palestine, which it governed under a mandate from the League of Nations, did Britain allow permanent settlement of Jews. Until 1936 the government facilitated refugee admissions under Palestine's existing immigration procedures. But, thereafter, Arab objections led to a policy of restriction, culminating in Britain's controversial White Paper policy of 1939, which set a ceiling of 75,000 admissions over the next five years, after which Jewish immigration would be permitted only with Arab consent.

The Home Office studiously avoided keeping its own statistics on the highly sensitive issue of Jewish immigration to Britain. This saved it from having to give precise answers to embarrassing questions asked in Parliament and the press about the numbers of Jewish refugees in the country. Of course, the government was keenly interested in such information and when Home Office officials required figures for their own use they obtained them from the organisation which the Jewish community had set up to deal with the refugees.

Each time the Nazis stepped up their persecution of Jews on the continent, the pressure for admission increased and further adjustments were made to British policy and procedures. These successive cycles of crisis and response up to the outbreak of war are documented in chapters 3 to 6. In the first cycle – from 1933 to early 1938 – Jewish leaders and Home Office officials evolved ways to accommodate much of the pressure for entry within the existing system of immigration control. For this reason, even though refugees were seen as a threat to jobs, the authorities turned back relatively few Jewish refugees from

British ports. Anglo-Jewish leaders negotiated terms and conditions for refugee admissions – primarily by guaranteeing the living costs of Jewish refugees during their stay in Britain. The government, in accordance with its established ban on permanent settlement of aliens, would offer only temporary refuge. The immigration authorities kept refugees under severe restrictions both on employment and on the length of their stay.

As the refugee problem became more urgent, the matter of selection of refugees for admission became all important. Chapter 4 deals with the second cycle, the crisis period immediately following the *Anschluss*, Germany's annexation of Austria in March 1938, when a sudden, savage and unremitting onslaught of persecution against Austrian Jews made the majority desperate to escape. The British government acted swiftly to restrict the influx of refugees from Austria and Germany by reviving visa requirements, which mandated pre-selection abroad and introduced strict new selection criteria for the precious British visas. Under the new rulings, most would-be refugees from Austria were ineligible for admission, but the British still made exceptions for certain categories, for example, people with guarantors and women who were prepared to become domestic servants. Chapter 5 continues the story through the further cycle following the Nazis' *Kristallnacht* pogrom in November 1938, when ministers decided to modify British policy to facilitate the temporary entry of several categories of refugee. Chapter 6 examines British selection of refugees from Czechoslovakia during the year following the crisis produced by the Munich Agreement of September 1938. It focuses in particular on selection policies which discriminated in favour of 'political' refugees and against non-political Jews, who were categorised as 'racial' or 'economic' refugees.

Throughout the period, little of the policy for managing the refugee influx was formally articulated. The lack of definition at the level of formal policy allowed officials to use discretion to resolve day-to-day policy issues as well as individual cases. A clearer policy approach, based on detailed directives, or perhaps quotas, as in the United States, would have been less flexible. Quotas enshrined in law could have been altered only by legislation. The British system allowed officials wide scope for decision-making in line with their perceptions of departmental objectives. Thus, they interpreted employment regulations generously in response to proposals from Jewish refugee organisations. They also developed new policies in the course of administrative practice. For example, in 1938, in order to reduce the time consumed by considering individual applications, officials acted to lighten the immigration conditions imposed on thousands of refugee domestics.

These officials concentrated on the management of their own caseload and on resolving the short- and medium-term issues raised by refugee admissions, such as maintenance of the refugees, and protection of the native labour market. Efforts to ensure that refugees re-emigrated were left to private initiatives. One result of the relative neglect of longer-term considerations was that refugees accumulated in Britain, but Home Office hopes that their arrival would be balanced by an outflow were disappointed. Some refugees re-emigrated overseas. Others returned to Nazi territory. Most, however, remained in Britain, having nowhere else to go.

Chapter 7 addresses policy during the early years of the war. The Home Office devised ways to speed the emigration of refugees from Britain. The government's war-time policy ruled out further humanitarian admissions of refugees. Britain's economic blockade of Germany offered further justification for ignoring the humanitarian plight of civilians in countries occupied by the enemy.

Having established these policies, and having maintained them without serious opposition in the first three years of the war, the government found itself from mid-1942 facing pressure to rescue European Jews from the Nazi programme of mass murder. The British response is the subject of chapter 8. After one narrow concession, the government resolved to resist further pressure to help Jews escape to Britain. Subsequently and in the face of unprecedented public pressure, the British government would not contemplate steps to rescue endangered Jews and carefully rationed its efforts to increase the scope of refuge. However, in 1944, new pressure from the United States and from within Whitehall led the government to make a modest contribution to saving Jews.

Britain's policy on refugees at the end of the war forms the subject of chapter 9. In 1945, some 60,000 refugee Jews remained in the country. By then, many had been absorbed into British society. They had contributed to the war effort. The case for allowing refugees to remain permanently was overwhelming, but the post-war government was reluctant to acknowledge refugees' claims with a formal policy decision. The government did allow some Jews to enter from the continent, but only if strict criteria on financial support could be met.

Reliable statistics on the war-time admission of Jews to Britain are elusive but the numbers were small. Overall refugee numbers went down because of large-scale emigration and deportation. However, the research for this study has led to an upward revision of the figures for refugees admitted to Britain between 1933 and 1939. The figure of approximately 56,000 given by Sherman has been replaced by perhaps 90,000, of whom 85 to 90 per cent were Jewish. This figure is arrived at as follows. On the outbreak of the Second World War in September 1939, over 78,000 refugees, most of them Jews, were present in the United Kingdom, not counting children who came with their parents. Of this number perhaps 70,000 were Jewish. Estimating that by this date up to 10,000 refugee Jews had entered and re-emigrated produces a final total of over 80,000 Jews from Germany, Austria and Czechoslovakia whom the government permitted to escape via the United Kingdom. Eventually, and despite the intention that most Jewish refugees would re-emigrate, about half this number settled in Britain. Over the period about 140,000 Jewish refugees entered Palestine – by both legal and illegal channels. No more than 250,000 refugee Jews were admitted to the United States in the years 1933–45. Taking into account that, of those who went to the USA, perhaps 20,000 came via Britain, it is possible to arrive at a figure of something under 450,000 Jews to whom these three countries gave refuge between them.

Selection and exclusion are basic to the operation of immigration control. Since refugee admissions were highly selective, these issues are central to this book. The process under scrutiny was designed to keep out large numbers of European Jews – perhaps ten times as many as it let in. This number reflects the difference between the estimated 500,000 to 600,000 family and individual case files in the archives of Britain's main Jewish organisation dealing with refugees and the number of Jewish refugees actually admitted, which totalled about 80,000.[30] The conclusion cannot be avoided: escape to Britain was an exception for a lucky few; exclusion was the fate of the majority. This point and the hostility that it is capable of arousing are not new. Over half a century ago, in December 1945, Viscount Samuel addressed the House of Lords on the record of governments, including the British government, in helping Jews escape from Nazi persecution. They had excluded Jews, he said, 'not as Jews, but by means of immigration restrictions'. He went on: 'And so we have had ten years of International Conferences, Committees and Commissioners, and out of that vast reservoir of misery and murder, only a tiny trickle of escape was provided.' In response to Samuel's remarks, first the Archbishop of York and then Viscount Cranborne, formerly a minister in Churchill's war-time coalition, asserted that Britain had done more than any other country to help the Jews.[31]

[30] Case files estimate by the director of the Central British Fund for German Jewry (CBF) based on CBF archives deposited in the Greater London Record Office, communicated to this author, July 1990.

[31] *Hansard*, House of Lords, vol. 138, cols. 493, 509, 529–30, 10 Dec. 1945.

Ever since, the British record has been obscured by selective memories and complacency over Britain's war-time role. The myth was born that Britain did all it could for the Jews between 1933 and 1945. This comfortable view has proved remarkably durable and is still adduced to support claims that Britain has always admitted genuine refugees, and that the latest harsh measures against asylum seekers are merely designed to exclude bogus applicants. The less heroic side of Britain's record is now receiving greater attention. For example, the collaboration with anti-Jewish policies in the occupied Channel Islands has been the subject of recent research and discussion in the press. Renewed discussion of the Holocaust, including the debate over whether to pass new laws allowing Britain to launch prosecutions for the murders of Jews, has helped to stimulate interest in the issue of Britain's record.

A gulf exists between the memory and history of that record. British kindness towards Jewish refugees is remembered fondly by those who gave generously – members of the public, refugee organisations, the Jewish community, the government – and the refugees who benefited from such kindness. We remember the touching photographs and newsreel footage of unaccompanied Jewish children arriving on the Kindertransports. There are no such photographs of the Jewish parents left behind in Nazi Europe, and their fate has made a minimal impact. The Jews excluded from entry to the United Kingdom are not part of the British experience, because Britain never saw them. In the aftermath of a devastating war which threatened the nation, the predominant mood was relief, mingled with pride at Britain's heroic struggle, and the predominant desire to rebuild and make the most of the peace. In this climate, memories of the unsuccessful public campaign to persuade the government to rescue Jews from mass murder faded quickly. The dissenters within government remained silent about their efforts to make British policy more generous. Telling the largely forgotten story of the exclusion of European Jews and of the battle to humanise British policy during the Holocaust is thus a task which falls to the historian, and it is not without risk. Because the story of exclusion and failure is not part of what most people remember, the historian who tells it may well be accused of neglecting the positive experience of refugees who came to Britain and the help they received from the British people and their government. *Whitehall and the Jews* recognises the sympathy British people felt for persecuted Jews. Indeed, this book shows how their concern increased the prospects for Jews to enter. It also emphasises that, without the pressure, organisation and finance provided by British refugee organisations, it is inconceivable that so many Jews would have found refuge in the United Kingdom. But that is only part of the story.

It falls to the historian to excavate the lost and forgotten parts of the past, as well as the truths we don't want to remember. The fact is that Britain did not welcome the refugees with open arms. This book explores the self-interested side of the British response to the plight of Jews under Nazism. Government policy ruled that escape to Britain was conditional on compliance with the country's requirements for immigrants. Britain selected from the Jewish masses the characteristics and skills it sought. The Home Office delegated much of the selection to representatives of refugee organisations which had their own reasons for limiting refugee admissions. This book, while respecting memories of British efforts to help Jewish refugees before the war, places the humanitarian elements of policy within their context – a context of self-interest, opportunism and an overriding concern with control. It shows the continuity between this approach and the ungenerosity of the British policy response to the Holocaust. It both confirms and amplifies the proof of that ungenerosity.

At the same time, the book also brings to light new evidence of humanitarian concern over the plight of persecuted Jews. It shows that within the Home Office, E. N. Cooper, an assistant secretary in the Aliens Department dealing with refugee matters, became a committed advocate for refugees. It brings out the responsibility of the prime minister, Neville Chamberlain, for Britain's agreement to expand temporary refuge for Jews following the outburst of orchestrated anti-Jewish violence in Germany in November 1938. Chamberlain persisted in his support for such a policy, in the face of opposition from the home secretary, Sir Samuel Hoare, much of whose reputation for generosity is, it emerges, undeserved. The book uncovers divisions within the circle responsible for British policy and shows how certain senior civil servants tried to make British policy more generous. Treasury officials were notable for their concern for the suffering of the Jews. They repeatedly expressed support for spending public funds on refugees. During the Holocaust, they challenged the narrowness of the government's policy and backed a British contribution to rescue. Home Office officials, too, supported letting refugees stay permanently in Britain after the war despite ministerial objections. The reputation of Sir Herbert Emerson, High Commissioner for Refugees and director of the Intergovernmental Committee on Refugees, whose efforts have been dismissed as almost comically ineffectual, is rehabilitated, with the help of new material from the records of the organisations he headed.

Whitehall and the Jews also offers further confirmation of the heartfelt public reactions to the revelation of the Nazi conspiracy to murder European Jewry. Many members of the public supported far more generous action than the government was ever prepared to contemplate. In thousands of letters and resolutions, British people begged their government to save Jews from wholesale slaughter – indeed a Gallup poll conducted at the height of the rescue agitation in early 1943 showed 78 per cent of those polled favouring the admission of endangered Jews.

What of other possible outcomes? Why, for example, was Britain not more generous in offering refuge? Could it have done more to rescue Jews from mass murder? If so, how much more? This book, in showing just where Britain drew the line in aiding persecuted Jews, reveals a number of situations when the government chose to do less than it had the power to do. Even within the existing system of priorities, more generous policies were sometimes possible, provided the will to carry them out was also present. The potential for different outcomes is implicit both in the range of possible decisions which were considered and in the spectrum of views among decision-makers about what was possible. This book criticises several British arguments for inaction during the Holocaust. It examines possible underlying reasons for the lack of a more actively humanitarian policy. It also assigns significance to evidence that strong humanitarian propensities were displayed by some policy-makers and not others. But British policy-making, while hardly populist, was not a conspiracy perpetrated on an unsuspecting public. It was, in the end, an expression of the values of the society that produced it. Radically different policies would have required a different set of values. The record of British refugee policy suggests that humanitarianism was hardly one of the determining values of the political civilisation from which it sprang.

The issues this story raises, then, are central to the history of Britain. Our responses to others teach us to understand ourselves. The analysis of British reactions to minorities and outsiders shows how British identity is created and interpreted. The importance of immigration and immigrant ancestry within British identity calls for a corresponding emphasis on the history of immigration. This study aims to fill a major gap in that history. In important ways, its focus is on the host community rather than the refugee experience. For the story of the refugees is not only a chapter in the history of the Jews – rather, the plight of the Jews and the British response to it are necessary starting points for an understanding of British values.

2 Immigration control: law and administration

The story proper opens in 1933, when hundreds of refugees from Nazi Germany, most of them Jews, arrived in the United Kingdom. Our starting point is a little earlier. This is because Whitehall policy on the new influx of aliens was made in the context of immigration restrictions dating from 1905. It is in that year that we begin, with a brief history of immigration law, policy and practice, including an explanation of how each change affected the position of refugees. Having thus established the context for British policy-making, we then turn to the Jews from Germany and Whitehall's response.

The year 1905 saw Britain take the first step in creating its modern system of immigration control. Prior to this time, immigration itself was not subject to legal controls, although records were kept of immigrant landings.[1] The Aliens Act 1905 was designed to stem the influx of Jews from eastern Europe. It introduced port controls, operated by immigration officers who inspected aliens on arrival. The new controls were highly selective. The vast majority of alien passengers were not subject to inspection. The act's inspection provisions applied only to aliens travelling steerage class – used by the poorest passengers – and then only on a ship carrying more than a specified number, in practice twenty, of alien passengers in that class. So small groups of steerage class passengers escaped inspection. No cabin class passengers were inspected. Aliens subject to inspection had to pass a poverty test. Failure made them liable to be refused entry as 'undesirable immigrants'.[2] The mad, the diseased and the criminal were also to be excluded. Aliens refused leave to land had a right of appeal to Immigration Boards.

Concern to preserve the United Kingdom's tradition of granting refuge led to the inclusion in the 1905 act of a limited concession for asylum seekers. It took the form of an exemption from refusal on grounds of poverty. The exemption was confined to refugees seeking entry:

[1] Vaughan Bevan, *The Development of British Immigration Law* (London, 1986), pp. 63–5.
[2] Aliens Act 1905, s. 1 (3).

solely to avoid prosecution or punishment on religious or political grounds or for an offence of a political character, or persecution, involving danger of imprisonment or danger to life or limb, on account of religious belief.[3]

No mention was made of racial persecution or religious persecution which fell short of endangering liberty, life or limb. The practical impact of the exemption was further limited by the fact that most refugees, like most other immigrants of the period, either passed the poverty test or were not inspected.

The Conservatives passed the act, but it was implemented under their Liberal successors, who interpreted the exemption generously. In 1906 pogroms in Russia reached new extremes and over 500 refugees entered under the exemption. In subsequent years the figures were much lower. Overall, the period from 1906 to 1914 saw a decline in alien admissions, partly because the new law had a deterrent effect. But by now most Jews emigrating from the continent preferred other destinations, particularly the USA.[4]

The mass entry of aliens ceased at the start of the First World War. The Aliens Restriction Act 1914 introduced sweeping powers to restrict alien immigration and to provide for deportation. After the war the Aliens Restriction (Amendment) Act 1919 extended the 1914 provisions into peace-time and added severe new restrictions. These two acts constituted the statutory basis for immigration control in the inter-war period. Detailed regulations were set out in the Aliens Order 1920 and adjusted over the years. The post-war system was comprehensive, subjecting all aliens to entry controls. Alongside the statutory code, certain prerogative powers of the crown continued and the government of the day exercised them without the need for parliamentary approval. These powers enabled the Home Office to take arbitrary action against aliens and rendered lawful the internment of enemy aliens. Aliens could apply for naturalisation as British subjects, normally after five years' residence.[5]

In 1919 both the right of appeal to Immigration Boards against refusal of leave to land and the provision exempting refugees from the poverty test were abolished. No trace of legal protection for refugees remained on the statute book. The home secretary, J. R. Clynes,

[3] *Ibid.*

[4] Lloyd Gartner, *The Jewish Immigrant in England, 1870–1914* (London, 1960); Bernard Gainer, *The Alien Invasion: The Origins of the Aliens Act of 1905* (London, 1972); John Garrard, *The English and Immigration: A Comparative Study of the Jewish Influx, 1880–1910* (Oxford, 1971); Jill Pellew, 'The Home Office and the Aliens Act, 1905', *Historical Journal* 32, no. 2 (1989), 369–85; Sir Edward Troup, *The Home Office* (London, 1925), pp. 143–4.

[5] British Nationality and Status of Aliens Act 1914, as amended.

explaining his refusal to admit Leon Trotksy in 1929, was one of a long line of Home Office representatives who emphasised that the only right in law was that of the state to grant asylum if it saw fit.[6] This discretionary control, so they assured members of Parliament and Jewish representatives, was an adequate safeguard for special cases. The Home Office exercised its discretion flexibly. Sympathetic consideration was given to applications from refugees, thereby maintaining in practice the essence of the British asylum tradition. It would therefore be unnecessary to revive the abolished refugee exemption or right of appeal. It would also be problematic. The hugely expanded scale of inspection would make appeals impractical to administer. Furthermore, ministers needed unfettered discretionary control over port decisions in order to enforce the current policy of strictly limiting admissions for settlement.[7]

Home Office discretion, then, was the only hope left to refugees. The British tradition of asylum still counted for something, despite having no legal basis. It was invoked repeatedly during the years of Nazi persecution. The government would assert that British policy remained in accordance with tradition as far as possible. Its critics would counter that the humanitarian claims of refugees were not satisfied by treating them no worse than other foreigners. Aliens were, after all, now subject to the most stringent controls.[8]

In truth, the basis of policy had changed beyond recognition since pre-war days. Britain was no longer a country of immigration. Strict controls on aliens were now the rule. Entry leading to permanent settlement was restricted to two categories of foreigners only: those whose presence offered some benefit to the country or people with strong personal or compassionate grounds. Inter-war governments, whatever their political complexions, maintained the ban on primary immigration. As the permanent under secretary at the Home Office, Sir John Anderson, said in 1930, immigration, 'in the ordinary sense of the term', was no longer allowed.[9] The immigration authorities were

[6] H. H. C. Prestige, memorandum, 'The Right of Asylum', 11 July 1929, PRO HO 45/15156/541506; J. R. Clynes, *Hansard*, House of Commons, vol. 230, cols. 1441–3, 24 July 1929; HO to under secretary of state, 22 Dec. 1932, PRO HO 45/15156/541506/2; Paul Grey, memorandum on asylum, 10 Jan. 1935, PRO FO 371/19653, W291/7/98, f. 8; Roger M. Makins, minute, 16 Feb. 1935, PRO FO 371/19675, W1370/356/98, f. 113.

[7] See n. 10.

[8] Sir John Gilmour, *Hansard*, House of Commons, vol. 276, cols. 2557–8, 12 Apr. 1933; Sir Samuel Hoare, *ibid.*, vol. 333, cols. 991–4, 22 Mar. 1938; Makins, minute, 16 Feb. 1935; Sir John Hope Simpson, *The Refugee Problem: Report of a Survey* (London, 1939), p. 345.

[9] Sir John Anderson, minute, 2 Jan. 1930, PRO HO 45/24765/432156/56.

aware that Anglo-Jewish leaders had no interest in bringing back unrestricted mass Jewish immigration. The strict system was mitigated for deserving Jewish applicants by informal arrangements for exceptional consideration.[10] By 1933 Britain was struggling to shake off depression. Unemployment was high. Severe restrictions on aliens entering for work or settlement remained in force. Other western European countries had adopted similar policies. Thus, when Jews in Germany began to consider escaping abroad, they found the countries of potential refuge already entrenched behind highly restrictive immigration policies.[11]

The administration of immigration control under the Home Office reflected the new climate of restriction. From 1912 B Division, which included the Aliens Division, later the Aliens Department, was charged with implementing the system. The immigration inspectorate was in the Aliens Branch, later known as Immigration Branch, which was attached to the Aliens Division. The inter-war immigration service was headed by the chief inspector of immigration, assisted by several inspectors. About 150 immigration officers handled controls at ports.[12]

All passengers required passports or other papers establishing nationality and identity from the time of the First World War onwards. The War Office's Military Intelligence Department ran an elaborate system of surveillance of alien passports by means of visas. After the war, the government decided to continue the visa system, for security purposes as well as for immigration control. A visa is a form of entry clearance. This means that, where a visa is a prerequisite of entry, anyone arriving at a port without one is normally refused admission. In the inter-war years, aliens from designated foreign countries, whatever the purpose of their journey, needed to obtain visas at a British post abroad before setting out. A visa was issued, on payment of a prescribed fee, provided the alien's plans complied with the Aliens Order and there were no personal objections. Normally, visa decisions were made on the spot by passport control officers (PCOs), who were responsible to the Passport Control Department (PCD) of the Foreign

[10] Correspondence, 19 Nov. 1929–5 Feb. 1930, *ibid.*; J. R. Clynes to Josiah Wedgwood, 22 July 1930, PRO HO 45/24765/432156/64.

[11] Strauss, 'Jewish Emigration from Germany' (I).

[12] *British Imperial Calendar and Civil Service List* (London), annually; W. Haldane Porter, minute, 11 Dec. 1929, PRO HO 45/24765/432156/56, and memorandum, 'The Control of Passengers and Alien Seamen in Time of War', 31 Jan. 1921, Sub-Committee on Treatment of Aliens, Committee of Imperial Defence, Standing Sub-Committee on the Co-ordination of Departmental Action on the Outbreak of War, 29 Mar. 1923, PRO CAB 15/10, pp. 21–4, CID paper No 411B.

Office but received their instructions, in effect, from the home secretary.[13] PCOs had discretion, but certain decisions were referred to higher authority in London.

A passenger arriving at a port of entry with a passport containing the appropriate visa would be admitted, provided nothing appeared to invalidate the grant of the visa. On granting leave to land, the immigration officer marked the alien's passport with details of any restrictions being imposed. In the 1930s no formal conditions of entry were imposed on the vast majority of alien travellers. Where extra caution seemed appropriate, the immigration officer prohibited or restricted taking employment, or imposed a time limit, or both. The use of such conditions grew dramatically, although they were still only applied to a fraction of all alien entrants. Aliens coming for residence or employment were required to register their addresses with local police. A Central Register of Aliens based on registration records, in conjunction with a card index of all aliens landing, helped the Home Office to keep track of their movements.[14]

A number of other departments were involved in immigration control. Policy was primarily made by the Home Office. At moments of crisis, the home secretary consulted his ministerial colleagues, and Cabinet committees were set up. The Treasury participated through its control of public expenditure. The Foreign Office operated largely as an intermediary, helping with implementation. Its Treaty Department supervised the Passport Control Department and dealt with the diplomatic and formal aspects of international agreements, passports, visa questions, nationality and deportation. Foreign Office policy on refugees came under a specialist League of Nations department until early 1939, when it was re-allocated to a Refugee Section, later the Refugee Department. The Ministry of Labour issued the labour permits aliens coming for employment needed to produce on landing. The Home Office, in consultation with the ministry, dealt with applications from aliens already in the United Kingdom for permission to take employment. A 'black list' contained details of undesirable aliens and of rogue employers. In business cases, the Board of Trade was consulted. The police's Special Branch provided information on aliens' politics. The secret service organisations MI5 and MI6 proffered advice in particular

[13] 'Control of Passengers', cited n. 12; H. R. Foyle to W. Wilson, 5 May 1939, PRO T 162/847/E20500/3.

[14] Aliens Order 1920, articles 1 (4) and 1 (3) (b); Hoare to R. Morrison, 22 June 1933, PRO FO 372/2949, T7159/509/378, f. 288; 'Memorandum on United Kingdom Immigration Laws and practices and the present policy of Her Majesty's Government on the reception of immigrants', CIE/CT/15, 8 July 1938, Intergovernmental Committee, Evian, July 1938, Technical Sub-Committee, PRO FO 919/9.

cases.[15] For example, in May 1933, MI6 warned that two refugees from Germany who were suspected communists were intending to apply for visas in the Netherlands. The names went on the 'black list' and Passport Control was told not to grant them visas without reference to London.[16]

Visa abolition agreements were concluded with many European countries including, by 1928, Germany and Austria, but not the Soviet Union and Poland. The British security authorities saw Bolshevism as the key external threat and saw exclusion of Bolshevik agents as one of the chief functions of the post-war system of passport controls. Intelligence and port controls would be closely interwoven. Colonel Vernon Kell, the head of MI5, explained: 'the surveillance of persons in transit . . . will provide not only the cover necessary, but the bulk of the material for records'.[17] The secret services continued to value the intelligence role of passport control. Many passport control officers held military rank. Thus, the Passport Control Department's head in the late 1930s was Captain Maurice Jeffes. His deputy, Reginald T. Parkin, a solicitor by profession, had an MI5 background.

Soon after the end of the First World War, planning for future wars commenced. The Committee of Imperial Defence (CID) assumed the Soviet Union would be the next enemy. This would make enemy aliens of Britain's estimated 92,000 Russian residents, perhaps half of whom lived in London's east end. Most were Jews who had entered before 1914. They had thus long completed the five years' residence requirement for naturalisation. But many still had Russian nationality, often because they could not afford the fee for naturalisation. Moreover, the Home Office covertly and systematically delayed 'Russian' – that is Jewish – applications for up to fifteen years beyond the period of statutory residence.[18] In 1920 the authorities agreed that the 'Russians' in the east end would in war-time need to be interned en masse.[19]

[15] F. H. Hinsley and C. A. G. Simkins, *British Intelligence in the Second World War*, vol. IV, *Security and Counter-intelligence* (London, 1990), pp. 3–26.

[16] Copy correspondence, May 1933, PRO LAB 2/2084/ETAR/4174/33.

[17] Aliens and Nationality Joint Standing Committee (ANJSC) minutes and memoranda (4 vols.) and files, 1919–32, esp. minutes of meeting of sub-committee, 27 Feb. 1919, vol. 1, f. 35, Report of Passport Control Sub-Committee, 15 Sep. 1919, V. Kell to Haldane Porter, 28 Aug. 1919, Memorandum no. 67, ANJSC, vol. 2, PRO HO 45/19966; correspondence, PRO HO 45/11043/121116/20.

[18] Sir J. Pedder, minute, 28 May 1924, PRO HO 45/24765/432156/17. On Pedder, see Pellew, 'Home Office', 374–5; correspondence 1929–30, n. 10 above; David Cesarani, 'Anti-Alienism in England After the First World War', *Immigrants and Minorities* 6, 1 (1987), 5–29, esp. 17.

[19] Shorthand note of meeting on 8 June 1920, CID Sub-Committee on Treatment of Aliens in Time of War, Report, Proceedings and Memoranda, PRO CAB 15/10, pp. 64, 66.

Similarly, in the late 1930s, it was presumed that, if there was war with Germany, the mass of refugees from Nazism would immediately be interned as enemy aliens.

The Aliens Department of the Home Office was responsible for dealing with foreigners after landing. It also formulated immigration policy. In 1933–9 an assistant secretary, Sir Ernest Holderness, handled much of the policy work. His eventual successor, Ernest Napier Cooper, formerly a factory inspector, entered the immigration field on the outbreak of the First World War, as a superintending aliens officer in Liverpool, whose task was to examine alien seamen. After seven years as a superintending inspector in the Aliens Branch, Cooper became a permanent member of the Aliens Department in 1932, with the rank of principal. In 1940 he became an assistant secretary, his rank on retiring in 1943.[20]

'It has always been a mystery to me how Mr Cooper is able to do what he does with so small a staff', wrote the chief inspector of immigration, William Haldane Porter, in 1917.[21] Staff shortages were a perennial problem. By 1930 the Home Office was making administrative economies, for example, reducing controls on domestic servants and lengthening the periods of stay given to visitors. However, additional controls, such as conditions designed to prevent aliens admitted as visitors from taking employment, entailed more work.[22] Further manpower savings were made by reducing follow-up, simplifying procedures, involving other departments, obtaining secondments of immigration officers, using customs officers and giving junior staff extra responsibility. In 1935 Holderness described the department as overburdened with correspondence, interviews, the need for immediate decisions and the problem of persons who made a visit a pretext for prolonging their stay indefinitely.[23] In 1937 officials hoped the numbers of people calling in person might decrease when the division moved to less accessible premises in Horseferry Road.[24] Home Office chiefs repeatedly requested extra staff.[25] During the 1938–9 refugee crisis, increases in manpower were sanctioned, but the Home Office never contemplated

[20] Anderson to secretary, 16 Dec. 1929, PRO T 162/846/E20500/1; 1929 correspondence, PRO HO 45/24773/19 and 20; *British Imperial Calendar*.

[21] Haldane Porter to Pedder, 27 June 1917, PRO HO 45/10732/255987/231.

[22] Correspondence, PRO HO 45/25773/22 and 23.

[23] Sir Ernest Holderness, memorandum, 'General System of Aliens Control', 1935, PRO HO 213/328.

[24] HO minute, 1 Nov. 1937, PRO HO 213/2.

[25] Correspondence, 1904–39, PRO HO 45/24773 and 1909–22, PRO HO 45/11043.

taking on numbers to match the huge growth in casework. The expansion took place in the voluntary sector.

The Home Office recruited into its aliens work people who held leading positions in the Jewish community. From 1919 Jewish leaders participated in the Aliens and Nationality Joint Standing Committee (ANJSC), helping to resolve the problem of large numbers of foreign Jews who remained in Britain after the war.[26] Work with Jewish war refugees was an extension of the work of the Jews' Temporary Shelter (JTS), which had been established in London's east end by Anglo-Jewish leaders following the increase of Jewish immigration in the 1880s. The JTS specialised in working with Jewish transmigrants from Europe as they passed through Britain on their way to settle overseas. Transmigrants arriving at ports and railway termini were met by JTS representatives offering short-term accommodation and financial support. The flow of transit passengers through Britain was a source of profit for British shipping lines; consequently there was no call for stringent controls. A system of bonding under the 1905 act had exempted transmigrants from inspection.[27] Likewise, the Aliens Order 1920 exempted transmigrants from many restrictions. As long as the masters or owners of the ships which brought the transmigrants to Britain had given security, usually in the form of a bond, that such passengers would be properly maintained and controlled during transit and would not remain in the country for any other purpose without permission, no visas were required.[28] The compliance of transmigrant Jews with immigration controls was also supervised by the JTS, relieving the Home Office of the burden. Close working relations grew up between JTS officers and Aliens Department officials.[29] The Jewish leader most trusted by the Home Office was a Frankfurt-born City stockbroker named Otto Schiff, president of the JTS, and the leading figure in Anglo-Jewish charitable work for aliens.

In 1932, the home secretary set up a new Aliens Deportation Advisory Committee (ADAC) to review deportation decisions. Composed of non-official persons, it included a Jewish member, recommended by Schiff. But the ADAC was not a success. Affronted by the rare challenges from the ADAC, senior officials soon decided to starve it of cases. The record of Home Office chiefs' dealings with the ADAC illustrates their ingrained preference for relying on their own discretion,

[26] ANJSC records, n. 17 above; *Report on the Work Undertaken by the British Government in the Reception and Care of the Belgian Refugees* (London, 1920), pp. 26–7, 52–8.

[27] Aliens Act 1905, s. 8.

[28] Aliens Order 1920, art. 4 (i).

[29] Haldane Porter to Pedder, 'Checking of transmigrant traffic', 11 May 1921, PRO HO 45/11043/72; JTS *Annual Reports*; London, 'Jewish Refugees, Anglo-Jewry and British Government Policy', esp. pp. 167–8.

their readiness to ignore legal technicalities to achieve control and their view that outsiders enlisted to help should not interfere and so cause extra work.[30]

The Home Office's use of discretion in enforcing immigration controls and its practice of co-operating with Jewish organisations would crucially shape the government's response to Jews in flight from Nazism.

[30] Correspondence, 1929–30, PRO HO 45/24765/432156/56; F. A. Newsam to Viscount Samuel, 17 Feb. 1932, PRO HO 45/14909/617473/2; PRO HO 45/15171/552811 and subfiles 1, 7, 9; correspondence, 1932, PRO HO 45/14909/617473/9; A. Maxwell, memorandum, 29 Feb. 1936, PRO HO 213/239.

3 Control without visas: the first five years of refugee immigration, 1933–1938

From 1933 onwards the immigration of Jewish refugees from Germany to Britain was controlled by a partnership between the Home Office and voluntary committees. The most significant of these organisations were the Jewish Refugees Committee (JRC) and its associated funding bodies, set up by Anglo-Jewish leaders in response to the first wave of refugees in the spring of 1933. The Jewish organisation undertook the management of the refugee influx and underwrote its costs. Having shouldered these risks and responsibilities, Jewish leaders also expected to have a say on refugee admissions. Indeed, they made several important interventions which led the Home Office to adjust its approach to the Jewish refugees' cases. But the crucial aspect of the relationship was the advantage it offered the government. Over these years, the government came to rely on the Jewish insurance against any risk to public funds when considering applications from Jews from Germany. This arrangement required no formal changes in the established system of control. Nor did the government commit itself to a policy of granting asylum. Indeed, it believed that keeping refugee policy to a minimum was a way of avoiding unwelcome obligations to refugees. Practice and policy both evolved, but in a piecemeal way, the product of the pressures of the moment and decisions on particular cases.

The refugee exodus from Germany began almost as soon as the Nazi Party gained control of the government. Adolf Hitler took office as chancellor of the German Republic on 30 January 1933. From this moment, the Nazi regime struck at individuals and groups it saw as enemies. It singled out socialists, communists, trade unionists and Jews for persecution. It began to undermine the German constitution and civil liberties. In March, using new emergency powers, it imprisoned thousands of people and placed detainees in concentration camps. Jews became the special targets of Nazi propaganda and assaults. Nazi thugs and storm-troopers made violent attacks on Jews and Jewish enterprises. A Nazi-organised boycott of Jewish businesses and professionals on 1 April was something of a fiasco. But the regime was engaged on a more systematic assault on the position of Jews in Germany. It dismissed Jews in government posts and the professions. It institutionalised discrimination by passing laws excluding Jews and political opponents from the civil service and banning Jews from legal practice. Anyone with a Jewish parent or grandparent was re-categorised as 'non-Aryan'. The 'non-Aryan' law invoked religious affiliation to resolve cases of racial ambiguity. Other laws excluded 'non-Aryan' professionals and academics from a range of government posts and instituted 'non-Aryan' quotas in schools and universities. Many Jews reacted to this persecution by seeking refuge abroad.

Refugees from Germany, most of them Jews, started to arrive at British ports at the end of January 1933. The immigration authorities reported that up to 400 Germans, most of whom were thought to be Jews, had been admitted as visitors by 30 March. A handful had been denied entry – refusals stood at fewer than ten. Then, in early April, a further 150 or so entered in just three days.[1] These figures were unsettling for the Home Office, not only because of the dramatic increase, but also because of the financial implications.

British policy towards the refugees revolved around the issue of finance. On 5 April 1933, the home secretary, Sir John Gilmour, raised refugee matters in the Cabinet for the first time; he emphasised the problem of refugees who were completely destitute, or might soon be so. He explained that, although most of the Jews entering under the Aliens Act were 'persons of the professional classes on temporary visits', some were 'Jews who were completely destitute'.[2] The Home Office wished to give a speedy response to an initiative from Jewish leaders which appeared to remove the risks entailed in admitting destitute Jews. The Jewish leaders were offering a guarantee that the Jewish community would undertake responsibility for refugees. Gilmour said that representatives of the Jewish community had visited the Home Office 'with a scheme to provide money and work for destitute Jews'.[3] They were also asking whether controls could be relaxed to ease the entry of

[1] Holderness, 'Copy of note given to S of S for use at the meeting of the Cabinet on 5th April 1933', 4 Apr. 1933, PRO HO 213/1630; Conclusions, Committee on Aliens Restrictions, AR (33) 1st Cons., 6 Apr. 1933, PRO CAB 27/549. This file contains the committee's records: its composition and terms of reference; Gilmour, memorandum, 'The Present Position in regard to the Admission of Jewish Refugees from Germany to this Country', 6 Apr. 1933; the record of its sole meeting, Conclusions, Committee on Aliens Restrictions, AR (33) 1st Cons., 6 Apr. 1933; its report, CP 96 (33), 7 Apr. 1933; and other documents.

[2] Cab. 23 (33)5, 5 Apr. 1933, PRO CAB 23/75.

[3] *Ibid.* This evidence is further discussed in London, 'British Immigration Control Procedures and Jewish Refugees, 1933–1942', Ph.D thesis, University of London (1992), pp. 78–80.

refugees.[4] Ministers agreed to set up a new Cabinet committee chaired by the home secretary to examine the Jewish proposals.

The Cabinet Committee on Aliens Restrictions met for the first time on 6 April. The issues for consideration were set out in a memorandum signed by the home secretary. The main problem was the difficulty that leave to land as visitors had been given to a number of persons who, it was believed were, 'in fact, Jews whose journey has been prompted by the desire to escape from prevailing conditions in Germany'.[5] Indeed, many of the suspected refugees admitted before 30 March had presented themselves as visitors but had admitted to the immigration officer that they were refugees. They were still allowed to land on the basis that they qualified for admission as visitors. However, since 30 March the authorities had applied a tighter approach to port controls in such cases. Now, when the immigration officer granted leave to land to a newly arrived passenger from the continent who seemed to be a refugee, he would routinely attach a short time condition – usually one month – plus a condition forbidding employment. Conditions like these were normally reserved for aliens whom the authorities suspected of planning to stay for longer than a visit or to seek unauthorised employment – most aliens were not subject to any conditions. Thus, the Home Office was treating refugees with extra caution. Yet, it was also sympathetic, as is demonstrated by the admission of destitute individuals and the low refusal rate. That week at Harwich officials had enforced certain refusals, but had reversed others where some guaranteed support was available. In the case of a man believed to be a German Jew who had arrived without a passport and asked for refuge, Aliens Department officials considered that an initial refusal should be maintained since he had stated that, though in fear, he had not been maltreated and his father was very popular in his home town.[6]

The future scale of the influx could not be estimated accurately. Members of the committee heard that Otto Schiff, chairman of the JRC and one of the signatories of the Jewish proposals, expected up to 3,000–4,000 Jews, mostly of the professional classes. But there were already signs that this might be an underestimate. Fresh telegrams from the British ambassador in Berlin, Sir Horace Rumbold, confirmed that a large-scale exodus of Jews to neighbouring countries was in progress.

[4] Neither this last request nor any mention of 'work' appears in the written proposals from the Jewish leaders. It is possible that they raised them when they called at the Home Office.

[5] Gilmour, 'The Present Position', n. 1 above.

[6] *Ibid.*; AR (33) 1st Cons., Holderness, 'Copy of note', 4 Apr. 1933, n. 1 above.

Rumbold also passed on a report that, at a recent meeting of the German Cabinet, at which an informant had been present, Hitler had asked 'for information about the number of Jews who had left Germany recently and remarked that he hoped, in time, to get rid of every Jew in the country', seemingly unaware that other countries' immigration restrictions would curtail any Jewish exodus.[7] Gilmour read the telegrams out to the meeting. The effect can only have been to increase the desire for caution and, in its advice to the Cabinet, the committee included a warning that, if Jews in Germany continued to be deprived of their employment, increasing 'pressure to emigrate' might be expected.[8]

The Jewish proposals were set out in a document signed by Neville Laski KC, president of the London Committee of Deputies of British Jews, better known as the Board of Deputies, Lionel L. Cohen KC, chairman of the Board's Law, Parliamentary and General Purposes Committee, Leonard G. Montefiore, president of the Anglo-Jewish Association, and Otto Schiff. The most important element in its seven short paragraphs was the guarantee that no refugee would become a burden on public funds: 'all expense, whether temporary or permanent accommodation or maintenance, will be borne by the Jewish community without ultimate charge to the state'.[9] The guarantee was open-ended. No limit was set on the numbers to whom it would apply, but it was not designed to lead to long-lasting commitments.

Jewish leaders intended the refugees' stay to be temporary. Re-emigration played a crucial part in their proposals. They stated that negotiations were in progress 'with a view to the ultimate transmigration of the refugees to countries other than England'. The community would look after refugees, from the moment they landed until their eventual departure. Representatives of the Jews' Temporary Shelter (JTS) would meet all continental trains. The authorities were asked to telephone with advance details of Jewish refugee arrivals. Emergency accommodation had been secured for up to 500 at the JTS and other hostels. More permanent homes would be found amongst the Jewish community. An organising committee chaired by Schiff would supervise the new arrangements. The illiberal proposal that it be made a con-

[7] Holderness to M. H. Huxley, 5 Apr. 1933, PRO FO 371/16720, C3159/319/18, f. 177. I gratefully acknowledge Peter Longerich's advice that the lack of any record of this exchange in published reports of German Cabinet meetings suggests it did not take place. Both telegrams were dated 5 April. The one quoted here was not appended to the committee's report but both were appended to the record of the meeting.

[8] CP 96 (33), 7 Apr. 1933, n. 1 above.

[9] 'Proposals of the Jewish Community as regards Jewish Refugees from Germany', n.d., Appendix I to Gilmour, 'The Present Position', n. 1 above (original in PRO HO 213/1627).

dition of entry that newly arrived refugees register at the JTS was not taken up by the government.[10] The package of proposals bore the hallmark of the Anglo-Jewish tradition, in which charitable aid to poor Jewish migrants went hand in hand with minimising the embarrassment they caused. However, the grand commitment of the guarantee was without precedent.

In return, Jewish leaders wished the government to throw open its doors. First, as the Home Office reported, they asked, 'that all German Jewish refugees from Germany should be admitted without distinction'. Secondly, 'those already admitted for the purpose of visits or who may be admitted in the future should be allowed during the present emergency to prolong their stay indefinitely'.[11]

These requests bristled with difficulties. The government was being asked to bestow a new right of asylum on all German Jewish refugees. Moreover, the Jewish guarantee, while open-ended, was aimed at emergency admissions on a temporary basis. The Jewish request that the government allow open-ended admissions in return confused the matter of temporary versus indefinite stays. The Home Office warned that further admissions could lead to the presence of a considerable number of German Jews who wished to remain indefinitely. In theory, the Home Office could refuse extensions of stay. In practice, it might prove difficult to insist that refugees return to Germany unless conditions there changed. Eventually, the question of maintenance or work was bound to arise. The possible transfer of the centre of the fur trade from Leipzig to London would create room for some Jewish fur traders. But, for the rest, if the numbers in Britain grew, how feasible were the plans of the Jewish community to send refugees to other parts of the empire? The Home Office was confident that the Jewish community could afford to implement its guarantee of temporary maintenance. The main long-term issue for the Cabinet committee was, therefore, the possibility that admissions might ultimately result in 'a considerable addition to the permanent population of this country'.[12]

However, an immediate decision was needed on the current issue of control. Should immigration restrictions be relaxed as the Jewish proposals envisaged? Alternatively, should controls be tightened? Neither course appealed to the Home Office. It preferred to leave the controls more or less as they were. The meeting agreed. The committee confirmed that the imposition of strict landing conditions should continue. It also accepted a new proposal put forward by Sir Ernest Holderness of

[10] *Ibid.* [11] Gilmour, 'The Present Position', n. 1 above. [12] *Ibid.*

the Home Office, that refugees be required to register with the police immediately on arrival, rather than after the usual three months.[13]

For the government, the great attraction of the Jewish initiative was the offer of finance. So, while the committee rejected the Jewish suggestion of granting a right of asylum and recommended telling Jewish leaders that there could be no question of relaxing entry restrictions for German Jews, it wished to make use of the Jewish guarantee. It therefore suggested that the reply should also say that, in the cases of refugees already admitted temporarily, applications for further extensions would be considered 'provided that the Jewish Community were prepared to guarantee, so far as might be necessary, adequate means of maintenance for the refugees concerned'. This form of words literally made consideration of all future extensions dependent on the guarantee.[14]

Reliance on the Jewish guarantee would add to admissions and thus to the numbers who might ultimately need absorption. However, there seemed little scope for employment or settlement. Home Office and Board of Trade representatives on the Cabinet committee had claimed that 'there did not appear to be much weight in the argument that new businesses might be brought to this country by the refugees'. The minister of labour had refused to support 'any measures involving a perceptible increase in the unemployment figures', warning that the government would face severe criticism if British workmen lost their jobs to refugees.[15]

On 12 April the Cabinet accepted the committee's recommendations and the government's response was conveyed to the Jewish leaders. The government had resolved the immediate problem of control in a highly advantageous manner. The Jewish guarantee allowed the Home Office to admit new arrivals and grant extensions without fear of financial repercussions. It included retroactive cover for the cases of hundreds of refugees already admitted, whose departure might be difficult to enforce and whose presence might otherwise become embarrassing. No criticism need be feared about refugees becoming a public liability. These gains cost the Home Office nothing. It made no commitment to admit anyone who did not appear eligible or to grant extensions in all cases. Thus it obtained instant benefits without incurring a single obligation.

The Cabinet's concern about Britain's image abroad made it unwilling to force refugees who were eligible for entry as visitors to return to Germany. Some enthusiasm was even expressed for invitations to

[13] CP 96 (33), AR (33) 1st Cons., n. 1 above; Aliens Restriction Act 1914, s. 1 (1) (f), and Aliens Order 1920, art. 6.

[14] CP 96 (33), AR (33) 1st Cons., n. 1 above. [15] *Ibid.*

distinguished individuals displaced by persecution. Yet the uncertainty about future numbers dictated caution.[16]

Ministers intended the committee to monitor refugee admissions and report further if necessary, but it never met again.[17] The immediate problem posed by the refugees was solved. Their fate in the long run was not. The interim arrangements agreed in April 1933 governed refugee admissions for nearly five years, during which the Cabinet did not discuss the subject again. Meanwhile, the demand for settlement grew steadily, but it was granted only in selected cases.

The overwhelming majority of refugees recorded by the JRC as arriving between March 1933 and October 1934 – over four-fifths out of a total of some 4,000 – were of German nationality.[18] The *Jewish Chronicle*, Anglo-Jewry's weekly newspaper, had told its readers in April 1933 that the bulk of the new arrivals, according to a spokesman for the JTS, were 'highly cultured people and Germans by birth, only a few being Poles'.[19] A substantial minority of Jews in Germany, including many born there, held Polish nationality. They were in general poorer and far less assimilated than the German Jews.[20] The Nazis persecuted Polish and other non-German Jews with particular venom. However, as the Jewish exodus swelled in the spring of 1933, the British authorities withheld visas from non-German or stateless Jews if they suspected them to be refugees from Germany. The Home Office argued that non-German nationals could return to their own countries.[21] This policy of discrimination by nationality was relatively easy to enforce, since most non-Germans required visas, while Germans did not.

In July 1933 the Foreign Office learned that 'on arrival no refugee admits to being other than an ordinary visitor' and that the Home Office did not 'hear of their existence till they come round for an extension 500 of wh. have been granted'.[22] The immigration authorities were conscious of the difficulty of distinguishing refugees from other visitors, but they did not as yet suspect every Jew coming from Nazi Europe of being a refugee. Many refugees were indeed visitors, in the sense that they did

[16] Conclusions, Cab. 27 (33)8, 12 Apr. 1933, PRO CAB 23/75; CP 96 (33), n. 1 above.

[17] *Ibid.*; Sherman, *Island Refuge*, pp. 32–3; minutes, 4 and 10 Oct. 1933, PRO FO 372/2949, T4351/509/378, f. 273.

[18] JRC, monthly information circular, May 1934, Archives of the Society for the Protection of Science and Learning (hereafter SPSL), Bodleian Library, Oxford, Box 116/2.

[19] 'Refugees in London: The Work of the Jews' Temporary Shelter', *Jewish Chronicle*, 14 Apr. 1933, p. 21.

[20] Jack Wertheimer, *Unwelcome Strangers: East European Jews in Imperial Germany* (Oxford, 1987), pp. 1–74.

[21] Gilmour, 'The Present Position', n. 1 above.

[22] J. V. W. Perowne, minute, 24 July 1933, PRO FO 371/16740, C6632/1621/18, f. 356.

not plan to stay long in Britain. Some did not yet even consider themselves refugees.[23] State persecution of Jews in Germany was a recent phenomenon. Jews everywhere hoped that the emergency would not last long. After several months, as the worst of the Nazi onslaught appeared to subside, many Jews returned voluntarily to Germany from countries of temporary refuge such as Britain.[24]

The British government regarded persecution of Jews as an obstacle to Anglo-German relations, but did not wish to overemphasise this in public. On 12 April the Cabinet decided against publishing a despatch from the ambassador in Berlin, Sir Horace Rumbold, detailing German persecution of Jews and other groups. Nevertheless, ministers agreed that in the next day's Commons foreign policy debate the foreign secretary, Sir John Simon, would voice British concern at the treatment of Jews in Germany.[25] Simon's remarks, while hardly inflammatory, still caused embarrassment within the Foreign Office.[26]

Rumbold was strongly anti-Nazi and concerned about Nazi persecution of Jews. He wrote a penetrating analysis of Hitler's *Mein Kampf* which became required reading within the Foreign Office. In May 1933 he even subjected Hitler to a disapproving lecture about his anti-Jewish policies, with what Rumbold himself interpreted as a beneficial result.[27] Yet, because of his own anti-semitic assumptions, he found German anti-Jewish attitudes understandable. In despatches, he insisted that he was seeking to explain Jewish unpopularity, not to condone outrages, but his explanations often condoned the prejudice behind those very outrages. For example, he blamed the sufferings of 'good' Jews in Germany on the misconduct of 'bad' Jews, particularly immigrants.[28] Following his retirement in August 1933, Rumbold helped refugee Jews while continuing to air his anti-Jewish prejudices.[29]

Neville Chamberlain, who became prime minister in 1937, was appalled at the barbarity of the *Kristallnacht* pogroms of November

[23] Susanne Horwell, interview with the author, 19 Apr. 1988.
[24] JRC, monthly information circular, May 1933–Oct. 1934, SPSL 116/2.
[25] Cab. 27 (33)8, 12 Apr. 1933, PRO CAB 23/75.
[26] Sir John Simon, *Hansard*, House of Commons, vol. 276, cols. 2808–10, 13 Apr. 1933; Michael Heatley, minute, 28 Apr. 1933, PRO FO 372/2949, T4295/509/378, f. 241.
[27] Martin Gilbert, *Sir Horace Rumbold* (London, 1973), pp. 377–81.
[28] London, 'British Immigration', p. 92; Sir Horace Rumbold to Simon, 28 Mar. 1933, PRO FO 371/16720, C3074/319/18, f. 140; Rumbold to Simon, 13 Apr. 1933, PRO FO 371/16722, C3594/319/18, f. 1.
[29] Gilbert, *Sir Horace Rumbold*, pp. 444–7; Kushner, 'Beyond the Pale? British Reactions to Nazi Anti-Semitism', in Kushner and Ken Lunn (eds.), *The Politics of Marginality: The Radical Right and Minorities in Twentieth-Century Britain* (London, 1990), pp. 143–60.

1938. Yet, he too accepted anti-semitic stereotypes. He privately acknowledged finding prejudice against Jews understandable and that he himself felt it. He regarded German anti-semitism as a fact of life, but did not see why it should take the form of excessive violence. He believed that decent relations with Nazi Germany would be possible if extremes of persecution could be avoided. His horror at Nazi atrocities was therefore combined with frustration at the damage they caused to Anglo-German relations. Later chapters will return to Chamberlain's views. Their relevance here is that they illustrate how the faith that the Nazi regime could and would keep its anti-Jewish actions within limits allowed the United Kingdom to maintain friendly relations with Germany. On numerous occasions during the 1930s – even after *Kristallnacht* – British diplomatic observers concluded that anti-Jewish violence had passed its peak. They seized eagerly on signs that the Nazi authorities were curbing the excesses of their followers. Public protest in Britain at Nazi atrocities was restrained by the belief – assiduously fostered by the Nazis – that foreign criticism would only provoke further outrages. For example, in 1933 Sir Herbert Samuel and Lord Reading even signed a declaration playing down atrocity reports and deploring attempts to boycott German goods, in a vain attempt to prevent the Nazis' anti-Jewish boycott of 1 April.[30]

British determination to limit public criticism of Germany's internal affairs was matched by concern to prevent the refugee issue from damaging relations with Germany. British spokesmen insisted that it was Germany's duty to solve the refugee problem it had created and that it could not expect other nations to take up this burden unaided. But they also sought to limit the scope of international action on the refugee problem, for fear that it might reinforce Germany's isolation from the international community or lead it to withdraw from the League of Nations.[31]

Britain might disclaim responsibility for helping refugees, yet the Foreign Office could not altogether escape the problems faced by Jews in Germany. For example, in April 1933, British directors of the Anglo-Persian Oil company, in which the British government held a majority of the shares, asked the Foreign Office if the government would have any objection to their plan to force the retirement of Jewish directors of their German sales subsidiary. They explained that they feared that sales would suffer and Nazi employees would become insubordinate if the company retained its Jewish employees. The government threw the decision back on the company. The company first dismissed the

[30] Correspondence, 31 Mar.–7 Apr. 1933, PRO FO 371/16720, C2998/319/18, f. 97.
[31] Sherman, *Island Refuge*, pp. 35–84.

German Jews. Later, deciding that the presence of Jews of any nationality would prejudice sales, it proceeded to dismiss all non-German Jews. Later, a Jewish MP sought Department of Overseas Trade backing for sacked Jewish employees, who had given the company many years of service, with a view to reinstatement or transfer amongst the concern's numerous non-German subsidiaries, but the government would not intervene. Nowadays, the company trades as British Petroleum.[32]

In Germany, British Jews faced increasing discrimination. The case of a London-born British Jew, Dr Ernst Kapp, driven by successive anti-Jewish measures to abandon his dental practice in Germany and move to London, where he planned to re-qualify, led the Foreign Office to conclude that commercial treaty law did not entitle a British Jew to claim the right to exercise a profession closed by German law to German citizens of the Jewish race. A British fruit dealer, who was Jewish and had been given notice to quit his stall in the Berlin market pursuant to anti-Jewish legislation, fared better. A protest by the British consul resulted in revocation of the notice by the market authorities, who explained that they had not known that the man was a British subject. After this, the Foreign Office considered raising Kapp's case on the basis that it was not fair suddenly to deprive a British subject of his livelihood, but by then he was back in England. Then, an accountant employed in Berlin by the British firm Peat Marwick Mitchell asked whether to comply with the local chamber of commerce's request for a statutory declaration that neither his parents nor grandparents were non-Aryan. Following the line of reasoning it had taken in Kapp's case, the Foreign Office concluded that there was no basis for protesting against such requirements and no redress if non-compliance caused British subjects to lose their jobs in Germany.[33]

British people in Germany were arrested, searched and harassed. The British embassy in Berlin received a grovelling apology from the German Ministry of Foreign Affairs after its assistant archivist was assaulted for failing to salute Nazi flags. In Frankfurt a group of Nazi storm-troopers knocked down and injured a British South-African naturalised Jew for failing to salute the Nazi flag. The victim, a farmer, visiting Germany, his native land, to get a cure for malaria, had been addressed as 'You Jewish swine', though, the British consul said, 'He

[32] Correspondence, 19–26 Apr. 1933, PRO FO 371/16750, C3768/C6784/3768/18, f. 274.

[33] Correspondence, 14 Aug.–12 Sep. 1933, PRO FO 371/16740, C7239/C7566/C8290/1485/18, f. 297; 20 Apr.–17 Aug. 1933, PRO HO 45/19985/39; 8 May–2 June 1933, PRO FO 371/16750, C4240/3768/18, f. 282; Ralph Wigram to B. C. Newton, 4 Aug. 1933, PRO FO 371/16746, C6660/3112/18, f. 131.

does not even look typically Jewish.'[34] The German government promised to deal firmly with attacks on foreigners, blaming them on Marxist or communist agents provocateurs.[35] British nationality thus afforded Jews no protection against Nazi hooligans and scant redress for damage to their livelihoods from anti-Jewish measures.

The Foreign Office's intense preoccupation with Anglo-German relations is illustrated by a controversy involving both politics and sport, which mobilised the national preoccupation with football in support of the goals of British diplomacy.[36] The dispute concerned an Anglo-German football match in North London, fixed for early December 1935. The venue of the proposed match was White Hart Lane, the ground of Tottenham Hotspur football club. Many of Spurs' supporters were – as they are today – Jewish. Several weeks before the game, trade union and anti-Nazi groups protested about it. Their principal objection was that the arrival of thousands of German supporters – expected to be mostly Nazis – would be interpreted as a gesture of British friendliness to the Nazi regime. Furthermore, the occasion would be used for Nazi and fascist propaganda purposes and clashes would occur between German fans and anti-fascists and Jews. Handbills protesting the match were to be distributed at Saturday games a fortnight before.

The Foreign Office did not wish to intervene. It unofficially suggested to the German Embassy that its government act to forestall trouble from visitors accompanying the team. But it did not wish to appear to be taking any official initiative in the matter. The Home Office position remained that the police would keep control and that the fear of disturbances was insufficient to justify cancellation. Sir John Simon, the home secretary, became worried about the political implications, but failed to persuade the Foreign Office to take responsibility for cancelling. Simon remained unhappy, but the Home Office saw no threat to public order even when the estimate of the number of visitors grew to 9,500. The plans of protesters gave no cause for concern. An objector who wrote threatening that he would 'definitely fly overhead and make the game in more than one way unpleasant and damaging' turned out to be a forty-year-old Jew of foreign extraction. There was no record of this man's possessing an aeroplane or a pilot's certificate, but the Special Branch nevertheless saw and

[34] Robert T. Smallbones to FO, 10 Oct. 1933, PRO FO 371/16746, C8931/3112/18, f. 215.

[35] Newton to FO, 18 Sep. 1933, PRO FO 371/16746. C8285/3112/18, f. 204; Sir Eric Phipps to FO, 18 Oct. 1933, *ibid.*, C9257/3112/18, f. 252.

[36] The episode is covered in PRO HO 45/16425/68814 and PRO FO 371/18884, C7175/C7348/C7495/C7737/C7757/C7974/C7975/C8128/C8362/7175/18, f. 343.

cautioned him.[37] The police thought any disturbance inside the ground during the game was 'likely to be promptly stifled by other spectators'.[38] Moreover, the Home Office had no powers to prohibit an unspecified group of foreigners from entering for a lawful purpose. The government's stance remained that the match should not be prevented. Soon it was too late to call it off.

The match's political implications were the subject of protest from Sir Walter Citrine, general secretary of the Trades Union Congress (TUC). Citrine's involvement led to a sudden metamorphosis of the affair into a point-scoring exercise over who was guilty of bringing politics into sport. The national press took it up. Simon said the government attached no political importance to the visit and no one else should do so. Two days before the match, he received a deputation from the TUC General Council. A conciliatory Citrine, anxious that the TUC should not be seen as importing politics into sport, pronounced himself satisfied by Simon's assurances.

Foreign Office officials saw this controversy in the light of their obsession with improving Anglo-German relations. They were hostile to the objectors. The Home Office refused the German Embassy's request to ban protest posters, so the Foreign Office gave the press an informal briefing to back up German denials of reports that at a German–Polish match in Upper Silesia a Jewish member of the Polish team had been attacked by the crowd and beaten to death. The Foreign Office's underlying concerns are apparent from a minute by Ralph Wigram, head of the Central Department: 'It is difficult, isn't it, to conceive a public statement in which we would say that the match had not been put off because we were afraid of the effect in Germany.'[39] In public the Foreign Office followed Hoare's advice to 'say as little as possible and intervene as little as possible'.[40] Its line was that the only issue for the government was public order. The police were satisfied, so there was no reason to intervene, especially since the German ambassador had undertaken to see that the visitors caused no trouble. Hitler, for his part, announced that any question of cancellation was entirely Britain's initiative.

The match passed with only minor skirmishes and seven arrests. The result was, as the British press had predicted, an easy (3–0) victory for the home side. Jews were advised to stay away, but a *Jewish Chronicle*

[37] A. Canning to acting commissioner, M. Drummond to Newsam, 22 Nov. 1935, Canning, report, Drummond to Newsam, 29 Nov. 1935, PRO HO 45/16425/68814/3.
[38] Canning to acting commissioner, 28 Nov. 1935, PRO HO 45/16425/68814/21.
[39] Wigram, minute, 21 Nov. 1935, PRO FO 371/18884, C7757/7175/18, f. 371.
[40] Hoare, minute, 24 Nov. 1935, *ibid.*

reporter who had kept close watch outside the ground conceded that 'there were too many young men who passed through the turnstiles who could not be mistaken for non-Jews'. Some of the German visitors were Jews. Of 800 guides provided for the visitors' charabanc tours round London, some 150 were German Jewish refugees, only too glad 'of an opportunity to earn a small fee'. J. Lyons & Co., reportedly branded by *Der Stürmer* as 'a Jewish concern which good Nazis should not patronise', provided catering for the German fans. German supporters greeted the anthems before the match with the Nazi salute and waved hundreds of small swastika flags during the game.[41] Later, the Germans announced that this successful occasion had led to match invitations from the Irish and Scottish Football Associations.

The Foreign Office was not displeased by the bad press the TUC suffered for allegedly bringing politics into sport. Soon afterwards, Sir Eric Phipps, British ambassador in Berlin, reported on the Nazis' tightening hold on sport. He cited a new manual for German sportsmen which advocated hostility to Jews, distorted facts to fit Nazi ideas and emphasised the political importance of sport. Phipps observed, 'The Trade Union leaders, had they been in possession of this book when they made their protest against the recent Anglo-German football match, would have had a stronger case.'[42] The Foreign Office's success in appeasing the Germans on this occasion gave little relief from worry over Anglo-German relations. Wigram fretted over pro-German activists giving 'the wrong impression of this country'.[43] Reginald Leeper, head of the Foreign Office's News Department, gloomily observed:

> Isn't our experience of Anglo-German relations simply this – that we shall always produce people here who will mislead the Germans and that the Germans will always be misled by them? The only answer is a steady policy which makes our position clear, & then all the rest becomes merely froth and bubble.[44]

To let the game proceed was easier than calling off a big match and thus courting unpopularity in the run-up to November's general election. But what message did the government's 'business as usual' approach send to Germany's Nazi leaders? As Hitler secretly prepared to violate the Versailles treaty by remilitarising the Rhineland, a step he took in March 1936, Britain's conciliatory behaviour over a mere sporting event must have underlined its desperate anxiety to avoid conflict with Nazi Germany. In mid-December, Hoare's forced resigna-

41 Cutting from *Jewish Chronicle*, 6 Dec. 1935, in PRO HO 45/16425/68814/20.
42 Phipps to Hoare, 16 Dec. 1935, PRO FO 371/18884, C8362/7175/18, f. 391.
43 Wigram, minute, 22 Nov. 1935, PRO FO 371/18884, C7737/7175/18, f. 368.
44 Reginald Leeper, minute, 22 Nov. 1935, *ibid.*

tion as foreign secretary was brought about by the storm over the Hoare–Laval plan for ceding Italy a valuable portion of Abyssinia in return for Mussolini's ceasing to attack that country.

In the mid-1930s, Britain's Jewish leaders clung to the hope that German persecution of Jews would diminish. They made speeches and wrote pamphlets in defence of German Jews.[45] They tried to dissuade Jews in Britain from advocating boycott tactics against Nazi Germany.[46] As the position of Jews in Germany worsened, however, Anglo-Jewish leaders increasingly felt they must help them to emigrate.

In the 1930s most Jewish emigrants from Europe came from the eastern regions and their most important destination was Palestine. This broad pattern of Jewish migration exerted an important influence on responses to the German exodus. The policy Anglo-Jewish leaders adopted towards the German refugee problem reflected pre-existing patterns of Jewish migration. They expected the greater part of the emigration from Germany to take the form of an orderly transfer of the younger people to destinations overseas, especially Palestine. Jewish leaders were deeply divided over the political future of Palestine and the prospects for Jewish assimilation within Europe. Yet Zionists and non-Zionists agreed that their priority was to encourage immigration into Palestine and that it should occupy the pre-eminent position as a refuge for Jews from Germany.[47] In the context of the refugee problem, Anglo-Jewry perceived the British government less as the holder of the keys to the United Kingdom than as the guardian at the gates of Palestine.

Asylum in 'countries of first refuge' such as the United Kingdom and other western European states was seen as transitional. Both Jewish leaders and the British government intended Britain to play a peripheral role, as a temporary haven. They gave high priority to limiting refugee numbers and reducing them where possible. This policy reflected both fear of enlarging the Jewish population and the view that refugees could not be allowed to threaten British jobs at what was already a time of high unemployment. Furthermore, ministers, especially Hoare when he was home secretary, claimed that to admit many more refugee Jews would provoke an unacceptable increase in anti-semitism. This argument was based on the assumption that anti-semitism was, at least in part, caused by Jews and that it was therefore necessary to restrict Jewish immigration

45 Leonard Montefiore wrote three pamphlets on the subject in 1934–5.

46 M. Hankey, minute of meeting with Montefiore and Neville Laski, 22 Mar. 1933, PRO FO 371/16720, C2978/319/18, f. 82; G. Lebzelter, *Political Anti-Semitism in England, 1919–1939* (London, 1978), pp. 136–54; G. Alderman, *The Jewish Community in British Politics* (Oxford, 1983), p. 121.

47 London, 'Jewish Refugees', pp. 166–8.

and select new entrants with care. The more foreign-seeming and unassimilated the immigrants were, the greater the problem. These assumptions and the restrictions they legitimated were not challenged by the leaders of British Jewry. Indeed, they supported them, partly because they accepted that the government would permit refuge only on these terms, but also because they themselves opposed any large-scale or long-term immigration of refugee Jews.

The leaders of Anglo-Jewry feared that any significant increase in Britain's Jewish population would produce an anti-semitic backlash. They remembered all too well how the British Jewish community, itself struggling for acceptance, had been burdened and embarrassed by the influx of poor Jews from Poland and Russia in the years around the turn of the century. The JTS and other Jewish charities which organised aid for Jewish emigrants from eastern Europe passing through Britain in tens of thousands annually in the 1930s were run by the same old-established leaders who orchestrated the community's efforts for refugees. For example, Otto Schiff had been the president of the JTS since 1922.

In March 1933 Schiff set up the Jewish Refugees Committee. The JRC's activities were limited to helping refugees in the United Kingdom. Its funds were provided by the Central British Fund for German Jewry (CBF), established several weeks later, following a meeting of Jewish leaders at the Rothschild bank's headquarters in the City. The CBF, as opposed to the JRC, had a broad perspective, aiming to foster reconstruction rather than relief. The JRC's needs had the first claim on its funds, but relief in the United Kingdom was only one of the CBF's commitments and the sums allocated to the JRC were small, compared to the large-scale outlay on expanding emigration to Palestine.[48] The emigration of German Jews to Palestine became Jewish Agency policy in the spring of 1933 and was pursued with special zeal by Zionists within the CBF.[49] Moneys allocated to Palestine largely went to finance development projects, such as housing, paving the way for the authorisation of new Jewish immigration, which depended on economic absorptive capacity. Many immigrants to Palestine now came from Germany.

The organisation of Anglo-Jewish refugee work took account of the conflicting opinions held by British Jews on Zionism and the future of Palestine. The CBF owed its inception to a decision by Zionists and

[48] Norman Bentwich, *They Found Refuge: An Account of British Jewry's Work for Victims of Nazi Oppression* (London, 1952); Joan Stiebel (Schiff's private secretary), 'The Central British Fund for World Jewish Relief', *Transactions of the Jewish Historical Society of England* 27 (1982), 51–60; Amy Gottlieb, *Archives: The Central British Fund for World Jewish Relief* (London, 1988), introducing microfilm publication.

[49] Strauss, 'Jewish Emigration from Germany' (II), 353–7.

non-Zionists to co-operate over fund-raising for refugees. The basis of this co-operation was an agreement over the division and control of the proceeds of appeals. The Zionists agreed to suspend their regular appeal for funds; in return, a portion of all moneys raised would be applied for Palestine purposes under Zionist control. The fund-raising truce was reflected in careful balancing of Zionists and non-Zionists within the CBF. The partnership weathered conflict between the two factions, and continued, despite Zionist uncertainty whether it constituted too great a compromise, when, in early 1936, Anglo-Jewish leaders set up the Council for German Jewry (CGJ) to organise a massive programme of permanent emigration overseas to places other than Palestine.[50] Establishing the CGJ was the most ambitious of several unsuccessful efforts to draw in American Jewry as a senior partner in the financing of refugee work. The American Jewish Joint Distribution Committee (AJDC) had many other calls on its funds. Its leaders, who were unsympathetic to Zionism, also felt serious disquiet about the dominance of Palestine projects and Zionists in Anglo-Jewish refugee work.[51]

The Board of Deputies of British Jews, the major body representing organised Anglo-Jewry, did not engage formally in refugee work, but its leadership had links with the Jewish refugee organisation.[52] The Board's Aliens Committee received regular reports from Otto Schiff, who handled most negotiations with the Home Office on refugee matters. Board leaders preferred to represent Anglo-Jewry as a whole and to work on fostering good relations between Jew and non-Jew. For them, admission of refugees to Britain was a subsidiary aspect of the German crisis. The Board's Joint Foreign Committee (JFC, joint with the Anglo-Jewish Association), which non-Zionists controlled, saw cessation of persecution in Europe as the solution to the refugee problem. Yet, the Board accepted that emigration was a necessity for many Jews. Its support for Palestine's pre-eminent role in refugee settlement was ratified at a conference called by the JFC in October 1933.

Leading members of the Anglo-Jewish elite, notably members of the Rothschild family, played key roles in the organisation and funding of Jewish aid to refugees. The offices of the Rothschild merchant bank were the venue for innumerable meetings and lunches, at which policy was decided and compromises negotiated. The dynamic and flexible

50 David Cesarani, 'Zionism in England, 1919–1939', DPhil. thesis, University of Oxford (1986), pp. 355–69.

51 David M. Bressler to Joseph C. Hyman, 1 May 1935, Archives of the American Jewish Joint Distribution Committee, 1933–44, New York (hereafter AJDC), 559; Morris C. Troper, 'Memorandum re: conversation with Lord Samuel', 17 Feb. 1939, AJDC 575.

52 London, 'Jewish Refugees', pp. 168–9.

Rothschild organisation offered an alternative forum to the formal institutions of Anglo-Jewry. Members of the family were also major providers of funds.

Anthony de Rothschild and his elder brother Lionel, who died in 1942, presided over the family organisation. In late 1939 Anthony also took over as chairman of both the CBF and the Central Council for Jewish Refugees (CCJR, as the CGJ was renamed in war-time). He took pains to disclaim a representative role and to deny that he or members of his family had influence in Jewish matters. Nevertheless, he was seen as an exceptionally significant representative of British Jewry and provided an informal channel of communication with the British government. In November 1941, for example, Chaim Weizmann, the Zionist leader, recounted that Foreign Secretary Anthony Eden would consult de Rothschild, 'wheedle private opinions out of him' over dinner and then confront Zionists with the claim that these views were representative of large sections of British Jewry. Weizmann found this unfair, since de Rothschild was the leader of a section of Anglo-Jewish opinion which was non-Zionist and assimilationist.[53] In October 1941, Lord Moyne, the colonial secretary, asked de Rothschild what British Jews thought about the possibility of limiting post-war emigration to Palestine and was reassured that he did not accept that Weizmann could justify demands for the entry of some three million refugees. On the same occasion, the permanent under secretary at the Colonial Office questioned de Rothschild about Selig Brodetsky and his new position as president of the Board of Deputies, 'adding that he thought it had been a very great mistake that a foreigner like this should be appointed to this post'.[54] In February 1942 Brodetsky himself consulted de Rothschild about approaching Eden in connection with helping Romanian Jews to emigrate.[55]

De Rothschild's refugee work benefited from his good connections with ministers. He also enlisted former public servants. He contributed generously to refugee appeals and aided many individuals. Other members of his family also helped Jews escape. For example, in early 1939 Lionel de Rothschild offered four Jews in Germany the chance to work as trainee gardeners on his Hampshire estate. He later supported

[53] Lord Rothschild, note of lunch with Chaim Weizmann on 14 Nov. 1941, Rothschild Archive (hereafter RA), X1/35/61.

[54] Lord Moyne to A. de Rothschild, 9 Oct. 1941, A. de Rothschild, 'Memorandum of interview with Lord Moyne', 16 Oct. 1941, RA XI/35/61.

[55] Selig Brodetsky to A. de Rothschild, 3 Feb. 1942, A. de Rothschild to Brodetsky, 4 Feb. 1992, A. de Rothschild to Lionel Cohen, 6 Feb. 1992, Cohen to de Rothschild, 11 Feb. 1942, RA XI/35/62.

one refugee gardener, Ernst Guter, in studying economics. Deported to Canada in 1940, Guter later became an economist.[56]

The efforts of the Anglo-Jewish elite did not, however, substantially change the emigration prospects. For most refugee Jews, coming to the United Kingdom was an emergency measure, a temporary substitute for permanent refuge overseas. In 1933 the British government shared the Jewish view that Palestine could make a more substantial contribution than the United Kingdom to solving the Jewish refugee problem. It took care not to inflame Arab hostility to Jewish immigration by allowing in large numbers of German refugees. Nevertheless, to facilitate the entry of German Jews, it announced adjustments to Palestine's immigration procedures, covering both immigrants in the labouring category and persons possessing defined amounts of capital.[57] Later, the Colonial Office estimated that, in 1933–6 alone, 32,754 German Jews had been admitted to Palestine.[58] In the five years from 1933 to 1937, Palestine provided permanent homes for perhaps four times as many Jews from Germany as the estimated 10,000 who were temporarily in Britain by the end of that period.[59] Understandably, therefore, a senior Foreign Office official in 1935 described Palestine as 'our contribution to the refugee problem'.[60]

The empire also seemed to offer possibilities. In the inter-war years Britain co-operated with dominion governments to support migration to Canada, Australia and New Zealand. Immigrants of British stock were preferred and certain emigrants could obtain assisted passages, but by 1933 such arrangements were at a low ebb.[61] Jewish organisations and the British government, largely motivated by the wish to reduce refugee numbers in the United Kingdom, decided to explore the possibility of resettling German Jews in the dominions and colonies.[62]

In the summer of 1933, Humbert Wolfe, principal assistant secretary responsible for the Ministry of Labour's Employment and Training Department, approached the Canadian government about settling Jewish doctors in remote areas of Canada. When this failed, he explored

56 Ernst Guter, interview with the author, 7 May 1989.

57 Conclusions, AR (33)1, n. 1 above; Simon, *Hansard*, House of Commons, vol. 276, cols. 8210–12, 13 Apr. 1933.

58 Sir J. E. Shuckburgh to Makins, 30 June 1938, PRO FO 371/22538, W8786/104/98, f. 6.

59 Strauss, 'Jewish Immigration' (I), table I, 346; Strauss, 'Jewish Immigration' (II), table X, 354–55.

60 M. D. Peterson, 18 Feb. 1935, PRO FO 371/19676, W1370/356/98, f. 113.

61 Empire Settlement Act 1922; Civil Estimates, Class II, 7, 'Oversea Settlement', PRO DO 175/14508/4, pp. 1–10.

62 Fuller details are in London, 'British Immigration', pp. 103–13.

possibilities with the other dominions, but was met there too by the re-affirmation of strict immigration regulations. Wolfe next involved Malcolm MacDonald, parliamentary under secretary to the Dominions Office and chairman of the Overseas Settlement Department. He sent him a list provided by the CBF with details of eighty-five refugees in the United Kingdom who were 'likely to be useful citizens'. The Ministry of Labour's objective, he explained, was to prevent 'any avoidable addition to our unemployment register'. It would, therefore, 'welcome any reasonable scheme which could absorb some of the refugees'.[63] The CBF agreed to pay the expenses of bringing back refugees who failed to make a living in the dominions. A letter signed by the dominions secretary, J. H. Thomas, went off to the high commissioners for Australia, Canada, New Zealand and South Africa. An eloquent accompanying letter from Simon Marks, of the retail chain Marks and Spencer and a member of the CBF's appeal committee, presented refugees in the United Kingdom in a favourable light and suggested how much they had to offer any country that accepted them.[64] In reply, New Zealand and South Africa merely reaffirmed their restrictive immigration policies.[65] Australia and Canada did not reply at all. Eventually the Dominions Office decided to let the matter drop. The episode illustrates not merely the dominions' intransigence, but also Dominions Office reluctance to put pressure on these autonomous governments.

The precise reasons dominion governments gave for their lack of enthusiasm varied, but all were worried about Jewish immigration. Lord Bledisloe, governor-general of New Zealand, expressed sympathy, especially for 'German scientists of Semitic origin', but stated that, even if there were openings, his government would be reluctant

> to take any step . . . from humanitarian motives which might leave the impression that German Jews of any description were being welcomed to this Dominion during a period of acute economic depression to the possible detriment of New Zealanders.

He feared 'that immigrants from Germany might be at heart, if not openly, Communists, and spread revolutionary propaganda to the social unsettlement of the local community'.[66] Cooper informed dominion governments of steps the Home Office had taken to prevent 'Commu-

[63] Humbert Wolfe to Malcolm MacDonald, 22 July 1933, PRO LAB 2/1189/ETAR/5513/1933.

[64] J. H. Thomas to high commissioners, 13 Sep. 1933, enclosing Simon Marks to Thomas, 14 July 1933, *ibid.*

[65] For South Africa's reply, see PRO DO 5/10, referring to file now destroyed 14414/10; Lord Bledisloe to Thomas, 22 Dec. 1933, PRO DO 57/175/14414/11.

[66] Bledisloe to Thomas, 22 Dec. 1933, PRO DO 57/175/14414/11.

nists and other undesirable aliens from Germany' entering 'in the guise of refugees'.[67]

Dominion governments were disinclined to surrender any part of their controls. They kept a grip on refugee arrivals by handling cases on their individual merits and refusing to commit themselves to admitting certain classes or specified numbers. The Australian Department of the Interior opposed group immigration schemes for Jews, claiming that Jews as a class were not desirable immigrants because they did not assimilate and generally preserved their identity as Jews. Australian Jewish organisations also preferred to restrict the size of groups entering the country. But discreet small-scale emigration to Australia of selected refugees was arranged, with Anglo-Jewish leaders providing much of the impetus. Michael Blakeney's research has shown that Australia reduced requirements for landing money in the cases of individuals, especially those nominated by persons or organisations guaranteeing that they would not be a charge on the state. This arrangement, modelled on the Anglo-Jewish guarantee, apparently flowed from suggestions made by Norman Bentwich, a prominent figure in Anglo-Jewish refugee work, in an attempt to promote refugee emigration.[68] Bentwich 'sifted' Jews in Germany to assess their suitability to emigrate to Australia.[69] Cooper and Schiff agreed a scheme for German Jews to come to Britain for a few months to learn English before re-emigrating to Australia, basing admissions on a 'pool' system, whereby new entrants had to be balanced by departures.[70] But despite Cooper's contacts in the Canadian High Commission, a modest Jewish scheme for agricultural trainees to come to the United Kingdom pending re-emigration to Canada never got going, since Canada clung rigidly to its immigration regulations.[71]

British officials and Jewish leaders concluded in March 1937 that, 'any attempt to force the pace, or to do anything spectacular, would only result in increased restrictions, as had been the case in South Africa'.[72] In 1933–5 South Africa had admitted over 1,000 Jewish refugees. But when refugee immigration increased in 1936, agitators alleged that the country was being flooded by 'unassimilable' Jewish immigrants. Severe restrictions ensued. The cash deposits now de-

67 References to destroyed DO files of 18 Sep. and 17 Oct. 1933, PRO DO 5/10.

68 Michael Blakeney, *Australia and the Jewish Refugees, 1933–1948* (Sydney, 1985), pp. 103, 109–61; Norman Bentwich, note, forwarded to DO, Department of External Affairs, to E. T. Crutchley, 28 Nov. 1936, PRO DO 175/14414A/3.

69 Norman Bentwich, *Wanderer Between Two Worlds* (London, 1941), p. 270.

70 London, 'Jewish Refugees', p. 174.

71 Correspondence, Oct. 1936–July 1937, PRO HO 213/267.

72 Sir John Loader Maffery, permanent under secretary, CO, minute, 24 Mar. 1937; G. F. Plant, memorandum of meeting with Felix Warburg, 31 Mar. 1937, PRO DO 57/175/14414A/3.

manded from intending immigrants were beyond the means of Jews from Germany, prohibited from taking out more than a twentieth of the required sum. Jewish organisations in Germany, with financial help from the CGJ and other Jewish relief organisations abroad, chartered a boat, the *Stuttgart*, which succeeded in landing 537 refugees in Cape Town, just ahead of the deadline for the new deposits. The boat's arrival led to further anti-refugee agitation and a hastily passed Aliens Act introduced an Immigrants Selection Board, with absolute power to grant or deny permits. Among other requirements, aliens had to show that they would become 'readily assimilable' with the country's white inhabitants and not pursue an overcrowded occupation. The numbers of German Jewish immigrants fell off dramatically, although restrictions eased slightly after *Kristallnacht*. In all, South Africa admitted between 6,000 and 7,000 refugees in the 1930s.[73]

Immediately after *Kristallnacht*, Britain approached dominion governments again. Canada was unmoved. The high commissioner stated that 'unfortunately the Jews were not generally good settlers on the land, they hastened into towns and cities'. In places like Toronto with large numbers of Jews 'any increase would start an anti-semitic movement'.[74] Canada took non-Jewish refugees from Czechoslovakia in 1938–9, but could only accommodate negligible numbers of European Jews – under 5,000 between 1933 and 1945.[75] Australia offered to take 15,000 over three years (the high commissioner, S. M. Bruce, had urged his government to agree to 30,000), but less than half arrived.[76] In all, Australia took some 10,000 refugees from Nazism, not counting those included in war-time deportations of internees from Britain.[77] The dominions held to their position throughout and even after the war.

Unlike the dominions, the British government was prepared to admit substantial numbers of refugees. But its awareness of the closed doors confronting refugees abroad did not lead to a softening of the regulations at home. At least officially, the government required refugees to fit into existing immigration policy. Home Office spokesmen claimed that refugees were admitted or denied entry as foreigners, rather than because they were refugees or Jews. If they could qualify like other

[73] Frieda H. Sichel, *From Refugee to Citizen: A Sociological Study of the Immigrants from Hitler-Europe Who Settled in Southern Africa* (Cape Town, 1966), pp. x, 13–25.
[74] MacDonald, memorandum of meeting with Vincent Massey, 29 Nov. 1938, PRO DO 121/2.
[75] Abella and Troper, *None Is Too Many*, pp. xxii, 131.
[76] MacDonald, memorandum, 1 Dec. 1938, PRO DO 121/2.
[77] F. Straton to official secretary, Office of High Commissioner for the UK, 28 Mar. 1945, PRO DO 57/1331/M1164/5; see also Blakeney, *Australia*.

aliens, or show that their individual circumstances justified an exception to the regulations, they might be admitted. Failing this, their plight did not, of itself, give them a claim to enter. Home secretaries would not give guidance on how German Jews might qualify for entry. They preferred the well-worn formula that each case would be considered 'on its individual merits'.[78]

Despite the government's reluctance to spell out a refugee policy, it developed policies relating specifically to refugees. It took no formal steps to recruit refugees or facilitate their entry, but certain departments adopted a special, discretionary approach which favoured particular cases or categories. The divergence of day-to-day practice from formal policy reflected an ambivalence at the heart of the government's thinking. Policy-makers agreed that they had to be seen to be taking a firm line; nevertheless, the decisions affecting individuals were often generous. These conflicting approaches could coexist because the details of day-to-day decision-making were hidden by the cloak of ministerial discretion and the confidential nature of individual cases. The more generous aspects of the government's practice went largely unacknowledged.

Employment policy is a case in point. The possible economic benefits of letting in refugees did not lead to any initiatives by the government. In April 1933 ministers recognised the potential gain from the transfer to the United Kingdom of certain industries, such as Leipzig's fur trade, but the Cabinet committee was dismissive. No action resulted from Cabinet instructions to follow up the idea of offering hospitality to distinguished men unable to continue their careers in Germany.[79] The Home Office, preoccupied with issues of control, was far from seeking to attract additional immigrants. In the Commons, Sir Herbert Samuel gently suggested 'a little relaxation of the very severe conditions of admission into this country' and Sir John Simon argued that Britain could combine self-interest with sympathy by encouraging the selective immigration of economically active refugees.[80] But the government made no active moves to encourage the entry of refugees who might prove useful. The task was left to non-governmental bodies.

The Ministry of Labour combined a policy of severe restriction and a stern public stance with readiness to bend the rules to let certain refugees take employment. Officially, it limited refugees to taking only employment which complied with the Aliens Order, for example, in

[78] Gilmour, *Hansard*, House of Commons, vol. 276, col. 2558, 12 Apr. 1933.
[79] AR (33)1, n. 1 above; Cab. 27 (33)8, 12 Apr. 1933, PRO CAB 23/75.
[80] Samuel and Simon, *Hansard*, House of Commons, vol. 276, cols. 2807 and 2810–12 respectively, 13 Apr. 1933.

domestic service. Many cases received exceptional consideration, however. In October 1934 a ministry official considered that, out of a recorded total of 773 refugees who had been permitted to take employment, 215 were really 'refugee' cases, namely those in which 'the humanitarian and compassionate aspect of the case has been the deciding factor'. Examples included au pair domestics, clerks, au pair teachers and nurse trainees, who would 'in normal times' have been rejected and had succeeded only through the exercise of discretion. The rest fell into three groups: 230 'ordinary' work permit cases'; 186 'professionals', mainly university cases under the aegis of the Academic Assistance Council (AAC; see more below); and 142 'training scheme' cases. The number of cases refused was not known, since some ultimately succeeded after several refusals.[81]

The majority of those allowed to work had originally entered as visitors.[82] The occupational condition imposed on arrival meant refugees needed specific authorisation to work. In August 1933, R. E. Gomme, of the Ministry's Aliens Restriction Branch, outlined employment policy to date in a memorandum designed to encourage dominion governments to accept refugees from the United Kingdom. Permission had been 'freely' given to undertake various forms of study, including the acquisition of British qualifications by lawyers and doctors. Some of the more distinguished academics had been allowed to accept research posts subsidised by the AAC. Businessmen had been permitted to engage in manufacture, import and export, and the fur trade. Sympathetic consideration had been given to cases where,

> the employment is of a minor character or the post is in effect being created in special circumstances . . . Jewish women have been allowed to take up posts of a domestic or semi-domestic character, i.e. as domestic servants, nursery governesses and teachers of the German language, in private houses.

Firms had been authorised to employ refugees 'over and above their actual requirements' and there was a new JRC trainee scheme. The refugees, Gomme concluded, were in the main 'a very good type', yet, the possibilities of absorption were 'necessarily limited' because they were mainly professional men and students.[83]

The proportion of refugees to the United Kingdom who belonged to the professional classes was roughly 50 per cent, far higher, for example, than in Czechoslovakia and the Netherlands, where they constituted

[81] Ministry of Labour, memorandum, 'Refugees from Germany irrespective of nationality', 3 Oct. 1934, PRO LAB 8/78.
[82] Holderness to under secretary, 26 Oct. 1934, *ibid.*
[83] R. E. Gomme, memorandum, 'German Jewish Refugees' n.d. Aug. 1933, PRO LAB 2/1189/ETAR/5513/1933.

15 and 12 per cent respectively. Those countries took far more workers. Britain also had a higher ratio of students. Ernest Cohen, who compiled these figures in late 1933, ascribed the disparities to the higher cost of travel to the United Kingdom and the attraction it held for the highly educated.[84]

The United Kingdom was the first refuge for perhaps half the 2,200 refugee scholars who had emigrated from Germany by 1938.[85] In May 1933 William Beveridge, director of the London School of Economics, set up the AAC, which in 1936 became the Society for the Protection for Science and Learning (SPSL).[86] The AAC helped displaced scholars and scientists to pursue their careers through information about possible openings at academic institutions and the provision of modest maintenance grants. But the AAC regarded only the elite of displaced scholars as within the scope of its work. Thus, it assisted research physicists with job-hunting and funds, but if other professionals, such as school-teachers, succeeded in gaining short-term permission to enter, the AAC was unable to help on a formal basis and advised re-emigration.[87] Many British scientists subscribed to the AAC and helped individual refugees with recommendations, funds and hospitality.[88]

Contacts established before the Nazi era between physicists in Germany and Britain paved the way for the admission of several researchers in low temperature physics, a field in which Germany held a leading position. They were recruited by Professor Frederick Lindemann, later Lord Cherwell, with financial backing from Imperial Chemical Industries (ICI). Lindemann already had links with the research group of Professor Franz Simon in Breslau. He had obtained a hydrogen liquefier from Simon and later arranged for a miniature helium liquefier designed by Simon in collaboration with Kurt Mendelssohn to be brought over and installed by Mendelssohn at Oxford University's Clarendon Laboratory. A few months later both Simon and Mendelssohn arrived in Oxford as refugees.[89] Simon's recommenda-

84 Ernest Cohen, 'Some notes on the problem of Jewish refugees from Germany', Dec. 1933, E. N. Cooper to Gomme, 13 Dec. 1933, PRO HO 45/15883/666764/77.

85 Gerhard Hirschfeld, ' "A High Tradition of Eagerness . . .": British Non-Jewish Organisations in Support of Refugees', in Mosse, *Second Chance*, pp. 599–610, esp. p. 604.

86 William Beveridge to Simon, 21 Apr. 1933, SPSL 111/5, f. 266.

87 Herta Leng, SPSL 333/7, ff. 279–307; Leng, entry, H. A. Strauss and W. Röder (eds.), *International Biographical Dictionary of Central European Emigrés, 1933–1945*, 3 vols. (Munich and London, 1980–3), vol. II (1983), p. 708; Gustav Kürti, SPSL 333/4, ff. 103–35.

88 Norman Bentwich, *The Rescue and Achievement of Refugee Scholars: The Story of Displaced Scholars and Scientists 1933–1952* (The Hague, 1953); William Beveridge, *A Defence of Free Learning* (Oxford, 1959); Hirschfeld, '"A High Tradition"', pp. 600–6; London, 'British Immigration', pp. 120–6.

89 F. Lindemann and T. C. Keeley, 'Helium Liquefaction Plant at the Clarendon

tions helped several former students, including the author's father, Heinz London, to come to Oxford with ICI fellowships. The refugees enhanced the Clarendon's reputation in the low temperature field.[90]

As a rule, academics were not allowed to take permanent posts. They were expected to re-emigrate and many physicists, including the majority of the most eminent, did so, going mostly to the USA.[91] Strictly, the Ministry of Labour policy that refugees should not cause unemployment meant refusing permission unless no suitable British person could be found to fill the position. But the regulations were applied to refugees selectively. Thus, a ministry official told an AAC representative in May 1933 that permission to remain permanently was only for 'persons of unquestioned repute e.g. Professor Einstein' (who chose residence in the USA). He added that it would be hard to defend flexibility towards the 'rank and file' of refugee academics, who represented 'a greater threat to British labour'.[92]

By mid-1935, 148 refugee academics had found temporary posts. Only sixty had permanent academic positions.[93] The AAC focused increasingly on transmigration and funded job-hunting trips to the USA.[94] Yet, in late 1935 Sir John Simon, who had been friendly to academic refugees from the outset and was now home secretary, personally approved the grant of settled status to thirty-one selected AAC protégés and their families, although they had less than the minimum four years' residence required in normal employment cases. To avoid possible embarrassment the lucky thirty-one were to be asked to keep their privilege secret.[95] But for most refugee scholars, especially after

Laboratory', *Nature*, 11 Feb. 1933. The author is indebted for this information to David Shoenberg, 'Early Low Temperature Physics in Cambridge', unpublished manuscript in Dr Shoenberg's possession of talk given at the Royal Institution, 26 Oct. 1988, at the Institute of Physics' History of Physics group seminar, 'Chapters in the History of Low Temperature Research in Great Britain'.

90 F. Simon, entry, Strauss and Röder, *Biographical Dictionary*, p. 1085; Lady Charlotte Simon interview, Imperial War Museum, Department of Sound Records, *Britain and the Refugee Crisis, 1933–1947*, tape 4529; Lady Simon, interview with the author, 22 Sep. 1985; N. Kurti, 'Oxford Physics: Opportunity Lost in 1865?', *Nature* 308, 5957 (1984), 313–14; Lindemann was instrumental in the award of an ICI fellowship enabling Heinz London's elder brother, Fritz, an established theoretical physicist, to continue his research in Oxford: Kostas Gavroglu, *Fritz London: A Scientific Biography* (Cambridge, 1995), pp. 105–10.

91 Paul Hoch, 'Some Contributions to Physics by German-Jewish Emigrés in Britain and Elsewhere', in Mosse, *Second Chance*, pp. 229–41.

92 Gent, memorandum of interview with Gomme, Aliens Restriction Branch, 26 May 1933, SPSL 113/5, ff. 731–2.

93 Hirschfeld, '"A High Tradition"', p. 604.

94 Esther Simpson (secretary of the AAC), interview, Imperial War Museum, Department of Sound Records, *Britain and the Refugee Crisis*, tape 4469.

95 Correspondence with HO, Nov.–Dec. 1935, SPSL 111/6, ff. 370–406.

1935, the United Kingdom functioned as a country of transit. Like the physicists, the majority went on to the USA, which by 1940 had become 'the real host country for German academics'. By 1946, only 400 academics from German-speaking areas remained in the United Kingdom, plus a further 200 from other areas.[96]

The pressure on the majority to re-emigrate demonstrated that, although the government perceived academics as an elite whose entry was advantageous, it was not committed to exploiting such perceived advantages. Instead, it subjected academics to its strict aliens' employment policies and to its need to be seen to be upholding them. The AAC agreed to Ministry of Labour urgings that it assume responsibility for the employment of refugees it helped financially. According to the ministry, the responsibility would be largely nominal: its real importance was that it would assist in the process of co-ordination and control. The AAC also agreed to make applications to the government on behalf of academic refugees.[97] Thus, the resources offered by these gifted refugees were secured without any government expense or risk, both of which were borne by the refugee organisations. As Hirschfeld observes, the ostensibly 'liberal' and exceptional policy of admitting a large number of academic refugees was an expression of self-interest, which 'amounted to nothing more than deriving the benefit without running any risks'.[98]

A training scheme approved in the summer of 1933 reflected JRC policy of helping refugees already in the country to maintain themselves and improve their qualifications so that they could soon re-emigrate overseas. The scheme's objective was to create employment opportunities, in the form of trainee jobs, for a limited number of young men, who had entered as visitors, subject to landing conditions which did not allow them to earn their living. An advantage of the scheme was that it would generate income for people who otherwise might well become the financial responsibility of the Jewish community before long. The scheme was aimed at men aged eighteen to twenty-five with previous professional training, mostly as clerks or in the legal profession, who had been forced to leave their posts in Germany.[99]

The scheme illustrates the government's readiness to make minor exceptions in connection with refugee employment, while keeping risks

96 Hirschfeld, '"A High Tradition"', p. 605.

97 Gomme to Walter Adams, 22 Sep. 1933, Adams to Gomme, 27 Nov. 1933, SPSL 113/5, f. 741.

98 Hirschfeld, '"A High Tradition"', p. 604.

99 Correspondence, 20 May 1933–3 Jan. 1934, PRO HO 45/21069/675231/1/2/3/4/5; Schiff to Lord Beaverbrook, Schiff to Cooper, 25 Sep. 1933, PRO HO 45/15882/666764/25.

to the minimum. Thus, firms might provide industrial training facilities for up to 100 refugees at any one time. Trainees would be taken on for a minimum of twelve months, but told they could not stay in Britain in the long term and required to confirm in writing that they understood this. The JRC would select trainees, provide financial help and assist with emigration at the end of the training period. The Home Office later assented to Schiff's proposal that trainees be placed in posts pending its approval of their training applications. Cooper also agreed to firms' taking on trainees for short trial periods.

Later, Cooper discovered the JRC using unfair methods to stop refugees from giving up trainee jobs. Bernard Davidson of the JRC, who ran the scheme, had persuaded R. E. Gomme of the Ministry of Labour to write a letter threatening that trainees who left their posts would face cancellation of their permission to stay in Britain. Cooper made it clear that refugees, who had not been admitted on condition that they enter training, could not be ejected merely because they chose to give it up. He reminded Gomme that Home Office policy was:

> not to raise objection to the prolongation of stay of German Jewish refugees so long as they have means to support themselves without employment, unless, of course, in particular cases, you [the Ministry of Labour] are able to recommend to us that their employment should be permitted.[100]

Of course, Cooper's rectitude cost the Home Office nothing. Davidson still had to worry about the cost to the JRC of maintaining unemployed drop-outs from the scheme.

Doctors and dentists constituted the largest occupational group among German Jewish emigrants to Britain recorded in 1933.[101] Dentists were in theory better placed to practice, since German qualifications were recognised in the United Kingdom, unlike those of doctors. Foreign dentists could apply for inclusion on a register kept by the General Medical Council. Admission to the register was a separate issue from permission for foreign dentists to enter or practice in the United Kingdom. Under the Nuremberg Laws of September 1935, Jews were being refused entitlement to practice medicine in Germany and requests for the registration of German dentists suddenly increased. The timing was propitious. Insufficient British students were entering the profession. About half the 15,000 British registered dentists were unqualified and the majority were, according to one Home Office official,

100 Cooper to Gomme, 21 Dec. 1933, PRO HO 45/21069/675231/5.

101 Doron Niederland, 'Areas of Departure from Nazi Germany and the Social Structure of the Emigrants', in Mosse, *Second Chance*, p. 59; Paul Weindling, 'The Contribution of Central European Jews to Medical Science and Practice in Britain, the 1930s to 1950s', in Mosse, *Second Chance*, pp. 243–54; Frank Honigsbaum, *The Division in British Medicine* (London, 1979), pp. 274–9.

'thoroughly bad dentists'.[102] Refugees' qualifications were often superior. The home secretary, Sir John Simon, wrote, 'The truth is that what this country wants is *better* dentists: when you have the toothache, it is extraordinary how little you care whether you are relieved by Jew or Gentile.'[103]

But British dentists and their professional organisations would not agree to permission to practice being given to more than sixty-one refugees already accepted on to the register. They persuaded the Home Office to close the door on further applicants and to admit none without prior consultation.[104] Their victory was well publicised. Home Office officials turned down further applicants, seeing no point in consulting the dental organisations. The only exceptions contemplated were for dentists of great eminence with backing from leading British colleagues.[105] By May 1937 only seventy-eight dentists had been allowed to practice. The figure for doctors was 183, comparably low.[106] Thus, notwithstanding the scope in the Aliens Order for suitable aliens to supply something the country lacked, the Home Office protected bad British dentists rather than offend the dental lobby.

For refugee women, however well qualified, jobs in domestic service proved the easiest to find and gain permission to accept. Such work was freely available because British women had rebelled against the oppressive conditions of life in service. Of course such jobs meant adapting to unfamiliar British ways plus the occupational hazard of having to provide sexual services to men in the household.

A 1935 novel, *Fires in May*, by Ruth Feiner, herself a refugee from Germany, suggests the pressures which could face a refugee domestic.[107] The novel's 22-year-old heroine, Vera, arrives in London, able to offer secretarial skills and teach German, piano or gymnastics, but reluctantly accepts a domestic service post. Lonely and naive, she falls for a scoundrel. The consequences pile up: loss of her respectability and consequently her post; a pregnancy ended by abortion; working without permission; a Home Office warning that if she persists she will have to leave the country; disapproval of her conduct ruining her chance to find a teaching post; Home Office pressure to leave; rejection by the family of her beloved English fiancé. Ultimately, Vera abandons romance and gets the Home Office off her back with a marriage of convenience.

102 Hoare memorandum, 'German Jewish Dentists', 8 Nov. 1935, PRO HO 213/264.
103 Simon, minute, 21 Nov. 1935, *ibid.* 104 Hoare, minute, 11 Nov. 1935, *ibid.*
105 Memorandum, minutes, 12–19 June 1936, PRO HO 213/265.
106 Weindling, 'Contribution', p. 248.
107 Ruth Feiner, *Fires in May* (London, 1935).

Feiner's decision to make Vera non-Jewish is misguided and her characterisations are generally weak. Yet, the novel accurately portrays the pressures on lone refugee women. The author castigates charitable organisations for imposing moral sanctions on women refugees, but concedes that, once the respectability considered essential in domestic service is lost, a woman might not find other work acceptable to the Home Office. The notion of entering a 'pro-forma' marriage to put an end to her immigration problems – marriage to a British man bestowed the right to citizenship and thus freedom from aliens' controls – both repels and tempts Vera. She hears of other refugee women who have done the same thing. Apparently such marriages were not confined to the realms of fiction.

These refugee cases tended to involve the immigration authorities in making fine judgements, which took time. The Home Office had insufficient staff to manage even routine immigration casework.[108] It introduced labour-saving measures, but staffing levels remained static, while aliens work expanded inexorably. The refugee influx placed further strain on resources, as Alexander Maxwell of the Home Office explained in late 1933:

> The German refugee problem cannot be met by any system of short cuts. The Home Office can only steer a middle course between the danger of opening the door too wide and the undesirability of refusing hospitality to refugees by considering individual cases on their merits, by granting limited extensions of time, and by reviewing such cases again and again at short intervals.[109]

In August 1935, Maxwell – justifying the appointment of an additional principal in B Division – emphasised the importance of interviews: 'The successful working of the Aliens order depends on the application of discretion to individual cases, and an interview is often the best method of securing information which enables a discretion to be exercised.'[110] Interviews of refugees were especially time-consuming because discretion played such a large part and each case was different.

The voluntary refugee committees carried out vast amounts of day-to-day casework which would otherwise have fallen to the lot of the already over-stretched Aliens Department. Prominent among these organisations were the JRC, the Germany Emergency Committee (GEC) of the Society of Friends, and the AAC, all set up in the spring of 1933. They worked in close co-operation with the immigration authorities, letting them draw on their records for information and statistics. The Home Office relied on these voluntary organisations to take responsibility for

108 HO memorandum, 21 Dec. 1934, PRO T 162/847/E20500/2.
109 A. Maxwell to R. R. Scott, 14 Nov. 1933, PRO HO 45/24773/30/37/62.
110 Maxwell to Scott, 6 Aug. 1935, *ibid.*

individual refugees and to ensure their compliance with immigration controls. These organisations also performed much of the work of screening refugees to assess which of them were desirable immigrants. The larger of these committees attained a quasi-official status, which reflected the scale of their operations and their ability to influence an individual's immigration prospects.

The authorities placed particular reliance on the Jewish guarantee. When Neville Laski, president of the Board of Deputies, hinted to the Foreign Office in July 1933 that the Jewish community might not be able to guarantee the ever-increasing number of refugees, officials recorded their determination that the promise be kept.[111] The Home Office saw the guarantee as the linchpin of its policy. Officials repeatedly invoked it to show that the situation was well under control. For example, in October 1933, Holderness reassured the Public Assistance Department of the London County Council (LCC) that refugees would not become a burden, saying

> I do not think that there is any reason for apprehension that any considerable number of the refugees who have been admitted to this country will become destitute. All those who have been admitted or granted extension of stay have satisfied us either that they have themselves sufficient means or that their friends and relatives in this country are prepared to accept responsibility for their maintenance or that their maintenance is guaranteed by the Jewish Refugees Committee. Any who cannot satisfy us in regard to their maintenance are refused admission . . . The bulk of those who have been admitted so far belong to the professional class, – doctors, lawyers, students, etc., and in a large number of cases they continue to receive remittances from their relatives in Germany for their support.[112]

Since London had by far the largest concentration of refugees, it was important to soothe municipal anxieties over possible claims for public assistance by refugees in the London area.

By 1935 the GEC reported: 'In London the applicants for help are more numerous and more desperate as time goes on.'[113] Much of the GEC's help was expended in preparing and helping people to emigrate. This reflected the problems in achieving permission for refugees to settle in Britain. In April 1935, a GEC deputation to the Foreign Office called for governments of countries of refuge to take a number of steps to improve the lot of refugees, such as allowing them to settle and granting

[111] N. Laski to R. G. Vansittart, 27 July 1933, Perowne, memorandum, 9 Aug. 1933, PRO FO 371/16756, C6860/C7633/6839/18, f. 171.

[112] Holderness to E. C. Blight (LCC), 19 Oct. 1933, PRO HO 45/15882/666764/46.

[113] George B. Jeffery, Report to Meeting for Sufferings, 1935, GEC minutes, 27 Mar. 1933–16 Dec. 1935, Central Archives of the London Yearly Meeting, Friends House, London (hereafter SOF), p. 261.

public assistance to those who were unemployable. A written submission from the deputation stated that the British authorities were issuing refusals, 'even in the cases of persons for whom private hospitality is available'.[114] By the autumn of 1935 the GEC, which specialised in aiding non-Aryan Christians and persons of Jewish origin with no Jewish religious affiliation, had helped a little over 600 families and individuals in Britain.[115] Towards the end of the year, the Society of Friends submitted to the experts' committee of the League of Nations a memorandum giving examples of cases in which difficulties arose:

(a) Germans who come in on a visit to look for work, and when they find it are told the work permit is not granted because they came in as visitors
(b) Germans who have had their passports and papers taken from them in Germany
(c) Members of so-called free professions who may be refused permission to accept engagements.
Example: A German doctor and author was commissioned to write a book by a well-known firm of publishers. The Home Office refused to extend his permit for three months to enable him to finish the book, although he promised to emigrate at the end of that period.

The memorandum argued that, because of 'occasional error', governments should allow the possibility of appeals against refusal to enter or settle. By way of illustration it cited the case of a Dr P. F. and his wife who came to England in the spring of 1934 on an invitation from the headmaster of a Quaker school. The headmaster came to meet them at Harwich and offered them hospitality for a few months, but they were refused entry and forced to return to Germany.[116]

The government felt it had fared comparatively well with the refugees whom it had allowed to enter. In late 1933 the Paris Embassy was told:

For your private information, the Home Office are not at all dissatisfied with the present position as regards the numbers and quality of refugees from Germany over here (which compares very favourably with that of some other countries including France). But we most certainly don't want present numbers increased and it is our policy therefore to do *nothing* to *encourage* further immigration.[117]

Refugee admissions, backed by the Jewish guarantee, created a steady and largely unsatisfied demand for absorption. This demand was further

[114] Memorandum, 2 Feb. 1935, *ibid.*, p. 253.
[115] 'Memorandum in support of proposals submitted by the Society of Friends', n.d. (late Nov. 1935), *ibid.*, p. 305.
[116] *Ibid.*; for the GEC generally, see Laurence Darton, *An Account of the Work of the Friends Committee for Refugees and Aliens, first known as the Germany Emergency Committee of the Society of Friends, 1933–1950* (London, 1954).
[117] Perowne to O. Peake, 4 Dec. 1933, PRO FO 371/16740, C10426/1621/18, f. 412; correspondence, 24 Nov.–5 Dec. 1933, *ibid.*, C10229/C10426/C10770/1621/18, f. 404.

reinforced by the government's decision in April 1935, in response to JRC representations about the obstacles to re-emigration, that permission to take or remain in employment should generally be granted to refugees recommended by the JRC who had by then been in the country a year or more, provided the terms of the employment were satisfactory and no question arose of displacing British labour.[118] The Home Office continued to claim that it was in control. In May 1935 an official stated: 'With the assistance of the Jewish Refugees Committee we expect to be able, within a reasonable time, to absorb the greater number of the refugees who have now been here for one year and upwards into the economic life of the country.'[119] Nearly three years later, with the refugee population at perhaps 10,000, the Home Office insisted that Germans seeking entry had not previously occasioned 'any real anxiety either as regards number or quality'.[120]

For the Home Office, sovereignty over immigration control was non-negotiable. It did not want a new organisation to be set up under the League of Nations to take responsibility for current refugee problems. Such an organisation, the Home Office said, might prove a source of embarrassment 'if it pressed us to admit more refugees to this country'.[121] British representatives also vigilantly opposed any development in international refugee law which might add to the pressure for entry. The United Kingdom delayed accession to the 1933 League Convention concerning the International Status of Refugees,

> largely owing to the fear that the convention, though itself covering only the categories of refugee dealt with by the Nansen Office, might form a precedent for some similar instrument in respect of other categories of refugees. It was felt it might be difficult, under the growing pressure from societies interested in the German refugee problem, to resist a demand for the extension of the terms of the convention to all refugees and Stateless persons, and the Home Office was particularly anxious to avoid any such commitment, which would appear to perpetuate the problem of German and other refugees.[122]

In 1936 the Home Office finally agreed to ratification, subject to reservations which left it a free hand in dealing with German refugees temporarily in Britain and future applicants.[123] The British stance remained that any agreement which eroded sovereignty and imposed

[118] Correspondence, Apr. 1935, PRO HO 213/1629.
[119] Hoare to Makins, 15 May 1935, PRO FO 371/19676, W4255/356/98, f. 334.
[120] HO memorandum, n.d., sent by J. R. D. Pimlott to O. C. Harvey, 15 Mar. 1938, PRO FO 372/3282, T3517/3272/378, f. 18.
[121] Hoare to Makins, 15 May 1935, PRO FO 371/19676, W4255/356/98, f. 334.
[122] Memorandum, original draft, C. H. Fone, 21 June 1935, PRO FO 371/19677, W5796/356/98, f. 28, esp. para. 30, printed 9 Aug. 1935.
[123] Correspondence, May–Sep. 1936, PRO HO 213/284.

pressure to absorb temporary cases would make the United Kingdom less willing to admit new refugees.[124]

Britain thus warded off the threat from international law. But it was about to face unprecedented pressure from another direction: an increase in Austrian refugees, especially in 1936–7, included Jews fleeing in anticipation of an *Anschluss*.[125] Once the Nazis finally pounced on Austria, what had been a refugee problem suddenly turned into a crisis.

[124] Cooper, draft statement for conference on German refugees, 21 Jan. 1938, PRO FO 371/22525, W985/104/98, f. 64.

[125] By 1938–9 Austrians were largely recorded as Germans.

4 New restrictions after the *Anschluss*, March to October 1938

Hitler's annexation of Austria in March 1938 unleashed a reign of terror against the Jews. The world was shocked by the extreme cruelty with which the Nazis persecuted the Jews of Austria. The Nazi regime launched a systematic assault on the Jews' economic position, while the Jews' neighbours joined Austrian and German Nazis in seizing opportunities to terrorise them and to steal their possessions. Austria's Jewish population, tormented, dispossessed, their livelihoods destroyed, saw emigration as the one chance of escape.

The response of countries of first refuge was to strengthen their defences. In Britain the Jewish refugee organisation swiftly announced that it was excluding future entrants from its general guarantee and instead asserted the right to select those it would support. The government moved rapidly to re-introduce a visa requirement to stem the influx of refugee Jews. Further entrants could be pre-selected and selection policy was for the first time crystallised in visa regulations which rendered most would-be entrants ineligible. The question of where refugees might settle permanently became increasingly pressing. Governments used international discussions on refugees to pursue agendas which had very little to do with helping Jews to find refuge. The record of international action was correspondingly lacking in humanitarian achievement.

German and Austrian passport holders coming to the United Kingdom had not required visas since visa abolition agreements between Britain and its two former enemies in 1927. When ministers discussed controls on refugees from Germany in April 1933 they had rejected the option of raising visa barriers once more. To restrict the immigration of Jews of German nationality the government would have needed to re-introduce the visa system for all German entrants. At that date the Home Office did not consider such a drastic measure necessary.[1] The position remained, therefore, that refugees holding German

[1] Conclusions, cited n. 1, ch. 3.

passports were processed on arrival at the ports. Meanwhile, the Home Office held in reserve the option of bringing back compulsory visas. To terminate the agreement with Germany would be a simple matter. However, it would entail serious disadvantages, since the Germans would certainly retaliate by re-imposing visas on British travellers. In both countries, visa procedures would impose inconvenience and expense on applicants and tedious extra work on officials.

In early March 1938, as an exodus from Austria seemed imminent, the idea of bringing back visas for Germans re-surfaced within the Home Office. C. B. McAlpine, a principal in the Aliens Department, put the case in favour. Refugee numbers in Britain were growing. Germans admitted as visitors were applying to remain as refugees. Austrian Jews were investigating refuge and an influx was to be expected. Getting rid of refugees would become increasingly hard. The numbers of stateless ex-Germans would grow as a result of a new German decree removing citizenship from exiles who failed to register at a consulate within three months. If Austrian Jews fled after a German takeover they might also become stateless either because of the new decree or because they would not be accepted as German citizens. Once stateless, people became undeportable. Refugees who still held a nationality were technically deportable, but an outcry could be expected if it became known that the government was deporting refugees to Germany. The Home Office did not want the extra work of large numbers of port refusals. Nor did it relish the inevitable criticism from a public which regarded forcible return to Nazi persecution as inhuman. Thus, it was difficult to enforce either expulsion or exclusion. The prospect of voluntary departures was also fading, since stateless and impoverished Jews found it increasingly difficult to gain admission abroad, even on a temporary basis. In early 1938 an estimated 10,000 Jewish refugees were present in the United Kingdom. McAlpine suggested that the benefits refugees had brought were outweighed by the danger of a spread of anti-Jewish feeling. The proper course, he concluded, 'if the restriction of Jewish immigration was deemed to be a national necessity', was to use a visa requirement, 'to prevent potential refugees from getting here at all'. It would then be possible to select immigrants 'at leisure and in advance'.[2] Other officials claimed that visas would not help and it was preferable to strengthen control at the ports.[3]

These leisurely deliberations were interrupted on 11 March 1938 by the news that Germany had annexed Austria. Immediately, arrivals of

[2] C. B. McAlpine, memorandum, 1 Mar. 1938, PRO HO 213/94.
[3] H. Jones, minute, 15 Mar. 1938, PRO FO 372/3282, T3398/3272/378, f. 8.

Jews with Austrian passports increased. A number were refused entry. More refugees were expected once Austria's borders re-opened. Within hours of the German occupation, the Home Office learned with dismay that the Jewish guarantee no longer held good for new admissions.[4] Schiff may have been the bearer of this devastating news. He was the signatory of a follow-up letter two days later stating regretfully that, in response to developments in Germany and recently in Austria, the CGJ had decided it must limit its liability under the guarantee given in 1933. His committee's expenditure on refugees from Germany, he pointed out, had amounted to over £60,000 the previous year and would reach the same figure in the current year. The CGJ would honour its commitments to refugees who had already entered. But it had decided that the guarantee would not extend to new admissions. The only exceptions would be for cases where the Jewish organisation had given its prior approval. Schiff added, 'we shall, of course, do our best to look after the welfare of all refugees who find themselves stranded here'.[5]

Any remaining hesitation about visas within the Home Office now evaporated. To adjust government policy took less than a week. The home secretary, Sir Samuel Hoare, raising the issue in Cabinet on 16 March, reported that 'many persons were expected to seek refuge from Austria'. Referring to visas, he said he 'felt great reluctance in putting another obstacle in the way of these unfortunate people'. He also mentioned a 'curious' MI5 report 'suggesting that the Germans were anxious to inundate this country with Jews, with a view to creating a Jewish problem in the United Kingdom'. The Cabinet assigned a small group of ministers to deal with the question. They were to adopt 'as humane an attitude as possible' and to avoid 'creating a Jewish problem in this country'.[6]

The Home Office's object was to prevent the unplanned accumulation of many more Jewish refugees in the United Kingdom. Total exclusion was not the intention. Rather, so the Home Office argued, a change in procedure was required to meet the new need to pre-select refugees abroad. Questions of quantity and quality had not posed a problem so far, but it had become necessary to address them.[7] Investigations by the

[4] William Strang, memorandum of telephone conversation with Holderness, 12 Mar. 1938, M. J. Creswell, Sir A. N. Noble, R. M. Makins, memoranda, 14 Mar. 1938, PRO FO 372/3282, T3272/3272/378, f. 1; Sherman, *Island Refuge*, pp. 86–93.

[5] Schiff to under secretary (HO), 14 Mar. 1938, PRO T 161/997/S45629; C. D. C. Robinson to Sir Nevile Bland, 14 Mar. 1938, PRO FO 372/3282, T3398/3272/378, f. 8.

[6] Cab. 14 (38)6, 16 Mar. 1938, PRO CAB 23/93.

[7] Memorandum regarding Austrian refugees, probably by Holderness, n.d., Mar. 1938, PRO HO 213/3.

passport control officer would have a better chance of picking out potential refugees than would controls at the ports, where the opportunities for making enquiries were too limited.[8]

On 1 April a Jewish deputation was given advance notice of the imminent changeover to visas. The home secretary explained his approach to the future selection of refugee entrants:

> It would be necessary for the Home Office to discriminate very carefully as to the type of refugee who could be admitted to this country. If a flood of the wrong type of immigrants were allowed in there might be serious danger of anti-semitic feeling being aroused in this country. The last thing which we wanted here was the creation of a Jewish problem.

The deputation reportedly said they 'entirely agreed with this point of view'. Indeed, Schiff endorsed the need for visas, for Austrians in particular:

> It was very difficult to get rid of a refugee . . . once he had entered and spent a few months in this country. The imposition of a visa was especially necessary in the case of Austrians who were largely of the shopkeeper and small trader class and would therefore prove much more difficult to emigrate than the average German who had come to the United Kingdom.[9]

When MPs subsequently raised questions about the barrier the visa requirement presented to refugees, ministers were able to cite the refugee organisations' support for reviving visas.[10]

The Aliens Department introduced new procedures for Austrian refugee cases, even before the visa requirement came into effect. In addition to being required to register immediately with the police and not to take employment, refugees would be admitted on three-month time limits. For the time being, all Austrian refugee cases would be referred to a principal, so that they would be seen by a relatively senior official before any final decision was made to issue a refusal.[11] But no public guidance was given on which applications would be granted. All the home secretary would say publicly was that sympathy would be shown to refugees but that a policy of indiscriminate admissions was not possible.[12]

The erection of a barrier to limit further admissions did not mean the Home Office had become less sympathetic to the needs of refugees who were already present in the country. On the contrary, officials agreed

[8] Robinson to Bland, 14 Mar. 1938, PRO FO 372/3282, T3398/3272/378, f. 8.
[9] HO minutes of meeting with deputation, 1 Apr. 1938, PRO HO 213/42.
[10] R. A. Butler, *Hansard*, House of Commons, vol. 335, cols. 843–4, 4 May 1938; Hoare, *ibid.*, vol. 338, cols. 2300–1, 21 July 1938.
[11] HO memorandum, n.d., Mar. 1938, cited n. 7, W. Jagelman, memorandum, 'Austrian refugees', 31 Mar. 1938, PRO HO 213/3.
[12] Hoare, *Hansard*, House of Commons, vol. 333, cols. 991–4, 22 Mar. 1938.

that refugees from Austria and Germany should not be forced to leave. Holderness went further, arguing that it was necessary to grant them asylum. He advised the Ministry of Labour that permission to work would have to be given freely, since refugees could not be made to return to their native country and most were unable to find openings overseas. The current practice of keeping such persons on time conditions served no useful purpose. It created unnecessary work for departments which had to keep reviewing conditions in consultation with one another. It also interfered with aliens' securing employment and led to complaints. Officials were, therefore, planning to phase out most time conditions and replace them by employment conditions administered by the Ministry of Labour. Holderness emphasised that even if a refugee took unauthorised employment 'there could be no question of making the man leave the country'. Adequate control could be exercised through employment conditions alone and the voluntary organisations would help supervise refugees' compliance.[13] Similarly, businessmen, rather than being restricted by time conditions, could be prohibited from engaging in any occupation without Home Office consent. Once some specific proposal was approved, the terms of the condition could be modified. Holderness also hoped that occupational conditions would be imposed on visitors.[14] Such measures, he argued, were 'long overdue and the only way to reduce the turnover of work without sacrificing control completely'. Holderness's views were endorsed by his superior, C. D. C. Robinson.[15] In the event, the planned reduction in the use of time conditions had to wait until the autumn. Meanwhile problems of overwork mounted in the Aliens Department.

The Home Office was reluctant to expel refugees, but it was not above using pressure and threats to get rid of them. Holderness recalled that, in the past, the Home Office had been able to turn out a few refugees who had shown themselves to be undesirable, but only after 'innumerable appeals, which mean much laborious work'. Often the only way in which the Home Office could get rid of refugees who could not get their passports renewed was 'to give a man a travel document and threaten him that if he comes back he will be deported to Germany'. But to get a visa to go to another country, the travel document had to be made valid for re-entry to Britain. Moreover, the threat to deport a refugee to Germany was empty. The Home Office felt 'more obliged than before to give asylum to persons once admitted to this country who cannot go elsewhere, and would be sent to a concen-

[13] Holderness to secretary, Ministry of Labour, 1 Apr. 1938, PRO HO 213/3.
[14] Holderness, memorandum, 6 Apr. 1938, PRO HO 213/3.
[15] Holderness, minute, 7 Apr. 1938, Robinson, minute, 27 Apr. 1938, *ibid.*

tration camp or otherwise ill-treated if they went back to Germany'. The imminent re-introduction of visas would provide 'a more effective control over the traffic' and 'exclude a number of persons who obtain entry under the guise of visitors'.[16] Holderness's views illustrate the crucial distinction for Home Office policy-makers: between refugees admitted to the United Kingdom, whom they knew, to whom they felt humanitarian obligations and whom it was humanly, politically and practically difficult to remove, and persons still abroad who could easily be prevented from entering. They felt no obligation to admit more than a select few persecuted Jews from the continent.

Holderness also acknowledged that once refugees entered they were likely to remain permanently. However, this realism was not for public consumption. It would be imprudent to admit openly the extent to which eventual absorption was contemplated. For a while, it seemed that any future influx could be kept within strict limits. But as the numbers unexpectedly multiplied over the next eighteen months, the Home Office increasingly looked on refugees as transitory residents.

Since the state of Austria was defunct, no question arose of giving notice of the changeover to visas. All that was necessary was the simple announcement that holders of Austrian passports landing after 2 May 1938 would require visas. A slightly later date was chosen for the change in respect of holders of German passports, because the German government was entitled to reasonable notice of termination of the visa abolition agreement. This was given on 21 April, to take effect on 21 May. In the intervening month, German embassy officials made strenuous efforts to avoid the imposition of visas on all German nationals. They tried to show that Britain's objective of selecting refugees in advance could be achieved by other means. Days before visas were due to come into effect, the Germans made a counter-proposal, offering to prevent unwanted entrants from coming to Britain by obstructing their departure from Germany. An aspiring emigrant would not get a passport valid for the United Kingdom without written evidence that the British government had authorised admission. Sir Nevile Bland, head of the Foreign Office's Treaty Department, where the disadvantages of visas were strongly felt, seized on this as a 'perfectly reasonable' alternative. He commented approvingly, 'under their proposals it is *we* who pass the refugee & the Germans only let him go when we have chosen him'.[17] However, Treaty Department pleas to suspend the change pending consideration of the German proposal left Home Office officials unmoved. They ruled out further discussion with the Germans,

[16] Holderness, memorandum, cited n. 14.
[17] Bland, minute, 19 May 1938, PRO FO 372/3283, T6620/3272/378, f. 304.

deeming the suggested collusion to detain people in the Reich unacceptable in principle. There were also practical objections, since the proposal did not make it possible to pre-select persons with valid German passports already outside Germany who could not be stopped from travelling to the United Kingdom. The Home Office was now fixed in its resolve to secure the control offered by visas.[18]

Shortly after the outbreak of war, Herbert von Dirksen, surveying his term as German ambassador in London from April 1938 to August 1939, interpreted British insistence on terminating the visa agreement, notwithstanding the German counter-proposal – which he claimed had met British technical objections – as a sign of anxiety to exclude persons suspected of Nazi leanings.[19] Certainly, distaste for the German regime was felt within the Aliens Department. It also appears that Cooper co-operated discreetly on refugee matters with non-Nazi elements within the German Embassy. Baron Wolfgang zu Putlitz, who was in charge of the Embassy's Consular Department from June 1934 to May 1938, claimed in his memoirs that he and others in the Embassy found ways to help refugees. Putlitz singled out Cooper for particular praise:

> Luckily for us, the Chief of the Aliens Department at the British Home Office, a Mr H. [*sic*] N. Cooper, was a man with his heart in the right place, and as I was in constant touch with him we soon became friends. Officially it was my duty to see that life in England should be made as difficult as possible for these wretched refugees, while the Nazis who wanted to work there should be given every assistance. 'Party Comrade' Bene, a former agent for the hair tonic 'Trylisin', who had risen to the rank of Group Leader, was often in my office dictating harsh instructions or listening to my protests to Cooper which I made sound convincingly Nazi. But since Bene was not particularly bright, he never realised that I was acting, or that Cooper never took any of my protests seriously. We had come to an agreement that I should give him the full details of the various cases privately, and then he could decide what action to take.[20]

The main concern Putlitz showed on learning of the decision to re-introduce visas was over the extra clerical work involved in issuing German visas for British passport holders. Treaty Department records betray no hint of complicity between British officials and Putlitz,

[18] Correspondence, Apr.–May 1938, PRO FO 372/3283, T5565/6053/6353/6620/6639/3272/378, f. 192, and PRO HO 213/95; Bland, minute, 21 Mar. 1938, PRO FO 372/3282, T3807/3272/378, f. 56.

[19] Herbert von Dirksen, 'Memorandum on the development of Political Relations Between Germany and Britain During my Mission in London, May 1938–August 1939', Sep. 1939, Document 29, *Documents and Materials relating to the Eve of the Second World War* (captured documents published by the Ministry of Foreign Affairs of the USSR), vol. II, *Dirksen Papers 1938–1939* (Moscow, 1948), p. 153; Dirksen, *Moscau, Tokio, London* (Stuttgart, 1949), p. 214, published in English as *Moscow, Tokyo, London* (London, 1951), p. 211.

[20] Wolfgang zu Putlitz, *The Putlitz Dossier* (London, 1957), p. 97.

although he was at the time providing high-grade intelligence on German re-armament to an agent of MI5.[21]

The Home Office proceeded to implement its new policy of pre-selection. Instructions to PCOs on investigating applicants left no doubt that the purpose of the new visa procedure was to regulate the flow of refugees. The regulations assumed that applicants 'who appear to be of Jewish or partly Jewish origin, or have non-Aryan affiliations' and claiming to be travelling to Britain for some temporary purpose were likely to be potential refugees, 'whose real object is to apply, after arrival, to be allowed to remain indefinitely'. The PCO's task was to distinguish such persons from *bona fide* applicants for visitors' visas. If a suspected emigrant persisted in claiming to be a visitor, he should be warned that he would be expected to leave at the termination of his visit and required to sign an undertaking to do so. He should also be warned that, if he overstayed, steps would be taken to compel his return, 'notwithstanding any plea to the contrary'. Once the PCO decided he was dealing with a refugee case, the applicant was usually ineligible for a visa unless he or she fell into the exclusive category of desirable immigrants set out in the new regulations. This elite consisted of people with international reputations in science, medicine, research or art, or successful industrialists wishing to make preliminary visits in connection with transferring their businesses to Britain, together with other persons of standing in these fields. Their applications were either to be granted on the spot, or not refused without sanction from London. At the opposite end of the scale stood the mass of potential applicants – the rank and file in commerce and the professions – who were not eligible for entry at all. However, exceptions might still be made – for political cases and for people who had offers of hospitality, or other means of temporary support in the United Kingdom. The scope for exceptions maintained a degree of flexibility, especially where safeguards were available against refugees becoming a public charge.[22]

In defence of the new visa system, Home Office spokesmen emphasised that it would save refugees the disappointment of fruitless journeys to British ports. Jews under Nazi rule who sought escape to the United Kingdom now experienced frustrations of another sort. In Vienna, Jews besieged the consulate, queuing, sometimes for days on end. There, they became targets for Nazi harassment and were subjected to many

[21] Creswell, minute, 26 Apr. 1938, PRO FO 372/3283, T5179/3272/378, f. 161; Peter Wright, *Spycatcher* (London, 1987), p. 68.

[22] PCD, circular, 'Visas for Holders of German and Austrian Passports entering the United Kingdom', 27 Apr. 1938, PRO FO 372/3283, T6705/3272/378, f. 326, esp. paras 1, 2, 3, 6–9.

indignities, for example, being forced to wash cars. One band of Nazi storm-troopers even announced the intention of entering the building and arresting all the Jews applying for immigration papers within, but the Consul-General forbade it.[23]

To establish whether a visa could be authorised involved endless correspondence with guarantors and educational institutions and the production of every kind of documentary evidence. Much of the groundwork was done by voluntary organisations, but applications generated volumes of extra work for the authorities, including a multitude of references back to London. Vienna became notorious as a bottleneck. Complaints about delays, discouragement and discourtesy at British consulates poured into the Foreign Office, forwarded by refugee organisations, public figures and indignant non-refugee travellers, many of them British.[24] The closure of the Vienna Legation after the *Anschluss* left only a Consulate-General, headed by Donald St Clair Gainer, who had been transferred from Munich. Answering complaints, Gainer pointed to the pressure under which his staff were operating. He conceded that accusations of favouritism had some foundation. All his staff had some 'pet Jew' whom they made extra efforts to help.[25]

The re-introduction of visas solved one problem for the Home Office even as it created another. The physical mass of refugees had been contained on the continent and difficulties at the ports largely avoided. Immigration officers were spared the distasteful duty of conducting endless quayside investigations, refusing Jews leave to land and forcing them to go back to the continent. The burden of initial face-to-face contact with applicants had been shifted abroad to passport control and consular officials, who came under the Foreign Office. In Germany and Austria, consular posts were overwhelmed with applications and people seeking advice. The Home Office was soon snowed under by an avalanche of paper – applications, certificates, photographs, affidavits and frantic, heart-rending letters. Officials, barely coping with the files of refugees in Britain, were now also burdened with applications referred back from Vienna, Berlin and elsewhere. Every day brought queries from friends and relatives of persons still abroad. Congestion in the Home Office interview room became a serious problem.[26]

As refugees and their friends scoured their connections in search of

23 *Jewish Chronicle*, 29 Apr. 1938, p. 18; Donald St Clair Gainer (consul-general, Vienna) to under secretary, 26 Apr. 1938, PRO FO 371/21635, C3944/1667/62, f. 170.

24 Sherman, *Island Refuge*, pp. 133–4.

25 Gainer to A. B. Hutcheon, 9 Aug. 1938, PRO FO 372/3284, T10774/3272/378, f. 258; correspondence, May–Aug. 1938, PRO FO 372/3283, T6515/3272/378, f. 287, PRO FO 372/3284, T7388/9533/9715/10728/3272/378, f. 47.

26 Holderness, minute, 22 June 1938, PRO HO 45/24773/435958/60.

someone to intercede on their behalf, officials in every corner of Whitehall were persuaded to forward queries to departments concerned with refugee matters. Members of the Foreign Office received letters from half-remembered acquaintances drawing attention to the plight of some refugee or would-be emigrant. The case of German architect Peter Moro, for example, was brought to the attention of a Foreign Office contact by fellow architect Denys Lasdun. Moro had entered in 1936 and had worked for the architectural partnership, Tecton, his permit being renewed at six-monthly intervals. He had intended to go to the United States, but when this proved difficult he left Tecton and, without obtaining Home Office approval, accepted a partnership in Britain. He was currently working on a job of considerable size and his financial position was good. The Home Office, objecting to Moro's unauthorised step, had ordered him to leave by the last day of the year. An official in the Treaty Department contacted the Home Office, which agreed to reconsider the case on the basis that Moro had found a new sponsor.[27] Moro's subsequent work includes London's celebrated Royal Festival Hall. Standing nearby is Lasdun's National Theatre.

The Aliens Department enlisted the aid of the Co-ordinating Committee, an umbrella organisation recently set up, with Home Office encouragement, by the main refugee organisations. The voluntary organisations helped by dealing with incoming correspondence and investigating visa applications. If persons wrote to the Foreign Office appealing for assistance or advice on entry to Britain, they were generally referred to the German Jewish Aid Committee (GJAC), as the JRC was now known; in other cases the correspondence itself was forwarded to the GJAC.[28] One consequence of having the voluntary organisations deal with letters was that the government itself never kept a systematic record of individuals who approached it for help. Departments were thus partly insulated from the desperate plight of Jews seeking escape from Nazism.

The Co-ordinating Committee provided a new vehicle for the articulation of grievances by refugee organisations. It put forward suggestions for more generous and imaginative treatment of refugees.[29] Activists emerged who were prepared to deal with the authorities in a more abrasive manner than the conciliatory Schiff. Mary Ormerod, a Quaker, and secretary of the Co-ordinating Committee, was particularly out-

[27] Correspondence, Dec. 1938, PRO FO 372/3286, T16178/3272/378, f. 628.

[28] Minutes, 1 Apr. 1938, PRO HO 213/42, p. 3; PRO HO 213/268; Simpson, *The Refugee Problem*, pp. 338–9; Sherman, *Island Refuge*, pp. 99–100.

[29] Memorandum from refugee organisations, 'The Treatment of Refugees in the United Kingdom', 3 May 1938, PRO HO 213/43.

spoken.[30] Ormerod made a complaint about the conduct of a clerk engaged in passport control work in Vienna. This woman, a certain Miss Stamper, had allegedly been rude to applicants, told them that no more Jews were wanted in England, voiced anti-semitic views and torn up the Ministry of Labour authorisation for a visa for a young Jewish woman in front of her face, after which the applicant was refused a visa.[31] Stamper defended her conduct, claiming to have helped Jews as much as possible, yet resigned soon afterwards. The consul-general concluded that many of the complaints arose from Stamper's conscientious performance of her job. For example, it was appropriate to ask applicants if they were Jewish, as different considerations applied to such cases. Stamper had been very overworked, he pointed out, and all staff were operating under great strain. He added that the majority of Jewish applicants left the consulate disappointed in their hopes of emigrating, which produced a sense of grievance which was 'inclined to vent itself upon persons rather than upon the regulations'.[32]

Ormerod also raised questions about the antiquated communications between London and Vienna. Since the *Anschluss*, communications were much slower because Vienna, downgraded to a Consulate, was reduced to a fortnightly diplomatic bag via Berlin, of which it was now an outpost. Although slow, the bag was secure and reliable and Ormerod asked for it to be made available for urgent and confidential communications about refugee matters. Delays in conveying results, she said, were leading to great distress. One case she cited had ended in suicide. The Foreign Office rejected her suggestion.[33]

The refugee committees' heavy reliance on volunteers resulted in amateurism and a lack of both systematic administration and effective financial controls. These weaknesses were later acknowledged by Sir Henry Bunbury, a retired senior civil servant and authority on public expenditure enlisted by the GJAC in late 1938 to provide desperately needed administrative expertise. By May 1939 Bunbury was director-designate of the Czech Refugee Trust Fund which the Home Office was setting up. Advising how the new organisation should be run, he insisted that experience had shown the need in such work for 'the type of trained ability which can usually only be obtained on a salaried basis, and for an office-trained and disciplined clerical staff'. Qualified staff were particularly necessary in key management posts, Bunbury

[30] Mary Ormerod to Makins, 10 June 1938, PRO FO 371/22527, W7582/104/98, f. 82.
[31] Ormerod to under secretary, 13 May 1938, PRO FO 372/3283, T6515/3272/378, f. 287.
[32] Gainer to under secretary, 31 May 1938, PRO FO 372/3284, T7657/3272/378, f. 61.
[33] Correspondence, June–July 1938, PRO FO 371/21751, C5809/2311/18, f. 190.

declared: 'Mediocrity, however well meaning, is always costly in the long run, and especially so when it is organising and directing the work of others.'[34] He also thought voluntary workers should be excluded from matters involving immigration and emigration. But, as the refugee committees expanded to meet the increased pressure after the *Anschluss*, they had no alternative to reliance on volunteers. Their funds were running short and the government refused to deviate from its principle of not providing financial help for refugees or refugee organisations.

As the resources for coping with casework became increasingly inadequate within both the private and public sectors, delay became the order of the day. Decision-making was interminably slow and notifying applicants of results was also plagued by delays. The backlog grew steadily. A *de facto* quota, the product of the poor capacity to cope with new applications and the meandering paths by which individual cases travelled through the system, limited the entry even of the narrowly defined categories of refugee for whom the Home Office was prepared to authorise visas.[35] Further complications resulted from a decision to seek the observations of MI5 on refugee visa cases; in order to avoid clogging its own machinery MI5 soon limited the cases it wished to see to aliens who might pose a security threat to re-armament work or war-time industries.[36]

The Home Office had claimed that the investigation of visa applicants would be a reliable way to identify potential refugees and select suitable entrants. Yet it had not solved the problem of distinguishing the emigrant masquerading as a visitor from the genuine visitor. Refugees were still getting through undetected. Desperate for any document enabling them to escape, people applied for visitors' visas, signing the requisite form of undertaking that they would not seek to extend their stay. The immigration authorities soon realised that many of these people, once they had achieved the object of gaining admission, would plead that they could not go back to Germany or Austria. In a bid to intercept such cases, preferably before they were given leave to land, PCOs were told in June 1938 to mark the passports of persons who signed these undertakings with a secret signal, which would be picked up by officials in the United Kingdom. However, the futility of demanding such undertakings in the absence of the will to enforce them

34 Sir Henry Bunbury, memorandum, 'Liabilities in respect of refugees from Czechoslovakia', 15 May 1939, PRO HO 294/39.
35 Simpson, *The Refugee Problem*, p. 339.
36 Correspondence, May–June 1938, PRO HO 213/1903.

subsequently was finally acknowledged in August, when the Home Office decided to abandon their use in refugee cases.[37]

Figures from Austria in the summer of 1938 give an idea of the scale of the demand for refuge. The director of passport control said in early July that a 'very large number of unclassified persons' had applied since the *Anschluss* for advice and taken away forms, but not so far put in applications. In addition, visas granted in the first half of 1938 alone to Austrian subjects totalled 2,740, refusals approximately 420, and 545 cases, including some already disposed of, had been referred for decision in London. The number of staff dealing with visas in Vienna had been increased from four to fifteen.[38] Locally engaged staff were employed as reception clerks to manage the crowd. By September, staff were dealing with 200 enquiries a day about emigration to various parts of the British Empire and accepting over 100 visa applications daily. From May to September 1938 the Consulate had also given out 16,000 forms in connection with possible emigration to Australia.[39]

As the situation of Jews on the continent deteriorated, the Home Office came under increasing pressure to re-examine admissions. Activists at home pressed the government for a more generous policy. It was also necessary to provide a British contribution to international discussions on the admission policies of countries of refuge and settlement at the forthcoming Evian conference, fixed for early July. In the preceding month the Home Office produced what was in essence a re-statement of existing policy. Nevertheless, it contained hints of movement towards a more positive approach. The statement said that numbers 'depended largely on the opportunities and rate of absorption, and, as regards artisans, on the attitude of the Trade Unions'. However, the Home Office was prepared to admit several classes of refugee: those prepared to start businesses; young people for training or education; professional persons; those with academic qualifications; and between 2,000 and 3,000 artisans per year.[40]

For the Home Office to make any detailed statement of the scope for

[37] Correspondence, May–June 1938, PRO HO 213/96; PCD circulars, 'Visas for Holders of German and Austrian Passports entering the UK', 10 June and 30 Aug. 1938, PRO FO 372/3284, T7056/3272/378, f. 1; Holderness to M. Jeffes, 19 July 1938, R. T. Parkin to PCOs Berlin and Vienna, 20 July 1938, PRO HO 213/98.

[38] Jeffes, minute, 9 July 1938, A. W. Urquhart, minute, n.d., mid-July 1938, PRO FO 372/3284, T9255/9423/3272/378, f. 167.

[39] P. Stanley Sykes to E. H. Rance, 5 Oct. 1938, attaching memorandum by G. W. Berry, Assistant PCO Vienna to inspector general of passport control, London, 26 Sep. 1938, PRO FO 366/1036, X9278/84/50, f. 52.

[40] Record of interdepartmental meeting, 'Intergovernmental meeting at Evian', 8 June 1938, PRO FO 371/22527, W8127/104/98, f. 150; Cooper to Makins, 2 July 1938, PRO FO 371/22528, W8853/104/98, f. 60.

admissions was in itself a departure, in view of its previous reluctance to spell out policy. The written submission to the Evian conference largely reiterated the existing categories for admission. Yet it put greater emphasis on training for re-emigration and referred to plans to extend arrangements with the voluntary organisations for the admission as trainees of a pool of refugees who intended re-emigration. The numbers who could be admitted would be subject to no absolute limitation, other than the amount of hospitality, maintenance and employment the voluntary organisations could arrange. However, strict limitations would be necessary on the numbers of doctors and dentists. In line with previous statements, no commitment was made to the admission of specific numbers. Nor was there any direct allusion to the practice of using discretionary powers to make exceptions for special cases.[41]

What was novel about the statement was the expansiveness of its tone. It talked of adopting 'a liberal attitude in the matter of admissions' and it offered greater flexibility and generosity in the interpretation of employment regulations. It also encouraged the voluntary organisations to seek out suitable jobs for refugees and to make an initial selection of suitable individuals to fill them. In addition, it hinted at prospects of settlement in the United Kingdom for a certain proportion, especially younger refugees, even though the terms of their admission for education or training required them to re-emigrate eventually.[42]

In reality, no move had been made to liberalise the substance of admissions policy, but the pressure to appear more liberal was being felt. The submission opened with the sonorous claim that Britain was now prepared 'on the ground of humanity to adopt an even more liberal policy in the matter of admission and employment', but confined within the narrow limits occasioned by domestic, demographic and economic problems and the fact that it was 'not a country of immigration'.[43] The object was largely exhortatory. The exaggerated, yet studiedly imprecise picture of Britain's contribution was designed to stimulate other nations to greater generosity. At the conference, Lord Winterton urged other countries of refuge to follow the United Kingdom in being ready to absorb a certain proportion of refugees.[44]

[41] 'Contribution which His Majesty's Government in the United Kingdom is able to make to the Problem of Emigration from Germany and Austria', 11 July 1938, 'Intergovernmental Committee, Evian – July 1938, Technical Sub-Committee, CIE/CT/15', PRO FO 919/9; see also 'Memorandum on UK Immigration Law and Practices and the Present Policy of His Majesty's Government regarding the Reception of Immigrants', 8 July 1938, *ibid.*; a later expanded version of the policy statement is in 'Memorandum', Cooper to under secretary, PRO FO 371/22534, W12713/104/98, 9 Sep. 1938, f. 1.

[42] 'Contribution', 11 July 1938, cited n. 41. [43] *Ibid.*

[44] Lord Winterton, speech, 6 July 1938, 'Intergovernmental Committee, Evian – July 1938, Verbatim Report of the First Meeting, CI/E/CRI', PRO FO 919/8.

The British presentations to the Evian conference had put the government's policy in a generous light. The reality remained that before they could get visas Jews needed means of support. Voluntary organisations could arrange this in some cases but not others. Control over admissions through pre-selection remained central to Home Office policy. Yet its control over the administration of the immigration system itself was slipping. At the same time, pressures for change were building up. To illustrate these developments, let us look at what was happening in the management of refugee immigration, especially the process of selection for entry.

There was intense anxiety within the Home Office over the short-term admission of persons who might seek permanent settlement. The Aliens Department therefore insisted on thorough investigation of all such applicants by passport control. In effect, Jews who might be refugees could not come on short visits unless their long-term plans had been scrutinised. Even refugee industrialists – who were considered desirable immigrants – had to undergo searching investigation before they could be allowed to make brief visits to discuss plans to invest in the United Kingdom.

A minority of refugees had been permitted to settle in Britain. For example, out of 142 refugee medical practitioners who had been allowed to work in private practice, 66 had all immigration restrictions lifted by September 1937.[45] The pressure for absorption of refugees already in the country was growing, prospects for re-emigration were shrinking and pressure for more generous admissions mounting. The Home Office responded by insisting that the cases of persons who might seek permission to remain permanently – and this category now encompassed virtually all Jews – must be scrutinised with the utmost care before permission to set foot in Britain could be granted. Thus, pre-selection was explicitly linked to absorption. The result was a system riven with contradictions. Refugees were granted admission on a temporary basis, yet people were required to have qualifications for permanent settlement in order to obtain merely temporary refuge. Many people who could only qualify for temporary refuge were refused admission, in case they stayed on. During the war and afterwards, people who had been led to believe that they would ultimately be allowed to settle were left in limbo and pressed to re-emigrate.

Earlier, a policy of fostering the immigration of refugee industrialists had developed from government promotion of investment and job-creation in depressed areas. The Special Areas Act 1934 set up commis-

[45] T. B. Williamson to R. Derenburg, 2 Sep. 1937, PRO HO 213/255.

sioners to attract new industries to designated parts of depressed areas in England, Wales and Scotland, but domestic manufacturers were slow to respond. Herbert Loebl, who has studied this topic extensively, dates the government's first invitation to refugee manufacturers to a ministerial statement in the House of Lords in March 1935. That autumn the government agreed, for electoral reasons, that the Special Areas Fund could be used for factory construction in three specified industrial estates and in March 1936 it agreed to encourage new industries to locate in the Special Areas. In the same month, Cooper accepted a Ministry of Labour suggestion that prospective foreign investors should be led to believe that their applications might be refused unless they agreed to go to the Special Areas. He even planned to bring pressure to bear in some cases, but Board of Trade representatives argued for caution and it was decided merely to inform applicants that location was a factor taken into consideration. The Home Office, nevertheless, contrived to let it be known in Germany, and later in Austria, that delays could be minimised for applicants willing to go to areas of high unemployment. Cooper also told the commissioners that permission would be granted more readily in such cases, thereby becoming, as Loebl notes, 'the first government department to attempt to implement a location of industry policy'.[46] In September 1936 the Ministry of Labour claimed that refugees had established industries which had given employment to more British subjects than the total number of refugees from Germany then in the United Kingdom.[47] In February 1937 the Home Office decided to put foreign manufacturers in direct contact with the commissioners and encouraged the commissioners to provide finance in cases where the applicant's capital was inadequate. An official recruitment drive among refugees developed, conducted in conditions of extreme confidentiality, designed to deceive the German authorities, who wished to prevent industry going abroad. Jews in central Europe who had not thought of becoming manufacturers previously began to work up applications in their search for refuge. In February 1939 the home secretary reported that 200 out of 300 firms established by refugee manufacturers were located in the depressed areas. Prior to emigration, one-third of adult male refugees from Germany and Austria, perhaps 4,000 persons, had been manufacturers. By no means all continued as manufacturers in the United Kingdom,

46 Herbert Loebl, 'Refugees from the Third Reich and Industry in the Depressed Areas of Britain', in Mosse, *Second Chance*, pp. 379–403, esp. pp. 381, 384–5; Loebl, 'Refugee Industries in the Special Areas of Britain', in Hirschfeld, *Exile in Great Britain*, pp. 219–49; Lord Londonderry, *Hansard*, House of Lords, vol. 98, col. 999, 31 Mar. 1935.

47 Sherman, *Island Refuge*, p. 73.

but by 1947 refugees were recorded as having established 1,000 firms.[48]

Correspondence in the papers of Anthony de Rothschild shows that in late 1936 he and other Jewish leaders expressed discreet support for the policy of encouraging refugees to go to the Special Areas. They also agreed to provide financial assistance for individual cases on their merits. They pledged their support at a confidential meeting with a businessman by the name of H. Powys Greenwood, who had set up the meeting at the suggestion of the Treasury's Sir Frederick Leith-Ross to explore what financial or other encouragement the participants would give to the settlement of Jewish refugees in the depressed areas. De Rothschild and his friends not only promised financial support, but endorsed the policy of discreetly publicising British liberality in the issue of permits for refugees going to these areas and offered to help disseminate information about such prospects, taking care not to alert the German authorities. De Rothschild was embarrassed to learn that a report of the meeting had been circulated among several Whitehall departments, one of which was arranging to discuss it. Schiff wrote on his behalf to Cooper disclaiming any intention of challenging the policy of considering all cases on their merits. The Ministry of Labour official who had circulated the report reassured de Rothschild that his purpose had been to obtain a decision on whether the meeting called for any alteration in government policy on the issue of permits.[49] More research would be required to establish a causal link between the Jewish offer of support and the Home Office's sudden shift to active recruitment of German manufacturers, but it seems highly probable. The offer of financial support from wealthy British Jews was bound to make the Home Office feel more secure about the admission of refugee manufacturers who were prevented by German restrictions and depredations from taking out much of their capital.

Many potential investors were still in Greater Germany. Rather than continuing to negotiate at a distance, the commissioners invited some of the more promising prospects to come over for exploratory interviews. But the Home Office began to insist that any visits by refugee industrialists required elaborate prior scrutiny. In July 1938 it refused to grant a visa to a man the commissioners for England and Wales had invited with

48 Loebl, 'Refugees from the Third Reich', pp. 379–80.

49 H. P. Greenwood to A. de Rothschild, 29 Nov. 1936, Greenwood to R. G. Somervell (Ministry of Labour), 9 Dec. 1936, A. de Rothschild to Greenwood, 6 Jan. 1937, Schiff to Cooper, 8 Jan. 1937, Greenwood to A. de Rothschild, 10 Jan. 1937, Somervell to A. de Rothschild, 13 Jan. 1937, A. de Rothschild, note of telephone call from Greenwood, 18 Jan. 1937, Greenwood to A. de Rothschild, 26 Jan. 1937, RA XI/35/46.

a view to setting up a factory on the Treforest Trading Estate in Wales. Cooper explained this decision by saying that another refugee had been allowed to land for four weeks on the basis of such an invitation and now wished to stay for at least another six months 'which I am afraid means for keeps'. The commissioners would embarrass the Home Office if they invited foreigners over for interviews without preliminary investigation of their cases abroad and it subsequently turned out that either applicant or proposal was unsatisfactory. Cooper wished applications of this type to be referred in the first instance to the Home Office. He warned that, having once gained entry, such persons were likely to seek asylum: 'These unfortunate German Jews get up to all sorts of dodges in order to gain a footing in this country, and as I have already said, once they are here they become refugees who cannot be got rid of.'[50]

Cooper's observations illustrate the lengths to which the quest for refuge drove some Jews. The desperation to get out of the Reich inevitably led unsuitable candidates to attempt to fit themselves into the limited range of categories for entry to Britain. The Home Office's exhaustive checks on the suitability of industrialists, who were overwhelmingly male, was in contrast to the relatively indulgent approach it adopted towards Jewish women who used domestic service as their avenue of refuge.

There was no question of surrendering the principle of pre-selection. However, the Home Office was prepared to ease certain aspects of procedure to facilitate the admission of refugees to work as resident domestics in private households.[51] The demand for women to undertake such work appeared inexhaustible. In fostering the immigration of refugee domestics, the government was acceding to middle-class pressure for more domestic servants and was overriding trade union objections to foreign labour, as Tony Kushner has pointed out.[52] Refugee organisations were enthusiastic because of financial considerations: 'for the expenditure of a comparatively small sum of money large numbers of Refugee girls could be placed in permanent employment in this country without further liability on any fund'.[53]

Domestic service became the principal avenue of entry for refugee

[50] Cooper to Owen M. Roberts, 6 Aug. 1938, Correspondence with commissioners for the Special Areas (England and Wales), Jul.–Aug. 1938, PRO HO 213/270.

[51] London, 'British Immigration', pp. 217–27, has a slightly fuller discussion of refugee domestics.

[52] Tony Kushner, 'An Alien Occupation – Jewish Refugees and Domestic Service in Britain, 1933–1948', in Mosse, *Second Chance*, pp. 553–77. Statistics in the next paragraph are drawn from Kushner.

[53] Minutes of meeting of Committee of Investigation into the Domestic Bureau of the Co-ordinating Committee, 26 Jan. 1939, attached to minutes of Co-ordinating Committee meeting, 31 Jan. 1939, records from the International Refugee Organisation (IRO)

women who needed to earn their living. Over one-third of all refugees who came to Britain in the 1930s, as Kushner has emphasised, entered as domestic servants, the vast majority being women. Of an estimated total of 20,000 refugees choosing this means of escape, 14,000 entered in the last year before the war, figures which explain why a majority of refugees coming from Germany and Austria – some 55 per cent – were women. A small number had permission to work in private homes as housekeepers, companions, nursemaids and governesses, but refugee women were mostly admitted for basic domestic work. Among them were the author's mother, Lucie Meissner, and a few months later her mother, both of whom arrived from Vienna in 1939.

The Home Office decided that the admission of refugees for domestic service should be expanded.[54] For this purpose it developed labour-saving changes to the conditions imposed on foreign domestics. The essential alteration was that domestic servants would in future be placed not on time conditions, but on occupational conditions restricting them to domestic service. These changes came into effect in two stages in the autumn of 1938. From September, aliens already admitted for temporary purposes who applied for permission to take paid employment or engage in business would have their time limit cancelled, as long as there was no objection to their remaining to work. A new 'occupational' condition would restrict taking any employment or engaging in any business, profession or occupation without Home Office authorisation. In November the same principle was applied to both the entry and extension applications of persons already authorised to take paid domestic employment, who would in future be subjected only to an 'occupational' condition – not to enter any employment other than as a resident in service in a private household. Authorisations took the form of either Ministry of Labour permits or visas authorised for domestic employment and marked 'Instructions R'.[55] These changes reduced the administrative burden, since immigration officers were obliged to furnish reports when landing aliens on time conditions, but not if imposing an employment condition only. Nor did employment conditions need regular renewal.

deposited at the Archives nationales, Paris, as AJ43 Organisation Internationale des réfugiés (hereafter AJ43), AJ43/14/114.

[54] Holderness to D. P. Reilly, 27 Oct. 1938, PRO FO 371/22535, W14096/104/98, f. 415, incorporated in Winterton, 'Disposal of refugees coming from Germany and Austria. Statement by the United Kingdom representative', L.I.C.14., 1 Nov. 1938, 'Intergovernmental Committee to develop and continue the work of the Evian meeting', PRO FO 371/22536, W15029/04/98, f. 236, para. 4.

[55] HO circulars to chief constables, 21 Sep., 9 Nov. 1938, Jagelman to J. E. Duff, 11 Nov. 1938, F. G. Ralfe (chief inspector of immigration) to HM ports, 15 Nov. 1938, PCD, circular no. S.5606, 'Domestic servants', 26 Nov. 1938, PRO HO 213/4.

Domestics whose time limit was cancelled were told that their stay was conditional on good behaviour and warned against making unduly frequent changes of employment. The police were instructed to make regular checks to ensure 'by discreet interrogation' that employment conditions were being complied with.[56] The Home Office asked the police to help by dealing with cancellation of time conditions. Chief constables outside London agreed, but the Metropolitan Police commissioner, Sir Phillip Game, objected to the work involved and claimed that it risked 'further slowing up a machine which already rivals the mills of God for slowness'.[57] The plan was ultimately abandoned. The Home Office had no wish to draw public attention to the new procedures. Game warned of adverse publicity if it became known that large numbers of refugees were having their time conditions cancelled, without the decision having gone through Parliament.

The principle behind the changes – that, if there was no question of enforcing a time limit, employment conditions gave adequate control – was spelt out by W. Jagelman of the Home Office: 'in the case of a foreigner to whose indefinite stay in this country there is no objection, there is no real purpose in reviewing his case at intervals as hitherto under a time condition, and all that is really necessary is to control his activity'. Refugees' time conditions would normally be removed at a much earlier date than usual: 'once it is definitely established that the foreigner is in fact a refugee and that plans for his future have been made to which the Home Office can agree, it follows that there is no objection to his indefinite stay'. If the foreigner had already been in the country more than four years, the time condition should simply be cancelled. But those who had been in the country less than three years, and who would now be subject to an occupational condition, would not be granted cancellation of this condition in future.[58] Thus, although recent arrivals would gain exemption from time conditions earlier than most aliens, their prospects of being granted unconditional leave were postponed indefinitely and the occupational condition chained them to domestic service. Overall, therefore, their position was worse than that of ordinary work-permit holders. Thus, although the Home Office planned to absorb refugee domestics into the labour force and assumed many would remain permanently, it treated the more recent arrivals as migrant labour rather than prospective permanent residents. In this way it expanded the use of refugees for domestic labour while avoiding any

56 See n. 55.
57 Sir Phillip Game to Maxwell, 6 Dec. 1938, correspondence with police, Nov. 1938–Aug. 1939, PRO HO 213/5.
58 Jagelman to Duff, 11 Nov. 1938, PRO HO 213/4, cited n. 55.

formal acknowledgement that they would constitute a permanent addition to the population.

In 1944 the Home Office legal adviser queried the legality of the practice of replacing time by employment conditions. Officials concluded that, in cases where the home secretary had varied landing conditions by introducing conditions of a type not imposed on entry, he had exceeded his powers. The new conditions were therefore *ultra vires* and unenforceable. However, an amendment to correct the illegality was proposed by an official in 1946, but did not progress beyond a draft.[59] Of course, it was not disclosed to refugees that the immigration conditions imposed on them were in many cases believed to be invalid.

Few refugees remained in domestic service if they had an alternative: most entered it only to escape from the Nazis. Home Office officials knew it would be impossible to keep refugees doing such work for very long, but hoped to tie them to it for a few years at least.[60] The exodus from domestic labour was rapid, hastened by job losses at the outbreak of war and then by mass internment and new war-time employment opportunities. By the end of the war few refugees remained in service. Yet, it remained one of the rare avenues by which Jewish survivors might enter.[61] British enthusiasm for this form of immigration did not prevent a significant rate of refusals in the period before the war, estimated at 15 per cent, partly accounted for by applicants who fell outside the age limits, a point made by Kushner. He notes that the story of the admission of refugee domestics strikingly embodies both the humanitarian elements and the deeply self-interested side of British policy.

In the latter half of 1938 the Home Office handed over the task of investigating domestic service applicants to the refugee organisations. They had lobbied for such powers as a means of obtaining more control over the selection of entrants. The voluntary organisations received many complaints about unsuitable refugee domestics and, in the frequent cases where employment arrangements collapsed, the women were thrown on to their charity. Consequently, they felt they had a proprietary interest which entitled them to vet admissions. In October the Co-ordinating Committee went further, complaining that the Home Office was admitting refugees without the approval of its constituent members.[62]

Under new arrangements finalised in October 1938, the Home Office

[59] Legal adviser, minute, July 1944, D. Parkinson, 'Memorandum on the subject of the variation by the Secretary of State of conditional landings imposed by the Immigration Officer', 5 Oct. 1946, PRO HO 213/601.

[60] Holderness to Major General Sir H. de C. Martelli (governor of Jersey), 4 July 1938, PRO HO 213/281.

[61] Kushner, 'An Alien Occupation', p. 575.

was to take over from the Ministry of Labour the processing of all applications from refugees to be admitted for employment. Prospective employers of refugee domestics would be referred to the Co-ordinating Committee's Domestic Bureau, whose recommendations would become the basis for Home Office visa authorisations. The Home Office had proposed that the Co-ordinating Committee should establish an office in Vienna to vet applicants for the United Kingdom and dominions, including domestic service cases. Cooper even offered space in the British Passport Control Office, but stipulated that the people doing the vetting should be 'thoroughly British and not people of German or Austrian origin who have settled down here'.[63] Although agreed in principle, the projected Vienna office was never set up, so the suitability of domestic applicants in Austria was investigated either by the Kultusgemeinde (the Jewish communal organisation in Vienna) or by the Society of Friends, which had a centre in Vienna. If they reported favourably, a visa would be authorised; if refugee organisations refused support, the application would be referred. In addition, applicants already approved by the Ministry of Labour should be 'closely interrogated' by the PCO to ascertain whether they were potential refugees; if this seemed to be the case, the application would be delayed for investigation and approval by the Domestic Bureau.[64]

The refugee bodies had now gained unprecedented control over admissions. The Home Office thought the Domestic Bureau did a better job of investigating refugee applications than the Ministry of Labour. However, the quality of domestic applicants remained a source of controversy. Jeffes, returning from a tour of European passport control offices, complained to Cooper in June 1939 about the 'bad type of refugee' he had met in Vienna, who nevertheless possessed authorisations from refugee committees and ministry permits. He had interviewed several women with domestic service permits 'who were so filthily dirty both in their person and their clothing that they were utterly unfit to go inside a decent British home'.[65] The PCO in Vienna, G. W. Berry, asked how to deal with applicants who clearly had no intention of remaining in domestic work. Home Office officials were well aware that the refugees were 'not domestic types' but took a tolerant view of many applicants' evident unsuitability and lack of enthusiasm for the work.[66]

Several expert advisory committees were set up to make recommen-

62 Sherman, *Island Refuge*, pp. 99, 155–7.

63 Cooper to Ormerod, 6 Sep. 1938, Ormerod to Cooper, 16 Sep. 1938, AJ43/14/114.

64 Jagelman to Ormerod, H. J. Neden and Jeffes, 21 Oct. 1938, PRO HO 213/99; PRO LAB 8/82 and 83; 'Report by Mrs Beer on her recent visit to Germany', Minutes of Co-ordinating Committee meeting, 1 May 1939, PRO HO 213/268.

65 Jeffes to Cooper, unsigned marginal notes, 5 June 1939, PRO HO 213/107.

dations to the Home Office on the admission of refugees in professional occupations. The entry of doctors from Austria produced a difference of opinion: a Medical Advisory Committee composed of doctors and representatives of refugee organisations insisted that the numbers should not exceed fifty, selected from about a thousand applicants, who would be allowed to re-qualify. The home secretary wished to admit 500 but felt unable to override the doctors' opposition. Hoare felt sufficiently aggrieved to complain about this in his memoirs.[67] Another committee restricted the admission of dentists from Austria to forty. The Home Office arranged for informal advice through the Tavistock Clinic about the admission of foreign psychoanalysts and other practitioners of psychological medicine.[68] While most medically qualified refugees were not allowed to practice, shortages during the war led to emergency regulations permitting the temporary employment of refugee doctors and dentists in hospitals and clinics.[69]

The vast majority of refugees seeking entry to Britain felt they had no alternative but to pursue immigration through the normal channels, however limited the opportunities were and dangerous the delays caused by the pre-selection process. Those few refugees who attempted to evade immigration controls were dealt with sternly. Three Austrian Jews who reached Bristol as stowaways in July 1938 were sent back to France, despite support from members of Parliament and offers by a Bristol Jewish congregation to pay their passage to South America.[70] Three other refugees who had entered without leave were imprisoned by a London magistrate who recommended them for deportation.[71] In the summer of 1939 five Jewish stowaways off a ship from Antwerp were prosecuted, remanded in custody, recommended for deportation and deported.[72] A German and an Austrian crossing the channel in a ten-foot dinghy which capsized were rescued and deported to Belgium.[73]

A British woman arriving by air from Rotterdam in the summer of 1938 was arrested and prosecuted by Customs for attempting to smuggle in jewellery belonging to Jewish friends in Vienna. The prose-

[66] *Ibid.*; Cooper to Jeffes, 15 Aug. 1939, PRO HO 213/107; R. T. Parkin, memorandum, 'Visas for United Kingdom granted to refugees', 8 May 1939, PRO FO 371/24100, W7740/3231/48, f. 63; Kushner, 'An Alien Occupation', pp. 563–5.

[67] M. G. Russell, memorandum, 15 Mar. 1939, PRO HO 213/261; Viscount Templewood (Sir Samuel Hoare), *Nine Troubled Years* (London, 1954), p. 240.

[68] Dr H. V. Dicks to Jagelman, 9 Aug. 1938, Russell, memorandum, 6 Nov. 1938, PRO HO 213/342.

[69] PRO MH 76/236.

[70] *Jewish Chronicle*, 22 July 1938, p. 20, 29 July 1938, p. 22.

[71] Sherman, *Island Refuge*, pp. 125–7.

[72] *Hansard*, House of Commons, vol. 350, col. 1979, 31 July 1939, col. 2808, 4 Aug. 1939.

[73] *Jewish Chronicle*, 4 Aug. 1939, p. 8.

cution was intended to deter smuggling by and on behalf of refugees, which was said to be prevalent. Schiff made representations on behalf of the woman, a worker with the GJAC, claiming that publicity would prejudice negotiations for the establishment of an emigration office in Vienna and guaranteeing payment of any fine. Support for leniency came from both the Home Office and Foreign Office, and Customs agreed that the prosecution would be withdrawn.[74]

The Czech crisis of September 1938 created further pressure for admissions. People from Czechoslovakia started to arrive at the ports and some were refused entry. It was not possible to re-introduce visas for holders of Czechoslovak passports quickly, since revocation of the visa abolition agreement required three months' notice which had to be given on a quarter-day. On the first possible date the Czechs were notified that visas would be required as from 1 April 1939. Meanwhile, Holderness warned that Czech nationals faced close interrogation at the ports and the likelihood of refusal.[75] Admitting large numbers of refugees from Czechoslovakia was regarded as out of the question.[76]

By October 1938, the policy of restriction could be said to be working only in the sense that it was keeping out most refugees who wished to enter. The demand for refuge was running at an unprecedentedly high level. Neither the Home Office nor the refugee organisations could cope with the ever-growing pressure of work, despite efforts to spread the burden by involving other departments. The system inevitably delayed all cases that passed through it. Representatives of the refugee organisations told the Home Office that the system was at breaking point. Although voluntary organisations were acquiring a greater measure of control over admissions, they lacked the administrative capacity to cope. The government would not provide the extra funds they needed.[77] The Co-ordinating Committee stated that there was 'a complete breakdown on the official side, of the policy of selected immigration through the approved voluntary organisations'.[78] It sent a deputation which complained that the government was admitting persons not previously authorised by the voluntary committees. Winterton found himself in the odd position of defending the Home Office's right to admit aliens not approved by the refugee bodies.[79] On 28 October, Schiff and Davidson

[74] J. S. Sutton to Chancellor of the Exchequer, 1 Sep. 1938, Wardle to Makins, W. Hayter to Cooper, 2 Sep. 1938, Cooper to Hayter, 3 Sep. 1938, PRO FO 371/22573, W11929/11929/98, f. 198.

[75] Holderness to W. I. Mallet, 2 Nov. 1938, PRO FO 371/21586, C13325/11896/12, f. 253.

[76] Makins, minute, 27 Oct. 1938, PRO FO 371/21585, C12940/11896/12, f. 47.

[77] *Jewish Chronicle*, 9 Dec. 1938, pp. 7, 21; Bentwich, *They Found Refuge*, pp. 54–5.

[78] Ormerod to Winterton, 18 Oct. 1938, PRO HO 213/1636.

told Cooper that the government had admitted too many refugees from Austria who should not have been admitted at all because they seemed to have no prospects of suitable employment or of emigration. Schiff suggested calling a halt to admissions, at least temporarily, until those already admitted had been assimilated or re-emigrated. This could be done without announcing any change of policy.[80]

The government's waning ability to deal with the workload was clear from the arrears in the processing of naturalisation applications. The Home Office was already badly behind when the applications of refugees who completed the statutory five years' residence were added to its pile of work. By May 1938 the arrears figure was over 2,000. An official seeking Treasury sanction for staff to reduce the backlog reported that the home secretary had recently expressed horror at the time it took to complete the case of the husband of the actress Elisabeth Bergner.[81]

The Treasury sanctioned loans of staff from the ports and other minor additions to the Home Office establishment, but these made little dent in the growing quantities of refugee work.[82] Further paid overtime was authorised because of extra work and disruption during the Munich crisis, when the belief that war was imminent led to the packing of files for evacuation and led many aliens to request the return of their passports so they could go home. Lord Winterton, describing the pressure at the Home Office, said it had received 'hundreds and thousands of applications', but it was 'impossible to grant more than a proportion of them'.[83] By late October the department had an estimated 15,000 files awaiting action. The figure was likely to rise to 20,000 but even this estimate, Holderness warned, might prove 'very conservative'.[84] The volume of admissions had increased from 200 per week in September to 100 per day in October.[85] By the third week of November there was a backlog of 10,000 pending visa applications.[86] The introduction of visas had created an administrative catastrophe.

Since the early days of the exodus from Germany, the government had been under pressure to participate in international action on refugees. Following the *Anschluss* the pressure intensified. British government

[79] Correspondence, 20–8 Oct. 1939, *ibid.*

[80] Cooper, memorandum, 29 Oct. 1938, *ibid.*; Sherman, *Island Refuge*, pp. 155–8.

[81] Correspondence, 21–7 May 1938, PRO HO 45/24773/435958/58; correspondence, Aug. 1937–Nov. 1938, PRO T 162/582/E4080/2.

[82] Correspondence, Sep. 1938–May 1939, PRO T 162/847/E20500/3.

[83] Winterton to MacDonald, 18 Oct. 1938, PRO FO 371/22535, W13882/104/98, f. 366.

[84] Holderness, minute, 28 Oct. 1938, PRO HO 45/24773/435958/61.

[85] T. W. E. Roche, *The Key in the Lock: A History of Immigration Control in England from 1066 to the Present Day* (London, 1969), p. 27.

[86] Cooper, memorandum, 19 Nov. 1938, PRO HO 213/1638.

policy towards international action on refugees from 1933 until war broke out in 1939 was shaped by two overriding considerations: first, to maintain sovereignty over refugee policy; secondly, to contain the size of the refugee problem.

The question of how the international community should respond to the refugee problem at first involved the League of Nations. From 1933 onwards, however, Britain made efforts to minimise the League's role, limiting its ratification of the 1933 and 1938 League Conventions on refugees, in order to protect British sovereignty over admissions. The League's decision in 1933 to establish a high commissioner for refugees coming from Germany, for example, was acceptable to Britain only on condition that the high commissioner be separate from the League itself, that his work be financed by private organisations and that he not have power to negotiate with Germany. The policy of denying the high commissioner government funds, except for administrative expenses, effectively confined him to providing juridical protection for refugees. The first high commissioner, James McDonald, an American, expressed his frustration at these limitations in a much-publicised letter of resignation in late 1935. His replacement, Sir Neill Malcolm, a British candidate thought to be more sympathetic to the British government's priorities, was equally constrained and his achievements were minimal.[87]

In early 1938 Britain set out its position on the proper role of the League on refugee issues. At that time a new League convention on refugees was being finalised. The Home Office wished to limit new obligations under the convention and expressed fears of excessive flows of German refugees to the United Kingdom. William Hayter of the Foreign Office criticised Home Office opposition to protecting persons who left Germany after the date the convention would come into effect. At the Geneva conference in February 1938 for conclusion of the new convention, Britain's representatives opposed any modification obliging it to allow refugees temporarily in the country to remain and establish themselves. In a statement drafted by Cooper, the United Kingdom delegate, the British government insisted on its right to decide these

[87] A League Provisional Arrangement of July 1936 made provision for a uniform legal status for refugees from Germany, on the pattern of that provided for 'Nansen' refugees by a convention of October 1933. The United Kingdom ratified the 1933 convention in October 1936, with reservations. In February 1938 the League adopted a new convention designed to give a more permanent form to the provisional arrangement; Sherman, *Island Refuge*, pp. 35–84; Lord Duncannon, 'A Summary of the Activities of the High Commissioner for Refugees coming from Germany in Questions of Emigration', 14 June 1938, Duncannon to Makins, 14 June 1938, PRO FO 371/22527, W7706/104/98, f. 93.

matters for itself, adding that it might withdraw concessions for other refugees if the new convention created an obligation to absorb temporary residents.[88] Cooper argued that Britain was already acting generously without any compulsion from international obligations. He told a private conference session that it had been possible 'in quite a large number of cases to agree to refugees remaining and establishing themselves', despite the difficulty of absorbing foreigners in a highly industrialised and densely populated country.[89] The United Kingdom signed the 1938 convention, but entered reservations which nullified the effect of provisions benefiting persons admitted on a temporary basis.

The Home Office saw a proposal for a new International Commission under the League as yet another source of unwelcome pressure. A new, autonomous body, Cooper wrote, might pursue 'an idealistic or adventurous policy which would not recommend itself to the countries of temporary refuge'. He advocated the exploration of settlement possibilities overseas.[90] When a League Council Committee of Three, including a United Kingdom representative, met in Paris in mid-February 1938, and recommended a policy of absorption of refugees in countries of refuge and the creation of an intergovernmental body for this purpose, the British response was similarly negative. Holderness told Roger Makins of the Foreign Office that the Home Office was worried about the proposal and would not accept it 'unless we are satisfied that it will serve a useful purpose and will not concern itself in the internal affairs of other countries'.[91]

Thus, the Home Office adopted a defensive posture towards any proposals to extend the scope of the existing international machinery. Its spokesmen also mounted a spirited defence, at home and abroad, of the existing domestic machinery for dealing with refugees. At the February 1938 League conference, Cooper argued that the relationship between the Home Office and the voluntary organisations was an acceptable alternative to specialised machinery created by certain other countries. Belgium, for example, had set up an Advisory Commission to pronounce on individual cases and express opinions on asylum decisions. Cooper argued that, in view of the close collaboration between the government and charitable organisations, 'it might be said that an

88 Cooper to Hayter, 12 Jan. 1938, Hayter, minute, Holderness to under secretary, 14 Jan. 1938, Cooper, draft of statement, 21 Jan. 1938, Hayter to Cooper, 22 Jan. 1938, PRO FO 371/22525, W511/637/985/104/98, f. 19.

89 League of Nations, Conference for the Conclusion of a Convention, Provisional Minutes of First Meeting (private), 7 Feb. 1938, PRO FO 371/22526, W2318/104/98, f. 27.

90 Cooper to Hayter, 11 Jan. 1938, Hayter, minute, 15 Jan. 1938, PRO FO 371/22525, W527/104/98, f. 38.

91 R. C. Skrine Stevenson, minute, 16 Feb. 1938, Holderness to Makins, 4 May 1938, PRO FO 371/22526, W2244/5829/104/98, f. 101.

advisory commission exists in the United Kingdom in fact, if not in name'.[92] His implication that the voluntary organisations performed an independent role as guardians of refugees' interests was far from the truth. In reality, these organisations were hardly impartial, but pursued their own agendas, which could and often did conflict with the aspirations of refugees. Still, the government saw no objection to relying on the voluntary agencies for leadership. In May 1938, when Eleanor Rathbone demanded the creation of more formal policy-making machinery, Prime Minister Neville Chamberlain countered with the claim, drafted by the Home Office, that the government's close collaboration with the voluntary bodies fulfilled this purpose and that ministers were relying on the recently formed Co-ordinating Committee to produce constructive policy proposals.[93] Thus, where humanitarian aid to refugees was concerned, the government surrendered its policy-making potential to the refugee organisations at home. Abroad, it doggedly resisted being told what to do by international agencies.

The League's work for refugees was reorganised in September 1938: a single organisation would replace the Nansen International Office, which protected people from several countries who had become refugees in the aftermath of the First World War, and the high commissioner for refugees coming from Germany. Accordingly, as from January 1939, refugees hitherto coming under the jurisdiction of these agencies would be dealt with by a newly appointed high commissioner of the League of Nations. One of his duties was to maintain relations with the newly established Intergovernmental Committee on Refugees (IGC).[94]

The IGC was the result of an initiative by President Roosevelt. The United States had not been particularly welcoming to Jews from Germany, although, after the *Anschluss*, Roosevelt increased the scope for Austrians to obtain a US visa, by ordering the combination of the small Austrian quota with the far larger German quota. The refugee crisis assumed new diplomatic significance in late March 1938 when Roosevelt called for an international meeting on the refugee problem, to launch a new committee of government representatives, 'for the purpose of facilitating the emigration from Austria, and presumably from Germany, of political refugees'.[95] Nations where refugees had found, or

92 League of Nations, conference for the Conclusion of a Convention, Provisional Minutes of Sixth Meeting (private), 7 Feb. 1938, PRO FO 371/22526, W2318/104/98, f. 27, pp. 9–12.

93 Chamberlain, *Hansard*, House of Commons, vol. 336, cols. 834–6, 23 May 1938.

94 League of Nations, 'International Assistance to Refugees: Report of the Sixth Committee to the Assembly', A.54.1938.XII., Geneva, 28 Sep. 1938, resol. 4, PRO FO 371/22535, W13140/104/98, f. 144.

hoped to find, a haven agreed to gather at Evian in France in early July to discuss collective action on the refugee problem.[96]

As the danger of a European war came closer, the Foreign Office was alert for signs that the isolationism of the Americans might be giving way to a readiness to become involved in European problems. Thus when Roosevelt suggested the conference, the attractive possibility of boosting Anglo-American co-operation led to agreement within Whitehall that, 'on political grounds alone', it was desirable to accept the American proposals in principle.[97] As Makins recalled, he and his colleague 'grabbed' the opportunity.[98] But British policy-makers were suspicious of the proposal for the new agency. The proposed Intergovernmental Committee on Refugees (IGC) was bound to create potential problems and unwelcome pressures. The British at first tried to prevent the new agency from coming into existence, but, once they realised that it would be difficult to stop, they acquiesced in its formation at the Evian conference.

In previous years the Foreign Office and the Treasury had agreed that to spend money or establish machinery for dealing with the refugees would risk perpetuating the problem, so such activities should be left to the private organisations.[99] Jewish organisations had provided the funds of the high commissioner for refugees. British government spokesmen continued to assert that public money would not be spent on refugees from Germany, whether for relief or for settlement abroad. This policy was not challenged by the American proposals, which also envisaged that emergency emigration would be financed by private organisations.

It was clear, nevertheless, that little could be done if the matter remained in private hands.[100] After all, private organisations could find jobs for refugees but could not organise their admission abroad. The head of the committee set up by the Evian meeting might be able to do something to facilitate the departure of people still in Germany.

Whitehall officials also feared that helping people in the Reich would provoke additional problems for Jews in Poland, Romania and elsewhere, including Hungary. At the May 1938 session of the Council of the League, Poland and Romania had already mentioned their desire for aid to help reduce their Jewish populations. Before the Evian confer-

95 US Embassy, memorandum, 24 Mar. 1938, Noble to E. A. Shillito, 28 Mar. 1938, PRO T 160/842/F13577/01/1.

96 Sherman, *Island Refuge*, pp. 95–7, 100–23.

97 Minutes of interdepartmental meeting, 28 Mar. 1938, PRO T 160/842/F13577/01/1.

98 Lord Sherfield (Roger Makins), interview with the author, 13 Dec. 1990.

99 See e.g. Herbert Brittain (Treasury) to Strang, 31 July 1935, PRO FO 371/19677, W7002/356/98, f. 172.

100 Minutes of 28 Mar. 1938 meeting, n. 97 above.

ence, Sir John Hope Simpson, director of the Royal Institute of International Affairs' Refugee Survey, argued that, if the proposed IGC failed to act to relieve the acute position of the Jewish populations in these countries, persecution was sure to follow. He regarded this problem as more serious than the problem faced by German and Austrian refugees.[101] Foreign Office officials shared Simpson's concerns, but came to the opposite conclusion, namely that any action by the IGC to relieve the position of Jews in these countries would be a cue for further persecution. At Evian they therefore tried to convince Polish and Romanian observers that their governments should not look to the IGC for assistance.[102]

The government, reluctantly, was being drawn into establishing new international machinery on the refugee problem. It still had to decide whether to propose financial aid to refugees. In mid-June, Edward Playfair, then a principal within the Treasury's finance division, produced the first draft of the financial instructions to the British delegation at Evian, advising that it would be unwise to abandon the policy of opposing expenditure on refugees from Germany. It was true that British funds had been spent very recently on assistance to Assyrian refugees, but this could be distinguished as a special case. If the principle of spending League funds on refugees was conceded, it would widen the scope of demands on the League and its contributing governments. Playfair underlined the potential for further claims on British funds if the countries represented at Evian showed readiness to make financial contributions towards the emigration of Jews expelled from Germany. Countries such as Poland and Romania would 'take further measures to expel Jews, once they know that someone else is prepared to come to their aid . . . In the interests of the Jewish population of those countries, it seems that too open a hand is inadvisable.' He concluded that policy should therefore remain unchanged.[103]

However, several higher-ranking Treasury officials were prepared to support expenditure on refugees. Playfair's senior, S. D. Waley, a principal assistant secretary concerned with finance, and a Jew, was not hopeful about the outcome of the conference:

101 Makins, minute, 'Consideration of the Refugee Question at the 101st Session of the Council', 14 May 1938, Simpson to Makins, 8 June 1938, PRO FO 371/22527, W6714/7399/104/98, f. 47.

102 Skrine Stevenson, minute, 6 July 1938, PRO FO 371/22528, W8851/104/98, f. 31; Makins, minute, *ibid.*, quoted in Sherman, *Island Refuge*, p. 116.

103 Edward Playfair to Imperial and Foreign Division (Treasury), memorandum, 7 June 1938, Playfair, memorandum, 'Attitude of HM Government in the United Kingdom', Playfair to Imperial and Foreign Division (Treasury), P. G. Inch to Playfair, Playfair to Waley, 15 June 1938, PRO T 160/842/F13577/01/1.

I am afraid that the Evian Conference is bound to be somewhat of a fiasco. Few governments seem likely to promise to take more refugees than they are doing at present, or to commit themselves to any definite number. The Conference seems, therefore, likely to do no more than express platonic sympathies and to set up an Intergovernmental Committee, which does not seem likely to serve any useful purpose, and may do actual harm by hampering the activities of the new high commissioner.

Waley's view was 'that we ought not to rule out of court the possibility of later on giving some financial assistance in order to obtain such constructive results as are possible'. Perhaps some understanding might be reached with Jewish leaders over limiting Jewish immigration to Palestine. Perhaps an offer of limited financial help might get countries which were trying to get rid of Jews to agree to take steps making it possible for them to make a new start abroad, rather than arriving destitute. Germany might allow refugees 'to export sufficient capital in the form of goods and capital equipment', said Waley, though he was more hopeful that arrangements of this type could be made with Hungary, Romania and Poland. Such assistance as Britain and other states could give would put them in a stronger position to urge 'that the problem of reducing Jewish populations should be undertaken in a gradual and orderly way and not by brutal methods and wholesale expulsions'. Waley concluded with a disclaimer: 'Frankly, I cannot pretend to be objective on this topic and am rather apologetic for expressing any views at all.'[104]

Sir Frederick Phillips, Treasury under secretary, shared Playfair's concern that Poland and Romania were poised to enlarge the scale of the Jewish refugee problem. He advocated that the conference confine its agenda to refugees from Germany and Austria: 'the more facilities are provided the more refugees there will be to provide for'. But he followed Waley's suggestion of a flexible approach. The position finally adopted was that the United Kingdom should be prepared to match any contribution the United States was ready to make. However, the British delegation should refuse to discuss governmental contributions until the US government, which had convened the conference, had decided on such action. Phillips warned: 'the Americans are past masters at pushing other people into obligations and then backing out themselves'. He concluded with the warning, 'We are *not* in the long run likely to escape some governmental assistance either by grant or guarantee but we had better safeguard our position very carefully at this stage.'[105]

[104] S. D. Waley to Sir Frederick Phillips, memorandum, 'Evian Conference', 17 June 1938, *ibid.* (title, 'Political refugees from Germany and Austria', added in Warren Fisher's hand).

Submitting the proposed line for ministerial approval, the permanent secretary of the Treasury, Sir Warren Fisher, put his personal stamp on the recommendation:

The principal element is of course the Jews who are exposed to unspeakable horrors. It is clear that, however much we may sympathise, we cannot provide a solution of this terrible problem (which is not confined to Germany). But our historic role of an asylum for political outcasts and our position as the mandatory Power for Palestine shd [*sic*] make us ready to do what we can consistently with the legitimate interests of our people at home and of the Arabs in Palestine. (On a wholly lower plane of thought I may mention that this country has frequently been the gainer by providing refuge to foreigners highly qualified in various walks of life.)

While, therefore, I wd [*sic*] start in at the conference apparently square-toed about the American exclusion of Government Finance from any scheme of help, I think we shd [*sic*] be well advised from every point of view – if not for reasons of humanity – to keep open minds (without avowing it) & be on the look-out for any opportunity of intelligent assistance. (This of course won't help the majority of these poor people.)[106]

The Chancellor of the Exchequer, Sir John Simon, initialled these suggestions, without comment.

The final brief, therefore, contained the reservation that delegates should not bring up the issue of governmental finance unless and until the United States had explicitly declared it would be providing such funding.[107] 'The hand will not be an easy one to play', Makins observed. He assumed the Treasury instructions to mean that some form of British government finance would ultimately be available, should the US government favour this approach.[108] He emphasised 'the overriding importance of co-operating with the United States Government in this matter to the fullest extent', and sought authority to agree to a commitment. He was told that, if the United States refused to abandon the idea of setting up an intergovernmental committee, the United Kingdom government should 'in the last resort' agree to the proposal, presuming that any contribution to the IGC's expenses and staff would involve a relatively small amount. However, no sign should be given of envisaging any further financial obligation. If such a prospect was raised, the delegation should seek instructions.[109] The Treasury thus opposed any British initiative on funds. But although policy-makers felt the United Kingdom should not take a lead, they recognised the crucial importance

105 Phillips, memorandum, 21 June 1938, *ibid.*
106 Fisher to Chancellor of the Exchequer, 21 June 1938, *ibid.*
107 Playfair to Makins, 27 June 1938, *ibid.*
108 Makins, minute, 28 June 1938, PRO FO 371/22528, W8388/104/98, f. 207.
109 Makins to Inch, 2 July 1938, Inch to Makins, 4 July 1938, FO minute, 'Final memorandum of instructions for the United Kingdom Delegation to the meeting of an

of government finance. For example, R. A. Butler, parliamentary under secretary at the Foreign Office, told an interdepartmental meeting shortly before the conference that, without government funding, 'the whole scheme would fall through', since private organisations were in no position to finance emigration of Jews from Germany and Austria on a large scale.[110]

In comparison with civil servants in other Whitehall departments, notably the Foreign Office, Treasury officials displayed unusual readiness to articulate the humanitarian issues involved in the refugee problem and to respond to them in a constructive manner. We have seen senior Treasury officials up to the permanent secretary expressing humanitarian concern for refugees. In terms of material support, they backed the principle of spending public funds to help Jews escape, even though it would constitute a break with established policy. Of course, the sums being contemplated at this stage were relatively small. As for the IGC, the Treasury officials' cautious response may reflect their highly developed concern with value for money which was bound to make them wary of supporting a new agency with poor prospects of accomplishing its stated objectives. Indeed, Waley feared that the IGC's very existence might damage other efforts to help refugees.

At Evian, Makins felt burdened by having as the British delegate the unimpressive Winterton, whom he dismissed as obtuse. He worked with officials from other countries to salvage something from the gathering. He exercised considerable influence over the proceedings and drafted the conference report. He recalled being reasonably satisfied with the outcome.[111] The British representatives acceded, albeit reluctantly, to the American plan to set up the IGC. The brief of the IGC was to use diplomatic means to persuade the German government to contribute to the cost of expelling its Jews by letting emigrants retain some of their capital. This, it was hoped, would result in a more orderly emigration from Greater Germany. In addition, the IGC's director was to approach other countries with a view to expanding opportunities for permanent settlement.[112] In the absence of any American motion that governments should make a financial contribution, the British, as instructed, maintained silence on this issue.

Inter-governmental conference at Evian on July 6th to discuss the question of emigration from Germany and Austria', 5 July 1938, PRO FO 371/22529, W8851/8885/8886/104/98, f. 31.

110 'Record of interdepartmental meeting on 30th June 1938', PRO FO 371/22538, W8713/104/98, f. 281.

111 Lord Sherfield, interview, cited n. 98.

112 Sherman, *Island Refuge*, pp. 112–36; Joshua B. Stein, 'Great Britain and the Evian Conference of 1938', *Wiener Library Bulletin* 29 (1976), 40–52; Breitman and Kraut,

Having resigned themselves to the IGC's formation, Foreign Office officials shifted their energies to containing the impact of the new agency by controlling its activities and limiting its scope as much as they could. One tactic was to link IGC officers closely to the work of the League high commissioner for refugees. Another was to treat the IGC more as the host for a series of infrequent meetings than as an ongoing body with a permanent secretariat.

There was a logic behind the apparently contradictory postures which British policy-makers adopted towards the IGC. The logic becomes apparent once it is understood that the government did not assign vital importance to the IGC's success; as mentioned, the government's overriding objective was rather to ensure that the IGC did not interfere with British sovereignty over refugee policy. The Foreign Office also wished to discourage the growth of the refugee problem on the continent and to limit its impact on the United Kingdom. It was therefore determined to show the German government – and other interested spectators, Poland and Romania in particular – that the United Kingdom could not be blackmailed into taking destitute Jews off other nations' hands. The priority, therefore, was not to help refugees. It was to force Germany – and other governments wishing to unload their Jewish populations – to play according to internationally agreed rules. British ministers and officials were determined that no aspect of the government's refugee policy would be dictated by any external force – be it a foreign state, an international organisation, or even the sheer pressure of the refugee exodus. In this context, the Evian conference could be viewed as a success for British policy. The demands of Poland and Romania for help in getting rid of their Jews had been consigned to the sidelines. The question of Palestine had been kept off the conference agenda. The United Kingdom had not been forced into any new commitments. There was even a chance that improvements in the situation of refugees might ensue.

Waley had been right to expect that the conference would produce little of value for refugees. His prediction that the IGC might have a negative practical effect also proved correct. Indeed, the main impact of the IGC was to undermine other work on behalf of refugees. Governments invoked the IGC's existence – and the illusory prospects of an IGC-negotiated agreement on the export of refugee capital from the German Reich – to deflect all other proposals for action. The likely failure of the proposed IGC to achieve anything had been Waley's reason for not excluding alternatives. This argument was turned on its

American Refugee Policy, pp. 58–62; for German policy, see Breitman, *The Architect of Genocide: Himmler and the Final Solution* (London, 1991), pp. 46–65.

head by Foreign Office officials in the months after the conference and used to dismiss any proposals outside the IGC's own narrow remit as a threat to its success. They claimed that to make funds available from countries outside Germany would play into the hands of both the Germans and other governments seeking to dump unwanted Jews on the charity of other nations.

Other Treasury officials joined Waley in his scepticism about the IGC's chances of achieving anything. Sir Frederick Leith-Ross, who had wide experience of international negotiations, tried to support the IGC's early attempts to set up talks with the German government, but was not optimistic. Expressing his reservations to Dean Acheson of the United States and Lord Winterton, the IGC's British chairman, Leith-Ross said he feared 'that the problem of getting butter out of a dog's mouth is a comparatively simple one as compared with getting foreign exchange out of Germany at the present time'.[113] Waley, who had been working closely with Leith-Ross, later explained Treasury doubts about the IGC's prospects to the Cabinet Committee on the Refugee Problem.[114]

In October 1938 Waley and the Foreign Office tried to overcome Board of Trade objections to schemes designed to facilitate the transfer of refugee capital to Britain. Such schemes were commercially unattractive, since they entailed conceding a reduction in export earnings.[115] A. W. G. Randall of the Foreign Office thought the Board of Trade should nevertheless relax 'their present rigid attitude' and drop their objections. His main reason was political: it 'would help Anglo-American relations if His Majesty's Government could offer a substantial contribution . . . having welcomed the American initiative at Evian and given the Intergovernmental Committee hospitality in London, we have accepted a certain responsibility for seeing that their work does not come to a complete deadlock'. The concessions currently in question, he argued, 'could not strictly be called financial'. He concluded that the 'overriding consideration' was Britain's 'moral responsibility' to try to find a solution of the refugee problem.[116]

While Foreign Office officials voiced support for the IGC, they showed little faith in its prospects. Indeed, they took steps which were

113 Sir Frederick Leith-Ross to Dean Acheson and Winterton, 10 Sep. 1938, PRO T 188/225.

114 Cabinet Committee on the Refugee Problem, 24 Jan. 1939, Conclusions, CRP (39) 1st Meeting, PRO CAB 98/1.

115 A. E. Lee (Board of Trade), 'Transfer of Property of German Refugees' (note of meeting on 6 Oct.), Waley to Wilkinson, 12 Oct. 1938, PRO FO 371/22535, W13549/13588/104/98, f. 258.

116 A. W. G. Randall, minute, 25 Oct. 1938, PRO FO 371/22535, W13673/104/98, f. 315; Randall, minute, 19 Oct. 1938, Lord Halifax to Stanley, 3 Nov. 1938, *ibid.*

calculated to undermine the new agency. In view of the difficulties of dealing with the Germans at anything below the summit level which had delivered the Munich agreement, officials considered unpromising the low level at which the IGC proposed to conduct negotiations. George Rublee, the IGC's director, did suggest that Chamberlain might raise the matter with Hitler.[117] But Foreign Office officials were concerned about diplomatic damage resulting from a German refusal to co-operate with the IGC. Worry that IGC initiatives might upset the delicate state of Anglo-German relations without achieving anything led officials to delay and undermine Rublee's proposed mission to Berlin. It was suggested that Rublee should wait until he had details of the numbers of refugees which individual countries would accept. But when Rublee then proposed that the British Empire match the US contribution of 27,000 quota admissions annually, the British reacted with fury at the very idea of being asked for specific numbers: as a sop, Rublee was confidentially provided with some figures for past admissions.[118]

The Foreign Office even suggested to the Americans that the IGC be effectively closed down as a separate body and that it would take over the IGC's responsibilities.[119] After six months, Rublee, frustrated by lack of support from the British and from Roosevelt, made good his threat to resign. Makins, the Foreign Office official most involved in refugee matters, had found Rublee unimpressive. He preferred the more amenable Sir Herbert Emerson, formerly governor of the Punjab, who had already been chosen in September as League high commissioner for refugees. Emerson, the Foreign Office's own candidate to succeed Rublee, was appointed as the IGC's director from the start of 1939. Once Emerson took over, the Foreign Office felt more hopeful about harmonious co-operation with the IGC in the service of British interests.[120]

As regards the proper role for privately funded aid for refugees, Lord Winterton and Foreign Office officials shifted uneasily between contradictory stances. On the one hand, they relied on private funds to achieve a solution of the refugee problem. On the other, they opposed the expansion of private fund-raising as a threat to the IGC's work. The Foreign Office even tried to curtail the success of Lord Baldwin's fund-

117 Williamson, 'Note of Discussion at the Home Office on 5/10/38', 5 Oct. 1938, PRO FO 371/22535, W13305/104/98, f. 206.

118 Correspondence, 4–20 Oct. 1938, PRO FO 371/22535, W13304/13405/13673/13860/13882/104/98, f. 202.

119 See ch. 5.

120 Lord Sherfield, interview, cited n. 98; correspondence, 22–9 Sep. 1938, PRO FO 371/22535, W13160/13699/104/98, f. 151.

raising appeal broadcast, in case it raised so much money as to cast the IGC's prospects into the shade.[121]

From a humanitarian perspective, the Foreign Office moves to limit private aid to refugees further undermined the only practical avenues of escape. British officials consistently discouraged proposals for refugee emigration outside IGC auspices.[122] Yet the IGC failed to produce any increased prospects for refugees. Meanwhile Sir John Hope Simpson, whose first study on the refugee problem appeared in the summer of 1938, persistently and publicly underlined the need for governments to recognise that the response of private charity was providing the only means of escape. He also emphasised that private efforts could deal with only a small part of the problem and called for action by governments before it was too late. Simpson had been rejected as a candidate for the post of director of the IGC – he was seen as too critical – but his analysis of the IGC's practical limitations remained unanswerable. Hayter advised Emerson to read Simpson's work.[123]

The IGC's limitations as an instrument for achieving humanitarian ends did not greatly worry the Foreign Office. After all, the department's primary objective in relation to the Evian proposal – maximising the opportunities it offered for developing closer Anglo-American relations – was being satisfactorily realised. And if the IGC threatened to muddy diplomatic relations with Germany, it could always be deflected, even dismantled.

Thus, British policy towards these international agencies was ruled by priorities formulated in terms of the national interest. These priorities made Britain hostile to the development of international agencies to engage effectively in humanitarian work. On the occasions when the British government did act to aid refugees, it tended to do so unilaterally. It also tried to draw other governments into bilateral arrangements in which a pledge of aid from one nation was conditional on similar commitments from others.

National concerns shaped British policy on every aspect of aid to refugees. As regards immigration, the government doggedly upheld its sovereign right to choose how many refugees it would admit and to decide cases on their individual merits. Spokesmen further claimed that only a very limited number of refugees could be absorbed, because the

121 See ch. 5.
122 Randall, minute, 7 Nov. 1938, PRO FO 371/22536, W14468/104/98, f. 58.
123 Report of speech at a Royal Empire Society dinner, *Jewish Chronicle*, 11 Nov. 1938, p. 24; Hayter to Stevenson, 10 Oct. 1938, PRO FO 371/22535, W13544/104/98, f. 250.

United Kingdom was 'not an immigration country' – a place of first refuge and transit, yes, but not of permanent settlement.

The government never envisaged mass settlement within the empire. The dominions' continuing reluctance to admit Jewish refugees was scarcely challenged.[124] In late 1938 and 1939 certain colonies, especially British Guiana, Kenya and Northern Rhodesia, were put forward publicly by ministers as possible places of settlement. Makins wished that these offers were genuine; he personally viewed Northern Rhodesia as the best possibility. But he acknowledged that talk of such prospects was largely bluff: 'In all fairness it has to be admitted that the offer of British Guiana and Tanganyika is largely an illusory one, and this must inevitably become apparent in due course.'[125] Palestine had been allowed to take in a relatively large number of Jewish refugees on a permanent basis until, in response to Arab opposition, Britain imposed increasing restrictions in the controversial White Paper of May 1939 and finally established a quota for Jewish immigration.[126] When the notion was floated that the IGC could require a commitment to absorbing specific numbers in any part of the empire, Britain rejected that too. British policy-makers' failure to act to provide settlement prospects for refugees from Nazism reflected fears that to do so might stimulate Poland and Romania to force out their Jewish populations in a state of destitution. The main use to which government put the IGC was thus negative: it would support nothing except action by the IGC; the IGC achieved nothing, so nothing was done. Thus it turned out that, for British purposes, a key function of the IGC was to contain both the size of the refugee problem and the demand for refuge and to do so merely by existing, rather than by acting. Similarly, in early 1943 the mere existence of Anglo-American discussions on refugees would be used by British policy-makers to justify their turning a deaf ear to suggestions for rescue attempts. Thus, the largely illusory prospects of intergovernmental action proved effective in helping the government to resist public pressure for humanitarian aid to Jews during the two periods when it was at its most intense.

As far as finance was concerned, British policy maintained that relief, emigration and settlement should be paid for by refugees themselves or by private organisations and not by governmental contributions. Any departure from this policy was believed to risk increasing and perpetu-

124 DO, 'Memorandum as to the attitudes of the Dominions towards the proposals to be discussed at the International Conference at Evian', June 1938, R. A. Wiseman to Makins, 20 June 1938, PRO FO 371/22527, W8012/104/98, f. 136.

125 Shuckburgh to Makins, 30 June 1938, Makins, minute, 1 Dec. 1938, PRO FO 371/22538, W8786/15621/104/98, f. 6.

126 *Palestine: A Statement of Policy*, Cmd 6019, May 1939.

ating the refugee problem, by encouraging the emigration and expulsion of destitute Jews. As the crisis deepened, Treasury officials questioned strict adherence to a zero-cost policy, but for the moment the policy remained intact.

British policy took a similarly cautious stand over diplomatic initiatives on the refugee problem such as efforts to influence the policies of the German government. The Foreign Office preferred to restrict the role of international agencies so that they did not interfere with conventional diplomacy. British fears for diplomatic relations with Germany even produced anxiety over possible repercussions if Nazi anti-Jewish policies were criticised at Evian. The British ambassador in Berlin suggested that such criticism might also produce a worsening of the treatment of the Jews.[127]

Reluctance to become involved in solving refugee problems in Europe led the government to adopt a cautious and defensive stance towards the role of international agencies in helping Jews emigrate. Yet the high priority given to fostering Anglo-American relations made it desirable to be involved in any international co-operation on refugees with which the US government was associated. The result was a policy of limited participation. The government could not avoid playing an active role on the international stage if it wished to exert a restraining influence on the scope of any internationally agreed action. Furthermore, British policy aimed to foster, by example and by diplomacy, greater commitment to aiding refugees on the part of other nations, in particular the United States. However, the difficulty underlined by Phillips – of getting the Americans to commit themselves to doing anything concrete on the refugee problem – remained. Over the next few years, British policy-makers launched several unilateral initiatives in the hope of giving the Americans a 'lead' which they would follow, preferably on a more generous scale. But the US government repeatedly failed to follow British leads in every area of refugee policy.

On the eve of war, the British government was dragging its heels on the intergovernmental scene and refusing to act under international direction. It offered little in the way of refuge and nothing in the way of settlement schemes or finance. Would any alteration in British policy result from further Nazi outrages against the Jews?

[127] Sir Nicholas Henderson to FO, 4 July 1938, PRO FO 371/22529, W8887/104/98, f. 73.

5 From *Kristallnacht* to the outbreak of war, November 1938 to September 1939

The Nazi regime now launched a terrifying new onslaught against Jews in the Reich. It began with a move timed to anticipate the imminent statelessness of Polish Jews in Germany. The Polish government, in order to exclude Jews who had been living abroad, had acted to withdraw their citizenship. Three days before this measure was due to take effect, the Germans suddenly rounded up some 10,000 Polish Jews and expelled them en masse to the frontier with Poland. There, border guards barred the way forward and the Germans the way back. Unable to proceed into Poland, the Jews were forced to remain in inhuman conditions in a no man's land on Polish soil at a place called Zbonszyn. Some people died, others lost their reason. The fate of the survivors remained uncertain. It took many weeks before most were admitted to Poland. Meanwhile a seventeen-year-old Polish Jew named Herschel Grynszpan, then living in France, learned that his parents had been caught up in the expulsions. He himself was under threat of expulsion from France. The distraught youth called at the German Embassy in Paris and fired a pistol at a third secretary, wounding him fatally.[1]

The assassination was denounced in Germany with menacing threats against Jews and wild allegations that British politicians were implicated. Fearful that a pogrom was imminent, Germany's Jewish leaders sent an eleventh-hour plea, delivered by no less a messenger than Weizmann, asking the British government to select 'some prominent non-Jewish Englishman to go to Berlin immediately' to try to prevent it.[2] But officials in London and Berlin agreed that such action would, if anything, make matters worse for Jews in Germany and that to meddle in 'a wasps' nest' could only detract from British prestige.[3]

The murder was the pretext for an outburst of violence against Jews

[1] Lucy S. Dawidowicz, *The War Against the Jews, 1933–1945* (tenth anniv. edn; Harmondsworth, 1987), pp. 135–6.

[2] Strang to G. Ogilvie-Forbes, no. 521, 9 Nov. 1938, PRO FO 371/21636, C13660/1667/62, f. 234.

[3] Ogilvie-Forbes to Strang, no. 662, A. G. M. Cadogan, minute, 10 Nov. 1938, PRO FO 371/21636, C13661/1667/62, f. 236.

which erupted simultaneously throughout Germany and Austria on the night of 9 November. Authorised by Hitler and orchestrated by the German authorities, the pogrom became known as *Kristallnacht*, because so much glass was smashed in attacks on Jewish homes and businesses.[4] Details of the ill-treatment of Jews filled many telegrams from the British chargé d'affaires in Berlin, George Ogilvie-Forbes, and consular officials. From Vienna, Gainer reported waves of arrests of Jewish men attempting to visit the British consulate.[5] Official instructions for measures against the Jews issued by Reinhard Heydrich, head of the SS (Schutzstaffel), stated that Jews ordered to be arrested and taken to concentration camps should not be ill-treated.[6] The German government later denied that Jews had been harmed. However, reports of violence against thousands of Jews told a different story. The Germans murdered nearly 100 Jews. Many others were driven to suicide. About 30,000 male Jews were taken to concentration camps.[7] A certain number were later released, so Ogilvie-Forbes reported, if they could prove that they were 'in a position to leave the country forthwith'.[8] The new wave of persecution was, he observed, 'on a scale and of a severity unprecedented in modern times'.[9]

Within hours, the head of the Foreign Office's Central Department, William Strang, was convinced that the pogrom in Berlin had been planned by the German authorities.[10] This remained the Foreign Office view. The distribution of culpability within the German leadership was less clear. Makins saw no reason to disbelieve a report that Goering and the Ministry of Economics wished for milder policies towards the Jews and to negotiate with the IGC, but had acquiesced in violence for which Goebbels was responsible. Ogilvie-Forbes considered that the pogrom had been 'instigated and ordered' by the German government and that recent events had 'only accelerated the process of elimination of the Jews which has for long been planned'.[11] The measures of official

4 Breitman, *Architect of Genocide*, pp. 46–55.

5 Ogilvie-Forbes to FO, nos. 661, 663, 10 Nov. 1938, no. 666, 11 Nov. 1938, Gainer to FO, no. 43, 10 Nov. 1938, PRO FO 371/21636, C13651/13706/13723/13729/1667/62, f. 232; Ogilvie-Forbes to FO, nos. 670–1, 673, 11 Nov. 1938, nos. 676, 679, 12 Nov. 1938, PRO FO 371/21637, C13775/13792/13841/13814/13815/1667/62, f. 1.

6 Reinhard Heydrich, 'Measures Against the Jews Tonight', 10 Nov. 1938, in Y. Arad *et al.* (eds.), *Documents on the Holocaust* (Jerusalem, 1981), pp. 102–4.

7 Dawidowicz, *War Against Jews*, pp. 136–8.

8 Ogilvie-Forbes to FO, no. 679, 12 Nov. 1938, PRO FO 371/21637, C13815/1667/62, f. 15.

9 Ogilvie-Forbes to Halifax, 16 Nov. 1938, PRO FO 371/21637, C13815/14108/1667/62, f. 144.

10 Strang, minute of telephone conversation with Ivone Kirkpatrick (Berlin) on 10 Nov. 1938, PRO FO 371/21636, C13768/1667/62, f. 257.

11 Ogilvie-Forbes to FO, no. 681, 13 Nov. 1938, PRO FO 371/21637, C13833/1667/62, f. 23.

punishment meted out to the Jews of Germany in the aftermath of the violence included a fine of 13 million marks for destruction and damage which they were alleged to have provoked.[12] Ogilvie-Forbes thought the proceeds of the fine should be used to assist Jewish emigration.[13]

Reports of the onslaught against the Jews led to outraged protests in Britain. The prime minister told the Commons that the government would be 'taking into consideration any possible way by which we can assist these people'.[14] On 14 November a meeting of the Cabinet Committee on Foreign Policy convened by the foreign secretary, Halifax, discussed the worsening state of Anglo-German relations since Munich and the possibility of war.[15] The question of whether to make any specific response to Germany's persecution of the Jews was raised by the home secretary, Hoare. He said that 'unless something was done there were signs that the House of Commons and the country might get out of hand'. Hoare's only suggestion concerned the USA, whose German immigration quota was fully earmarked for the next five years and could not be increased without legislation. He thought it might be possible to arrange to surrender part of the undersubscribed British annual quota of 60,000 – of which only about a quarter was used – in aid of German Jewish immigration. The meeting rejected several other ideas. Chamberlain dismissed proposals of putting pressure on Germany to modify its harsh internal policies. He saw little public demand for the government to act in this way and emphasised that Britain was 'not in a position to frighten Germany'. However, he wished to respond to the 'very general and strong desire that something effective should be done to alleviate the terrible fate of the Jews in Germany. Some such action, taken in collaboration with America, would ease the public conscience.' Hoare appeared to feel that all Britain needed to do was to get the United States to act, perhaps through the quota transfer he had suggested. He said it was not true that the USA was admitting many Jewish refugees while Britain was 'doing nothing':

> A powerful and responsible Jewish organisation in London was dealing with individual cases at a cost of £5,000 a week and about 75 refugees were being daily admitted to this country. The organisation was anxious that these figures should not be disclosed as they would be criticised both by those who would think them inadequate and by those who would regard them as excessive.

[12] Ogilvie-Forbes to FO, nos. 532, 533, 13 Nov. 1938, no. 534, 14 Nov. 1938, no. 537, Makins, minute, 16 Nov. 1938, PRO FO 371/21637, C13836/13837/14014/14049/1667/62, f. 18.

[13] Ogilvie-Forbes to FO, no. 681, n. 11 above.

[14] Chamberlain, *Hansard*, House of Commons, vol. 341, col. 505, 14 Nov. 1938.

[15] Conclusions, Cabinet Committee on Foreign Policy, FP (36) 32nd Mtg, 14 Nov. 1938, PRO CAB 27/624.

The discussion showed that some action was felt to be necessary but there was no clear idea of what it should be. Halifax worried over arousing anti-Jewish prejudice. Oliver Stanley thought pressing the United States for a quota transfer would be a mistake unless Britain was taking 'some comparable action to admit German Jews into the United Kingdom'. It was said that Winston Churchill thought British policy should assist the Jews – he favoured settlement in some colony such as British Guiana. Chamberlain was sceptical. Opening up an undeveloped tropical country was, he said, 'a long and very expensive business'. The settlement of 250,000 Jews in British Guiana had been proposed, 'but it was quite clear that under the most favourable conditions the settlement of anything like this number must take a very long time'. Chamberlain thought the dominions contained the most suitable places for settlement of European Jews within the empire. The discussion ended with no resolution.[16]

The following day Chamberlain received a deputation of Anglo-Jewish leaders led by Viscount Samuel.[17] He was accompanied by the chief rabbi, Dr J. H. Hertz, Viscount Bearsted, Lionel de Rothschild, Neville Laski and Chaim Weizmann. The Jewish leaders estimated that 500,000 Jews remained in Germany, of whom 300,000 might emigrate if given the opportunity. They asked Chamberlain to facilitate the urgent temporary admission of children and young people aged up to seventeen years for education and training, with a view to ultimate re-emigration. Jewish organisations in Britain would give a new collective guarantee in support of the young people's entry and would take full responsibility. The deputation announced that the CGJ had launched an immediate appeal for funds, which for the first time would be directed to non-Jews. Samuel pressed for the authorisation of extra staff to deal with the emergency and reduce the 'extreme congestion' in administering refugee casework. Chamberlain expressed deep concern and sympathy, but made no firm promises. He suggested that Samuel take up the question of extra staff with the departments concerned, promising his 'benevolent interest'. Entry to Palestine was the subject of a separate request by Weizmann. He sought the eventual admission of 6,000 young men then in German concentration camps, who might go to refugee camps in the Netherlands in the interim; he also asked for the immediate evacuation to Palestine of 1,500 children. Chamberlain

[16] Afterwards, Hoare's quota transfer proposal was followed up, but dropped when the US State Department proved unreceptive: FO to Sir R. C. Lindsay, no. 823, 16 Nov. 1938, Lindsay to FO, no. 423, 18 Nov. 1938, PRO FO 371/21637, C13994/14092/1667/62, f. 82; Makins, minute, 14 Oct. 1938, PRO FO 371/21535, W3823/104/98, f. 348.

[17] Herbert Louis Samuel (1st Viscount Samuel), *Memoirs* (London, 1945), pp. 254–6, 276–9.

promised to consider this sympathetically if the colonial secretary raised it with him.[18] The next day, Chamberlain's office circulated the record of the meeting, asking departments whose responsibilities were principally affected to consider points coming within their province.[19]

On 16 November, the full Cabinet discussed 'The Jewish Problem'. Ministers were conscious of the pressure to take some action in response to Germany's persecution of the Jews. Halifax claimed that the view that the government was not doing enough was damaging Britain's reputation, especially in the USA. He suggested that

> the position could be restored if this country would give a lead which would force the United States in turn to take some positive action. He hoped that it might be possible on the course of the next day or so for us to lend our support to fairly wide promises of help to the Jews.

Ministers discussed making land in the empire available for Jewish settlement. Halifax expected political gains to flow from such a gesture. But the colonial secretary warned against exaggerating the limited possibilities in the mainly agricultural colonies. Chamberlain contrasted the numbers who might benefit from temporary refuge in a colony with the smaller numbers who might be admitted for settlement. All agreed it desirable to make an offer of some territory. Most hope was placed on British Guiana, despite the limited possibilities it offered. The offer did not need to be unconditional – Chamberlain suggested retaining a measure of control by means of a long lease at a nominal rent. But by the close of their discussion of the settlement issue ministers were no nearer to being able to offer large-scale admissions to any colony in the foreseeable future.

Still, Chamberlain had, for the second time in two days, made ministerial colleagues face the fact that any proposed colonial settlement was unable to meet the immediate need for large-scale refuge. He next turned to the question of short-term refuge, saying that this had been the particular concern of the deputation of Jews the previous day. In response to his indication that the government would take some action on colonial settlement they had pointed out

> that time was the essence of the matter. It followed that anything which we could do in regard to a permanent settlement must also be accompanied by some effort to find a temporary resting-place for refugees while arrangements were made for their permanent reception.

[18] Samuel to Chamberlain, record of meeting, 15 Nov. 1938, PRO PREM 1/326; *Jewish Chronicle*, 18 Nov. 1939, p. 16; Minutes of Executive Committee meeting on 17 Nov. 1938, Archives of the Central British Fund for World Jewish Relief, (hereafter CBF), Weiner Library, London, reel 1, file 20.

[19] C. G. L. Syers to H. E. Brooks, G. H. Creasy, Pimlott, E. E. Bridges, Makins, 16 Nov. 1938, PRO PREM 1/326.

The two ministers most concerned with refugee questions showed no enthusiasm for making Britain such a resting-place. Winterton fended off American criticisms of British inaction. Certain countries in South America would act, he thought, 'if we could show them a good example'. But he insisted that no large-scale emigration could be effected unless IGC efforts succeeded in enabling Jews to take money out of Germany. Hoare advocated action in British colonies as the way to influence opinion and loosen purse-strings in the United States, and ultimately open the door into the country, which he saw as 'the key to the problem'. Entry to Britain, Hoare said, was the subject of 1,000 letters a day, but 'only cases which were recommended by the Jewish representatives were admitted'. Jewish representatives opposed large-scale admissions or the entry of Jews they had not approved, he said, 'since they were afraid of an anti-Jew agitation in this country'. They also feared the consequences of publishing admission figures. The meeting agreed that such a step was risky, yet wished to get credit for what Britain was doing, and so Hoare eventually agreed to consider communicating a figure privately to the Americans.[20]

Makins had warned Chamberlain that it was very doubtful that the Home Office would welcome an increase in the number of Jewish immigrants.[21] Certainly Hoare opposed a more generous entry policy. According to the minutes, Hoare said

> that we were going as far at present as public opinion would allow, and it was important to retain a check on individual immigrants. He thought, however, that we might agree to admit a number of young Jews for the purpose of agricultural training, with a view to their ultimate settlement elsewhere. He was also in favour of admitting a number of Jewish maidservants. These girls might replace the German domestics who had left at the time of the [Munich] crisis.

This was nothing new. Hoare was merely setting out existing policy. The only categories of Jews whose admission Hoare proposed were already being allowed in. Even before the Evian conference it had been Home Office policy to admit agricultural trainees and domestic servants. The availability of job opportunities had been the only brake on numbers. On the procedural side, Hoare was merely re-affirming the need for pre-selection. His overall position was opposed to an expansion of admissions – a stance he claimed had the backing of both public opinion and Jewish representatives.

20 Cab. 55 (38)5, 16 Nov. 1938, PRO CAB 23/96.

21 Makins, memorandum, 'Anti-Semitic Measures in Germany', 10 Nov. 1938, Cadogan, minute, 10 Nov. 1938, Sir Horace Wilson, minute, 14 Nov. 1938, PRO PREM 1/326.

Hoare cited the fears of Jewish refugee organisations but Chamberlain countered by pointing to the pressure for more open admissions from the high-ranking Jewish deputation he had seen the previous day. He ended by suggesting that, 'if, in addition to offering a territory overseas, we undertook to allow Jews to come here as a temporary refuge this would constitute a considerable contribution towards the problem'. According to the minutes, Hoare 'undertook to consider this point'. Several of the other ministers gave signs of realising that the climate had changed and that a more generous approach to admissions had gained the upper hand. Suddenly, Hoare showed concern about the plight of the elderly, saying that the Jewish refugee organisation was not attempting to deal with older people but concentrating on the younger generation. Halifax joined in, floating the idea of asking people to sponsor individual elderly Jews 'who would otherwise be left to an appalling fate in Germany'.

The meeting finally agreed that a statement outlining proposed action would be drafted by the ministers whose responsibilities were most affected and issued speedily.[22] The next day Hoare announced in the Commons that the Home Office was expanding the numbers of staff dealing with applications for entry by refugees and that everything possible would be done to eliminate delays, though these were largely due to difficulties in obtaining necessary information about applicants' cases.[23]

On the afternoon of 21 November the prime minister made a Commons statement. It was largely devoted to an enumeration of the steps the government was taking to survey the possibilities of settlement in the colonial empire, especially plans to lease large areas of British Guiana. On further admissions to the United Kingdom, Chamberlain merely reiterated that numbers were 'limited by the capacity of the voluntary organisations dealing with the refugee problem to undertake the responsibility for selecting, receiving and maintaining' refugees. He stated that since 1933 the government had permitted about 11,000 refugees to land, in addition to some 4,000 to 5,000 who had since re-emigrated. He dismissed as 'premature' the suggestion by Eleanor Rathbone MP of a loan for refugee maintenance. Other questioners were told to await the home secretary's speech that evening.[24] Chamberlain's statement was widely reported in the North American press. Hoare's speech would arouse much less interest abroad since it concerned domestic policy only.

[22] Cab. 55 (38)5, 16 Nov. 1938, PRO CAB 23/96.
[23] Hoare, *Hansard*, House of Commons, vol. 341, cols. 1037–8, 17 Nov. 1938.
[24] Chamberlain, *ibid.*, cols. 1313–17, 21 Nov. 1938.

Hoare set out the government's new approach later the same day during a Commons debate on refugee policy.[25] The need for careful selection was his starting point. He warned that mass immigration was likely to encourage the growth of fascism, although he did not use the word. He also stressed the importance of preventing 'an influx of the undesirable behind the cloak of refugee immigration'. The government therefore needed to check in detail the individual circumstances of adult refugees, a process bound to involve 'a measure of delay'. Individual cases would be investigated by voluntary organisations represented on the Co-ordinating Committee, whose recommendations the Home Office accepted. The main issue was whether refugees could support themselves. The 11,000 German refugees who had come to live in Britain in the years 1933 to 1938 had set up industries which provided jobs for 15,000 British workmen; they had thus improved rather than damaged British employment prospects. These benefits, Hoare claimed, were due to 'very careful selection'. In reality the creation of most of these jobs dated from the period prior to the revival of mandatory pre-selection.

Hoare admitted that the admissions system had been strained 'to breaking point' in the preceding ten days, but, with thousands of applications per day, strain was inevitable. The machinery was now being greatly expanded, he announced. Moreover, while the Home Office would stick to individual selection for persons who might stay permanently, selection procedures would be modified for people coming for temporary refuge, for whom a less detailed scrutiny was permissible. Those expected to re-emigrate were 'a class of case which we can deal with en masse', he said, and could be admitted on an unprecedented scale and more speedily. Transmigrants would be provided with a temporary home, on the understanding that, 'at some time in the future, they will go elsewhere for their permanent home'. The government would also look kindly on proposals for training for eventual resettlement in the colonial empire, such as an existing scheme to train 'Jewish boys for agriculture and Jewish girls for domestic service'. Large numbers of 'non-Aryan children' could be admitted without the individual checks used for older refugees, provided they could find responsible sponsors. All children whose maintenance could be guaranteed could come. Jewish parents would accept separation from their children to save them from danger in Germany. Hoare commended to his fellow countrymen this 'chance of taking the young generation of a great people'. He asserted the government's anxiety to help, promised 'the utmost support' for the voluntary organisations' work and vowed to

[25] Hoare, *ibid.*, cols. 1427–83, 21 Nov. 1938.

show 'that we will be in the forefront among the nations of the world in giving relief to these suffering people'.

Chamberlain and Hoare represented the two major positions on government action. Chamberlain's contributions to the ministerial discussion on 14 November showed his belief that Britain should act and his insistence on the distinction between long-term settlement prospects and immediate action. In the Cabinet meeting of 16 November Chamberlain steadfastly supported urgent action to provide temporary refuge. He insisted on the distinction between the immediate need for temporary refuge and long-term projects of permanent settlement overseas, emphasising the limited scope and uncertainty of settlement prospects in the colonies. The IGC's shortcomings were obvious and Chamberlain had seen warnings from Makins, the expert on the IGC, to the effect that the possibility of any useful contribution from that quarter looked more dubious than ever.[26] Chamberlain did not fall into the error of viewing the IGC's programme as a substitute for immediate action, nor were his views altered by Hoare's arguments. Such obduracy seems to have been a characteristic of the prime minister. The historian Ian Colvin could discover no example, in two and a half years of Cabinet meetings, in which Cabinet discussion had altered his mind on a subject.[27]

How do we explain the position which Chamberlain took on the refugee issue? Chamberlain had previously demonstrated his sympathy for the Jewish plight. After the *Anschluss* the celebrated violinist, Fritz Kreisler, an Austrian of partly Jewish origins, saw Chamberlain, an old personal friend, and enlisted his support in obtaining a German passport so that he could return to Germany.[28] Chamberlain's meeting on 15 November with Jewish leaders – the most distinguished deputation Anglo-Jewry had yet mustered on refugees – clearly impressed him. Colvin says that Chamberlain was known to alter his mind between Cabinets. Yet perhaps he did not so much change his mind on the immigration of refugee Jews – an issue in which he had so far shown little interest – as think hard about it, possibly for the first time.

Chamberlain's letters to his sisters show that the *Kristallnacht* pogrom horrified him. Still, his primary concern was with the questions it raised about his Anglo-German policy and his own dilemma over balancing his public comments on the recent events. He wrote to his sister Ida:

[26] Makins, 'Anti-Semitic Measures', cited n. 21.

[27] Ian Colvin, *The Chamberlain Cabinet* (London, 1971), p. 265.

[28] Syers to Chamberlain, memorandum, 28 Mar. 1938, Neville Chamberlain papers, Birmingham University Library (hereafter NC) 7/11/31/160; F. Kreisler to Chamberlain, 28 Mar. 1938, NC 7/11/31/161; Syers, note, 29 Mar. 1938, NC 7/11/31/162.

I am horrified by the German behaviour to the Jews. There does seem to be some fatality about Anglo-German relations which invariably blocks every effort to improve them. I suppose I shall have to say something on the subject tomorrow as there will certainly be a private notice question & it will be [? problem] how to avoid condonation on the one side or on the other such criticism as may bring even worse things on the heads of those unhappy victims. It is clear that Nazi hatred will stick at nothing to find a pretext for their barbarities.[29]

The difficulty of making progress with Hitler was a continuing and major worry. In mid-December Chamberlain deplored the 'continued venomous attacks by the German press, and the failure of Hitler to make the slightest gesture of friendliness'. He felt that discussions on any subject with Germany were impossible for the time being. However, he maintained an interest in discreet informal contacts with various German intermediaries.[30]

Months after the pogrom, Chamberlain was still trying to make sense of it. Writing to his sister Hilda, he essayed an analysis of German anti-Jewish persecution which revealed something of his own attitude to Jews. Hilda had sent him material showing that some Jews were still being given posts in Germany. Chamberlain replied:

Your enclosure from Mrs Sichel is very interesting. I had no idea that Jews were still allowed to work or join such organisations as the Hitler Youth in Germany. It shows, doesn't it, how much sincerity there is in the talk of racial purity. I believe that the persecution arose out of two motives, a desire to rob the Jews of their money and a jealousy of their superior cleverness. No doubt Jews arent [*sic*] a lovable people; I don't care about them myself; but that is not sufficient to explain the pogrom.

He then turned to speculating about Hitler's sanity, wondering if his moods were characteristic of a 'paranoid' but aware that they were not proof of any organic disease.[31]

Chamberlain's reactions show his practical nature. He tended to respond to events by trying to decide on his next step. He could not dwell on an issue for long without exploring its implications for him personally.[32] Thus his concern with Anglo-German relations shaped his response to the persecution of the Jews. He was not averse to showing

29 Chamberlain to Ida, 10 Nov. 1938, NC 18/1/1076; Ida to Chamberlain, 11 Nov. 1938, NC 18/2/1099.

30 Chamberlain to Hilda, 6 Nov. 1938, NC 18/1/1075; Chamberlain to Hilda, 11 Dec. 1938, NC 18/1/1079; Chamberlain to Ida, 23 July 1939, NC 18/1/1108; Chamberlain to Hilda, 30 July 1939, NC 18/1/1110.

31 Chamberlain to Hilda, 30 July 1939 1939, NC 18/1/1110.

32 For insights into Chamberlain's character I am indebted to Stephen Stacey, 'The Ministry of Health 1919–1929: Ideas and Practice in a Government Department', DPhil. thesis, University of Oxford (1984).

the Germans that their policies were isolating them, but he wished to develop good relations with amenable elements in Germany. He was prepared to show distaste for anti-Jewish persecution. For example, in the winter of 1938–9 he told the Deutsche Shakespeare Genossenschaft that his real reason for refusing an honorary presidency the society wished to confer on him was that it had expelled its Jewish members.[33] But he felt impelled to state his own ambiguous feeling about this 'unlovable people'.

After his forced resignation as prime minister in 1940, Chamberlain, now lord president of the Council, expressed concern in Cabinet over the handling of internment. He was sensitive about being chairman of a committee which decided to deport alien internees, and intervened in the deportation of two Jewish refugee boys to Canada, apparently helping to keep one in the United Kingdom.[34]

Chamberlain has received insufficient credit for his contribution to easing refugee admissions. On the other hand, excessive credit for the generous side of British policy has gone to Hoare. This is partly because, as home secretary, Hoare presided over the admission of Jewish refugees, and did so sympathetically. It is also because his failure to argue for a more open policy – indeed his opposition to it – in Cabinet discussions remained hidden in records which were not released for many years. As home secretary, Hoare was obliged to act and speak on refugees, but he carried out both decisions which were forced on him and decisions he supported. His remarks during the months following the decision to expand temporary refuge display his worry about the accumulation of refugee Jews in the United Kingdom and his preoccupation with searching for other places to send them.[35]

Chamberlain won Cabinet agreement to take urgent action to help German Jews, even as the search for long-term solutions continued. The United Kingdom's role as a temporary refuge would be expanded and delays caused by pre-selection abroad reduced. The role of public opinion in this change of emphasis is hard to establish. From mid-November on, the public showed intense interest in what Britain was doing about German persecution of Jews, but ministers drew contrary conclusions from it. Hoare insisted public opinion opposed further admissions. Chamberlain claimed the opposite. Home Office statements attempted to placate both extremes of opinion, offering concessions to

[33] K. Feiling, *The Life of Neville Chamberlain* (London, 1946), p. 390.

[34] Correspondence with Peake, 22–4 July 1940, NC 8/34/36–37; correspondence with Mrs Rogers, 16 July–23 Aug. 1940, NC 8/34/53–56.

[35] Makins, minute, memorandum (draft Cabinet paper), 'Emigration from Germany and other Central European Countries. Possible action by His Majesty's Government', 15 Nov. 1938, PRO FO 371/22536, W15095/104/98, f. 287.

advocates of a more generous policy together with reassurances that they entailed no loss of control.

What had changed since *Kristallnacht*? Ministers were more hopeful that an offer of settlement in the colonies might yield political benefits, by setting an example which reflected well on Britain. Other countries, the United States in particular, might feel obliged to follow suit. Still, ministers knew the danger of sounding too optimistic about British Guiana; Cadogan reminded them of a League committee's unfavourable report on the colony as a place of settlement for Assyrians. Makins and MacDonald now believed that the government should be prepared to make a loan to finance a colonial settlement scheme, but nothing was to be said to suggest that this was even contemplated.[36] While there might be political benefits in making some gesture of support for settlement projects, it carried political risks and offered no substantial benefits to Jews in Germany. In mid-November Makins itemised the objections. There was the expense; opposition could be expected from the dominions; financial support would tempt Poland and other European governments to persecute Jews further. In short, Makins saw no advantage to Britain in funding settlement overseas. Moreover, international discussions showed that no country was at present prepared to consider proposals for group settlement. Emigration, then, Makins concluded, was only feasible by the process of 'infiltration', the gradual process of the re-establishment of individuals in more developed countries. This, he stressed, had been the policy of the Jewish organisations, which had organised the largest quantity of emigration. Surveying prospects around the world, he noted the preference of South America and the dominions for agricultural workers and South Africa's prejudice against Jews. Except for a small-scale experimental CGJ scheme in Kenya, little progress had been made within the colonial empire.[37]

Makins saw no positive role for the IGC. Indeed, he was concerned to prevent it from creating extra difficulties in relations with Germany. He suggested that the proposed visit to Germany by Rublee, the IGC's director, had been rendered undesirable by the recent actions of the German government. Destitute refugees were now unavoidable: the continuing burden of the fine imposed after *Kristallnacht* plus the fall in

36 Record of interdepartmental meeting, 16 Nov. 1938, PRO FO 371/22537, W15119/104/98, f. 295.

37 Makins, 'Emigration from Germany', minutes, 18 and 19 Nov., correspondence with Antoni Balinski, 19 Nov., Randall, minute, 20 Nov. 1938, PRO FO 371/22537, W15095/104/98, f. 42; MacDonald to Winterton, 4 Nov. 1938, PRO FO 371/22536, W14805/104/98, f. 141. The force of fears regarding Poland was promptly illustrated by the action of the Polish ambassador in pressing for the IGC to deal with Poland's Jews and the 10,000 recently expelled from Germany.

the realisable value of their assets had reduced Jews in Germany to a condition where they were no longer 'desirable immigrants'. In these circumstances, the work of the IGC must be reviewed. Although Makins denied that there was any question of dissolving the IGC, he made proposals aimed at suspending the committee's work indefinitely. He argued that Germany's non-cooperation rendered the orderly emigration envisaged at Evian impracticable. There was therefore little point in having a full-time director. He suggested that Rublee return to the United States, leaving the IGC to be minded by his deputy, Robert Pell, for whom Makins had much more respect. The British government should not itself propose the IGC's partial suspension, but keep that recommendation in reserve, hoping that the Americans would themselves tire of the committee and its problems. With the IGC put to one side, Makins saw two alternative approaches to the refugee issue: either to take no action, or to start thinking along different lines, with or without German co-operation, always bearing in mind the dilemma 'that the more emigration is increased the greater is the temptation to increase pressure on Jews in Central Europe'.[38] He welcomed news that the poor prospects for Rublee's talks had led the Americans to re-examine the IGC's role and consider alternative proposals.[39] He warned, however, that the government would be criticised if any failure of the IGC became public, even though it could be blamed on Germany. Despite these reservations, the IGC remained on the scene, and Makins remained a key adviser to Lord Winterton, its chairman. Indeed, the two worked together in early December to try to curtail the effectiveness of the forthcoming broadcast appeal for funds for refugees by the former prime minister, Lord Baldwin, lest it cloud the IGC's prospects.[40]

The decision to expand the scope of temporary refuge in the United Kingdom which had been reached between the closing stages of the Cabinet meeting of 16 November and the ministerial announcements of 21 November was a unilateral act by a sovereign state. It had nothing to do with the IGC, except, perhaps, in reflecting the ministers' lack of faith in the committee's ability to achieve anything. The new policy was at odds with the principles agreed upon at Evian. It could be seen as a capitulation to German robbery and persecution of Jews. Hoare had

[38] Makins, memorandum, 'Effect on position of Intergovernmental Committee and its Director of Anti-Semitic measures in Germany', 15 Nov. 1938, PRO FO 371/22536, W15069/104/98, f. 269; Lord Sherfield, interview, cited ch. 4, n. 98.

[39] Makins, minute, 'Inter-Governmental Committee', 15 Nov. 1938, PRO FO 371/22536, W15056/104/98, f. 266.

[40] Makins to Sir Geoffrey Fry, 5 Dec. 1938, PRO FO 371/22539, W16055/104/98, f. 54; Sherman, *Island Refuge*, p. 185.

stated that to obtain entry Jews needed to be able to support themselves. Still, the government's readiness to accept Jews lacking independent means of support, and who would be largely reliant on charity, reduced the pressure on Germany to co-operate over letting Jews depart with sufficient means if it wished to achieve Jewish emigration. Lastly, it provided dangerous precedents in relation to central Europe, as Makins tirelessly warned. In the context of Anglo-German relations generally, the decision can be seen as reflecting British pessimism about the prospects of negotiating agreement with Germany, on refugees or anything else.

It appears that Chamberlain's only effort to use diplomacy to influence Germany's position on Jewish emigration was at his mid-January meeting with Benito Mussolini in Rome. Having rejected direct approaches to Berlin as unprofitable, he was hoping to secure the Italian leader's good offices with Hitler.[41] When Chamberlain raised the refugee issue, Mussolini defined the problem as general rather than local, suggesting the long-term solution would be the creation of an independent sovereign Jewish state in a large area of territory. Halifax asked if Germany might be persuaded to allow departing Jews to take money out, and Mussolini agreed to try to use his influence in that direction. He said the Germans were determined to get rid of the Jews and would be ready to do anything to expedite their departure. He assented to Chamberlain's suggestion that Rublee should make an approach to the Germans.[42]

As Chamberlain was raising these matters in Rome, Rublee arrived in Berlin. In mid-December, Hjalmar Schacht, president of the Reichsbank, had come to London, with Hitler's approval, bringing a plan that envisaged financing emigration by means of an international refugee loan raised from Jewish contributors and entailed increased exports of German goods. The Berlin talks on the Schacht plan lasted three weeks. Schacht himself was removed from his position halfway through the talks. The plan itself was cynical in the extreme, involving German confiscation of the bulk of Jewish wealth without compensation and a boost for German exports. Seized Jewish assets would be retained by the German authorities as a trust fund, a quarter of which could be used by emigrants to purchase supplies and travel facilities from German companies. The bulk of resettlement costs would be borne by outside Jewish

[41] Cab. 60 (38)4, 21 Dec. 38, PRO CAB 23/96.

[42] Mutilated copy document from R434/1/22, 'Record of the first conversation with Signor Mussolini and Count Ciano at the Palazzo Venezia on the afternoon of January 12th. Conversations between British and Italian Ministers, Rome, January 11–14, 1939', PRO FO 371/22962, C1190/15/18, f. 212.

sources through a bond, for which the trust fund would be the collateral.[43] The Foreign Office regarded the plan as unsatisfactory but continued to use it as a basis for negotiation, since it at least provided further contacts with the Germans, including moderates like Schacht. These contacts continued until shortly before the outbreak of war, but the plan and its subsequent variations produced nothing which facilitated Jewish emigration.[44]

Once Rublee was replaced by the more tractable Emerson, there was less fear that the IGC might undermine Anglo-German relations. The contacts with Germany were hardly rewarding. The Foreign Office was, however, charmed with the opportunities the IGC presented for closer contact with the Americans and was determined to exploit them.[45] Thus, Britain continued to use the IGC as a tool of foreign policy rather than as a means to help persecuted Jews.

In early November, when refuge was sought for German refugees being turned out of Yugoslavia, Holderness had said, 'We are not prepared to be made the dumping ground of Europe.'[46] Cooper considered that the November pogrom had been designed to rouse sympathy abroad so that the doors of receiving countries would be opened to admit larger numbers than they had previously been prepared to accept, and that this hope had been largely fulfilled.[47] But the Home Office remained totally opposed to the mass immigration of refugees and totally committed to pre-selection. Home Office ministers steadfastly resisted the idea of setting up a facility similar to Ellis Island in the USA, where persons whose entry had not been approved could remain while their cases were being investigated. Hoare told the Commons that it was undesirable to allow a 'stagnant pool' of refugees to develop in the United Kingdom.[48] The Home Office continued to require admissions to be linked to jobs or re-emigration.[49]

The Home Office had accepted the principle of letting in large numbers of children. Samuel had returned from the Jewish leaders' 15 November meeting with Chamberlain in a hopeful frame of mind. He reported to the CGJ's Executive Committee that he felt the prime

[43] Breitman, *Architect of Genocide*, pp. 59–60.
[44] Chamberlain, note of private conversation with Hjalmar Schacht, 15 Dec. 1938, PRO PREM 1/326; Sherman, *Island Refuge*, pp. 194–203.
[45] Reilly, minute, 17 Nov. 1938, PRO FO 371/22537, W15370/104/98, f. 146.
[46] Holderness to Makins, 4 Nov. 1938, PRO FO 371/22536, W14633/104/98, f. 93.
[47] Cooper, memorandum, 16 Dec. 1938, PRO HO 213/1639.
[48] Hoare, *Hansard*, House of Commons, vol. 342. col. 3082, 22 Dec. 1938; *ibid.*, vol. 345, cols. 2455–7, 3 Apr. 1939.
[49] Record of interdepartmental meeting, 16 Nov. 1938, cited n. 36.

minister appreciated the difficulties of the situation and wished to help and that, where the entry of children was concerned, Chamberlain would support any suggestion approved by the Home Office. Mrs Rebecca Sieff, having spoken to Cooper, was convinced that the home secretary would be prepared to waive formalities. In preparation for expanded immigration, a new appeal, chaired by Lord Rothschild, was being launched in the Jewish press. Plans were outlined to bring 5,000 children from Germany. Schiff also suggested approaching trades unions, adding that, if refugees could not work, they might come for training for re-emigration.[50] Jewish leaders' assessment of Chamberlain's position, several days prior to Samuel's meeting with Hoare, is consistent with Cabinet records showing Chamberlain's key role in widening refugee admissions. The crucial Jewish promise was the collective guarantee of financial responsibility for children given to Chamberlain on 15 November. On 21 November, the date of the refugee debate, Hoare reached agreement with Samuel and several Jewish and other religious workers on streamlining children's admission. Samuel recorded in his memoirs that Hoare agreed that children could enter 'without the slow procedure of passports and visas' and that Jewish leaders gave a guarantee 'that they should be emigrated as soon as they were old enough and conditions allowed'.[51]

Fundamentally, the policy of expanding temporary refuge was humanitarian. It was a response to the escalating persecution of Jews in Germany and the concern it aroused in Britain. Jewish leaders had offered a new guarantee to provide financial cover for additional children to enter. Considerations of Anglo-American relations added a political motive. Yet the policy offered only short-term solutions. As far as permanent settlement was concerned, immigration considerations still applied.

Until this moment, precedent and policy had militated against openly humanitarian admissions, even on a temporary basis. Certainly, there was a humanitarian strand in Home Office and Ministry of Labour practice, but it had gone largely unacknowledged. It was no accident that the expansion of temporary refuge was brought about by Chamberlain. How else could it have happened? Only an intervention from the top could alter policy tradition. Chamberlain possessed the tenacity and the authority to nullify Hoare's opposition and swing the Cabinet behind a change of emphasis. The home secretary's reluctance to concede the case for a humanitarian policy had stemmed partly from his own limited sympathies and partly from his departmental preoccupation with firm

[50] Minutes, Executive Committee meeting, 17 Nov. 1938, CBF, reel 1, file 20.

[51] Samuel, *Memoirs*, p. 255.

controls. Once the decision was made, however, Hoare played his part in carrying it out and was rewarded by gratitude from refugees.[52]

Let us digress briefly to compare these developments with Britain's response to refugees from the Spanish Civil War. In May 1937 the United Kingdom gave temporary refuge to some 4,000 Basque children from Bilbao in northern Spain. The National Joint Committee for Spanish Relief (NJCSR) requested the children's admission and made itself fully responsible for selecting the children, bringing them to Britain and caring for them after arrival. It gave guarantees required by the Home Office that the children would not become a public charge and would be carefully selected according to age, sex and political balance. Temporary refuge only was offered and the NJCSR would make efforts for the children's re-emigration.[53]

The vast majority of Spanish refugees went to France, which was considered more suitable. Why was it relatively easy to persuade the British government to make an exception for the Basque children? Part of the answer is that the NJCSR was an effective pressure group. Moreover, the refugees inspired the sympathies of the foreign and home secretaries, Eden and Simon. Hoare, then first lord of the admiralty, raised objections, but failed to prevent the initial influx, although, soon afterwards, when he became home secretary, he ruled against further admissions of women and children. There was a clear humanitarian case for urgent action since Bilbao's population was undergoing bombardment, and the attack on Guernica shocked the British public. With the surrender of Bilbao to the insurgents the situation changed once again. The British consul advised that the surrender would save children and that priority now be given to evacuating adults.[54] But it was evacuation of children that conformed with the British government's non-intervention policy, since it assisted non-combatants only and could be politically balanced, so neither side could complain of discrimination. There were also political gains to be made. As Chamberlain said in Cabinet later that year, it was good to be seen helping people, especially children, and it was necessary to get on good terms with the Spain of the future.[55] In addition, providing escorts for refugee ships asserted Britain's naval power at a time when its international prestige needed bolstering.

[52] Werner Rosenstock to Hoare, 6 Dec. 1951, Templewood Papers, Box XVII/8, Cambridge University Library.

[53] PRO HO 213/287–9.

[54] James Cable, *The Royal Navy and the Siege of Bilbao* (Cambridge, 1979), p. 108.

[55] Cab. 47 (37)2, 12 Dec. 37, PRO CAB 23/90. The context was funding for a British scheme to feed children of insurgent supporters in Spain.

Crucially, the Spanish children required only short-term refuge. They would return home once hostilities subsided, although, in the event, they stayed longer than expected. The Home Office was much less welcoming to adult Spanish refugees who would need permanent resettlement. In 1939, when defeated republicans sought asylum, stringent conditions were laid down and only a small number of 'very respectable' refugees were to be admitted.[56] It was Spanish adults, therefore, not children, who raised issues comparable to those posed by Jews of all ages. Britain was minding the Spanish children on behalf of their parents, who soon began to ask for them back. Jewish children were being surrendered by their parents.

It soon became feasible to organise the admission of large groups of Jewish refugee children. Following Hoare's Commons statement on 21 November, a number of changes to the entry process were implemented. Admissions were simplified and speeded up by means of procedural shortcuts. Extra staff resources were found. For months, Home Office staff worked around the clock on refugee cases. The scope for admissions widened as the non-Jewish public began to contribute funds and sponsorship, especially after the broadcast appeal by Lord Baldwin.

The streamlining of procedures and expansion of refugee committees' participation in the mechanics of admission pre-dated the November pogrom, although it now had extra impetus. The voluntary organisations had steadily increased their involvement in pre-selection, especially in relation to domestics. Jewish refugee organisations and the Home Office were already modifying procedures for transmigrants, although it is not clear exactly when these discussions began. Now wide discretion was given to PCOs to grant visas to refugees seeking temporary admission prior to re-emigration. To satisfy the Home Office that proper financial arrangements had been made for transit cases, the GJAC had arranged for counsel to draft a form of bond for guarantors, who would agree with the CBF to defray the costs of maintenance and re-emigration. Evidence of entry into such a bond had to be presented to the PCO, along with documentary evidence showing the applicant would eventually be granted permission to enter the USA, or some other country, for permanent residence. Other arrangements covered young people coming for training for re-emigration. They did not require evidence of emigration prospects, but their visas had to be authorised by the Home Office and could not be granted on the PCO's discretion alone. Certain types of case, including those of transmigrants and unaccompanied children, were expedited by the introduction of a

[56] Correspondence, Feb.–Mar. 1939, PRO FO 371/24153, W2082/2082/41, f. 160.

system which made it unnecessary to open a file for each individual. The system was based on case cards, in different colours according to the category of admission and serially numbered. The cards were used as documents which could be endorsed with authorisation for entry. After being stamped at the Home Office they were sent out to refugees for submission to the PCO.[57]

British consular officials in Germany exerted themselves to speed up departures for the United Kingdom. The PCO in Berlin, Captain Frank Foley, acting without instructions, arranged with the American consul to grant visas to persons stopping in Britain in transit to the USA, but was asked to await new procedures developed by the Home Office.[58] British officials based in Germany knew that evidence that a British visa had been authorised could secure a man's release from a concentration camp. Thus it was important to grant visas quickly and to minimise the time lag between visa authorisation and release. The consul in Frankfurt, R. T. Smallbones, had an agreement with the local secret police that they would release prisoners on being told that a visa had been granted. Even though Hoare was enthusiastic, Makins failed to interest Home Office officials in developing more systematic procedures for notifying the German authorities of visas granted to detainees. Cooper argued that it was up to the prisoner's friends and family to do this. He opposed the idea of intervention by British representatives in the hope of securing a man's release, advising that it would be unlikely to help the prisoner and would, moreover, produce delays in Germany while the case file was removed from its normal place for investigation. Nevertheless, the chargé d'affaires in Berlin was authorised to intervene in the case of a distant relative of Lord Reading.[59]

The voluntary committees could now select a wide range of refugees for entry. The representatives they sent to the continent worked in conjunction with German Jewish organisations, notably the Reichsvertretung, identifying suitable candidates. Lists of approved names were then submitted to the Home Office. These lists, or 'nominal rolls', largely replaced the elaborate process of individual visa applications, notably in children's cases, and made possible the use of group visas. Other refugees still came under the standard visa system, but recommendations from

[57] Correspondence, 22–30 Nov. 1938, PRO HO 213/100; Co-ordinating Committee, minutes of extraordinary meeting, 21 Dec. 1938, AJ43/14/114; Cooper to Brooks, 28 Mar. 1939, PRO FO 371/24076, W5248/45/48, f. 210.

[58] Correspondence, 24–8 Nov. 1938, PRO HO 213/100.

[59] Correspondence, 18 Nov.–28 Dec., 29 Dec. 1938–12 Jan. 1939, PRO FO 371/21753, C14141/14718/16070/2311/18, f. 165; correspondence, 9 Nov.–23 Dec. 1938, PRO FO 371/21757, C13766/15535/2412/18, f. 349; for Home Office views, see correspondence, PRO HO 213/101.

the voluntary organisations were often accepted in lieu of investigation by the authorities. The Home Office also arranged with the GJAC that people aged thirty-five to fifty selected to enter on the basis of guarantees would be required to prove only suitability for emigration, or in special cases absorption in the United Kingdom, rather than the existence of firm and valid arrangements to re-emigrate within two years.[60]

In a special effort to save men from German concentration camps, the CGJ set up a refugee transit camp at Richborough in Kent on the site of an abandoned army camp. The American Jewish Joint Distribution Committee agreed to subsidise some 20 per cent of upkeep costs. A Jewish worker in Berlin recalled that the lucky ones who went to Richborough were chosen from over 10,000 applicants. Julian Layton, an Anglo-Jewish representative who helped with selection in Germany, felt a strong personal commitment to assisting men who did not have means but who would be suitable for re-emigration. Layton and his companions successfully proposed a policy of releasing CGJ funds to help such men and in early January the project obtained approval from the Home Office. Men aged eighteen to forty-five going to the camp were accepted as transmigrants. The endorsement on their passports described them as admitted 'pending re-emigration'. However, the reality of these re-emigration prospects was often questionable and in some cases fictitious. For example, Werner Rosenstock, who worked for the Reichsvertretung in 1939, and arrived in the United Kingdom just before the war, recalled that statements by refugees that they planned to re-emigrate to Shanghai were often based on nothing more than the fact that Shanghai did not require visas. The camp filled rapidly. It had been intended to accommodate 5,000 refugees, but a lower limit of 3,500 was agreed. Some 3,350 men and 220 women and children were temporarily lodged at Richborough when war broke out. Only 100 had re-emigrated by November 1939.[61]

There was no quota for children. However, a sub-committee set up by the CGJ to promote large-scale children's emigration considered the admission of about 10,000 as an upper limit. The numbers climbed from 1,544 in January 1939 to 9,354 by the end of August.[62] The vast

60 Co-ordinating Committee minutes, 31 Jan. 1939, AJ43/14/114.

61 Julian Layton, interview with the author, 20 Apr. 1988; correspondence etc., Jan.–Nov. 1939, CGJ, 'Report by Mr Layton, Mr Gentilli and Mr Baron on the selection of refugees for the Richborough Camp' (n.d., covering visit 19 Feb.–3 Mar. 1939), AJDC 592; Hubert Pollack, 'Was nicht in den Archiven steht', n.d., 497/55 01/17, Yad Vashem Archive, Jerusalem; Dr Werner Rosenstock, interviews with the author, 19 Apr. 1988, 6 May 1989.

62 *Movement for the Care of Children from Germany: First Annual Report, 1938–1939*, PRO HO 213/302.

1 Members of a party of 200 unaccompanied refugee boys and girls between the ages of twelve and seventeen arrive at Harwich from Vienna on 2 December 1938. As they come ashore an official examines the labels they are wearing.

2 Some of 235 Jewish refugee children on arrival at Liverpool Street Station, London, from Vienna, on 14 July 1939.

majority – 7,482 – were classified as Jews, the rest as Christians (1,123) and 'undenominational' (749). The large number of arrivals in late 1938 led to the utilisation of summer camps as short-term accommodation. The camps were impossible to heat properly, but the children had warm clothes, so few needed the additional clothing donated by Marks and Spencer.[63]

Admission saved the children's lives. Exclusion sealed the fate of many of their parents. Three-quarters of the unaccompanied children in England by July 1939 had parents left behind in Greater Germany, in most cases with no means of support. Distress at parting from their parents pervades the following extracts from a BBC programme, 'Children in Flight', broadcast in February 1939, in which the children, lodged at Dovercourt camp near Harwich, interviewed one another in English:

Brigitte from Westphalia: Oh we had a very good journey, but we must make it quite alone. No one was allowed to come with us and I must carry my luggage always and it was very heavy. My mother was very sad that she must not come

[63] Correspondence, Dec. 1938–12 Jan. 1939, PRO MH 55/689.

3 Refugee boys gather around the 'Post Office' at Dovercourt Bay Camp. The holiday camp was used from late 1938 to accommodate large numbers of unaccompanied refugee children temporarily until homes were found for them.

on the platform and say goodbye to me. It is nice to be in camp with all the other children – I feel not so alone.

Sixteen-year-old Kate from Hamburg: We are all waiting to come to homes in England where we stay till our parents will leave Germany. I will not stay in England for ever. My parents go to USA but it is terribly difficult for them to emigrate because the quota is filled and they will have to wait till next year . . . happy as I am to be in England but my greatest sorrow is how to get my parents over.

Marion: Yes, that's it. There is no possibility for our parents to emigrate and we don't know when we will see them again.

Kate: It's true. Only to make it easier for them we left our home and went to England and we are so very happy to have got a permit from the British government to enter the country. How do you like the English, Marion?

Marion talks of the kindness of the English and how grateful the children are. She then asks: 'Kate, why did you leave home?'

Kate: I knew that this was the only way to help my parents and to help me and I don't regret it. What are you going to do here in England, Marion?

Marion: I hope soon to come to an English family where I can live and begin to learn till my parents will emigrate and I can go to them.

4 Jewish boy and girl refugees newly arrived at Liverpool Street Station from Vienna (via Harwich) on a transport organised by Rabbi Solomon Schonfeld on 24 December 1938. They were taken from the station to a Schonfeld hostel in Amhurst Park, London N16.

Strains of children's voices singing a musical setting of *Dona nobis pacem* accompanied the programme.[64]

The children were busily corresponding with parents whom many would never see again. The impact of these partings on parents is conveyed in a report by Stella Renny-Tailyour to the Society of Friends on the activities of twenty workers based at its Vienna Centre:

> To watch, as I did, the departure of one of their children's transports gives a very good idea of the problem with which they are faced. The smiling courage of the parents, during the two hours when they had to stand on the platform and keep the children happy, was wonderful. But the picture changes when the train has gone. The worker's problem is to keep up that courage when there is no longer any incentive to action. They find that the Jews, when they are unable to get away, change beyond all recognition if they are left for long to face alone a future without money, work or hope but with the perpetual fear of what tomorrow may bring forth.
>
> There seems to be a growing need that English people should go over there and run hostels for all those people who have very little hope of getting away.[65]

[64] 14991/LP 2035 b 6–8/2047–8, National Sound Archive.

[65] Stella Renny-Tailyour, 'Notes on impressions received from my visit to Germany and

The organisers of this exodus knew they were separating families in circumstances where parents abandoned to Nazi persecution had little prospect of survival. This must qualify our view of the admission of unaccompanied children as humanitarian. To admit the children without their parents was regarded as less onerous. Adding good white stock to the population was seen as demographically advantageous at a time of worry about the declining birth rate. The children would be Anglicised, growing up speaking English and thus less likely than adults to arouse xenophobia.

The question of whether children were expected to re-emigrate remained contentious. Hoare's speech of 21 November 1938 suggests that he envisaged the children would obtain permanent homes in the United Kingdom. The children's migration committee of the CGJ, the Movement for the Care of Children from Germany (MCCG), understood that the Home Office was prepared to accept the permanent unofficial adoption and residence of younger children and of girls who entered domestic service or married British citizens. The MCCG estimated in May 1939 that it would be necessary to arrange the emigration of 80 per cent of the boys but only 20 per cent of the girls.[66] The issue caused rifts within the Jewish community: the Zionist organisations saw the children as pioneer material for Palestine but their view was not universally shared.[67] Furthermore, many British people took refugee children into their homes believing the arrangement would be permanent. The resulting confusion meant many children had no idea whether they would re-emigrate or remain. The Home Office made no attempt to relieve their uncertainties.

By July 1939 about 1,300 of the children had already started to pay their way in jobs and youth agriculture camps. Before the end of the year, nearly 300 had re-emigrated and many more had plans to do so. The United Kingdom was the country which played the greatest part in succouring unaccompanied young people from Germany. Figures from July 1939 show that 7,700 refugee children unescorted by relatives had arrived in Britain, while the Netherlands had 1,850, France 800, Belgium 700 and Sweden 250. A campaign to change US immigration laws to facilitate the entry of refugee children after *Kristallnacht* had failed.[68]

Austria', appended to minutes of meeting of 9 May 1939, GEC Executive Committee minutes 1938 (Dec.)–1939 (Dec.), SOF, pp. 67–8.

66 MCCG, *First Annual Report*.

67 Norman Rose (ed.), *Baffy: The Diaries of Blanche Dugdale, 1936–1947* (London, 1973), pp. 116–18; MacDonald, 'Conversation with Dr Weizmann on the 12th December', PRO FO 371/21868, E7548/1/31, f. 374.

68 Wyman, *Paper Walls*, pp. 75–98.

To gain entry, children needed financial sponsors. Much of the finance for Jewish children's immigration came from the Baldwin appeal. This national appeal, launched in December 1938 by the former prime minister, Earl Baldwin, raised some £500,000. About half the proceeds were allocated to the Jewish organisation and largely spent on helping child refugees.[69] Certain urgent cases, known as 'unguaranteed children', constituted a limited exception to the requirement for guaranteed finance, since they were financed by the Baldwin appeal. The vast majority had to be 'guaranteed' by cash deposits from private sponsors which would cover maintenance up to the age of eighteen. In the spring of 1939, as funds dwindled, the MCCG introduced new mandatory deposits of £50 per child to cover the cost of re-emigration, but this requirement was rescinded after the CGJ agreed in June to accept full responsibility for the re-emigration of children then arriving. The Baldwin appeal's success in raising funds competed with other bodies seeking to raise funds for refugees with the result that in May 1939 the Co-ordinating Committee resolved that it be closed down and its funds distributed to other organisations.[70]

Financial support was of the utmost importance. Failing sufficient means of one's own, or an offer of approved employment, funds had to be raised through private sponsorship. The need for guarantees of support grew as the refugee organisations became increasingly unable to assist people without resources. Of course, since the *Anschluss* the JRC had ceased to underwrite admissions generally. The rule was that refugee organisations would not themselves undertake financial responsibility, although they might expend funds on the basis of a guarantee. Their role was to drum up opportunities and bring refugees together with people who might support or employ them. Once arrangements had been agreed, the refugee committee would submit the details to the authorities.[71]

The standard system of guarantees was geared towards offers of help from people willing and able to make a large financial commitment. However the sums required were too great for less affluent individuals to raise on their own, so that potential aid was going to waste. At the end of 1938 the GJAC considered proposals for a more flexible arrangement for collective guarantees. Prior to this, the GEC had adopted a practice of accepting a formal guarantee from a person of substance, knowing that he had a group behind him sharing the financial responsibility. A

[69] MCCG, *First Annual Report*, pp. 6–7.

[70] Co-ordinating Committee Resolution, 22 May 1939, minutes, Co-ordinating Committee meetings, 27 May and 22 June 1939, PRO HO 213/268.

[71] GJAC monthly reports, Feb.–June 1939, AJDC 587.

5 Guarantors await the names of newly arrived refugees whose keep they are guaranteeing in Liverpool Street Station gymnasium. This photograph was taken on 20 April 1939, when 150 refugees who had travelled from central Europe via the Hook of Holland arrived at the station on a special train. On arrival the refugees were taken to the gymnasium where they met their guarantors.

pacifist group, War Resisters' International, which did refugee work with people who had suffered in Germany and Austria on account of their pacifist ideals, evolved a scheme for spreading the responsibility for guaranteeing its cases. Each person who gave a guarantee for a sum of up to £250 – they included Baron Cadbury, Ruth Fry and the author Laurence Housman – agreed to guarantee all the cases. The scheme was agreed with the Home Office on the basis of a pool system which envisaged that no more than twenty people (later doubled to forty) would be in the country at any one time and that the organisation was responsible for ensuring their eventual re-emigration.[72]

A common criticism of the guarantee system was that the assurances being demanded were excessive in relation to the risk involved. The Co-ordinating Committee decided to complain to the GJAC over its demand for an unlimited guarantee for persons applying for transit visas, even when hospitality was available for the limited period required.[73] But not even the prime minister could persuade the home secretary to dispense with the requirement for guarantees in the cases of particularly distinguished or well-qualified people.[74] The Archbishop of York, William Temple, complained to the Home Office about the delays caused by requirements for the deposit of actual sums of money and signed guarantees. Because of its inability to deposit funds, the York committee found itself unable to use offers of hospitality: 'Not only are the poor refugees hindered from coming, but the hosts are discouraged and lose heart.' Refugee organisations answered critics of the guarantee system by retorting that they, too, found such conditions irksome in the extreme, but they were a product of Home Office requirements for funds to cover re-emigration. Thus, the International Student Service required banking of £200 per case. The MCCG required guarantees for maintenance, education and training up to the age of eighteen, plus £50 to cover re-emigration. The GJAC was increasingly accepting deposits of cash and securities in place of unlimited guarantees. To relax such conditions with regard to private guarantees would impose an impossible strain on charitable resources as long as government policy required most refugees not to work or become a public charge and to re-emigrate within a reasonable time. As Bunbury of the GJAC emphasised, it was necessary for opportunities of emigration to expand or for large-scale finance to be provided from new sources. The system of guarantees could be dispensed with only if the whole basis of refugee

[72] Correspondence, 1939, PRO HO 213/285; Co-ordinating Committee, minutes of extraordinary meeting, 21 Dec. 1938, AJ43/14/114.
[73] Minutes of Executive Committee meeting, 16 Jan. 1939, AJ43/14/114.
[74] Correspondence, 13 Feb.–2 Mar. 1939, PRO HO 213/1641.

admissions was altered. The Home Office knew there was no chance of this. Maxwell finally replied to Temple that the Home Office stood by its conditions, but would consider any proposals his committee might put forward to share liability amongst groups of sponsors.[75]

Many guarantees were not honoured, or honoured only in part. In 1940 the Refugee Children's Movement took over responsibility for 109 children and partial responsibility for another 168.[76] By 1941 half of the 2,000 guarantees had lapsed. Refugee organisations and the Assistance Board spent much effort in trying to hold defaulters to their promises.[77] Eventually, the Treasury Solicitor advised that the agreements signed by guarantors were not legally enforceable, since an essential ingredient of a binding contract was lacking because no consideration moved from the refugee committee to the guarantor. The author of this advice thought the guarantees had never been intended to confer real rights, enforceable either by a refugee committee or the government, but had been 'in the nature of credentials which the Home Office required before refugees were permitted to land'.[78] The JRC's Guarantee section was also advised that group guarantees given by poorly paid domestic workers were unenforceable in the courts. Some refugees who lived in guarantors' homes were in fact unpaid domestic servants.

The demand for support far exceeded the supply. The financial pressure was unrelenting. Jews wrote from addresses all over the Reich seeking sponsors. They placed classified advertisements in the *Jewish Chronicle*, such as the following:

Urgently seek for uncle (55) in daily danger fearing return to Dachau, generous rescuer providing short-term guarantee until emigration overseas.

Urgent appeal, old couple (63 and 60) American visas 1940 to be expelled from Germany 1.4.39., threat concentration camp. Maintenance 1 year in England needed.

Which Jewish family would take a 14 year old boy from Germany, whose emigration to America is assured, during his stay here?[79]

But countless people failed to surmount the hurdle of sponsorship.

Earlier, many German Jews had emigrated without assistance. The AJDC estimated that perhaps 105,000 had already done so by July 1938. However, the agency predicted correctly that, with the steady pauperisation of German Jews, a much larger proportion of emigrants

[75] Correspondence, Apr.–June 1939, PRO HO 213/286.
[76] MCCG, *First Annual Report*, p. 6.
[77] J. E. Micklewright to district officer, London IV, 19 Aug. 1941, PRO AST 11/82.
[78] R. W. A. Speed to R. A. Ellefson, 28 Oct. 1941, PRO TS 27/467.
[79] *Jewish Chronicle*, 17 Feb. 1939, p. 3.

would need assistance in future.[80] For this reason the policy of the refugee organisations became increasingly crucial in determining who could escape.

Being persecuted because of one's Jewish ancestry was never a sufficient qualification for aid to come to Britain. To obtain assistance from a refugee organisation one had to fit its criteria of suitability. Before any question of occupation came the question of affiliation. The Nazis persecuted Jews on racial grounds and categorised them on the basis of their ancestry, almost completely regardless of religious affiliation. But when the persecuted looked for refuge, religious affiliation became highly significant. The religiously defined organisations which provided most of the help directed their philanthropic efforts where they felt their duty lay – towards their co-religionists. Jewish organisations aimed to help selected members of specific Jewish communities. The ultra-orthodox specialised further, focusing on the like-minded. Thus Jewish organisations focused on helping affiliated Jews, rather than persons of Jewish origin. Persons of Jewish origin who were Christians were regarded as having forfeited their claims to Jewish charity through their desertion of the community.

As a result, vast numbers of people with Jewish ancestry were excluded from the operations of Jewish organisations. Many were categorised as full Jews under the Nuremberg laws and therefore subject to the harshest discrimination. Certain people of partly Jewish origin were designated by the Nazis as *Mischlinge*, a status which was further subdivided into first and second degrees according to the precise configuration of Jewish elements. *Mischlinge* were exempted from important discriminatory measures against Jews. Many could summon help from non-Jewish connections to mitigate the impact of Nazi persecution. While being in a comparatively privileged situation themselves, such people often had strong reasons for seeking to escape Nazi rule. Spouses, too, even if not categorised as Jewish themselves, were caught up in the pressure to emigrate. Precise figures are elusive, but the partially Jewish population of Germany in 1933 has been estimated at up to 500,000.[81] Figures provided at Hitler's request in April 1935 putting 'racial Jews', including the converted, at about 775,000, and *Mischlinge* of the first and second degrees at 750,000, making a non-Aryan total of 1.5 million, are agreed to be a gross overestimate.[82]

[80] AJDC, statement for Evian conference, July 1938, AJ43/13/56.

[81] Werner Cohn, 'Bearers of a Common Fate? The "Non-Aryan" Christian Comrades of the Paulus Bund, 1933–1939', *Leo Baeck Year Book* 33 (1988), 327–66.

[82] John A. S. Grenville, 'Neglected Holocaust Victims: The Mischlinge, the Jüdischversippte, and the Gypsies', in M. Berenbaum and A. Peck (eds.), *The Holocaust and*

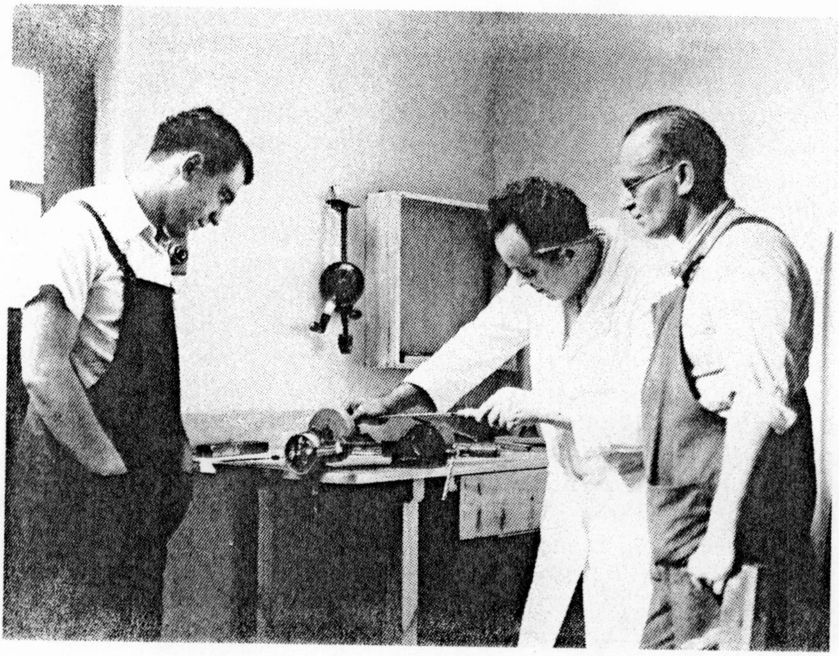

6 Retraining refugees for manual occupations. This war-time photograph shows Hans Eisenwagen, himself a refugee from Austria, instructing refugees in carpentry at the Society of Friends' Agricultural Training Settlement at Tyn-y-cae, Brecon, Wales. The Carpentry Training Centre, originally set up at Offenham, Birmingham, in 1939, moved to Tyn-y-cae in March 1941.

In Germany, people with Jewish ancestry inhabited a wide range of religious identities, often within one family. Many Christians of Jewish origin, sometimes known as 'non-Aryan Christians', were categorised as full Jews by the Nazis. German Jewish leaders estimated in early 1939 that there remained in Germany and Austria 470,000 professing Jews along with at least 320,000 dissidents, agnostics and Christians of Jewish origin. The figures are conservative; since Christian non-Aryans had never organised, there was a tendency to underestimate their numbers. But it seems Christians made up at least one-third of the total needing assistance to emigrate.[83]

Non-Aryans had been helped since 1933 by the Society of Friends' Germany Emergency Committee (GEC). The 'non-Aryan Christians'

History: The Known, the Unknown, the Disputed and the Reexamined (Bloomington, 1998), pp. 315–26.

[83] Jonkheer Baud to T. Robbins, 28 Mar. 1939, AJ43/14/114.

received relatively little help from British sources, compared with Jews of the Mosaic faith. This was partly because the Friends had fewer resources than the Jewish organisations. It was also because other Christian bodies were tardy in offering assistance to fellow Christians of Jewish ancestry. After the war, Christian organisations expressed regret and shame that, despite having recognised the need, they had done little compared to the generous effort of the Jews.[84]

Early in 1939 the Co-ordinating Committee began to express concern at the lack of provision for non-professing Jews and non-Aryan Christians. It decided to set up a special organisation in Germany, parallel to, but separate from, the Reichsvertretung, to enable Christian churches in Britain to assist non-Aryan emigrants.[85] Thomas Robbins was sent to Berlin with details of a proposed central organisation, with branches in the provinces, to help 'non-Aryans who are not of the Mosaic faith, such as non-Aryan Christians, Dissidents and agnostics who are racially 100% Jewish but are not accepted by the Jewish communities as co-religionists'.[86] He submitted the proposal to the German authorities and sought their co-operation. But the German government, as Bentwich observed, 'recognise[d] only a racial criterion and treat[ed] "full non-aryans", that is those who have two Jewish parents or four Jewish grandparents, whatever their creed, as Jews'. The Nazis were uninterested in distinctions of faith which meant so much to religious organisations. Indeed, the Germans were planning a new structure for emigration, dissolving the Reichsvertretung and setting up a supreme authority, the Reichsvereinigung, to which 'all Jews by race, irrespective of faith, would be forced to belong'. At a meeting with the Nazi authorities Robbins requested a separate department within the new structure to deal with 'non-Christians and other Jews who are not of the Mosaic persuasion'. He also asked permission for Co-ordinating Committee representatives to select candidates for jobs and other opportunities for emigration created in Britain and elsewhere by Christian organisations. The German officials appeared interested. Robbins concluded that the proposed reorganisation would make for a simplified and more efficient emigration process. Bentwich, however, expressed concern that the expanding numbers of persons of other confessions who would be forced to emigrate 'would increase the difficulty of finding openings for

84 A. Freudenberg, report on ecumenical refugee work since 1939, Appendix A to minutes of first meeting of Ecumenical Refugee Commission, 5–7 June 1946, AJ43/19/1092.

85 Minutes of Executive Committee meeting, 23 Jan. 1939, AJ43/14/114.

86 Robbins, memorandum, 10 Feb. 1939, PRO FO 371/24080, W3348/520/48, f. 64.

the Jews "in our sense"', but claimed that Christian and Jewish organisations were prepared to work together in the new Reichsvereinigung.[87]

However, the remaining Jewish authorities in Germany resisted Nazi attempts to integrate the administration of the forced migration of Jews and non-Aryan Christians. The leading German Jewish rabbi, Leo Baeck, together with the Reichsvertretung, unsuccessfully opposed the proposal that Jewish organisations should exercise authority over Christian non-Aryans. Later elaborating on his attitude towards Christianised Jews, Baeck described them as deserters from the Jewish community.[88] The Jewish authorities in Germany had good reason to fear what the new structure would mean in practice. The Nazis were trying to force the pace of the Jewish exodus to double its existing rate. The chaotic and panic-stricken emigration from Austria since the *Anschluss* under the emigration organisation Adolf Eichmann had set up in Vienna gave a frightening foretaste of things to come.

The CGJ limited its commitment on the basis of nationality, saying its funds had been collected for German Jews. We have seen how swiftly it acted after the *Anschluss* to curtail its commitments to Austrian Jews. In September 1938 Schiff even drafted proposals that one among the recognised refugee committees should have the final say over the admission of Austrians.[89] The Jewish organisation similarly refused to take formal responsibility for Jews of Czech nationality. Also outside the scope of its aid were European Jews threatened by anti-semitism, but not as yet under Nazi rule. Schiff made it clear that, while the GJAC would help Jews from Germany and Austria who went to Italy, he did not approve of the admission of Polish and Italian refugees 'as that would only encourage these communities to get rid of further people'.[90]

Illness was another problem for the GJAC. Nazi persecution took a terrible toll on people's sanity. If the signs of damage were already obvious, people were not considered emigration material. In June 1939 Bernard Davidson of the GJAC turned to Cooper for assistance in excluding the mentally ill. He suggested that, before a visa was granted, all applicants should be examined by a doctor acting for the government and should pay a fee for this. He gave an example of the problem: a refugee in Birmingham had turned out to be suffering from an incurable mental disease, making him unemployable. If the JRC could not get his relatives to support him, it would have to undertake that liability, 'which,

[87] Robbins, memorandum dictated 16 Feb. 1939, *ibid.*; Bentwich, note on visit to Germany 17–19/2/39, sent to Cooper, 22 Feb. 1939, PRO FO 371/24080, W3779/520/48, f. 96.

[88] Baud to Robbins, 28 Mar. 1939, cited n. 83.

[89] Schiff to Cooper (draft), 14 Sep. 1938, CBF, reel 18, file 91.

[90] Minutes, Co-ordinating Committee meeting, 3 Jan. 1939, AJ43/14/114.

as you know, may last many, many years'. L. Clayton of the Home Office was unimpressed:

> It is hardly for HO to protect the GJAC from liabilities of this kind, but for them to satisfy themselves before assuming responsibility. But it is disturbing, to say the least, that refugees are coming here in increasing numbers in a condition which appears to call for a refusal of leave to land under article 1 (3) (e).[91]

Schiff expressed concern at suggestions that the Ministry of Health was prepared to admit persons known to be mentally deficient as long as the Jewish committee recommended the case.[92] The ministry was concerned about cases where mental and physical problems, including a number of tuberculosis cases, made an immediate or future charge upon public funds practically certain. An extra worry was the likelihood that Germany would be particularly anxious to get rid of all its mentally and physically defective population. Pointing out that Britain would probably 'never be able to re-emigrate them', the chief inspector of immigration, F. G. Ralfe, supported medical examinations.[93] After discussion between Cooper, Ralfe and Ministry of Health officials the idea was raised with the GJAC. Schiff was enthusiastic. He estimated that the GJAC would bring 1,000 refugees per month from Germany over the next two years. He did not envisage the risk of pressure being put on medical examiners to relax their standard in especially pitiable cases. It was impossible to rescue every Jew in Germany, he said, and his committee considered it would be most unwise to try to bring out 'the halt and the lame' and, in any case, there were insufficient funds.[94] By this time it was already mid-August and the war intervened before anything more could be arranged.

Political refugees held a special attraction for the Left, the Labour Party and trades union circles. These groups responded sympathetically to the plight of the left-wing opposition in Germany and Austria and felt concern over the fate of social democratic opponents of German claims to Czechoslovakia's territory. The British Left had been actively involved in the Spanish Civil War and in aid to Spanish refugees. Eleanor Rathbone MP was tirelessly active on behalf of refugees from both political and racial persecution. Generally, however, the Left tended to focus on political cases.

Thus, the response to the need for rescue was limited and compartmentalised – on the basis of religion, nationality, health and politics.

91 Davidson to Cooper, 21 June 1939, L. Clayton, minute, 4 Aug. 1939, PRO HO 213/317.
92 Schiff to C. F. Roundell, 12 July 1939, PRO MH 57/386.
93 Ralfe, minute, 9 Aug. 1939, *ibid.*
94 Correspondence, 15 Aug.–29 Sep. 1939, *ibid.*

The piecemeal provisions which resulted were far from providing humanitarian aid to all who needed it. The proportion of prospective applicants to entrants is impossible to estimate precisely. It varied according to the category under which people applied. Thus, only 50 out of 1,000 Austrian doctors were admitted, but the refusal rate for domestic applicants was much lower, at 15 per cent. The CBF had files on between 500,000 and 600,000 cases, while the number of Jewish refugees present in the United Kingdom when war broke out is estimated at between 60,000 and 70,000. On this basis, we may conclude that perhaps one applicant in ten succeeded in gaining entry.[95] Of course, a proportion of the visas authorised were not used. Cooper claimed in May 1939 that most of 57,000 Reich refugees to whom visas had been issued over the past year had never arrived in Britain.[96]

In the last months before the war the British authorities realised that the influx of refugees was getting out of control while hardly any were leaving. Samuel intimated to the CGJ in late 1938 that the Home Office felt unease about the establishment of transit camps, 'as they feared that a pool of refugees might be formed in England'.[97] The Home Office had given permission for Richborough Camp, but, by January 1939, Hoare already regarded the accumulation of transmigrants as a problem. A new Cabinet Committee on the Refugee Problem, set up under his chairmanship, held six meetings before the outbreak of war. Hoare used the committee to promote the reduction of refugee numbers in the United Kingdom. At its first meeting he complained about the 'very embarrassing' delay in arriving at a detailed scheme for the permanent settlement of refugees allowed in on a temporary basis. Making specific reference to the training camp at Richborough, he expressed concern that a 'stagnant pool of refugees' remained in the country – in fact the camp was not yet ready to accept inmates.[98] A few weeks later Hoare suggested earmarking some of the men training at Richborough for settlement in British Guiana. He sought Foreign Office action to curtail irregular immigration to British colonies or Palestine by parties of Jewish refugees without visas. Such immigration, he said, was causing difficulties in his own department – presumably he meant that it was using up opportunities for re-emigration from the United Kingdom. Randall told him the Foreign Office had concluded that it was a waste of

95 Estimate by director of the CBF, based on CBF archives deposited at the Greater London Record Office, communicated to this author July 1990.
96 Minutes, Co-ordinating Committee meeting, 1 May 1939, PRO HO 213/268.
97 Minutes, CGJ Executive meeting, 29 Dec. 1938, CBF reel 1, file 2.
98 CRP (39)1st meeting, 24 Jan. 1939, PRO CAB 98/1.

time to try to influence the German government to stop stimulating the exodus of Jews without visas.[99]

The committee's interim report to the Cabinet in July 1939 stated that the refugee organisations were in no position to finance colonial settlement schemes such as the British Guiana project. Indeed, there was a danger that their funds would be inadequate to meet existing commitments. Of some 40,000 refugees in the country, the majority were transmigrants, admitted on the strength of guarantees that the cost of their maintenance would not fall on public funds. The funds of the refugee organisations which had undertaken responsibility for these guarantees had been strained to the utmost, principally by delays in re-emigration. Unless a large number emigrated soon, refugees were likely to fall on public assistance, an outcome the Home Office was most anxious to avoid. The report concluded that in these circumstances the government should no longer refuse to offer financial support for refugee settlement and re-emigration. It advised agreeing in principle to make funds available on a basis proportional to amounts subscribed privately, provided other governments would also contribute, although the only country whose co-operation should be regarded as essential was the USA. The United Kingdom should take a lead on these issues at the forthcoming meeting of the IGC 'in view of the gravity of the situation in this country'.[100] Hoare's committee advocated this major reversal of previous policy because it considered that the United Kingdom now had a refugee problem, which should be solved urgently through the provision of settlement opportunities abroad. It should be done at government expense because no other source was available.

The new position, while it represented an important turnaround regarding public funds, was also aimed at saving future expenditure on public assistance. It was consistent with the policy of keeping the United Kingdom as a country of transit. The proposed injection of British finance was aimed at increasing opportunities to emigrate from the United Kingdom, not at expanding the chances of escape from Nazi territory. In mid-July the Cabinet agreed these proposals in principle.[101] The government communicated its offer of funds first to the Americans, then to the IGC, reiterating the concern that without such action countries of refuge would 'be left with large numbers of refugees who cannot be absorbed'.[102] But it was too late. In September, war broke out,

[99] CRP (39)3rd meeting, 1 Mar. 1939, 4th meeting, 9 May 1939, *ibid.*; Randall, minute, 1 Mar. 1939, PRO FO 371/24080, W3734/520/48, f. 89.

[100] Hoare, Interim Report, Cabinet Committee on the Refugee Problem, CP 151 (39), 7 July 1939, PRO CAB 98/1.

[101] Cab 37 (39)11, 12 July 1939, PRO CAB 23/100; Sherman, *Island Refuge*, pp. 242–50.

[102] Text of statement by UK representative to IGC on 19 July 1939, LIC 32, AJ43/37/48.

rendering British contributions for settlement projects inconceivable in the foreseeable future. In October Britain formally withdrew the offer.[103]

In the absence of real possibilities of colonial resettlement, re-emigration remained the only means of reducing refugee numbers in the United Kingdom. However, compared with admissions, refugee re-emigration was negligible. Every month, a few hundred refugees left, but several thousand arrived.[104] A major obstacle to re-emigration was the US government's refusal to relax entry controls in order to accelerate the admission of refugees who had arrived in the United Kingdom in transit to the United States. Many would be unable to depart for years, if ever, because the American quota system operated to hold back applicants from European countries where the demand for visas far exceeded the quota. For example, a person registered after July 1938 on the German/Austrian quota would not be in line for a US visa until March 1940. In early 1939, American consular representatives in Europe explained to the British authorities that the quota system was having this impact. The US State Department insisted that delays must be expected and no exceptions could be made for persons in danger. The Home Office responded with more stringent entry conditions for applicants in transit. From April 1939, they needed to show a reasonable chance of admission to the USA at a not too distant date and evidence of backing from a voluntary organisation.[105]

The Home Office made other moves to tighten up admissions. In June 1939, for example, it discontinued use of the quicker card procedure mentioned earlier (pp. 114–15) for applicants residing in France, who were not thought to be in danger. It introduced more rigorous selection procedures for refugees in France applying to come for domestic service, after the British PCO in Paris, G. W. Courtney, doubted the suitability of many applicants. He cited the example of an upper middle class doctor, who, on being told that his proposal to work as a tutor did not constitute domestic service, announced that he would work as a butler: 'This', Courtney declared, 'is absurd, as butlering requires a lifelong experience.'[106]

[103] CRP (39)6th meeting, 25 Sep. 1939, PRO CAB 98/1.

[104] Sir John Hope Simpson, *Refugees: A Review of the Situation Since September 1938*, (London, 1939), p. 71; Cooper to Brooks, 28 Mar. 1939, PRO FO 371/24076, W5248/45/48, f. 210.

[105] Correspondence, 17 and 26 Jan. 1939, PRO HO 213/115; Douglas Jenkins to Cooper, 13 Feb. 1939, PRO HO 213/116; correspondence, 16 Feb.–3 Apr. 1939, Aliens Department circular, 'Refugees desiring to come to the United Kingdom temporarily while waiting for US visas', Apr. 1939, PRO HO 213/117; correspondence, 2 Mar.–21 Apr. 1939, PRO HO 213/118.

[106] G. W. Courtney to Jeffes, 8 Mar. 1939, 'Instructions to Passport Control for Paris', 2 June 1939, Russell to Schiff, 5 June 1939, PRO HO 213/105.

For all the tightening up of admissions, the Passport Control Department emitted a stream of complaints that the Home Office was undermining the basis of control and allowing Britain to be swamped by refugees. In February 1939 the home secretary received a memorandum detailing PCOs' grievances. A major grouse was persistent overwork. Despite large reinforcements of staff in Berlin, Vienna, Prague and Budapest, officers were 'being daily submerged by crowds of excited and insistent refugees'. Visas were being issued on a grand scale: between May 1938 and the end of January 1939, some 50,000 had been granted to refugees, many covering more than one person. Of these, 13,500 had been granted in Vienna and 34,000 in Berlin. Refugees received five-sixths of all visas granted at these posts. In January alone, some 4,000 Home Office authorisations had been sent out to PCOs, plus authorisations such as Ministry of Labour permits. The PCOs expressed concern at the 'poor type of refugee' whose admission was being authorised under new procedures. This category included individuals previously refused visas. They further protested that the Home Office was overruling their objections to issuing visas. Hoare asked whether the safeguards could be improved. His officials' response was negative. They claimed that the new selection procedures were reliable and that PCOs' discretion to refuse visas was respected. They rejected a suggestion from Foley that medical certificates and police certificates be made a condition of granting visas. The director of passport control, Captain Maurice Jeffes, agreed that Foley's proposal was misconceived. But he too had many reservations: his report on a recent tour of European passport control offices included complaints about the quality of refugees being authorised for entry under revised procedures.[107] Individual PCOs also raised problems. In mid-June, W. H. Hindle, the Budapest PCO, warned against 'the swamping of the UK with Hungarian and other refugees' and sought authority to limit the validity of visas to one month in doubtful cases, in order to stop Jewish businessmen from acquiring visas and keeping them in reserve as 'a key to the back door out of Hungary'. No action was taken on this suggestion.[108] The PCO in Prague, Captain V. C. Farrell, complained:

> The tendency appears to be to get refugees into the United Kingdom under any pretext whatsoever, so long as the Home Office and the Ministry of Labour are prepared to issue some sort of authorisation which provides a cover for refugees to 'dig' themselves in in British territory.

[107] PCOs' memorandum, Hoare, minute, 14 Feb. 1939, PRO HO 213/103; correspondence, starting 1 Feb. 1939, PRO HO 213/104; Jeffes to Cooper, 5 June 1939, PRO HO 213/107.

[108] W. H. Hindle to director, PCD, memorandum, 'Limitation of visas', 15 June 1939, Cooper to Jeffes, 15 Aug. 1939, minutes, 25 and 26 Sep. 1939, PRO HO 213/107.

The immigrants, he claimed, were usually ignorant of the conditions attached to their stay, which were based on 'plausible assurances given by bankrupt Refugee organisations and guarantors who are unable to accept financial liability for their protégés'. Like Hindle, Farrell saw Jewish applicants for business visas as potential emigrants, since anti-semitic measures would soon exclude Jews from earning a living. He was denying visas unless applicants provided 'incontestable proof' of the intention and means to return to Czechoslovakia.[109] The Home Office decided to tell Farrell that, if authorisation was under 'Instructions R' (the special refugee guidelines), the PCO need not concern himself with the alien's subsequent plans.[110]

Jeffes reported satisfactory improvements in managing refugee cases. In Vienna, 100 visas were being granted daily, 200 people a day interviewed and the queue nuisance and most complaints had been eliminated.[111] Earlier that year both the Home Office and refugee organisations had been concerned to establish a more effective organisation in Vienna to examine prospective immigrants.[112] The Home Office was worried that applicants were not being examined by the PCO. In an unpublished history of inter-war refugee policy a retired Home Office official noted that, unlike the 'thoroughly westernised' German refugees who were business and professional men, the Austrian Jews were mostly shop-keepers and small traders and thus harder for Britain or overseas territories to absorb:

> and many of them had recently moved into Austria from Poland, Romania and other East European countries and were therefore much nearer the Ghetto mentality. This had the further consequence that a number had relatives who had settled in England (before 1914 when entry was easier), and these exerted every sort of pressure in their power to get them admitted.[113]

The Co-ordinating Committee, seeking to improve the selection of women for domestic service, sent Robbins to make enquiries. Another Co-ordinating Committee concern was over the PCOs' practice of allowing women granted domestic service visas to bring their children with them. Cooper still hoped the Co-ordinating Committee would appoint British representatives to select refugees in Vienna and he had

109 V. C. Farrell, memorandum, 'Withholding of visas by examiners', PCO Prague to director of passport control, 7 June 1939, PRO HO 213/111.
110 Clayton, minute, 14 Aug. 1939, *ibid.*
111 Jeffes to Cooper, 5 June 1939, PRO HO 213/107.
112 Co-ordinating Committee, minutes of executive committee meeting, 9 Feb. 1939, AJ43/14/114; Cooper, memorandum of meeting with Schiff, 6 Feb. 1939, PRO HO 213/1642.
113 A. J. Eagleston, 'The Refugee Question, 1918–1939', 1942–1956, PRO HO 213/1772, p. 18; for February 1939 comments see PRO HO 213/1642.

suggested a similar plan for Berlin. He told Bentwich he hoped these proposals would not be

> steamrollered by the German authorities. I am sure you will be in entire agreement with our view that it is essential, in the best interest alike of immigration countries and the Jews in Germany, that the governments of countries receiving these people should have the determining voice in the selection of the persons who can be most readily admitted to their territories and it will be little short of disastrous if the Gestapo try to unload the wrong type of emigrant upon other countries.[114]

This nervousness over the dumping of undesirables was evident in Cooper's reluctance to exempt passengers on the *SS St Louis* from pre-selection. The ship had left Hamburg in mid-May 1939 with over 930 passengers, mostly Jewish refugees bound for Cuba, where they planned to wait to enter the USA under the German quota. On arrival in Havana the passengers' landing permits were not honoured and the ship was refused permission to dock. The Cuban authorities had sent a fore-warning of their intentions before the *St Louis* left Hamburg and Sir Herbert Emerson had told the ship's owners not to let her sail. A frantic search for another haven commenced. Meanwhile, the Cubans kept raising their financial demands for admitting the refugees. The US government would permit no one to land and sent coastguard vessels to stop anyone swimming ashore. Thus the *St Louis* began her return voyage to Hamburg in a glare of publicity, as western governments were bombarded with pleas to offer the passengers refuge.[115]

Cooper saw the voyage as a German ploy to unload refugees on other countries, upsetting IGC plans for orderly emigration. He advised that, since a proportion of the passengers would be undesirable, all should be required to return to Germany, where refusal would be much easier than enforcing the return of refugees after admission to the United Kingdom. He told Schiff no admissions were possible without individual examination by a British representative in Germany, but consideration of the cases would be expedited. Cooper believed Schiff agreed with his firm line. However, Schiff told AJDC representatives that he thought the Home Office would agree to temporary admission of refugees with documents for re-emigration to the USA on the basis of a guarantee from the AJDC to maintain them in the interim. The admission of between 300 and 350 passengers was finally agreed on this basis. The GJAC also promised to maintain a proportion of the passengers. The agreement was made dependent on confirmation of offers by Belgium, the Netherlands and France to admit the remainder. Home Office

114 Cooper to Bentwich, 24 Feb. 1939, PRO FO 371/24080, W3779/520/48, f. 96.
115 Breitman and Kraut, *American Refugee Policy*, pp. 70–3, 232.

officials and ministers seized on the fact of the *St Louis* passengers' already having visas to justify the exception and stop the decision from becoming a precedent for admitting refugees who had not made definite arrangements for their reception before setting out. Insisting that emigration must proceed in accordance with an orderly programme, they asked all governments concerned to impress on the Germans that this was the last such concession. The AJDC announced that it would abstain from staging a rescue should similar circumstances arise in future.[116]

The *St Louis* saga was not a clear-cut case of illegal dumping of refugees, because of the existence of the Cuban landing permits. The AJDC had decided to offer the Cubans a ransom of up to $500,000 to let the refugees land, despite the danger of encouraging similar demands from other governments, especially of Latin American countries which were potential destinations. The US government resisted AJDC pressure to intervene with the Cubans or to modify its own immigration procedures. President Roosevelt possessed the power to authorise admission, but would not risk setting a precedent. Despite its unbending stance, the US government was embarrassed by the *St Louis* crisis and the interest it was arousing. The State Department pressed Pell to use IGC resources to achieve admissions to western Europe.[117] The IGC subsequently received more credit than its insignificant role seems to justify. The admission of the passengers to the four countries was achieved mainly through the AJDC's willingness to offer finance and the efforts of its energetic negotiators. Britain's acceptance of a share of the passengers helped to rescue the US government from the embarrassing consequences of its own inflexibility.

The four receiving countries made their selection of passengers on board ship in Antwerp. The process was observed by Joseph Harsch, an American journalist then working for the IGC. He reported to Pell that the British group had singled out passengers who had relatives in the UK offering to maintain them, and thus

> had rather skimmed off the cream of the list at the outset. Then when it came to dividing up the balance difficulties developed. The French refused to accept any Poles at all, although they did willingly take all the Czechs. No one wanted the

[116] Cooper, minute, 9 June 1939, Randall, minute, 12 June 1939, PRO FO 371/24101, W9189/9189/48, f. 11; Hyman, minutes of Executive Committee meeting, 8 June, ADJC London to AJDC New York, 9 June, 'Record of discussions re St Louis', 9 June, 'Memorandum of Discussions and meetings re S/S St Louis', 12 June 1939, P. Baerwald to Hyman, 13 June 1939, AJDC 378; Peake, *Hansard*, House of Commons, vol. 348, cols. 1111–12, 13 June 1939.

[117] AJDC to Baerwald, 9 and 10 June 1939, AJDC 378; Bauer, *My Brother's Keeper* pp. 278–89; Breitman and Kraut, *American Refugee Policy*, p. 232.

'Statenlos', and equally avoided those with no evidence of prospects in the United States. It of course happened that the majority of the 180 selected at the outset for England did have the best prospects and the best credentials. The Belgians and the Dutch in particular felt that things were not going as planned or in accordance with the original agreement that each country would accept a proportion of the undesirables. The upshot was that in the end neither Belgians nor Dutch took the original agreed quotas. The British having had first choice were forced, most reluctantly, to accept the final residue of undesirables to a total of 287.

Harsch was favourably impressed by the bulk of the passengers who 'seemed to be readily assimilable anywhere' and able to 'disappear into the normal population'. He ascribed this to the fact that

the shipping line had filled its list from the individuals in the German-Jewish community who still have some money and some position left. Other subsequent groups might not be as desirable . . . The passengers all looked well fed and physically in excellent condition. A picture of Hitler on the walls of the tourist smoking room was undamaged, evidence of restraint on the part of the passengers unless one assumes a large supply of replacements.[118]

It seems Hitler's picture was removed at passengers' request when a religious service was due to take place and put back up the next day.[119]

Two former women passengers have recollected how they and their relatives managed to secure their inclusion in the British contingent. One of the young women knew English and shorthand and had served as secretary on board ship to the British selection team. Learning that she and her mother and sister had been allocated to one of the other countries, she pleaded with a British official to include them. He told her to stay behind. They were last off the boat and were put into the group destined for England.[120] Most passengers who came to Britain could not expect admission to the USA for several years and many were too old to work. In the end, their expenses proved costly for the AJDC.[121]

The *St Louis* was only the most notorious of several refugee ships without a haven. The German authorities were known to be implicated in hastening the departure of Jews who had no certainty of admission elsewhere. British officials and refugee organisations became increasingly involved in efforts to stop illegal refugee boats and transports. Illegal migration overland was also seen as a serious problem. The

118 Copy Pell to J. Pierrepont Moffat, 20 June 39, AJ43/36/40; Randall and Wright, correspondence, 14–15 June, Reilly, minute, 16 June 1939, PRO FO 371/24101, W9189/9470/9189/48, f. 11

119 Information from film, *The Voyage of the St Louis*, Maxiar Bahari, Gala Films, 1996.

120 Gisela Feldman and Gisela Thomas, interviews with the author, 14 July 1996.

121 Correspondence with CCJR, Apr.–June 1941, AJDC 379; Troper to E. M. Morrissey, 17 Mar. 1942, AJDC 381.

7 An elderly Jewish refugee disembarks from the *Rhakotis* at Southampton on 21 June 1939. After journeying from Germany to Cuba and back across the Atlantic in search of a haven, the Jewish refugee passengers on the *St Louis* were eventually offered refuge by France, Belgium, the Netherlands and the United Kingdom. Kept on board ship in the harbour at Antwerp, refugees were allocated to specific countries. The *Rhakotis* brought those refugees coming to Britain to Southampton.

continuing influx into Shanghai, where refugees did not require visas, gave growing concern to the British government. Cooper, for example, cited the need to discourage the Germans from sending refugees to Shanghai to justify his strict line on the *St Louis* passengers. He saw the readiness of American organisations to maintain refugees there as consent to German blackmail.[122]

Palestine was increasingly a destination for illegal immigrants. The government rode out the storm of protest which greeted its clamp-down on immigration in the White Paper of May 1939, which limited Jewish immigration to 75,000 over the next five years, after which no more would be permitted without Arab consent. The Colonial Office added a six-month suspension of admissions to Palestine as a punishment for illegal immigration. The Home Office failed to get the ban lifted in the case of refugees in transit to Palestine who were now stranded in the United Kingdom.[123]

Emerson sought the co-operation of foreign governments and refugee organisations in curbing illegal emigration. He stressed the need for orderly arrangements sanctioned by the IGC. The government's favourable report on settlement prospects in British Guiana was published one week before its devastating Palestine White Paper, in the vain hope of countering Jewish despair.[124] In reality, neither British Guiana nor IGC negotiations produced avenues of escape. The way out of Nazi Europe, if not by emigration to Palestine or Shanghai, which was often illegal, was through infiltration into developed countries. The money came, as it had always done, from such means as emigrants could salvage and from private charity.

The numbers in Britain grew, but so did the obstacles to admission. Delays and inefficiency added to the difficulties of fulfilling the conditions for entry. As war approached, channels of sponsorship dried up, as Cooper had predicted. Given that refugee organisations operated on the principle of transferring to Britain, to quote Cooper, 'as many refugees as they feel able to deal with', it is understandable that the Jewish organisation, its funds almost exhausted, felt duty-bound to resist pressure to comply with the Nazi timetable for Jewish emigration.[125]

Norman Bentwich of the CGJ has left us an account of his extraordinary meeting with Adolf Eichmann in Vienna in mid-August 1939. Eichmann was in charge of organising Jewish emigration in Vienna and

[122] Cooper, minute, 9 June 1939, PRO FO 371/24101, W9189/9189/48, f. 11; David Kranzler, *Japanese, Nazis and Jews: The Jewish Refugee Community of Shanghai, 1939–1945* (New York, 1976).

[123] Wasserstein, *Britain and Jews*, pp. 1–39; Sherman, *Island Refuge*, pp. 242–3.

[124] Sherman, *Island Refuge*, pp. 230–5.

[125] Cooper to Brooks, 28 Mar. 1939, PRO FO 371/24076, W5248/45/48, f. 203.

had recently acquired a similar responsibility in Bohemia and Moravia.[126] By this date, Vienna's population of confessional Jews had fallen from 165,000 in April 1938 to 67,000. In the Austrian provinces the total had collapsed from 15,000 to a mere 370. The Jewish death rate – one-eighth due to suicide – was four times what it had been in 1937. Now the Nazis planned to eliminate Jews from Vienna by early 1940. Bentwich attended the meeting together with a leader of the Jewish Kultusgemeinde. He told Eichmann that the CGJ could not continue its current level of funding to assist the Kultusgemeinde. His organisation, he said, was unwilling to help carry out a policy 'which was only multiplying the problems of the countries to which the refugees were forced out'. It could help only if there was 'an ordered emigration over a longer period', which required German co-operation. Eichmann, on the other hand, required complete evacuation of Jews from Austria in the shortest possible time. He dismissed the possibility of ordered emigration. His only concession was that between 20,000 and 25,000 persons over sixty-five who could not emigrate, pensioners and the very poor might stay; the remaining 45,000 should be cleared out over the next six months.

In his report on this meeting Bentwich showed that emigration opportunities were not available on the scale Eichmann required. Shanghai and Italy were regarded as closed. Future admissions to the USA and Britain were estimated at the rate of only 1,000 persons per month each. Of the categories for admissions to Britain, the scope for admitting children and Richborough Camp cases was nearly exhausted, leaving only the categories of women for domestic service and cases for which private guarantees could be found. With 1,700 estimated monthly places contributed by other countries, the monthly grand total of just 3,700 places was only half what Eichmann proposed. Meanwhile, providing relief for Jews remaining in Austria would tax Jewish resources heavily.

This confrontation between Jewish representatives and Eichmann illuminates the unresolved conflict over Jewish emigration. Efforts to persuade Eichmann to moderate his demands and talk of orderly emigration were a melancholy echo of the Evian conference. The CGJ faced an agonising dilemma. Should it try to comply with Nazi pressure for Jewish emigration while pleading for time? Or had the moment come to call a halt? Several weeks before war broke out, the Jewish refugee organisation decided to accept no more cases. It asked the British government to halt new admissions.[127]

126 Bentwich, 'Report on a visit to Vienna', 17 Aug. 1939, CBF, reel 4, file 25.
127 Sherman, *Island Refuge*, p. 255; Wasserstein, *Britain and Jews*, pp. 81–2; Cooper to Randall, 18 Sep. 1939, PRO FO 371/24100, W13792/3231/48, f. 120.

6 Refugees from Czechoslovakia

The British response to Jews seeking to escape from Czechoslovakia was less generous than the response to Jews from Germany and Austria. This is the crucial respect in which the Czech episode diverges from our story so far. But there are several other differences. The UK government for the first time committed funds to help refugees and thus involved the Treasury closely with refugee policy. Furthermore, the Home Office unexpectedly found itself taking over the main British organisation for refugees from Czechoslovakia.

This chapter examines how, in the aftermath of the Munich settlement of September 1938, the government and refugee organisations responded to pressure to admit refugees from Czechoslovakia to the United Kingdom. In particular, it explores discrimination against Jews over access to refuge. Such discrimination was based on the principle of opposing mass Jewish emigration from Czechoslovakia. The Home Office and British refugee organisations held to this principle and used it to justify withholding funds which could have enabled more people to escape.

In September 1938, German designs on the Sudeten areas of Czechoslovakia appeared to be taking Europe to the brink of war. Britain and France put pressure on the Czech government to give Hitler what he would otherwise take by force of arms. All the Czechs could do was capitulate. Britain breathed a sigh of relief. Its emergency war preparations could be called off. Chamberlain's diplomatic coup in achieving a settlement with Hitler was an occasion for national rejoicing.

The Munich settlement resolved the international crisis and put off war for the moment. But it immediately worsened the refugee problem which was already developing within Czechoslovakia. During September thousands of people, fearing the worst, had fled from the Sudeten areas. After the agreement at Munich, the Sudeten areas were ceded to Germany and occupied from 1 October. The refugee exodus continued. People abandoned the ceded areas and headed for the rump of Czechoslovakia – the provinces of Bohemia, Moravia and Slovakia.

The Czech authorities forcibly returned thousands into the German areas, whilst others returned home voluntarily. The total of refugees in the Czech areas fell, but estimates of their numbers fluctuated.[1]

The refugee crisis was complicated by provisions in the Munich agreement. Exchanges and transfers of population were to take place between the territory of 'new' Czechoslovakia (the areas remaining under Czech rule after Munich) and the areas newly acquired by Germany. The way of implementing these changes was through the exercise of rights to opt for Czech nationality. The agreement gave such rights only to certain groups. Many ethnic Germans from the Sudeten areas who were denied the right to this option feared what might happen to them in the newly German areas. Indeed, the agreement entitled the Czechs to send non-citizens back into these areas.

The enfeebled Czech state was ill equipped to deal with the economic and social costs of resettling large numbers of the Sudetenland's former inhabitants in 'new' Czechoslovakia. The Czechs soon showed that they did not intend to respect the rights of certain groups to opt for Czech nationality. In particular, they were disinclined to accept Jews as full citizens. It became obvious that the Munich provisions gave no protection to people the Czechs did not want.

How was Britain to respond to this volatile situation, a direct outcome of the Munich settlement? The British Foreign Office tried to stave off further Czech expulsions and emphasised the need to respect refugees' rights under the Munich agreement to a guaranteed future in new Czechoslovakia. But it became clear that legal rights to Czech nationality were largely irrelevant to the immediate dangers and difficulties faced by thousands of refugees. Many were now seeking urgent assistance from foreign governments. It was therefore necessary to establish criteria for adjudicating between them.

Refugees and potential refugees fell into three principal groups. First came the Sudeten Germans, who were mostly supporters of the anti-Nazi German Social Democratic Party. Their homes had been in the Sudetenland and they were of German ethnic origin. Their opposition to the Munich agreement and their German origin made them unpopular with the Czech government and the population at large, still smarting from having been forced to capitulate to Germany. Sudeten Germans had no right to opt for Czech nationality. Communists, Jews and some persons of Czech origin also belonged to or were associated

[1] J. W. Bruegel, *Czechoslovakia Before Munich* (Cambridge, 1973); Cab. 47 (38), 30 Sep. 1938, PRO CAB 23/95; Sherman, *Island Refuge*, pp. 137–59; Sir Walter Layton to Halifax, enclosing memorandum, 'Emigration of refugees from Czechoslovakia', 28 Oct. 1938, PRO T 160/1324/F13577/05/1.

with this group. The Sudeten Germans were regarded as the principal casualties of the Munich settlement. British representatives tended to designate members of this group as 'political refugees'. Selected individuals received high priority for British rescue efforts. The reason given was the risk that they might be forcibly returned by the Czechs to the German areas and persecuted there – a fate which befell many in the early weeks of the crisis. By late October, expulsions into the Sudeten areas and the return of other refugees without physical compulsion had produced a drop in the estimated numbers of these refugees from 40,000 to 15,000, only some of whom required resettlement abroad.[2]

The second group, refugees from Germany and Austria who were in Czechoslovakia, were also regarded as political victims of the Munich settlement. A term often used in referring to them, 'old Reich' refugees, will be employed here. By October 1938 some 5,000 to 6,000 old Reich refugees were present in new Czechoslovakia. Most had come recently, in the wake of Austria's annexation. The majority had found refuge in Czechoslovakian territory prior to the Munich crisis, mainly in Moravia and Bohemia. A minority had found asylum in the Sudetenland and later joined the mass exodus into the Czech areas. The greater part of the old Reich refugees were Jews. Among the non-Jews there were many political exiles. British representatives often divided old Reich refugees into 'political refugees' and 'Jewish refugees'.[3] In contrast to the fluctuating estimates of Sudeten Germans needing resettlement, the old Reich group was small and its numbers reasonably certain. The Czechs showed that they found the presence of these foreigners problematic. The British government sympathised with Czech difficulties over harbouring old Reich refugees, and supported efforts to resettle them abroad.

Jews from the Sudetenland constituted the third large refugee group. Some 22,000 Jews had lived there before Munich. The majority had now fled into Bohemia and Moravia. Their national status was mixed, but most had rights under the Munich agreement to opt for Czech citizenship and live in new Czechoslovakia. However, the Czech government soon showed its contempt for these rights. A pattern of bureaucratic discrimination against Jews from the Sudetenland emerged, and they were systematically denied access to funds they had brought out. British officials acknowledged the difficulties of Sudetenland Jews in the face of Czech anti-semitism. Nevertheless, they expressed considerable

2 'Emigration of refugees from Czechoslovakia', 'Report by Sir Neill Malcolm on his visit to Czechoslovakia, October 10th–12th, 1939', 13 Oct. 1938, PRO T 160/1324/F13577/05/1.

3 Sir Herbert Emerson, memorandum, 'Report on Visit to Prague', 17 Jan. 1939, PRO T 160/1324/F13577/05/3.

sympathy with Czech reluctance to accept them within the country's reduced and overcrowded boundaries, even agreeing that Czech Jews were not 'real' Czechs.[4] Officially, British policy was to press the Czech government not to discriminate against Sudetenland Jews and to accept them. To expel or exclude them would breach the Munich agreement and create a mass of potential refugees, whose problems in finding new homes would be at least as acute as those of Jews from Germany and Austria.

In the autumn of 1938 these three categories – Sudeten Germans, old Reich refugees and Sudeten Jews – constituted the main body of refugees believed to need resettlement outside Czechoslovakia. Estimates fluctuated, but the total was not greatly in excess of 40,000 persons, well over half of them Jews. However, the position of a far greater number of Jews – some 300,000 – normally resident in the areas of 'new' Czechoslovakia – Bohemia, Moravia and Slovakia – was already exciting concern. Although not as yet refugees, their position looked increasingly uncertain. The Czech authorities also refused to admit Czech Jews who were being expelled into their territory from areas surrendered to neighbouring states. Numerous Jewish expellees were confined in these frontier areas. The Czech government made it clear that Jews of Czech nationality were not wanted and put various forms of pressure on them to emigrate. British government observers recognised that the future for Jews looked problematic.[5]

The British government was affected by the difficulties of these groups and the Czechs' negative attitudes to them. For political and strategic reasons, British policy aimed to keep the shaky Czech state in existence and independent of its menacing German neighbour. At the same time British responsibility for implementing the Munich agreement included a commitment to uphold the rights of residents of territories now under German control – entitlements to opt for Czech nationality, to reside in Czech areas and to protection of personal and property rights. The British government decided on a policy of offering the Czechs financial help with the refugee problem. Such a policy took account of the Czechs' inhospitability towards refugees and would ease their severe economic and financial difficulties. Taking this approach also assuaged British guilt over the Munich settlement. Britain had obtained the peace it craved – refugees had paid the price. A significant section of the British public considered their nation to be under a moral obligation to mitigate the Czech refugee crisis. For these reasons the British government – which steadfastly refused to finance the exodus

[4] FO to Henderson, nos. 512, 513, 26 Oct. 1938, PRO T 160/1324/F13577/05/1.

[5] Cab. 50 (38)1, 26 Oct. 1938, PRO CAB 23/96.

from Germany and Austria – decided to fund relief and resettlement for refugees from Czechoslovakia.

Accordingly, in early October 1938 Britain agreed to advance to the Czechs funds totalling £10 million. Of this sum, £4 million was designated as a gift for the relief and resettlement of refugees within Czechoslovakia and overseas.[6] During negotiations with the Czechs over the gift fund, British representatives laboured the point that the money should be used to meet people's needs on a non-discriminatory basis and that refugees were not to be expelled into the German areas. Further financial assistance would be tied to British satisfaction on these points.[7] But there were disturbing signs that the cash-starved Czechs were only waiting to get their hands on the British funds before launching anti-Jewish measures.[8] Britain did not intend the money to finance the entry of refugees to the United Kingdom, but, in time, it came to be regarded as a means to this end.

The responsibility for supervising the advance involved the Treasury not only in control over expenditure, but with refugee policy. The original arrangements with the Czechs for the British advance were handled by the Treasury, working in conjunction with the Foreign Office. The government, wishing to monitor the Czechs' expenditure of British funds, announced in October the appointment of Robert Stopford as British liaison officer in Prague. Stopford was a last-minute replacement for the Treasury's Edward Playfair, who was unwell.[9] Stopford was not a civil servant but a banker. He and S. D. Waley of the Treasury were friends. He had recent experience of Czechoslovakia, having worked on the failed Runciman Mission. He was also instrumental in bringing about the decision to offer the Czechs the funds the expenditure of which he was now to supervise. Stopford had strong humanitarian instincts. He proved able to inspire trust and win friends on all sides in Czechoslovakia and became an effective advocate for refugees.

An important part of Stopford's brief was to make sure that there was no discrimination on political or racial grounds. He was also to collect information on the refugee problem in Czechoslovakia. His instructions

[6] Cab. 48 (38)1, 3 Oct. 1939, PRO CAB 23/95; Cab. 49 (38)2, 19 Oct. 1938, Cab. 52 (38)9, 2 Nov. 1938, Cab. 55 (38)7, 16 Nov. 1938, Cab. 57 (38)3, 30 Nov. 1938, PRO CAB 23/96.

[7] 'Note of a meeting between the Czecho-Slovak Financial Mission and representatives of HM Treasury, held on Saturday, 15th October 1938', 15 Oct. 1938, PRO T 160/1324/ F13577/05/1.

[8] Waley to Leith-Ross, 19 Nov. 1938, Waley to Makins, 23 Nov. 1938, PRO FO 371/ 21576, C14393/2320/12, f. 204; Cab. 57 (38)3, 30 Nov. 1938, PRO CAB 23/96.

[9] Sir Edward Playfair, interview with the author, 9 Apr. 1997.

required him to report to the Treasury with copies to the Foreign Office.[10] Stopford left for Prague in the second half of October. Soon, he was predicting that most Czech Jews would be forced to emigrate. His reports to Waley in the Treasury warned that a wholesale expulsion of between 150,000 and 250,000 Jews was possible. Waley decided to alert Anthony de Rothschild to the need for British Jews to make provision for guarantees to support the emigration of their co-religionists in Czechoslovakia.[11]

The severity of the problem Jews were already facing within the country – and British awareness of it – is underlined by secret provisions of the formal agreement regarding the British advance made with the Czechs in January 1939. The published agreement, to which the French government was a party, converted the sum of £4 million from the British government into a free gift to be used entirely for the emigration of refugees.[12] But secret provisions extended the agreement's benefits to Jews who had fled to Bohemia and Moravia from persecution in Slovakia, even though Slovakia was part of new Czechoslovakia.[13]

Several voluntary funds were launched for refugees from Czechoslovakia. The Lord Mayor of London, Sir Harry Twyford, started a fund and went to Prague to investigate the situation along with representatives of other organisations including the TUC and Labour Party.[14] The initial aim of the British fund-raising effort was to provide relief for refugees within Czechoslovakia. But the heavy demand for refuge abroad led to the formation in late October 1938 of the British Committee for Refugees from Czechoslovakia (BCRC) to allocate funds raised in Britain and to handle arrangements for refugees who might come to the United Kingdom.[15] The committee was a non-sectarian organisation. Its supporters had a particular interest in rescuing endangered 'political refugees', many of whom were Sudeten Germans and also took an interest in the plight of old Reich refugees.

10 Phillips to R. Stopford, 31 Oct. 1938, PRO FO 371/21576, C13311/2320/12, f. 56.

11 DO memorandum, 'Position of Sudeten German Social Democrat Refugees and other Refugees in Czechoslovakia', n.d., sent by Duke of Devonshire to high commissioners, 21 Nov. 1938, Waley to A. de Rothschild, 25 Nov. 1938, Waley to Stopford, 29 Nov. 1938, PRO T 160/1324/F13577/05/2.

12 'Agreements between His Majesty's Government in the United Kingdom the Government of the French Republic and the Government of the Czechoslovak Republic regarding FINANCIAL ASSISTANCE TO CZECHO-SLOVAKIA' (with exchange of letters with the Plenipotentiary of Czechoslovakia in London), 27 Jan. 1939, Cmd 5933; Czechoslovakia (Financial Assistance) Act 1939, 28 Feb. 1939.

13 Exchange of letters, Stopford and R. Zavrel, 27 Jan. 1939, B. Trend to Cooper, 1 Feb. 1939, PRO T 160/1324/F13577/05/3.

14 Cab. 48 (38)2, 48 (38)3, 3 Oct. 1938, PRO CAB 23/95.

15 For the BCRC's origins, see PRO HO 294/39; minutes of meeting, 13 Feb. 1939, PRO HO 294/50.

The British government was reluctant to undertake responsibility for mitigating the refugee crisis in Czechoslovakia by admissions to the United Kingdom. But in response to pressure it agreed to authorise entry in selected cases. Up to the end of October 1938, apart from some port admissions, the government's only concession was a single quota of 350 special visas. These visas authorised admission on a temporary basis only. Refugees and their families were required to show guaranteed maintenance during their stay. The BCRC negotiated the authorisation of the visas in accordance with its policy of giving priority to 'political refugees', allocating 250 to Sudeten Germans and 100 to old Reich refugees.[16] The quota satisfied only a fraction of the demand and the government faced pleas for further admissions. In January 1939, for example, Eleanor Rathbone noted the Czechs' susceptibility to German pressure to surrender refugees and urged immediate evacuation.[17]

To estimate the numbers and needs of refugee groups was difficult. It was often unclear who stood in the most serious danger. Refugee populations were constantly shifting. The Czechs were expelling some and refusing others entry. Neither their assurances nor their threats could be relied on. In the face of these uncertainties, BCRC and British government representatives evolved guidelines for the selection of individuals from among thousands seeking help and refuge.

The privately funded BCRC initially set the pattern of priorities in choosing candidates for its special visas. A similar system was followed later when public funds were being allocated to selected refugees from Czechoslovakia. Indeed, everyone concerned in determining who should qualify for British aid engaged in an unending process of listing various refugee groups in order of priority. Particularly convoluted formulations designed to exclude some refugees and include others were incorporated in the Anglo-Czech agreement. But whatever other details varied, 'political refugees' were always at the top of British lists. At the bottom were always Jews with no recognised political activism, who were defined as 'racial' or 'economic' refugees.

In choosing the objects of its help, the British government showed a sense of political obligation towards Sudeten Germans and old Reich refugees. The feeling that it was right to help the Czechs resettle these two groups abroad also reflected the fact that they were the groups in the most obvious danger. Sudeten Germans and old Reich refugees were menaced by the terms of the Munich agreement and by its aftermath. Their presence within new Czechoslovakia caused the Czechs expense and embarrassment. If the Czechs expelled them, they faced

[16] W. Layton to Halifax, 28 Oct. 1938, cited n. 1.

[17] Eleanor Rathbone, 'Note on Situation in Prague', 20 Jan. 1939, PRO HO 294/39.

deadly peril under the Nazis. The British government was also under pressure at home from humanitarians and opponents of the Munich settlement lobbying for admissions and expressing particular concern for the welfare of Sudeten and old Reich refugees.

The preference for Sudeten German refugees, then, reflected British sympathy for endangered political refugees. It was further reinforced by effective pressure mounted by the leader of the Sudeten German Social Democrats, Wenzel Jaksch, who arrived in Britain in early October 1938 hoping to secure havens abroad for up to 20,000 of his endangered followers. Proposals made by Jaksch for exploring refuge in the dominions were urgently taken up with dominion governments. Canada was seeking new immigrants, especially skilled craftsmen and agricultural workers, and eventually accepted several thousand Sudeten refugees. Many of the Sudetens entered the United Kingdom and departed again for Canada, within weeks in some cases. The terms of their entry to Britain were similar to those imposed on refugees from Germany and Austria. Sudetens were granted only temporary refuge and needed guarantees for maintenance and emigration as well as emigration prospects. The Canadians extracted from the British government an agreement to allocate landing money of C$1,500 per family, as a condition of acceptance.[18]

A further reason for Britain's readiness to help Sudeten refugees was that they were easier to resettle than Jews. Very few of the refugees from Czechoslovakia accepted by Canada were Jews. The Canadian government followed the advice of its high commissioner in London, Vincent Massey, that accepting substantial numbers of 'Aryan Sudeten German' refugees would make it easier to refuse to admit Jews.[19] The British government was aware that Canada wished its share of the emigration to be confined to Social Democrats of the Sudeten German community. Yet, in late April 1939 Waley told Maxwell that the Canadians had agreed to the inclusion of Jews 'provided that they are of a "non-ritualistic" type, but they look very much askance at Communists'.[20]

The BCRC's policy for allocation of its special visas emphasised danger as the criterion for rescue. As Mary Ormerod, a leading figure in the BCRC, said, the BCRC had been guided in its choice of Sudeten and old Reich refugees 'solely by the degree of danger in which they

[18] Copy, S. B. Pearson to Maxwell, 17 Apr. 1939, sent by J. Williams to Waley, 18 Apr. 1939, *ibid.*

[19] Abella and Troper, *None Is Too Many*, pp. 48–9.

[20] Waley to Maxwell, 19 Apr. 1939, PRO T 160/1324/F13577/05/8; W. Gillies to W. Layton, 24 Nov. 1939, PRO HO 294/52.

stood of being deported to Germany'.[21] The priority the BCRC gave to trades union and political figures reflected the same principle – that they were in special peril of persecution because of their politics and their own particular histories of activism. The consequences of such politically motivated persecution were perceived as more dangerous than the likely outcome of anti-Jewish persecution. The need of 'politicals' for refuge from persecution fitted the British conception of 'political' asylum much more closely than did the plight of Jews persecuted for what they were rather than for anything they believed or anything they had done.

Jews were also being forced back into the German areas, but as part of a general hostility to Jews as such. Jews were for the most part persecuted as Jews, rather than on political grounds. Of course, certain Jewish cases did have a political dimension, but in the great majority of Jewish cases there was no suggestion that the persecution flowed from hostility to particular individuals. Indeed, the Germans did not press for the return of Jews to the newly acquired Sudeten territories. On the contrary, they were busy expelling Jews or persecuting them in order to force their emigration.

The fact that Jews were wanted by neither the Germans nor the Czechs was not seen as sufficient reason to offer them refuge in Britain. The Munich agreement gave the Czech government no grounds to complain about the presence of Czech Jews. Furthermore, the policy of both the British government and the IGC was opposed to the forced emigration of Jews. For all these reasons, the BCRC and the British government treated Jewish emigration as a low priority.

These arguments against the need and desirability of Jewish emigration were reinforced by questions of its practicability. Emigration prospects for Jews were poor. As the Canadian example showed, prospects for emigration from Czechoslovakia were worse for Jews than for non-Jews. But there was opposition to pursuing a policy of singling out refugees from Czechoslovakia generally or Sudeten Germans in particular for special privileges merely because of their better emigration prospects. Makins objected to it and worried about the consequences of increasing commitments to Czech refugees. The government, as a Dominions Office official pointed out, was showing partiality by its action in assisting Czech refugee emigration to the dominions and admitting urgent cases to the United Kingdom.[22] When Winterton

[21] Ormerod, 'Notes on the liabilities of the British Committee for Refugees from Czechoslovakia', 22 Jan. 1939, PRO HO 294/39.

[22] Makins, memorandum, 27 Oct. 1938, PRO FO 371/21585, C12940/11896/12, f. 47; C. R. Price to Makins, 31 Oct. 1938, PRO T 160/1324/F13577/05/1.

proposed advertising the availability of the Sudeten Germans since non-Jews would be more attractive to possible countries of settlement, Rublee objected that such a policy was discriminatory and contrary to IGC principles.[23] Yet even Stopford felt that the likelihood that settling non-Jews abroad would be easier would justify releasing a lump sum from the new British loan to help endangered Sudeten Germans by financing their temporary asylum in the United Kingdom and subsequent settlement.[24]

A major impediment to the entry of Jews was that Jewish organisations in Britain refused to take responsibility for refugees from Czechoslovakia. The CGJ adhered tenaciously to the position that its funds had been collected for German Jewry.[25] The Jewish organisation was prepared to co-operate with the BCRC and be represented on its committees and some of its staff went to work for the BCRC.[26] But the CGJ and its associated bodies resisted, to the last, all pressure to get directly involved in arranging the entry of Czech Jews. This made it certain that relatively few would obtain refuge in Britain.

Jewish leaders in Czechoslovakia provided the British government with evidence of the persecution of Czech Jews and pressed for greater generosity towards them. Some of these requests concerned the defence of Jewish rights in Czechoslovakia. The Jewish leaders also made pleas for assistance in organising Jewish emigration, to Palestine in particular. Leo Herrmann, who represented the Jewish Agency in Czechoslovakia, suggested that part of the Czech loan be used for Jewish emigration to Palestine.[27] In January 1939 the British and Czech governments agreed that the Czechs would set aside a sum of £500,000 for this purpose, to finance the emigration of 2,500 Jews – only half the number the Czechs had originally hoped to include.[28]

In Britain, Erich Turk, who represented the Anglo-Jewish refugee bodies on the BCRC and would later be a trustee of the Czech Refugee Trust Fund, argued that Jews should be allocated more of the committee's special visas. In January 1939 he reminded fellow members of the BCRC's Finance Committee that the BCRC's original mandate required aid to be given to persons whose lives were endangered,

23 G. Rublee to Winterton, 26 Oct. 1938, PRO FO 371/22535, W13882/104/98, f. 24.

24 Newton to FO, 26 Nov. 1938, PRO T 160/1324/F13577/05/2.

25 Bunbury, 'The problem of Jewish Refugees from Czechoslovakia', 5 Apr. 1939, PRO HO 294/39.

26 W. Layton to S. Dixon, 9 May 1939, Dixon to W. Layton, extract, 10 May 1939, 'Questions of principle on which decisions must be taken', n.d., PRO HO 294/52.

27 Makins, memorandum, 21 Oct. 1938, Leo Herrmann, 'Memorandum on the position of Jews in and from the Sudeten areas', n.d., PRO T 160/1324/F13577/05/02.

28 Herrmann to Bunbury, 11 Aug. 1939, PRO T 160/1324/F13577/05/16.

'regardless of race or creed'. The Jewish position in Czechoslovakia was, he suggested, not fully understood. Turk stressed Jewish political activism, saying that members of the democratic and anti-Nazi Jewish Party faced danger at least as great as that facing communists and social democrats. He said that, being Jews, they were more likely than other citizens to be expelled and he asked that some of a block of visas currently being allocated be set aside for certain urgent cases supported by Jewish organisations in Czechoslovakia.[29] In February, Turk pressed the BCRC to give special consideration in future to the position of Jews since most political refugees in special danger would soon be evacuated and anti-semitism would increase in Czechoslovakia if Jews could not emigrate. He received a polite hearing, but the committee's practice did not change.[30] As before, Jews who were 'political' might get special visas, but non-political Jews remained a subsidiary concern for the BCRC.

Sir Herbert Emerson, the IGC's director, did not regard the difficulties facing Jews as a reason to help them emigrate. On his return from visiting Prague in mid-January he assigned top priority to old Reich political refugees, followed by German refugees from the Sudetenland. Non-political old Reich Jewish refugees he saw as a lower priority, considering their reasons to be economic rather than political. He still noted Czech anti-semitism towards these Jews and the Czech government's wish to be rid of them. He also acknowledged the intense Czech hostility to the presence of Jews from the Sudetenland and that the Czech government wished to get rid of any who did not possess Czech nationality.[31] Emerson did not yet consider it necessary to assign Czech Jews generally a position in his order of priorities.

By mid-March 1939 sanction had been obtained for the admission to Britain of some 2,900 persons in all, selected according to the priorities outlined above. The initial allocation of 350 special visas was followed by Home Office sanction of several further batches.[32] The authorisation of a large quantity of visas in February 1939 reflected provisions for emigration expenses and £200 resettlement grants in January's Anglo-Czech agreement. The extra funds made available took pressure off the voluntary funds collected by the BCRC, making expansion possible. The machinery for authorising entry was improved. It became possible for the Home Office to authorise visas by telephoning the PCO in Prague and for the PCO to grant block visas

29 E. Turk to Gillies, 12 Jan. 1939, PRO HO 294/52.
30 Minutes of meeting, 6 Feb. 1939, PRO HO 294/50.
31 Emerson, memorandum, 'Report on visit to Prague', 17 Jan. 1939, PRO T 160/1324/F13577/05/3.
32 W. Layton to Jagelman, 11 July 1939, PRO HO 294/52.

on lists of names supplied by a local BCRC representative.[33] However, the departure of a trainload of 450 people whom the BCRC managed to get out of Prague in mid-March turned out to be the last legal emigration for several weeks.

On 15 March 1939, Germany's troops occupied Czechoslovakia. The demise of the Czech state put an end to the agreement over refugee finance. By this date the Czechs had drawn about one-seventh of the money from the Bank of England account. Britain acted to prevent the balance from falling into the hands of Czechoslovakia's new masters. The funds in the account were frozen and a law passed prohibiting payment out of moneys connected with the former government without Treasury authority.[34]

The British government decided that the unexpended balance of the original £4 million gift should still be available for the purpose of enabling refugees to emigrate from Czechoslovakia. The provisions of the defunct agreement were treated as constituting the terms of a trust under which the remaining moneys were held in British hands. The fund, which stood at approximately £3.25 million, was to be administered by a new agency, the Czech Refugee Trust Fund (CRTF).[35] However, the CRTF was not set up immediately.[36] The BCRC, its own funds exhausted, offered to continue with its work if funds to cover liabilities and administrative expenses could be assured from the remaining balance of the gift fund. The government agreed that, pending the CRTF's creation, the Treasury would advance to the BCRC moneys which would later be repaid out of the fund.[37] This arrangement enabled the BCRC to continue bringing refugees to the United Kingdom, while its casework was carried out under increasing direction from the British government. In July 1939 the Home Office finally set up the CRTF and the trust absorbed the BCRC's casework functions. Maxwell, permanent under secretary at the Home Office, issued formal directions to the new CRTF trustees, Eward G. Culpin, a trustee of the Lord Mayor's fund, Erich Turk of the BCRC and Sir Malcolm Delevigne, a retired Home Office official.[38] In this way the government became involved in the business of financing and controlling refugee organisations.

[33] BCRC, report of the Executive Committee meeting held on 15 Mar. 1939, *ibid.*
[34] Czechoslovakia (Restrictions on Banking Accounts etc.) Act, 1939, 27 Mar. 1939, Waley, Czech Claims, 11 Sep. 1940, PRO T 210/20.
[35] Simon, *Hansard*, House of Commons, vol. 345, cols. 1299–1303, 22 Mar. 1939.
[36] For the CRTF's history, see PRO HO 294/5.
[37] M. Layton (BCRC) to Simon, 25 Mar. 1939, PRO HO 294/50.
[38] 'Note of Meeting in Sir A. Maxwell's room on 18th Apr. 1939, to discuss the setting up of a Trust to administer the Czech Refugee Fund', PRO T 160/1324/F13577/05/8;

The urgent need following the German occupation was to evacuate people. Temporary refuge was the most that was available for the majority of those seeking to escape from Czechoslovakia. But the gift fund had originally been designed to assist only those emigrants who were bound for a destination where they could settle permanently. The main barrier to gaining temporary refuge was finding the costs of maintenance. In early April the government decided to enlarge the purposes of the fund to cover temporary refuge. Accordingly, the government agreed that the fund's aim was primarily to secure the emigration and settlement of refugees from Czechoslovakia, but that a secondary objective was to maintain them. On this basis the government could promise the BCRC that it would be able to recover from the Treasury the cost of maintenance of refugees up to £100,000.[39]

After the German occupation, Stopford became the leading authority on the interpretation of the provisions of the gift fund. He also worked strenuously to get the flow of legal emigration moving again. His contacts in Prague included many Jews and he showed serious concern about anti-Jewish persecution. Stopford pressed for inclusion of Czechs, Jews and stateless persons in the definition of refugees covered by the fund. He advocated using the fund to help some, but not all, Czech Jews to emigrate. The new German authorities in Prague had told him that they were anxious for the work of the fund to continue, but one of their conditions for allowing this was the inclusion of Czech Jews in the definition of eligible refugees.

Most of the people embraced by the categories of refugee designated as eligible for help under the Anglo-Czech agreement had been persons with German or Austrian origins or affiliations. In addition, the government now decided that Czechs and Jews would also be eligible for inclusion as refugees.[40] Accordingly, the terms of the trust were expanded to include two new categories of persons from new Czechoslovakia, subject to the trustees' discretion and, in certain cases, to the home secretary's approval. The BCRC supported this expansion.[41] On the instructions of the Treasury, Stopford told the German

HO, 'Czech Refugee Trust Fund and Directions to the Trustees', 21 July 1939, Cmd 6076.

39 Report on Czech Situation, Co-ordinating Committee meeting minutes, 3 Apr. 1939, PRO HO 213/268; copy, Lord Hailey to Hoare, 6 Apr. 1939, sent by Jagelman to Waley, 12 Apr. 1939, Waley to Phillips, 15 Apr. 1939, PRO T 160/1324/F13577/05/8; Maxwell to Hailey, 6 Apr. 1939, Hailey to Maxwell, 14 Apr. 1939, PRO HO 294/39; 'Note of Meeting in Sir A. Maxwell's room', cited n. 38; Trust Deed, 21 July 1939, PRO HO 213/297.

40 Waley, draft telegrams to Stopford, 13 Apr. 1939, FO to J. M. Troutbeck, no. 123, 17 Apr. 1939, PRO T 160/1324/F13577/05/8.

41 Trust Deed, cited n. 39, para. 1; W. Layton to Simon, 25 Mar. 1939, PRO HO 294/50.

authorities that his government was prepared to include Czechs and Czech Jews within the scope of the trust. But he added that the original refugees were the principal concern of the British government.

The Home Office's new responsibility for overseeing the use of the gift fund gave officials an unprecedented degree of control over the British voluntary effort for Czech refugees. The search for an efficient director for the CRTF who would, Maxwell hoped, 'have real control over the voluntary workers' led to the selection of Sir Henry Bunbury.[42] In the four months between the end of the Czech state in March 1939 and the establishment of the trust in July, the Home Office became closely involved in ruling on which cases the BCRC should take up. Ultimately, the CRTF would take over responsibility for such cases; meanwhile, the costs were covered by moneys advanced to the BCRC. New BCRC cases needed to satisfy a number of requirements: to be eligible for help within the terms of reference of the fund as recently expanded; to be sufficiently deserving to merit the expenditure of a portion of the finite sum available from the free gift funds, and to comply with immigration policy. Of course, Home Office agreement to admission was required in all cases. Lastly, holders of Czech passports were required to obtain visas from 1 April 1939, the earliest date on which the Home Office had been able to re-introduce them.

The Home Office had thus acquired the responsibility for directing the policy of an organisation whose aim was to rescue refugees and bring them to the United Kingdom, but its overriding preoccupation remained with control. Accordingly, much of its effort went into limiting new commitments by the BCRC. The same pattern continued when the CRTF came into being. The Home Office's policy of trying to rein back British efforts for Czech refugees at the same time as funding refuge for a select minority involved officials in new controversies.

Once the Germans became masters of Czechoslovakia in March 1939, they openly pursued a policy of eliminating the Jewish presence and put intense pressure on Jews to emigrate. The majority of Jews could have departed openly. Their difficulty was not so much in leaving the country as in finding a refuge abroad. On the other hand, the Germans attempted to prevent the departure of political opponents, most of them non-Jews, who were therefore generally able to emigrate only by illegal channels. Legal emigration was largely confined to Jews.[43]

42 Minutes, BCRC General Council meeting, 15 May 1939; 'Czech Refugees', minutes of meeting on 23 May, PRO T 160/1324/F13577/05/9; minutes, BCRC, Executive and Finance Committees meeting, 24 May 1939, PRO HO 294/50.

43 'Report on the Czechoslovakian Refugee Problem', Odo Nansen, 31 Mar. 1939, PRO HO 213/268.

But it was possible to graduate from illegal to legal status. For example, Stopford and BCRC workers in Prague reluctantly agreed to disclose to the German authorities the whereabouts of a group composed mainly of wives or children who had gone into hiding. The decision to reveal the families' hiding places flowed from the conclusion that, to enable the families to leave at all to join their Sudeten German menfolk in Britain, it was necessary to co-operate with the Gestapo, who wished to address them first about the advantages of remaining.[44] As a result, after submission of their cases to the Gestapo, some 200 family members were able to leave for Britain by early May. But disappearances, arrests and deaths also occurred among the group of families. BCRC workers in Prague insisted that their new approach was justified and that departures depended on co-operation with the Gestapo.[45] William Gillies of the Labour Party submitted a list of high-sounding objections to co-operation with agents of the detested Nazi regime and also took exception to British assistance to help Czech Jews emigrate. His criticisms received short shrift from Stopford.[46]

The Gestapo rightly suspected that certain BCRC workers were helping people to leave the country illegally. Most illegal emigrants went to Poland – the only north-westerly route out of Czechoslovakia not across Nazi territory. They left Poland from the port of Gdynia. At the time of the occupation illegal emigration quickly developed: soon hundreds of refugees had entered Poland, the majority congregating in Krakow and Katowice. BCRC representatives went out to Poland and tried to select cases which merited British visas. The refugee situation was complicated by the Polish government's reluctance to harbour large numbers of refugees. Indeed, the Poles turned back many Jews who sought to enter the country illegally. But they refrained from expelling refugees sponsored by the BCRC and they were responsive to requests from the British vice-consulate in Katowice. A. W. G. Randall of the Foreign Office told Emerson that

> most of these refugees appear to be Jews who are not in any real danger, and some of them are certainly undesirables whom the Poles would be justified in refusing. Their illegal exodus prejudices the position of refugees who *are* in real danger, and if they stayed it should be possible to emigrate them legally later. In all the circumstances we doubt whether we can fairly ask the Polish Government

[44] Stopford to Ormerod, 16 Apr. 1939, Stopford to Waley, 17 Apr. 1939, PRO T 160/1324/F13577/05/8.

[45] DW, 'The Numbers now Remaining in the Protectorate: Wives and Children of Refugees now in England', n.d., written 29 Apr.–4 May 1939, PRO HO 294/52.

[46] Stopford to Trend, 1 May 1939, PRO T 160/1324/F13577/05/9.

not to turn back refugees who have no proof that they are in danger or that they are on the British or other lists.[47]

In late April, leaders of the BCRC and the Jewish refugee organisation, together with Emerson and Bunbury, agreed that a further 700 refugees from Poland would be selected. Top priority would be given to Sudetenland refugees, followed by old Reich refugees, refugees because of post-Munich boundary adjustments and other political cases. Additional persons might be selected on the basis of 'suitability for emigration or other means of livelihood or support in England' – the only chance for most non-political Czech Jews.[48] The investigation of applicants involved consultation with Jewish representatives, and Julian Layton and Maurice Baron representing Anglo-Jewry went to Poland to recommend refugees for visas. They reportedly agreed that Jewish economic refugees should not be encouraged to enter Poland from Czechoslovakia.[49]

Refugees denied British visas faced expulsion by the Poles. In mid-June Randall told Waley that Ormerod felt that the BCRC could not object to these expulsions. She asserted that many people the BCRC had rejected were neither refugees 'in the proper sense of the word' nor covered by the January agreement. Ormerod's view was opposed by a local BCRC representative, by the consul in Katowice and the British ambassador. Randall thought the government should not oppose Ormerod, but that she might be asked to include some additional people on top of those she had already selected. Waley advocated a tougher line, arguing that, notwithstanding the fact that Ormerod's committee had many friends in Parliament, the government should not let it determine what course of action to adopt with the balance of the fund. Stressing the need to establish facts, he observed that the Jews in Poland whom the BCRC did not wish to help appeared to dispute its view that they were economically motivated and not in any danger.[50]

The plight of refugees in Poland was urgent and Britain wished to maintain good relations with the Polish government. Consequently the Foreign Office pressed for prioritisation of Polish cases over those in Czechoslovakia.[51] Furthermore, Emerson had given the Polish

47 Sir H. Kennard to Halifax, 25 Apr. 1939, Randall to Emerson, 28 Apr. 1939, *ibid.*

48 'Revised memorandum of decisions of meeting held on 28th Apr.', 1 May 1939, PRO HO 294/52.

49 CM to C. Hollingworth, Katowice, 17 July 1939, W. Layton to Ormerod, B. Bracey, Gillies, 3 Aug. 1939, PRO HO 294/57; Kennard to Halifax, 25 Apr., Randall to Emerson, 28 Apr. 1939, both cited n. 47; Ormerod to Hailey, 5 May 1939, PRO T 160/1324/F13577/05/9.

50 Randall to Waley, 15 June 1939, enclosing copy of Kennard to Halifax, 8 June 1939, Waley to Randall, 16 June 1939, PRO T 160/1324/F13577/05/12.

51 Sir G. Mounsey to Maxwell, 24 May 1939, PRO T 160/1324/F13577/05/10.

authorities an undertaking that the BCRC would take responsibility for a large number of families in Poland.

Balancing aid to refugees who had fled abroad against helping those who remained in Czechoslovakia involved a further complication. British visas issued in Poland went largely to illegal emigrants while visas in Prague were issued to person emigrating lawfully. To help 'illegals' put departures from Prague at risk, since the German authorities had threatened to stop the BCRC's work there if its representatives did not desist from support to refugees who left illegally.[52] The question of whether trust funds should be used to support illegal emigration networks led to disagreements in London. Maxwell wished to help 'illegals' and was prepared to make concessions to BCRC pressure on their behalf.[53] Yet, as Stopford pointed out, to use the fund to help a small number of Czech politicals – who could only leave illegally – could endanger work for the original refugees and other persons whom the trust had already pledged to help, including Jews.[54] The issue was left in an ill-defined state which in practice enabled some assistance to 'illegals' to continue. Stopford managed to help both legal emigrants and 'illegals'. He maintained good enough relations with the Germans to work with them on legal emigration while providing discreet support for British workers and others involved with illegal emigration networks.

Of course, irrespective of whether their departure had been legal or illegal, all refugees coming to Britain needed Home Office authorisation. After the occupation, the Home Office had suspended the issue of approvals, pending release of the trust fund. The resulting hiatus in legal emigration lasted two months. Stopford played a key role in getting things restarted, negotiating in Prague with Czech and German officials and contributing to discussions in London on the future of the trust fund.[55]

In mid-April the voluntary organisations and the Home Office agreed general guidelines for future selection. Lord Hailey of the Co-ordinating Committee promised efforts to avoid bringing people to the United Kingdom and instead to arrange direct emigration overseas. Arrangements agreed for the 'systematic selection' of refugees in both Prague and Poland gave first preference to persons who,

[52] Stopford, memorandum, 20 June 1939, PRO T 160/1324/F13577/05/12.

[53] Minutes of meeting on 13 June 1939, *ibid.*; BCRC, minutes of meeting, 21 June 1939, PRO HO 294/50; Waley to Maxwell, 12 Apr. 1939, with note, 'Negotiations in Prague', PRO T 160/1324/F13577/05/08.

[54] Waley, draft memorandum sent to Sir R. Hopkins, 29 June 1939, Stopford, memorandum, 20 June 1939, Trend to Cooper, 19 June 1939, PRO T 160/1324/F13577/05/12.

[55] Stopford to Waley, 14 Apr. 1939, enclosing memorandum of 13 Apr., PRO T 160/1324/F13577/05/8.

either for political or other reasons, were in immediate danger from action taken by the German Government, or of being sent back to Germany by Poland. In the selection of others, and in particular in the selection of Jews, preference should be given to those who might be considered suitable for emigration or for whose maintenance in Great Britain satisfactory guarantees were forthcoming.[56]

The BCRC was discouraged from accepting fresh responsibilities. Still, it was allowed to promise visas to a limited number of new refugees, mostly political cases from Poland.[57]

The Home Office's policy was to resist Gestapo pressure for forced Jewish emigration, to discourage mass emigration of Czech Jews and to ensure careful selection of Jewish entrants. Cooper knew that in future the Germans were likely to allow little emigration from Czechoslovakia other than that of Jews, but he was against using the free gift exclusively to finance it. This, he said, would be to give preference to Jews from only one part of Greater Germany and would divert the gift from its original purpose in a way that was 'entirely incongruous and anomalous'. He suggested using any remaining balance in the fund towards the administrative expenses of voluntary organisations in Britain in respect of refugees coming from all parts of Greater Germany.[58] Maxwell, after speaking with the home secretary, planned to favour refugees who left illegally and to keep Jewish emigration within strict limits. He was against entrusting selection to the Refugee Institute in Prague. The institute had been set up before the occupation with funds from the Czech loan but was now under Nazi control and the people permitted to leave 'would be mainly Jews or undesirables whom the police wish to get rid of'.[59] Maxwell wished to spend most of the money to help persons who left illegally, 'because refugees of the political type for whom the money was originally intended are unlikely to get out at all unless they get out illegally'. He was even prepared to include a certain number of communists in Poland, since refusal would force the Poles to send them back to persecution in Czechoslovakia. But Maxwell was worried by the prospect of admitting people prepared to use 'lawless methods' for political ends and he ruled that people guilty of crimes of violence should be excluded and that the BCRC should also be asked to 'limit their selection so far as is practicable to persons who are suitable for emigration'. He claimed that most people who sought to leave because

56 Hailey to Maxwell, 14 Apr. 1939, PRO HO 294/39.
57 W. Layton to Cooper, 18 May 1939, Maxwell to W. Layton, 7 June 1939, PRO HO 294/52; 'Czech Refugees', minutes of meeting, 23 May 1939, PRO T 160/1324/F13577/05/9.
58 Cooper to Maxwell, 29 Apr. 1939, *ibid.*
59 Maxwell to Waley, 15 May 1939, and enclosed memorandum 'Czech refugees', n.d., *ibid.*

they were destitute in Czechoslovakia and wished to make a living elsewhere would be Jews, and added:

Jewish organisations here agree that it would be bad policy to encourage a general Jewish emigration from Czechoslovakia, and while we cannot entirely exclude Jews, we ought, I think, to say that those who have left Czechoslovakia merely for economic reasons should not be selected for assistance.

This basis for future policy was acceptable to Waley.[60]

Thus the Home Office opted for an approach diametrically opposed to that of the German authorities. It adopted a policy of blocking the Jewish exodus which the Gestapo desired, while creating escape routes for people the Germans particularly wished to prevent from leaving. The BCRC leadership might be irritated by Home Office delays and failures of communication and might complain that officials were unduly restrictive or downright unhelpful in granting visas for BCRC-supported cases, but they supported Home Office policies which limited the overall scope of emigration, particularly of Jews categorised as 'economic refugees'.[61]

Emerson's strong opposition to the mass emigration of Jews was in accordance with IGC policy. After the German occupation Emerson took the position that financial assistance for Jews to emigrate from Czechoslovakia would increase the difficulties of the Rublee plan.[62] Stopford, on the other hand, had few illusions about the Rublee plan's prospects. He did not rule out negotiations with the object of pressing Germany to contribute to arrangements for mass Jewish emigration, but in July 1939 he expressed concern that 'a blank refusal to help any Jews would lead to a breakdown of negotiations and increased persecution of the Jews themselves'.[63] Stopford found himself increasingly isolated in his commitment to help Czech Jews. The commitment brought him into conflict not only with Emerson, but with the BCRC, the trustees and Bunbury.

The total number of British-sponsored visas was limited by the amount of money available. Before the occupation the limit had been largely determined by the number of guarantees the BCRC succeeded in obtaining. Afterwards, the quantity of money remaining in the trust fund was the main limiting factor for BCRC-sponsored cases. The Home Office was holding up decisions on new applications pending clarification of existing liabilities.[64] The committee applied for 2,300 additional visas for persons whose immigration would be financed by

60 Waley to Maxwell, 16 May 1939, *ibid.*

61 W. Layton to Cooper, 8 June 1939, W. Layton to Bunbury, 26 June 1939, PRO HO 294/52.

62 Emerson on talk with H. Wohlthat, 19 July 1939, PRO CAB 98/1.

63 Stopford to Bunbury, 31 July 1939, PRO HO 294/70.

64 W. Layton to Cooper, 8 June 1939, *ibid.*

8 Members of a group of Jewish refugees from Czechoslovakia are marched away by police at Croydon airport on 31 March 1939. The refugees were detained at a police station because their documents were not in order. They were put on a flight to Warsaw but threatened to jump out of the window if the plane took off. The pilot refused to fly, so they were deported the following day.

the fund: some were to be taken from Poland; but most were family members still in Slovakia or the Protectorate, as Bohemia and Moravia were now known.[65] By 15 May 1939 the BCRC had undertaken liability for an estimated total of 7,100 persons, plus up to 2,000 who had taken refuge in other countries. The liabilities on the fund to date were calculated at approximately £2 million, plus the further £500,000 set aside for the emigration of Jews to Palestine. In addition, allowance had to be made for claims to the £200 resettlement grant to which refugees were entitled on re-emigration. Bunbury argued that in view of the difficulties in finding permanent settlement – especially for Jews – liabilities for maintenance might have been underestimated. He suggested that a portion of the fund be set aside against the possibility that refugees in Britain would be unable to emigrate.[66] The significance of

[65] Correspondence, PRO HO 294/7; Visa Committee papers, PRO HO 294/52.
[66] Bunbury, memorandum, 'Liabilities in respect of Refugees from Czechoslovakia', 15 May 1939, PRO HO 294/39.

9 Croydon airport departure hall, 31 March 1939: a Jewish refugee from Czechoslovakia in a state of collapse after having been told by the immigration officer that he will be allowed to stay, as an exception has been made in his case.

the exercise of estimating liabilities was that the more that existing commitments consumed the funds available, the less money could be spent on taking on new cases.[67]

Neither the GJAC nor the BCRC was prepared to take responsibility for Jewish refugees from Czechoslovakia. The BCRC undertook Jewish cases, but tried to minimise its involvement in them. After the German occupation, the BCRC opened its doors to refugees from Czechoslovakia who were in Britain, many of them Jews, and was overwhelmed by the flood of applicants. It took responsibility for a total of 1,200 persons who became refugees as a result of the occupation. Some were already in the United Kingdom. Others arrived soon afterwards with inadequate guarantees or none. In many cases the BCRC accepted only limited responsibility. Members of the BCRC's casework committee expressed their wish to cease dealing with Jewish cases, suggesting that the case department's work be split into two separate operations. A division of the work would facilitate a possible handing over of the 'racial refugee' cases to the GJAC, if and when it was able to take responsibility for them.[68] But the GJAC maintained its refusal to undertake this role. And nothing came of a suggestion by the Co-ordinating Committee that, as neither the GJAC nor the BCRC would undertake the responsibility, a separate organisation be created for Jewish refugees from Czechoslovakia.[69] Still, the BCRC's own casework was split into BCRC-sponsored visa cases and Jewish immigration, each handled at different locations.

The BCRC had a paid staff of 100.[70] Its procedure varied according to the category of case. Cases sponsored for committee visas were 'practically confined to the cases of refugees who are in danger on political grounds'. From May 1939 these were selected by a visa committee, after consultation with various Czech political leaders, and sent to the Home Office.[71] The Home Office controlled the quantity by numerical limitation. It gave block authorities to the BCRC from time to time, subject to the subsequent submission of individual names.

'Ordinary visas' were not financed from the fund. Such visas – the only option for most Jews – were obtained from the Home Office after examination by the BCRC's Immigration Department, based at Bloomsbury House alongside the other refugee committees. Ordinary visas were subject to the same conditions as those for refugees from

67 Waley to Maxwell, 16 May 1939, PRO T 160/1324/F13577/05/9.

68 Minutes of Case Committee meeting, 5 Apr. 1939, PRO HO 294/52.

69 Bunbury, 'The Problem of Jewish Refugees from Czechoslovakia', 5 Apr. 1939, PRO HO 294/39.

70 CRTF, memorandum, 'Short account of the work to be taken over from the late British Committee for Refugees from Czechoslovakia', 1 Aug. 1939, PRO HO 294/5.

71 Circular, W. Layton, 4 May 1939, PRO HO 294/52.

Germany and Austria.[72] Children's cases were similarly divided into guaranteed and non-guaranteed.[73] The BCRC set up an expert panel of businessmen to advise on guarantees. It also had a special committee which tried to arrange emigration from the United Kingdom.[74]

Selection of refugee Jews from Czechoslovakia, then, proceeded along the same lines as for Jews from Germany and Austria.[75] The BCRC performed similar functions to the larger GJAC. Many of the same difficulties cropped up, for example, domestic entrants who proved unsuitable.[76] The BCRC was equally conscious of the need to comply with Home Office guidelines. In June 1939, Elizabeth Acland Allen, secretary of the BCRC's visa committee, criticised the inclusion of Jewish professional men in a list of visa candidates forwarded by the Lord Mayor's fund. The Home Office, she said, had sent a written warning 'about the undesirability of applying for professional people, as they are very difficult to emigrate'. Allen asserted that 'most of the refugees were really all economic' and not any more in danger than thousands of others. The majority of the cases would therefore have to await submission to the visa committee after the whole question of new visas had been cleared up – for the past two months the Home Office had not granted the BCRC any visas for Czechoslovakia.[77]

A survey of BCRC visa allocation policy written by Allen in late August 1939 offers further insights into the BCRC's approach.[78] Allen said that the visa committee had selected cases on the basis of endangerment, contribution to public life and suitability for re-emigration, taking into account such matters as an applicant's age and profession. It also decided in what proportions to allocate visas to refugees in Poland, the Protectorate and elsewhere. Refugees, she said, were divided into 'Political and racial/Jewish'. Her explanation of the term 'political' was that it covered members of a wide range of organisations – trades unions and women's, peace and youth groups – in fact, any refugee 'who was organised, [and/or] – in consequence of his public activities – is in danger'. It embraced writers, artists and actors whose work was considered obnoxious by the German authorities. Large numbers of Jews were included under all these headings, Allen claimed. She estimated that at least three-quarters

72 *Ibid.*; BCRC, leaflet, 'Conditions for entering Great Britain', n.d., PRO HO 294/39.
73 Finance Committee minutes, 4 May 1939, PRO HO 294/50.
74 W. Layton correspondence, 4 May–23 June 1939, PRO HO 294/52.
75 Cooper to Waley, 9 May 1939, PRO T 160/1324/F13577/05/9.
76 Case Committee minutes, 19 July 1939, PRO HO 294/52.
77 E. A. Allen, memorandum, 'Candidates for Visas, forwarded by the Lord Mayor's Fund', 6 June 1939, *ibid.*
78 Allen, 'Memorandum on emigration to the United Kingdom pending final settlement of persons coming from Czechoslovakia', 20 Aug. 1939, *ibid.*

of political refugees coming from Poland to the United Kingdom were Jews 'according to the Nurnberg laws'. The term 'racial refugee', she said, was used 'to cover purely Jewish refugees' and did not include people endangered through their activities in Jewish organisations or in the Jewish communities, who were seen as political refugees.

Allen concluded that the categories for whom the government's grant had originally and primarily been intended had been very largely dealt with. She considered that there was still a need to apply for visas for family members in Germany and Austria. Little chance remained of 'getting any real political refugees out of the Protectorate', she said.[79] Permission to emigrate was, she claimed, obtainable only by Jews who had taken no part in public life. She said that most 'political' Sudetens, Germans or Austrians either had come to Britain or were in prison in Czechoslovakia or awaiting visas in Poland or elsewhere. Some visas, Allen advised, should be kept for people who might still emerge from the Protectorate. Indeed, the BCRC had received visa applications for a group of political refugees of various nationalities, all Jews, but the German authorities would allow them to leave only 'if their political activities are not considered of sufficient importance to outweigh the desire that all Jews should leave'.[80] But in Slovakia the demand for visas for people who had been active politically was very low, she said, since most had left after the Munich settlement.

Allen had no proposals to help non-political Jews. She said that the requirements of 'Czechs', meaning Czech Jews, were 'impossible to estimate', owing to the uncertain situation in the Protectorate. In Slovakia there were some 5,000 Jewish refugees of various nationalities, but their political status was not known and would be difficult to investigate, she said. Allen also reported that some 200,000 Slovakian Jews, now under similar threat to those in the Reich, would have to emigrate and the BCRC was collecting information about leading figures in the Jewish communities. By then Czech refugees were scattered throughout Europe and had been expelled by eight countries named by Allen. Among the applicants for British visas were a large number of recent arrivals in Latvia, many of whom had previously been rejected by the BCRC in Poland, she reported, as 'unsuitable either for moral or physical reasons or because there was better material already there'. The BCRC was applying for visas for the one group Allen described as 'really good material for emigration' – some 800 persons who had fought in Spain and were now housed in camps in the south of

[79] *Ibid.*; Willi Wanka correspondence with W. Layton, mid-June 1939, PRO HO 294/15.
[80] Allen, 'Memorandum on emigration', cited n. 78.

France, in appalling conditions. Eleanor Rathbone was willing to help find hospitality for them in Britain.[81]

Allen concluded that the task of rescue the BCRC had set itself had been largely completed. Her survey was designed to give the CRTF guidance in taking over the BCRC's responsibilities. In late July 1939 the BCRC was formally wound up and its liabilities and assets were transferred to the CRTF trustees.[82]

The establishment of the trust produced a new effort to get a grip on commitments. Bunbury, the director of the CRTF, tried to restrict the definition of eligible refugees to exclude Czech Jews. The result was a dispute between Bunbury and Stopford over whether the government had made a commitment to help Czech Jews emigrate and whether this came within the terms of the redefined trust. Stopford, emphasising his accountability to the aims of the original gift and to the Treasury, took a stand against the BCRC and the trustees and reminded Bunbury that the government was 'committed to the principle of including Czech Jews'.[83] Indeed, back in April, Waley, speaking for the Treasury, had told Stopford that 'Czechs and Jews are to be included as refugees'.[84] Stopford left his deputy, Walter Creighton, to approve cases in Prague and returned to London where he told Waley of his concern that the trustees might not wish to assist Czech Jews 'whom we have agreed to assist in limited numbers at Creighton's discretion'.[85] Bunbury claimed that the admission of Czech Jews was not yet authorised but that they still constituted up to 20 per cent of the cases Creighton was approving. He expressed concern that this would require retrospective sanction.[86]

Bunbury was right to be careful not to overspend the CRTF's limited funds. Yet, he did not back a move to increase them. In late July, Eleanor Rathbone led a campaign for part of the £6 million of the Czech loan which remained in the government's hands to be made available for additional emigration. The question of whether to finance a further exodus was discussed at a meeting between Cooper, Bunbury, Margaret Layton, secretary of the BCRC, and Farrell, the PCO from Prague. Those present expected that Adolf Eichmann's planned speed-up of Jewish emigration from the Protectorate – designed to reduce

81 Minutes, Visa Committee meeting, 23 June 1939, PRO HO 294/52.
82 General Council minutes, 27 July 1939, see PRO HO 294/50; for the Trust Deed, PRO HO 213/297.
83 Bunbury to E. G. Culpin, 7 July 1939, PRO HO 294/7; Stopford to Bunbury, 31 July 1939, PRO HO 294/70.
84 FO to Troutbeck, no. 123, 17 Apr. 1939, PRO T 160/1324/F13577/05/8.
85 Stopford to Waley, 3 Aug. 1939, PRO T 160/1324/F13577/05/16.
86 Bunbury to Stopford, 11 Aug. 1939, Stopford to Bunbury, 14 Aug. 1939, *ibid.*

numbers by 60,000 over twelve months – would be conducted in a disorganised way, using the same oppressive methods he had employed in Austria. In these circumstances, Rathbone's campaign for additional finance was 'a grave mistake in strategy':

> any suggestion of substantial financial assistance from Great Britain to Jewish emigration from the Protectorate would play straight into the hands of the Gestapo and would be far more likely to encourage persecution and terror than avoid it.

The meeting resolved to advise against further financial assistance, except under binding arrangements satisfactory to the government and the trustees.[87]

The plight of other categories of refugee also came up. It was felt necessary to persuade the German authorities to allow the departure from the Protectorate of some 130 wives and children of 'illegals' who had escaped. But the meeting decided that the trust should not assist political refugees who would continue to trickle illegally into Poland in spite of German efforts at prevention. Nor should it support the escape of 'non-political Jews in large numbers across the Polish frontier with at least the connivance of the German authorities'. To do otherwise

> would obviously create a intolerable situation for the Jewish people in general in Eastern Europe – for unless Great Britain were prepared to receive and maintain them freely (and this would give rise to a corresponding claim from Jewish people still in the Reich) an influx of Jews from Czechoslovakia would prove the last straw to the Polish Government and might well lead to persecution of Jews generally in Poland. Obviously there is no solution of the Jewish problem along these lines.[88]

Accordingly, the meeting resolved to close down the trust's operations in Poland. No further help for refugees was envisaged. Mention was made of the possibility extending to Czechoslovakia the scheme of orderly emigration in the plan the IGC was discussing with the German government, but this was hardly a practical response to the Jewish plight. Indeed, those present recognised that the Germans might seek to deprive Jews of the greater part of their wealth before agreeing such a scheme, if at all.

Cooper afterwards claimed that more funds would 'embarrass' the trustees. Waley, who supported an increase in expenditure, rejected this as 'untrue'. Cooper also claimed that 'It would be little short of a catastrophe if £6,000,000 or any lesser sum were made available by the British Government for assisting Jewish emigration from Czecho-Slovakia (and/or Poland) at the present time.' Waley's initial reaction was, 'This is surely rubbish.' He later moderated his language to say he

[87] Memorandum of 29 July meeting, 30 July 1939, PRO HO 294/7. [88] *Ibid.*

found Cooper's position 'unconvincing'.[89] In early August, notwithstanding Waley's views, the government rejected all proposals for extending the fund, including one from an all-party deputation of MPs. Eleanor Rathbone voiced the suspicion that the government was exaggerating the fund's existing commitments in order to present an artificially depressed picture of its resources and thus its capacity to help refugees.[90] Her hunch was correct. The residue of the British loan was later used for huge payments to a handful of selected refugees from Czechoslovakia under a scheme paying compensation for assets left behind.[91]

The arguments being invoked to justify the limitation of British assistance to refugees from Czechoslovakia to well below its full potential were not new. At Evian the previous year British representatives had argued that to aid one set of Jewish refugees would create more persecution and more refugees. Now, the same reasoning was invoked to support the same approach, namely, one of containing the size of the refugee problem. The organisations set up to aid refugees from Czechoslovakia – the BCRC and CRTF – were directly implicated in the government's policy of limiting refugee numbers. Both the government and the refugee bodies it was funding aimed to limit the commitments they faced. Their joint decision to refuse to co-operate with the Gestapo to achieve mass Jewish emigration from the Protectorate differed, in one crucial respect, from the refusal of the Jewish organisation to comply with Eichmann's timetable for emptying Austria of Jews described in the previous chapter. The Jewish organisation lacked the resources and could not provide the emigration opportunities which were necessary to enable Jews to leave Austria at the rate Eichmann demanded. The British government, on the other hand, had funds set aside for Czechoslovakia but it chose to withhold them. Reasons of policy, not practicability, led the government to refuse to help more Jews escape persecution in Czechoslovakia. It was wishful thinking to argue that the British decision to resist Nazi pressure to force the Jews out of Czechoslovakia would teach the Nazis to adopt a more acceptable way of operating. The Nazi regime's intransigence was soon put beyond a doubt. At the start of September, Germany invaded Poland, finally forcing Britain into a declaration of war.

89 Cooper, memorandum, 'Czech Refugees', marginal notes by Waley, Waley to M. Wilson Smith, 2 Aug. 1939, PRO T 160/1324/F13577/05/16.

90 Rathbone to Bunbury, 21 July 1939, Rathbone papers, Liverpool University Library, XIV.2.15 (35); statement regarding deputation, memorandum on the need for further financial provision for refugees from Czechoslovakia, 2 Aug. 1939, *ibid.*, XIV.2.15 (43).

91 Sherman, *Island Refuge*, p. 250; *Hansard*, House of Commons, vol. 350, col. 2906, 4 Aug. 1939; Czecho-slovakia (Financial Claims and Refugees) Act, 1940; Waley, 'Czech Claims', 11 Sep. 1940, Waley to Makins, 25 Sep. 1940, PRO T 210/20.

7 War-time policy: 1939–1942

From 3 September 1939 Britain was at war with Germany and the nation's war-time priorities were considered to require disengagement from the plight of persecuted Jews on the continent. The main focus of this chapter is the British government's changed approach to the entry of refugees to the United Kingdom. Before looking at how the question of new admissions was dealt with, let us briefly examine government policy towards refugees who were already in Britain, including the mass internment episode.[1]

The Home Office believed that there were already far too many refugees in the country. The result was a policy of speeding the departure of as many refugees as possible and of refusing any commitment regarding refugees' ultimate disposal. Before the war, the need to ensure the suitability of potential permanent residents had been the home secretary's justification for insisting that candidates for refuge endure the slow process of pre-selection abroad. Not surprisingly, the government's approach led many refugees to believe that they might ultimately be allowed to settle. But now the Home Office insisted that refugees' stay was temporary, thereby blurring the distinction between people who were genuinely in transit and those admitted with some expectation of eventual settlement. Even Cooper asserted that refugees had been 'admitted on the assumption that they would eventually re-emigrate'.[2]

An extra reason for boosting re-emigration was that public funds were now being spent on refugees. In December 1939 ministers accepted a Home Office proposal that funding from the public purse was necessary since the funds of the main Jewish organisation were finally exhausted. From then on, the government subsidised the costs of refugee maintenance and re-emigration and the Jewish organisation's administrative expenses. A monthly grant was paid to the Central Committee for

[1] A fuller treatment of policy towards refugees in Britain is in London, 'British Immigration', pp. 354–404.

[2] Cooper, memorandum, 20 Sep. 1939, PRO FO 371/24078, W14035/45/48.

Refugees (CCR), a new non-sectarian body approved by the Home Office, which distributed the money among the various refugee organisations. A special subsidy for emigration was included and kept secret by hiding the extra sum in the monthly grant payment, burying the arrangements in what Maxwell termed 'semi-official' correspondence and keeping the Commons in the dark about it. The Americans, whose laws prohibited payment of an immigrant's passage by outside bodies, appeared ready to turn 'a blind eye' to the subterfuge 'so long as it is not broadcast'.[3] In 1941 the Home Office loaned the Jewish organisation further funds for both re-emigration and administration costs, disguising the transaction by using an intermediary body. Maxwell observed that this would 'reverse the historic practice by which Governments have borrowed money from the Jews, and . . . introduce a new procedure by which the Government will lend some money to the Jews'.[4]

Most refugees, including many who were stateless in fact or law, were now regarded as enemy aliens. The Home Office decided not to proceed immediately with mass internment, but set up tribunals to review the cases of enemy aliens and Czechoslovaks, to decide who could be left at large and, if so, whether they should be subjected to restrictions. The tribunals exempted 64,244 persons – the vast majority – from both internment and special restrictions. But in the second week of May 1940 the British government finally resorted to mass internment. The home secretary, Sir John Anderson, and his officials had resisted demands for mass internment of refugees as unjustifiable: 'unnecessary on security grounds and inexpedient on grounds of general policy'. But once Winston Churchill replaced Chamberlain as prime minister and showed he was set on a policy of mass internment of enemy alien refugees, the Home Office gave way, although it still tried to delay implementation.[5]

Within a few weeks the harshness of the government's policy was being denounced. The dangers involved in the government's decision to deport shiploads of internees, including several thousand refugees, to the dominions became obvious in early July, when the *Arandora Star* was torpedoed in mid-Atlantic as it shipped internees to Canada. Hundreds perished. Many survivors were deported a second time, but now to Australia. Public opposition mounted. The mass internment of refugees was causing widespread outrage in government circles. John Maynard Keynes, who took up the cases of several interned fellow economists,

[3] Cooper, 'Brief for Supplementary Estimate: Grant-in-Aid to Central Committee for Refugees', 5 Nov. 1940, PRO HO 213/299; correspondence, Nov. 1939–Jan. 1946, PRO T 161/997/S45629/1; Maxwell to Emerson, 2 July 1940, PRO HO 213/298.

[4] Maxwell to Sir T. Barnes, 8 Dec. 1940, PRO TS 27/500; 1941 correspondence, *ibid.*

[5] Anderson, memorandum, 'Control of Aliens', WP (G) (40)115, 29 Apr. 1940, PRO CAB 67/6.

claimed he had 'not met a single soul, inside or outside government departments, who is not furious at what is going on'.[6] Indeed, civil servants supported Francois Lafitte in compiling his denunciatory study, *The Internment of Aliens*.[7] In July the War Cabinet shifted to a policy of release. A White Paper announced new categories eligible for release and the slow process got underway of scrutinising applications from internees seeking their liberty. Further detentions were suspended for lack of accommodation, and deportations ceased. Mass internment was never resumed.

In most cases internees seeking their freedom had to prove not merely that they were not a threat to security but also that furtherance of the war effort would result from their release – a far more difficult task. The threat of continued detention became an instrument of manpower control. For example, the Home Office directed internees to gaining release through joining the Army's Auxiliary Military Pioneer Corps (AMPC), rather than by obtaining better-paid civilian work for which the Ministry of Agriculture wished to recruit them. As enemy aliens, the men could not be conscripted. Still, indirect pressure to join the forces was applied in the form of a new ground for release which conferred eligibility on male internees of military age who applied to enlist in the AMPC and were rejected on medical grounds. The new home secretary, Herbert Morrison, supported the policy of making men of military age earn their liberty by joining up.

Re-emigration was another route out of internment. Many refugees with advanced re-emigration plans had been interned, despite instructions to the contrary. The Home Office, ever intent on reducing numbers, introduced a release category covering persons about to embark for emigration overseas. Internees with US quota numbers were taken under guard to the US Consulate for interviews. Once a visa had been granted and a passage obtained, the alien would be taken to the port of departure. A gentler approach of releasing people to make final arrangements to leave eventually made its way into the regulations. The departures of at least 10,000 refugees in 1940 were 'voluntary' in name, but the circumstances were often close to expulsion. A proportion of the interned refugees who were deported had also 'volunteered' to go. The JRC and Emerson agreed that refugees able to re-emigrate and not doing so should not be supported financially. Refugee re-emigration reached a peak in 1940 but continued at a lower rate throughout the

[6] John Maynard Keynes to Francis C. Scott, 23 July 1940, in Donald Moggridge, ed., *The Collected Writings of John Maynard Keynes*, vol. XXII, *Activities 1939–1945: Internal War Finance* (Cambridge, 1978), pp. 190–1.

[7] Francois Lafitte, *The Internment of Aliens* (London, 1988; original publication, 1940).

war. The Home Office pressured both children and adults to depart and it emphasised that there was no certainty of being allowed to remain after the war.

The Home Office showed sympathy and good will towards refugees in Britain and devoted substantial resources to their welfare. But endangered Jews on the continent were not the department's responsibility. To admit them could be seen as a security risk and any substantial increase in refugee numbers would be an extra burden on the Home Office. Nonetheless, a small number of Jewish refugees did succeed in gaining entry.

The war had dramatically curtailed the scope for the lawful emigration of Jews from Nazi Europe. European countries of refuge opposed a further exodus, not merely because of the security implications, but also because they wished that opportunities for permanent settlement overseas should be reserved for unwanted refugee Jews still sheltering within their own borders. When the United States re-allocated part of its German immigration quota to the United Kingdom, to enable Jewish refugees to re-emigrate from Britain, the escape prospects of persecuted Jews in Germany contracted yet further.[8]

On 25 September 1939, the Cabinet Committee on the Refugee Problem decreed that the concentration of Britain's energies 'upon the eradication of the root cause of the refugee problem . . . namely the existing regime in Germany' should now be regarded as the British contribution to its solution. Ministers suspected that the only refugees the Germans would allow out would be 'persons whose entry into other countries was desired for reasons connected with the war'. Therefore, the United Kingdom could not 'assist in any way' the exodus of enemy nationals, nor could it admit persons who had been in German-controlled territory subsequent to the outbreak of war, even should they later reach neutral or friendly territory. Ministers wished the IGC's wartime role to be confined to encouraging the emigration 'of refugees who had reached countries of refuge at the outbreak of war'. Should the IGC propose to do more than this, Britain would withdraw. Any negotiations with Germany over refugees were out of the question. The United Kingdom formally withdrew its recent offer to finance overseas settlement schemes and stated that it could undertake no new burdens in connection with the IGC's work. The government assumed that the IGC would be left in semi-suspension as long as the war lasted.[9]

8 Wyman, *Paper Walls*, pp. 170–1.

9 'Summary of Conclusions and Conclusions, War Cabinet, Committee on the Refugee Problem', CRP (39) 6th meeting, 25 Sep. 1939, PRO CAB 98/1.

At the outbreak of war the Home Office was ready with a new set of regulations for controlling aliens which came into immediate effect. All unused visas and authorisations were automatically invalidated. Enemy aliens could be refused leave to land, unless the Home Office had approved their visas, and could be detained, questioned and disposed of, by internment or otherwise. Alien admissions were severely restricted and evaluated by reference to the requirements of the war. The policy of not admitting refugees – alien or British – to the United Kingdom solely on humanitarian grounds was repeatedly affirmed at Cabinet level. The ban on humanitarian admissions was not seriously challenged in the first three years of the war.

Before we consider possible avenues of entry, the distinction between admission to the United Kingdom and to Palestine should be reiterated. Since before the war, European Jews' access to refuge in Palestine had been marked by continuing and bitter conflict over illegal immigration. Cooper had warned that the likely result of failure to mitigate the conditions of refugee emigration was

> more Gestapo pressure of the worst type, resulting in mass flight, forced voyages to Shanghai, attempts to land illegally in Palestine, etc. with the result that the receiving countries might almost be driven to abandon the whole problem if they saw all their plans thrown out of gear by both the open and subversive activities of the German Government.[10]

As Cooper had predicted, the early part of the war saw an increasingly chaotic Jewish exodus. The flight from Nazi territory was encouraged by the Germans and in some cases organised by them. At the same time Britain expended diplomatic and naval resources on curbing the transit of unauthorised Jewish immigrants to Palestine. The government continued to permit permanent Jewish immigration to Palestine. Furthermore, in October 1939 the colonial secretary, Malcolm MacDonald, decided to admit those holders of Palestine immigration certificates for the half-year just ended who had been unable to leave Germany before the war.[11] For this group of Palestine cases, then, MacDonald was prepared to lift the recent blanket ban on assisting the exodus of persons coming from enemy territory. Indeed, throughout the war Palestine provided the bulk of the exceptions to the ban on 'potential' refugees. The reason for the contrast between war-time policy on Jewish refugee admissions to Palestine and to the United Kingdom was the long-standing difference in the immigration policies Britain had for the two

[10] Cooper, memorandum, 'Refugee Conference in Washington', n.d. [mid-Aug. 1939], sent to Randall by Grant, 23 Aug. 1939, PRO FO 371/24078, W124558/45/48; f. 75.

[11] Note of interdepartmental discussion at CO, 3 Oct. 1939, PRO FO 371/24079, W14378/45/48, f. 272.

countries. British policy allowed Jewish families to be admitted for settlement in Palestine within the limits set by the 1939 White Paper. But it was opposed to the new settlement of alien Jews in Britain.

The case of the Sekel family illustrates the consequences of banning persons from coming to Britain from enemy territory. Miss Gertrud Sekel had found refuge in the United Kingdom before the war. She was also seeking a guarantor for the emigration to the USA of her 71-year-old German Jewish father. A guarantor was found, but in February 1940 the British authorities stated that since Miss Sekel's father was still in Germany he could not be granted a visa for temporary admission pending re-emigration. Miss Sekel's father had already suffered one incarceration in a concentration camp and she feared both her parents would be interned by the Germans. Her British-born mother did not require a visa, but remained with her husband because she did not wish to leave him to come to Britain alone, nor did the Home Office wish to encourage her to do so. Despite support from Foreign Office officials and the director of passport control, the Home Office refused to make an exception for Miss Sekel's father.[12] An official explained that the Home Office 'recognised the case as a hard one but there are many other refugees in this country who would like to get their parents out of Germany', adding that these old people were unlikely to be accepted as immigrants to the USA.[13] The Home Office had previously said the case could be considered if the parents were in a neutral country. But the difficulty lay in getting there. Neutral countries, as Miss Sekel found after applying to the Netherlands, Belgium and Switzerland, withheld transit visas from persons with no visa for their ultimate destination. The Foreign Office considered that it had no standing to intervene – Miss Sekel's mother, though British-born, was still a German national and so could not even be helped to obtain a transit visa while resident in German territory.

Like Miss Sekel, most refugees in Britain had relatives in enemy territory. As Emerson wrote in June 1941,

> it was comparatively rare for a whole family to be able to emigrate before the war. In fact, it was part of the German scheme to get the men out first so that when they were established elsewhere they could send for their womenfolk. Even when a man got out his wife and family, he would often have a brother or sister or other relative still left in Germany. And, of course, families got widely scattered between France, Holland, Belgium and other countries now under the rule of Germany.[14]

[12] Correspondence, Feb.–May 1940, PRO FO 372/3358, T1520/T3878/1520/378, f. 304.
[13] K. G. Davies to F. H. Cleobury, 6 May 1940, *ibid.*, f. 312.
[14] Emerson to Pell, 17 June 1941, AJ43/22/122 (the sentence 'In fact . . . womenfolk' is crossed out).

The British government justified the admission of close relatives as having the value of boosting the morale of persons engaged in the war effort. The one serious bid to reunify families was a scheme proposed by Maxwell and Cooper in December 1939 to promise visas to deserving pre-war applicants in enemy territory who were wives or children of refugees in Britain, if they could reach neutral territory. The Home Office parliamentary under secretary, Osbert Peake, although initially sympathetic, feared a flood of applicants and ruled against the scheme. 'The duty of playing the good Samaritan', he argued, 'rests more heavily on a neutral than a belligerent country.'[15] Thus Jews could not obtain or even be promised British visas while they remained in German territory.

Had the necessary visas been available, Jews could have emigrated. The German authorities did not finally prohibit all Jews from departing until the autumn of 1941. Indeed, they connived at continued Jewish emigration, legal and illegal. For example, they left the 'J' off passports of Jews attempting illegal emigration to Palestine. Certain British officials alleged that German agents had been helped to emigrate in the guise of Jews, with the Jewish 'J' marked in their passports. Indeed, Captain Liddell of MI5 considered all German Jews who could renew their passports to be under some form of German control and advised refusing them transit facilities, but the Passport Control Department took a more relaxed view and allowed consular staff to affix visas to such passports.[16]

Until Germany overran western Europe, the Home Office would grant visas in neutral territory to certain classes of enemy alien refugees, even if they had left enemy territory after the war began. From late 1939 on, however, this policy was not advertised. Moreover, Jews were generally unable to reach neutral territory to obtain a British visa.[17] In April 1940 the Home Office published details of categories of family members eligible to join close relatives in the United Kingdom provided there was no risk to public funds: wives joining husbands; minor children joining parents or a sole surviving parent or, in the case of orphans, other close relatives; and, in very exceptional cases, elderly mothers without relatives abroad joining children.[18] But the German

[15] Peake, memoranda, 11, 18 and 19 Dec. 1939, Maxwell, memorandum, 18 Dec. 1939, PRO HO 213/447.

[16] Correspondence, Jan.–Mar. 1940, PRO FO 372/3358, T2474/T3186/2474/378, f. 319.

[17] Cooper to Maxwell, 19 Dec. 1939, Grant to Cooper, 1 Jan. 1940, Aliens Department, Visa Instructions, 'Refugees from Germany, Austria and Czechoslovakia', 19 Feb. 1940, *ibid.*

[18] Circular, VR 21, 'Admission to the United Kingdom of Refugees from certain Central European countries', 25 Apr. 1940, PRO FO 371/29158, W5467/3/48.

military advance westwards led to a drastic clamp-down. Soon entry was confined to narrowly defined cases of children joining parents.[19]

In May 1940, as the Allied military situation on the continent deteriorated, the emergency along the coast nullified most arrangements for the examination of war refugees on or before arrival. Ports and reception centres became congested. Britain evacuated some refugees from Belgium who had entered north-west France. But ministers suspended earlier plans to admit up to 300,000 war refugees from Allied countries in the event of their being overrun and turned down further evacuation requests. For British ships, the priority was evacuating the British Expeditionary Force and getting food ashore for the troops.[20]

Most of the war refugees came without visas. Some were refused leave to land, but no records have been located suggesting actual removal.[21] The small number of Jews among the new arrivals included a few enemy aliens.[22] During the evacuations, British consular officials on the continent authorised the entry of selected civilian refugees. A memoir by Margaret Czellitzer, addressed to her two grandsons, vividly records how members of her family were saved by evacuation to Britain.[23] Before the war this German Jewish family – grandparents, parents, children and other relatives – had found refuge in the Netherlands. In May 1940 they fled, hoping to find refuge in England. In Antwerp the children's father was detained. Their grandfather (Mrs Czellitzer's husband) was arrested by police in La Panne, interned and later deported from Westerbork camp to death in the east. The women and children continued to France, making for the British consulate in Dunkirk. Both grandchildren possessed British nationality because their mother had deliberately travelled from Berlin to London shortly before each birth. The children's status as British subjects was the deciding factor for the consul. He granted their mother a permit to board an evacuation ship and eventually agreed to include the grandmother and two other female relatives. They left on a destroyer with bombs and shells exploding around them. On landing at Folkestone Mrs Czellitzer was interned. After several weeks in Holloway prison she was moved to join the boys and their mother in internment on the Isle of Man. Later the family went on to the USA and were

19 Regulations dated 15 June 1940, PRO FO 371/29158, W5467/3/48, *ibid.*

20 Correspondence, 21–2 May 1940, PRO CAB 63/133; Anderson, 'Dutch and Belgian War Refugees', WP (G) (40) 132, 19 May 1940, PRO CAB 67/6; WM 131 (40)12, 20 May 1940, PRO CAB 65/7; correspondence, 21–22 May 1940, PRO FO 371/24283, C6927/6927/4.

21 Correspondence, June 1940, PRO HO 213/556; Roche, *Key in Lock*, pp. 133–6.

22 Home Office figures to 31 March 1942, PRO HO 213/1347.

23 Margaret Czellitzer, 'Story of your childhood', n.d., circa 1948, ME 429, Leo Baeck Institute, New York.

reunited with the boys' father who had managed to escape from an internment camp in the south of France.

The pleas of Jews to be allowed to board boats taking people from French ports to the United Kingdom were often in vain. In his memoir of the fall of France, General Sir Edward Spears, who was in Bordeaux in mid-June as French resistance collapsed, recalled seeing 'men turned to jellies by fear'. He remembered that he had seen Jews

> with every justification for apprehension as to their fate at the hands of the Nazis . . . so transfigured by fear as to be totally unrecognisable. I saw two large flabby white fellows I knew whom I described to Campbell [Sir Ronald Campbell, Ambassador to France] as looking like a couple of blancmanges pursued by a Sunday-school treat. Some arrogant, aggressive men I had never thought were Jews came to beg for passages, proclaiming themselves as such, having ceased to be either arrogant or aggressive. Everything was done to try ensure the escape of those most justified in their fear of falling into Nazi hands, but the shipping space was far short of the demand.[24]

Allegations that French, Czech and Polish refugees had been given preference on British evacuation vessels, while Austrian and German refugees had been turned away were taken up with Clement Attlee, then Lord Privy Seal, by John Parker MP. Parker provided Attlee with the names of prominent refugees on French soil, including members of the International Brigade, who it was feared might fall into enemy hands. Attlee gave the curious reply that France was 'now completely in the hands of the Germans and there is no way in which we can get these people out, especially as there is no indication of where they are'.[25] In fact, south-east France remained unoccupied and functioned as a departure point for refugees for many months to come.

By the winter of 1940–41 the Home Office and the security services had established a policy of refusing to admit any more refugees.[26] Consequently, when the Luxembourg government-in-exile requested refuge within the empire for 700 of its own nationals, officials dealing with refugee matters in the Foreign Office did not even think the request worth raising with the Home Office. The entire Jewish population of occupied Luxembourg – some 2,000 people – had been told to leave the country or be deported to Poland. Approximately 150 Luxembourg

[24] Major General Sir Edward Spears, *Assignment to Catastrophe*, vol. II, *The Fall of France. June 1940* (London, 1954), pp. 260, 280–1.

[25] John Parker MP to C. Attlee, 25 and 27 June 1940, Attlee to Parker, 28 June 1940, PRO CAB 118/78.

[26] T. M. Snow, minute, 11 Dec. 1940, PRO FO 371/25243, W12102/7614/48, f. 593; Snow, minute, 2 Jan. 1941, PRO FO 371/25254, W12667/12667/48, f. 487 and see below p. 178; see also Snow, minute, 27 Jan. 1941, PRO FO 371/29158, W624/3/48.

Jews had already fled to Portugal and needed visas. Another 300, escorted out of Luxembourg on a locked train, had been turned back by the Portuguese and were now in a desperate situation in France. R. T. E. Latham, a temporary civil servant in the Foreign Office Refugee Department, initially thought 'next to nothing' could be done, since the government's current policy prohibited more admissions 'merely on humanitarian grounds'. The Luxembourg Jews' plight was 'pitiable', he said, but they seemed ineligible for exceptional treatment, being 'hardly war refugees in the sense that they are in danger because they have fought against the Germans but simply racial refugees'. The Foreign Office ruled against suggestions that the Luxembourg Jews might go to Tanganyika, or be admitted to the United Kingdom on compassionate grounds alone, although possibilities of admissions to the empire were being explored. Officials raised doubts about Luxembourg's status as a full ally, but once these were resolved Latham and his colleagues advocated that if Luxembourg nationals among the Jews could escape to Portugal they should be admitted. The government agreed to include suitable individuals among the Luxembourg group in a labour recruitment scheme limited to nationals of Allied governments based in London. A Ministry of Labour expert due to visit Lisbon in connection with the scheme would receive details of Jews from Luxembourg with high technical qualifications. Those deemed suitable would be unofficially encouraged to go to Lisbon. The Passport Control Department agreed to dispense with Home Office and MI5 concurrence, arguing that the refugees would not be getting exceptional treatment. Through these efforts, motivated principally by humanitarian considerations, a few Jewish refugees reached the United Kingdom.[27]

Reviewing the position some twenty months into the war, we see that the ban on humanitarian admissions was so well established that Foreign Office officials did not think it worth challenging, even for endangered Allied nationals. The response to the Luxembourg Jews underlines the advantage of having accredited representatives to draw their case to the attention of the government. But possession of Allied nationality was the indispensable prerequisite for inclusion in the labour recruitment scheme. We see, too, that refugee entrants needed either to fit into a 'war effort' category or to qualify on political grounds. The places from which applications for entry were received were also becoming fewer, and by late 1940 further requests for humanitarian admissions to the United Kingdom were largely confined to neutral territory, notably Portugal.

[27] Correspondence, 17 Dec. 1940–13 Jan. 1941, PRO FO 371/25254, W12667/12667/48, f. 487; Wasserstein, *Britain and Jews*, pp. 108–10.

Certain Czech refugees on the continent benefited from the existence of the CRTF and from the close relations between Britain and the Czech government-in-exile. The first year of the war saw the admission to the United Kingdom of groups of Czech refugees, including a number of Jews, who had fled east through Poland ahead of the invading Germans. Many of these refugees had ended up in Vilna (Vilnius), a Polish town which became part of Lithuania and was crowded with refugees in the early part of the war. In January 1940 British voluntary workers who remained in central Europe co-operated with the CRTF to enable thirty-five Czech refugees to obtain British visas in Lithuania on the basis that they had made contact with British organisations before the war.[28] A few refugees from Czechoslovakia were included in the Lisbon-based labour recruitment scheme.[29] Pressure from the exiled Czech leader Jan Masaryk led to the launch in April 1941 of a special and highly restricted scheme to assist Czechs who were allegedly in danger from German influence in Europe. The government authorised a grant of £100,000 from CRTF funds to the provisional Czech government-in-exile to provide maintenance that would assist people in getting visas, including British visas in some cases, to enable them to leave Lisbon. Latham wished to expand the scheme but found himself at loggerheads with Cooper, who was worried about such people coming to the United Kingdom. On paper the scheme constituted a rare exception to the policy of not funding aid to endangered refugees during the war, but its humanitarian aspects should not be overstated. The scheme was intended largely to benefit persons not in immediate danger – the presumption of danger from German influence in Lisbon in the instructions for implementing the scheme was highly artificial. The grant benefited the Czech government financially by enabling it to reclaim the cost of evacuations of its nationals. Moreover, the scheme's purpose was political as well as humanitarian, since it answered criticisms that the benefits of the trust fund should be distributed more evenly among the Czech community and it matched a similar sum allocated to Polish relief.[30]

There were also political ramifications to a scheme for the selective admission of potentially useful political refugees and their wives and children. The scheme, which the Home Office agreed in May 1941, explicitly included enemy nationals. All applications were to be vetted by the Home Office, the security services and the Foreign Office. The

[28] Correspondence, Nov. 1939–Jan. 1940, PRO HO 294/46.
[29] Correspondence, 14–29 Jan. 1941, PRO FO 371/29158, W624/3/48.
[30] Correspondence, 15 May–13 June 1941, PRO T 160/1324/F13577/05/19; correspondence, 2 June–5 Sep. 1941, PRO FO 371/29193, W8548/W8696/W10009/112/48.

Foreign Office largely delegated its task – to assess usefulness – to Allied governments-in-exile, thereby assisting these governments in putting forward candidates for admission.[31]

Large numbers of refugees had accumulated in neutral Portugal, making Lisbon the principal refugee centre on the continent. It was also feasible for refugees to leave Lisbon by ship. The Foreign Office had its own reasons for supporting refugee evacuations from Portugal because the Portuguese were using the continued presence of certain Jewish refugees as an excuse to refuse transit visas for Polish and Czech technicians wanted in the United Kingdom. Britain therefore agreed to evacuate a 'hard core' of some 200 Polish Jews from Portugal to Jamaica. Invariably, British representatives would not allow any evacuation to proceed until each Allied government whose nationals were concerned undertook financial responsibility for the refugees and also to accept them at the end of the war. Persons of doubtful nationality were covered by special guarantees. The AJDC provided much of the necessary finance and organisation for these evacuations, including guarantees of maintenance in Jamaica for refugees of Allied nationality. In early 1942 refugees of several nationalities eventually set sail for Jamaica.[32] The Colonial Office had agreed that the refugees be allowed to enter Jamaica but it did not wish the island to be used as a 'dumping ground', so Alan Walker of the Refugee Department reported, and he added:

> Neither do we – unless the Portuguese will allow more Czechs and Poles from unoccupied France who could be used either here or in Canada for the war effort, and not merely Jews for whom we appear to arrange a clean getaway to the States without any compensating advantage – to enter Portugal.

Walker was at that moment particularly angry that a group of Luxembourg Jews had succeeded in sailing for Jamaica just before the Foreign Office had planned to refuse them. Indeed, Silvain Hayum, one of the Luxembourg group, recounted to the author how he helped to organise the evacuation of himself and his family, bypassing the Refugee Department.[33] Walker's annoyance illustrates the Foreign Office obsession with

[31] Newsam to Cadogan, 6 May 1941, PRO FO 371/29158, W5467/3/48; PCD circular, VR 13853, 'Visas for Refugees of Political Importance', instructions to HM Representatives, 13 July 1941, minutes, 5–6 Dec. 1941, PRO FO 371/29159, W9549/14699/3/48; correspondence, 6 Jan.–3 Mar. 1942, PRO FO 371/32655, W568/205/48.

[32] Correspondence, 3 Feb.–17 June 1942, PRO FO 371/32655, W568/W2092/W2580/W3225/205/48; Feb.–July 1942, PRO FO 371/32656, W4887/4992/W8134/205/48; Emerson to Randall, 12 Nov. 1942, PRO FO 371/32681, W15303/4555/48; Randall to P. Rogers, 4 Dec. 1942, PRO FO 371/32682, W16060/4555/48.

[33] A. Walker, minute, 6 Apr., Walker to P. Garran, 9 Apr. 1942, Jeffes, minute, 13 Apr. 1942, PRO FO 371/32656, W4728/W4887/205/48; Silvain Hayum, interview with the author, 11 Jan. 1990.

extracting a compensating benefit for Britain from any humanitarian scheme for refugees.

The approach of the Foreign Office, then, was that any investment in aiding refugees was supposed to yield a return for the war effort. Evacuations were intended to make neutral governments more accommodating over the transit of escaping Allied personnel. The humanitarian aspects of such schemes had secondary importance. The officials who negotiated them were punctilious about protecting Britain from any financial, immigration or security liabilities – and correspondingly unconcerned at making refugees wait however long it took to tie up every last bureaucratic loose end.

Admissions for employment in war-time were ostensibly tied to the war effort. 'Owing to its scarcity, manpower became the vital factor – perhaps the most vital factor – in the planning of the war effort', the official history of the Ministry of Labour and National Service (MOLANS) asserts, and claims that requirements 'always outstripped the numbers available'.[34] Scarcities of skilled labour, technicians and scientists were particularly acute. The shortages of medical manpower included doctors, nurses and midwives. A succession of measures were introduced in an attempt to maximise labour mobilisation. But when we look at the entry of aliens for manpower purposes, we find interdepartmental differences, omissions and missed opportunities.

Planning for the recruitment of skilled technicians, if Germany should overrun the Netherlands and Belgium, was the responsibility of Sir Maurice Hankey, minister without portfolio in the War Cabinet.[35] Hankey encouraged the Ministry of Labour to set up an organisation which could recruit refugees, but his primary concern was to save the machine tool industry and other key continental industries and deny the rest to the enemy.[36] In May 1940, as civilians on the continent fled before the German advance, Hankey sought to recruit Belgian refugees before they became too scattered. The Cabinet thought such measures sufficiently valuable to outweigh anxieties about security and anti-alien opinion.[37]

[34] Sir Godfrey Ince, *The Ministry of Labour and National Service* (London, 1960), pp. 40–6.

[35] Lord Chatfield, memorandum, WP (39) 72, 27 Sep. 1939, PRO CAB 63/129; WM 40 (39)6, 7 Oct. 1939, PRO CAB 65/1.

[36] WP (39) 95, 23 Oct. 1939, PRO CAB 66/2.

[37] Correspondence, 23–4 May 1940, record of interdepartmental meeting, 11 June 1940, PRO CAB 63/130; War Cabinet 'Machine Tools: Employment of Belgians', S.50/7/3, 13 June 1940, PRO CAB 63/130; WM 162 (40)9 (5), 12 June 1940, PRO CAB 65/8; record of meeting between Hankey, H. Dalton and Prof. Hall, 12 June 1940, PRO CAB 63/132.

A last-minute British salvage operation helped extract a valuable haul of machine tools and diamonds from Belgium, as well as some leading diamond merchants and experts in the technology of warfare.[38] The government encouraged the entry of diamond manufacturers and workers, partly to salvage valuable stocks of diamonds but also in the hope of future dollar earnings from cut diamond exports.[39] One government plan envisaged that officials would go over to France to collect diamond merchants and their families, taking care to exclude undesirables, but officials emphasised that 'the essential thing was that they should bring the diamonds with them'.[40] All the diamond manufacturers who arrived were from Antwerp, the world centre for diamond cutting, and most were Dutch and Polish Jews.[41] Numerous refugee diamond workers from the Netherlands and Belgium, many of them Jews, also came to the United Kingdom. Penniless refugees with pockets full of loose and partly cut diamonds, which they claimed to be unsaleable, presented novel dilemmas for Assistance Board officials trying to assess their resources.[42]

There were immediate reasons for welcoming refugees involved in the diamond business because industrial diamonds had military importance. The United Kingdom scarcely possessed a diamond industry and therefore suffered from a shortage of skilled diamond workers. The refugee diamond workers' skills also had immediate application elsewhere, for example, in the cable industry. The development of cutting and polishing could also lay the foundations for a post-war diamond industry.[43] For all these reasons, refugee diamond workers obtained privileged admission to Britain. In September 1940, a Foreign Office official noted that, if several hundred Dutch and Belgian diamond workers, reported to be in Toulouse, could be brought over, 'they would be welcomed with open arms by the Ministry of Economic Warfare and the diamond industry'.[44] A Jewish refugee from Belgium employed as a diamond polisher succeeded in the summer of 1941 in arranging the grant in Lisbon of British visas to several family members from occupied France, including a brother who was also a diamond polisher. 'From

38 Correspondence, 13–26 June 1940, PRO CAB 63/130.
39 P. H. Brind to Mr Marshall, 21 Oct. 1941, PRO LAB 8/100.
40 Minutes of interdepartmental meeting at Board of Trade on 17 June 1940, PRO BT 11/1322.
41 Brind to A. Cartwright, 23 Dec. 1941, PRO LAB 8/100.
42 Correspondence, May–Oct. 1940, PRO AST 11/75.
43 H. C. Bull (MEW) to under secretary of state, 18 July 1940, PRO FO 371/24286, C8046/8046/4, f. 22.
44 Anthony Lambert, FO minute, 'Belgian and Dutch Diamond Workers in France', 6 Sep. 1940, J. G. Ward to Pritchett, 19 Sep. 1940, PRO FO 371/24286, C9629/9629/4.

Refugee Dept's point of view', an official explained, 'we don't want any more refugees here, but perhaps the enhancement of Mr Niewiazki's morale by having his children & the addition of a diamond cutter may make it worth while our pressing this request.'[45] Yet even this case took months before it obtained Home Office and Ministry of Labour agreement.

Diamond workers were an elite in war-time Britain. They were protected from call-up by Dutch and Belgian conscription and well aware of their scarcity value. The diamond workers' wage demands outraged their employers and worried the authorities. As the need for diamond workers' skills began to diminish, the Home Office was refusing visas for diamond cleavers, yet still granting them to diamond polishers. By May 1942, MOLANS considered there was no longer a need for additional diamond workers and had ceased to encourage their immigration.[46]

The demand created by the arrival of diamonds and machine tools from the continent was for refugees with specific expertise. Ministers also showed interest in the entry of people with skills which could be employed to enhance war production. For example, in late June 1940 Churchill called for an effort to ensure that admission was not refused to qualified technicians.[47] But little detail of the entry of other categories of specialised civilian workers during the summer of 1940 can be gleaned from the fragmentary Foreign Office and Home Office records relating to refugee admissions for that year.

Considerable documentation has survived of the MOLANS-sponsored labour mission which visited Portugal in early 1941 to recruit skilled refugees for the civilian war effort. A labour expert, Professor S. J. Davies, interviewed seventy-nine persons, of whom roughly two-thirds were accepted, including many professional engineers and several diamond workers.[48] On Davies's return the Home Office agreed that a recommendation from him would establish the national interest of a case. But after MI5 objections, the PCO in Lisbon was refused permission to grant visas without reference to London to persons who seemed to meet Davies's criteria. The consequent delays in processing referred cases gave an MI5 representative an opening to oppose the whole scheme on the basis that delays gave the Germans time to 'get at' applicants waiting in Lisbon – he advocated sending them to Canada,

[45] Sir Colville Barclay, minute, 1 Aug. 1941, PRO FO 371/29159, W9281/3/48.

[46] Correspondence, 23 Mar.–4 July 1941, 30 Jan.–12 May 1942, PRO LAB 8/100.

[47] WM 178 (40)2, 24 June 1949, PRO CAB 65/8.

[48] S. J. Davies, 'Report on interviews at Lisbon between 30.12.40. and 16.1.41.', 16 Jan. 1941, PRO FO 371/29194, W1008/115/48.

where potential sabotage would have less effect. He also proposed that entrants under the scheme be required not to change employment or residence without MI5 concurrence, but the Home Office established that this was not feasible.[49]

Once the refugee recruits arrived they had problems in finding work. On landing, they had their passports endorsed with restrictions the severity of which was outdated, as the home secretary later acknowledged. After complaints about difficulties faced by some of the Belgians, Lady Cheetham of the Refugee Department reported that T. T. Scott of MOLANS had discovered that only two were 'real Belgians' and they had refused good offers of employment. The rest were Russian Jews who had acquired Belgian citizenship by naturalisation. The refugees faced the problem that certain employers did not want to engage Jews – a Russian Jewess had been refused a job in Bradford for this reason. Scott said he thought it a great mistake that Davies had recommended these people for visas and voiced his suspicion 'that there was a great deal of "bunk" about it all'.[50] Randall acknowledged the existence of prejudice against all foreigners, particularly former Russian Jews, but said he was still inclined to blame the Belgians' own 'high falutin' ideas' for their employment difficulties.[51]

The officials involved in employment admissions from Portugal did not always agree about selection criteria. Latham criticised MI5, which carried out security vetting in all cases, for its incompetence, arbitrariness and lack of accountability. He tried unsuccessfully to mobilise support for calling MI5 to account for straying beyond its brief in the case of a Romanian Jewish electrical engineer in Lisbon, recommended by Davies, but rejected because of MI5 objections which were based on grounds other than security.[52] The International Labour Branch of MOLANS had felt it should be concerned only to establish that Allied national applicants from Lisbon had a promise of employment. But the Home Office, as emerged in March 1942, had been taking a different approach, applying the sole criterion of 'direct national interest' and relaxing this only in rare cases when Allied governments made representations through the Foreign Office. Certain Home Office officials,

[49] 'Minutes of meeting held on 29th January, 1941, to discuss the Recruitment of Foreign Technical Personnel from Portugal for employment in Industry in the United Kingdom', PRO FO 371/29194, W2036/115/48.

[50] P. Hayman to V. G. Lawford, 26 June 1941, H. S. Morrison to P. H. Spaak, 26 June 1941, R. T. E. Latham, minute, 3 July 1941, C. Cheetham, minute, 21 July 1941, PRO FO 371/29194, W8050/115/48.

[51] Cooper to Randall, 1 Aug. 1941, Randall to Cooper, 20 Aug. 1941, PRO FO 371/29194, W9573/115/48.

[52] Latham, minute, 21 Jan. 1941, PRO FO 371/29180, W962/63/48; correspondence, 27 Mar.–10 June 1941, PRO FO 371/29158, W3447/3/48.

including Cooper, expressed sympathy for admitting aliens falling outside the 'national interest' definition. But by now there were few opportunities to escape to Portugal and the Home Office was highly critical of applications from the western Mediterranean. This negative attitude was confirmed by a survey the previous year suggesting that refugees in the area were unpromising material for incorporation into the war effort. Consequently the numbers coming to the United Kingdom from Portugal and North Africa were quite small and consisted largely of people coming to join the Allied forces.[53] These debates among officials about whether to admit refugees show they sensed that any susceptibilities to humanitarian arguments needed to be kept under tight control.

As we have seen, ministers saw recruitment of skilled refugees from abroad as useful for the war economy. But departments questioned the value of such recruits and worried about the security implications. Employers also showed reluctance to take on Jews. The poor reception for Davies's mission even within the Ministry of Labour which sponsored it shows how little enthusiasm there was for recruiting highly skilled foreigners from abroad. If a British recruitment initiative was received so badly, it is not surprising to see unsolicited offers of help from abroad being rejected as marginal to the requirements of the war effort. Indeed, by June 1942, Paul Brind of the ministry's International Labour Branch was expressing the view, based on previous experience in bringing over highly qualified foreigners, that it would be 'very undesirable to encourage aliens to come over here for civilian work'. He claimed that the government should consider only 'specially qualified people whose particulars are submitted in advance and for whom we get a definite acceptance from an employer and definite approval by the Security Services'.[54]

The efforts of British diplomatic representatives in the Near and Far East to interest home front departments in the availability of local reserves of qualified refugees met with little success. The lack of response was mainly because departments did not consider the benefits of bringing such people over worth the effort, risk and expense involved. Departments preferred to use people whose value was already proven and they adopted a highly selective approach even to offers from British people abroad. Additional doubts were felt about aliens whose English might be inadequate and whose qualifications would be difficult to check. The result was that departments tended to reject proposals for which a good outcome could not be guaranteed.

53 Brind to Cooper, 17 Mar. 1942, Cooper to Brind, 23 Mar. 1942, PRO HO 213/693.
54 Brind to D. L. Stewart, 15 June 1942, PRO FO 371/32534, W7046/1695/49.

In October 1941 the potential contribution from refugees in Shanghai was the subject of a despatch to the Foreign Office from Sir Archibald Clark Kerr in Hong Kong:

> there is at Shanghai human material now lying idle and going to waste of which we might make good use. I refer to the German and Austrian Jewish refugees large numbers of whom are keen anti-Nazi and eager to serve our cause ... Among these sixteen thousand people there are (a) some 1,000 to 1,200 men between 18 and 35 physically fit for military duties (b) a number of doctors both male and female (c) nurses and (d) scores of engineers, electricians, mechanics, wireless experts, chauffeurs etc.[55]

It was 'imprudent to ignore this valuable material', Clark Kerr warned: 'If we make no use of it, it will fall into the hands of, and be absorbed by, Japanese if they occupy Shanghai.' Clark Kerr offered to create unobtrusive machinery to vet recruits. His plan had the agreement of the governor of the Malay States and local service chiefs. The proposal did arouse immediate interest from the government of India, which was experiencing great shortages of all technicians, including doctors and nurses. India adopted a more liberal admission policy than the United Kingdom in respect of Jews of enemy origin who were believed to be anti-Nazi and offered to accept technically qualified persons on Clark Kerr's recommendation.[56]

A new interdepartmental Committee on Overseas Manpower (COM), set up to co-ordinate overseas manpower, had by early 1942 acquired a wide brief which included manpower transfers between countries.[57] But the committee chose not to take up suggestions such as that made by Clark Kerr that refugees be brought to the United Kingdom. The committee echoed the general lack of interest in the services of persons other than British subjects and eventually reverted to considering British subjects exclusively.

In February 1942 the Foreign Office put to COM a proposal to obtain manpower from Greece by assisting skilled men to escape. Starvation conditions were then afflicting the population of occupied Greece. Indeed, the terms in which the Foreign Office advanced its proposal revealed its humanitarian and political dimensions: 'the better Greek achievements for the Allied cause place us under a moral obligation to think of the future of their race and save the health of as many as we can by evacuating them from Greece'.[58] T. H. Preston, the chief

[55] Sir A. Clark Kerr to FO, 9 Oct. 1941, PRO LAB 13/34.

[56] S. G. Pennells to Randall, 23 Jan. 1942, PRO FO 371/32670, W2865/831/48.

[57] Bridges, WP (G) (41) 108, 6 Oct. 1941, PRO CAB 67/9; Bridges, WP (42) 2, 2 Jan. 1942, PRO CAB 66/20.

[58] FO, memorandum, 'Manpower from Greece', OMP (42)7, 31 Jan. 1942, PRO FO 371/32670, W1332/831/48.

repatriation officer for the Middle East, questioned the manpower value of the scheme, expressing doubts whether sufficient skilled men were still available and pointing to the numerous skilled aliens, including many Jewish refugees, already available for employment in various parts of the eastern Mediterranean without the trouble of arranging an escape from enemy territory. The committee, nevertheless, agreed to the proposal, perhaps because the Foreign Office was so set on it, and it authorised giving assistance to escape to a small number of Greek mechanics, preferably men under forty with no dependants. It was further agreed that, to prevent escaping Greeks being turned back from Turkey, they would be transhipped in British craft via Cyprus to Haifa, and the committee resolved that a Middle Eastern labour bureau would be re-established, probably at Haifa, to recruit alien labour in the region.[59]

Thus British policy-makers put themselves out to assist the Greeks, to whom they felt an obligation, by promoting an escape scheme the manpower value of which was questionable, but which had an undeniable humanitarian element. The government's agreement to save Greek refugees from being turned back from Turkey was given in a period when British government policy was much less generous towards Jewish refugees who lacked permission to proceed to Palestine. In the case of Jewish refugees, the policy was to take no action to save them from being turned away by the Turks or from being deported from Turkey back to Europe. Britain refused to relax this harsh policy for several hundred Jewish refugees on board the *Struma*, which had sailed from the Romanian port of Constanza in mid-December 1941. For two months the Turks denied the ship permission to land or to proceed and it lay in the sea off Istanbul with all its passengers still on board while the British government tuned a deaf ear to pleas to authorise the Jews' entry to Palestine. Eventually in late February 1942 the Turks towed the ship out into the Black Sea and it sank with the loss of all but one of the passengers. In May 1942, the Cabinet still decided against acting to prevent Turkey from turning back Jewish refugees. Finally, in September of that year the government gave way to humanitarian pressure and undertook responsibility for finding refuge for Jews who reached Turkey.[60]

The war effort was regarded as the only legitimate basis for acting to aid refugees. The pervasiveness of this assumption is well illustrated by

[59] T. H. Preston, memorandum, 26 Mar. 1942, draft minutes, OMP (42) 3rd meeting, 14 May 1942, PRO FO 371/32670, W7452/831/48.

[60] Wasserstein, *Britain and Jews*, pp. 143–63, 340. The government withdrew this concession in December 1944.

the attitude of Anthony Lambert, a member of the staff of the British embassy to Turkey. Lambert had suggested that the United Kingdom accept the services of a Hungarian Jew named Strausz. Informing Lambert in June 1942 that Strausz had been rejected, the Refugee Department suggested reference to the Haifa bureau as 'the best means of helping Mr Strauss [*sic*] and other Jewish doctors, scientists, etc.'. Lambert was stung into insisting that he was not trying to assist these people but to 'try and recruit valuable talent for our own war-effort'.[61] When Lambert and his colleagues asked whether to continue sending home details of qualified technicians, only to have them rejected, the answer came that COM was now dealing only with British subjects and that MOLANS saw no grounds for bringing enemy alien technicians and specialists from Turkey to the United Kingdom. Embassy staff were advised to refer such skilled refugees to Cairo in connection with the planned Haifa bureau for overseas manpower.[62]

The Ministry of Health was similarly lacking in enthusiasm for refugee recruits from abroad. From 1940 on, the ministry recruited foreign doctors from the USA. But it refused offers of help from refugee doctors stranded in neutral territory all over the globe, claiming that their services could not be utilised. A group of eighty Polish doctors in Romania who were put forward by the British ambassador were among the refusals.[63] But a group of Polish medical students who intended to proceed to Palestine and Persia were allowed to enter on a temporary basis.[64]

Decisions not to utilise aliens in employment meant that the manpower itself was lost, sometimes irretrievably so, for example, with the Japanese occupation of Shanghai. A further worry for the Treasury was the expense of keeping unemployed refugees, including internees, in idleness.

The Ministries of Labour and Health interpreted their requirements so as to exclude numerous refugees well qualified in fields in which the country was experiencing serious shortages. Yet, these departments were not required to show great imagination or flexibility. Departments were entitled to reject options that appeared to involve disproportionate effort, risk or cost. The British officials who made these decisions were under no duty to take account of humanitarian considerations. Indeed,

61 Randall to Sir H. Knatchbull-Hugesson, 23 June 1942, Lambert to General Department, 21 July 1942, PRO FO 371/32670, W7948/W10775/831/48.

62 Lambert to General Department, 21 July 1942, Refugee Department to Lambert, 10 Aug. 1942, PRO FO 371/32670, W10775/831/48.

63 R. J. R. Farrow to under secretary, 1 Feb. 1941, PRO FO 371/29194, W849/115/48; correspondence, May–June 1941, PRO FO 371/29159, W6642/7094/3/48.

64 Correspondence, Sep.–Oct. 1942, PRO FO 371/32669, W13191/781/46.

the instructions under which these officials were operating did not treat humanitarian grounds as a sufficient reason for action.

When Foreign Office officials had cases they wished to support for entry, they criticised the Home Office's refusal to treat humanitarian grounds as sufficient. But their own motives were by no means simply humanitarian. The approach of Foreign Office officials is perhaps best characterised as a quest for some form of 'compensating advantage', in Alan Walker's phrase, for any assistance to refugees. The advantage in question varied from case to case: improved relations with another government; improved morale for persons involved in the war effort; better escape opportunities for persons whose services were required. These officials did cite humanitarian motives but they realised they could not put such motives forward as the primary justification for backing a case. For example, the 1942 proposal to help Greek technicians was put forward by Foreign Office officials on 'war effort' grounds, which were tenuous. The officials supporting this scheme gave it only secondary justification on political and humanitarian grounds, even though these appear to have provided the predominant motive.

The government's loss of control over the landing of war refugees during the evacuation emergency of May–June 1940 was short-lived. From then on, the Home Office and MI5 were largely successful in preventing admissions without visas and in curbing the grant of visas without reference. Procedural control was reasserted, then, but war-time priorities dictated that the Home Office's authority was circumscribed so far as the substance of admissions was concerned and tightly defined Cabinet policies left the Home Office with much less discretion than in peace-time. The security services made new incursions into what had formerly been Home Office territory. Admissions for the war effort were evaluated by ministries directly affected or were delegated to governments-in-exile.

This chapter has shown how in war-time humanitarian aid for refugees was relegated to the sidelines. By mid-1942 the government's policy of rejecting purely humanitarian action had been legitimated by three years of practice. Officials had learned to suppress and deny humanitarian motives. These officials were now adept at using the war effort to justify all actions and omissions. Before the war, immigration policy had provided the criterion of national interest against which possible aid to refugees was judged. Now, immigration concerns still remained important, but the overriding criterion was the needs of the war effort. After three years of war, the miserly character of British refugee policy formed part of a transformed system of values. The war effort had acquired the status of the supreme, if not the only, good. In the context of refugee admissions the war effort served a dual purpose – as the justification for supporting some admissions and for refusing others. Officials and ministers became fluent in arguing that whatever outcome they desired would benefit the war effort.

Given the way priorities had been set, how could additional refugees be perceived as anything other than a burden? The horizons of both the Home Office and refugee organisations had narrowed and they were concentrating their energies on dealing with the refugees within Britain and seeking ways to reduce their numbers. For officials to assess and investigate new refugee cases used up precious resources. The benefits to the British war machine of admitting any single individual could only be marginal. No public servant was allocated the duty to promote humanitarian aid to persecuted Jews or was offered any incentive to do so. It is impressive that even in these circumstances a number of individuals within the government laboured to explore the possibilities of admitting refugees to British territory. But it is hardly surprising that their efforts bore little fruit.

8 The response to the Holocaust

What remains unsaid about the British government's response to demands to rescue Jews from Nazi mass murder? The ungenerosity of British policy has been amply demonstrated by other authors. There is an emerging consensus that the government had many reasons for not acting to save Jews and detected no vital interest for Britain in doing so. Since the government did not regard rescue as a British problem, it tried to prevent it from becoming one. The British government ruled that there were to be no alterations in overall policy and no rescue attempts. The government's representatives cynically outmanoeuvred the rescue campaigners and went through the motions of investigating action, of which the most notorious is the Anglo-American Bermuda Conference of April 1943. Later, when the Americans adopted a more positive approach to rescue, the response of the British Foreign Office was obstructive.

The consensus over the negative character of British policy is now well supported by a growing body of research. But alternative approaches within Whitehall have not been explored. Such approaches, which reflected a more humanitarian way of thinking, will be explored here and the British contributions to rescue will be re-appraised. The efforts Britain made to rescue Jews arose in good part from tensions within Whitehall about British policy – tensions which have attracted little attention to date.

Before examining the British record on rescue, I shall consider the evacuation scheme to offer children relief from the war-time blockade – an episode which helps to explain the broader policy response to the Holocaust.

The child evacuation scheme

The British blockade was designed 'to lay squarely upon the shoulders of the enemy the responsibility for providing for the needs of the inhabitants'. The government resisted pressure to allow relief, even for underfed children, if it risked impairing the blockade or aiding the enemy.[1] For example, in June 1942, the War Cabinet vetoed a plan put forward by Eden, with support from the Ministry of Economic Warfare (MEW), to allow dried milk for children into enemy-occupied Belgium.

In October 1942, Eden proposed a scheme for the reception in Switzerland of children from Belgium and other Allied occupied territories. The concept of the scheme, which MEW and the Foreign Office had conceived as a sop to the Belgians, was to encourage the Swiss to develop existing arrangements to receive Allied children 'for recuperative visits'. The proposal involved offering to facilitate the import through the blockade of goods, over and above those normally allowed, to enable the Swiss to feed and look after additional children. Changes in blockade practice now required the Americans' agreement and they seemed strongly in favour of the plan and had already broached it to the Swiss. Eden admitted that the Germans were likely to find reasons to sabotage the scheme. But it represented 'a most desirable gesture on our part towards helping these children in some way without impairing the blockade or aiding the enemy'. For this reason, he concluded, 'and particularly in view of Field Marshal [Goering's] recent threat that the occupied countries must starve to feed Germany, this scheme is, I think, well worth proceeding with'.[2]

In January 1943, MEW put the idea to the Swiss. The entry of up to 100,000 children, largely from Belgium, was contemplated. The United Nations would subsidise the operation by paying for additional imports of goods through the blockade to Switzerland.[3] The Swiss were to organise and pay for the collection and housing of the children. The Swiss responded sympathetically.[4] The scheme had been presented to them as approved by both governments, even though the Americans had withdrawn preliminary approval in late 1942.[5] As originally envisaged, the scheme involved no expense falling directly on the British Exchequer, but it was now being suggested that it be financed by the

[1] MEW memorandum, 'Note on Blockade Policy respecting Relief', Jan. 1943, printed 24 Feb. 1943, PRO FO 837/1214, para. 1; W. N. Medlicott, *The Economic Blockade*, vol. II, (revised edn., London, 1978), United Kingdom Civil Series, *History of the Second World War*, pp. 254–81.

[2] A. Eden, 'Proposed Scheme for Reception in Switzerland of Children from Occupied Europe', WP (42) 463, 13 Oct. 1942, PRO CAB 66/29; for the scheme's origins, see correspondence, 16 June–24 Sep. 1942, PRO FO 371/32566, W9117/10003/12090/9117/49.

[3] Peter Quennell to W. L. Fraser, 16 Jan. 1943, enclosing MEW to Berne, no. 137 Arfar, 8 Jan. 1943, PRO T 160/1271/F18404.

[4] MEW to Berne, no. 241 Arfar, 15 Jan. 1943, *ibid.*

[5] Washington to FO, no. 6204, 23 Dec. 1942, PRO FO 837/1213; W. A. Camps to Walker, 16 Apr. 1943, PRO FO 371/36512, W5996/4/49.

British government alone. The Treasury objected to the requirement to find precious Swiss francs for a scheme which it regarded as 'still completely half baked', poorly planned and unlikely to bring Britain any benefit.[6] It was for Allied governments, the Treasury argued, to underwrite the cost of evacuations from their countries and to obtain any credit which might accrue. Treasury officials insisted that Britain could undertake any foreign exchange commitment resulting from the scheme only if Allied governments provided compensation in Swiss francs. This point was taken and a condition of compensation for any foreign exchange commitment was agreed, but MEW showed no sign of addressing the other objections.[7]

The British suggested that poor health be adopted as 'the sole criterion of priority' for inclusion in the evacuation scheme:

> the children most under-nourished or most prone to tuberculosis etc., should be chosen. Some such principle is essential if we are to avoid pro-German families getting priority. For the same reason it is desirable that Swiss Government as distinct from any Red Cross organisation should have responsibility for selection.[8]

The Swiss then proposed including a proportion of Jewish children. MEW suggested putting this idea to the Americans,

> as they may share our view that this is a valuable opportunity of bringing some relief to the suffering Jewish population of Europe, for whom much sympathy is felt, both here and in United States . . . in our view the inclusion of Jewish children who are in particular distress deserves to be considered, whether they are in Germany or in the occupied territories.[9]

MEW had seized on this idea as a means to sell the scheme to the Americans, whose agreement to the change in blockade practice was now essential.

The primary attraction of the scheme was political. Its practicability was a secondary issue. The scheme could be presented to those lobbying for relief through the blockade as a humanitarian gesture. And if, as the scheme's proponents hoped and expected, the Germans refused to make this gesture possible, the Germans' inhumanity would provide material for Allied propaganda. German rejection of the entire scheme – the preferred outcome – was even more likely if Jewish children were part of the package.

MEW officials did not merely expect the scheme to fail, but designed it for failure. Junior minister Dingle Foot, the scheme's chief advocate

6 R. A. B. Mynors to P. D. Proctor, 23 Jan. 1943, PRO T 160/1271/F18404.
7 C. H. M. Wilcox, memorandum, 'War Cabinet Paper WP (42) 463', 14 Oct. 1942, correspondence 20 Jan.–5 Feb. 1943, *ibid.*
8 MEW to Washington, no. 405 Arfar, 1 Feb. 1943, *ibid.*
9 MEW to Washington, no. 690 Arfar, 20 Feb. 1943, *ibid.*

within MEW, was seeking 'a chance for making capital out of a German refusal'.[10] Foot acknowledged that in responding to pressure for food relief the department was entering 'the realm of psychological rather than economic warfare'.[11] But he insisted that it would cause problems to try to feed hungry children in occupied Europe. Any scheme put forward should, he proposed, be designed

> (a) to make it as difficult as possible for the enemy to accept; (b) to avoid discrimination between one European ally and another; (c) to give each refugee government something that looks like a concession, which it can use for propaganda purposes; (d) to keep our commitment down to the smallest possible amount if the enemy accept; (e) to avoid raising throughout Occupied Europe hopes which we cannot satisfy.

He suggested offering to feed children and nursing and expectant mothers in selected cities on an experimental basis and simultaneously proposing the Swiss child evacuation scheme and a new Swedish scheme, and publicising both. He had little doubt that the enemy would refuse and he claimed: 'We should then be in a very strong position', while, if the enemy were to accept, 'we should run very little risk of conferring any substantial economic advantage on him'.[12] Foot's approach satisfied the minister of economic warfare, Lord Selborne. A Foreign Office official noted that one of the main arguments MEW adduced in support of the scheme was that 'the Germans might be expected to turn it down'.[13] MEW explained that it planned 'full publicity' for the scheme to coincide with the approach to the Axis: 'We should thus place onus of refusal publicly on the enemy.'[14]

The Americans' agreement was still lacking. In April 1943 the Americans agreed that the scheme could be explored further and MEW asked the Foreign Office to arrange for it to be discussed with American representatives during the refugee conference in Bermuda.[15] The message MEW wished to be passed to the British delegation emphasised the notion of including Jewish children:

> 100,000 children altogether could be looked after, of which 20–25% might be

[10] D. Foot to R. K. Law, 26 June 1942, C. E. Steel to Law, 10 July 1942, PRO FO 371/32566, W9117/9117/49.

[11] Foot, 'Memorandum on food relief for occupied Europe', Foot to Lord Selborne, 11 Apr. 1943, PRO FO 837/1214.

[12] Foot, memorandum cited n. 11; Foot, draft letter from the minister to the foreign secretary, n.d., approved by Selborne on 13 Apr. 1943, *ibid.*

[13] Washington to FO, no. 1507, 30 Mar. 1943, Selborne, minute, 11 Apr. 1943, Selborne to Eden, 13 Apr. 1943, *ibid.*; J. H. Le Rougetel, minute, 14 Apr. 1943, Eden, minute, 15 Apr. 1943, PRO FO 371/36512, W6189/4/49.

[14] MEW to Washington, no. 2095 Arfar, 30 June 1943, PRO T 160/1271/F18404.

[15] Correspondence, 19 Feb.–10 May 1943, PRO FO 837/1214.

Jewish. While such a scheme could not be regarded as even a partial solution of the Jewish problem it would at least be an earnest of our good intention.

Randall saw MEW's request before leaving for Bermuda to attend the conference but because of Foreign Office delays the message reached the island after the conference ended.[16] It was only in August 1943 that the Americans agreed to the child evacuation scheme. Finally, in September, the scheme was put to the Swiss for further discussion.[17] Treasury officials expected it to come to nothing. Edward Playfair commented: 'I am interested to see how this goes on – "till the conversion of the Jews", I expect.'[18]

At the end of 1943, Halifax, under growing pressure in Washington over blockade relief, pressed for an update on the negotiations over the scheme, asking, 'how far if at all it would be politic to refer to them publicly at this stage'.[19] Finally, in January 1944, MEW instructed the Berne embassy to ask the Swiss to raise the scheme with the Germans, seeking permission in principle for the children to leave occupied territory. The Swiss should be asked to include in their enquiry 'Jewish children from Germany and elsewhere in Axis Europe' and to make it clear that selection of children should not be left to the Germans or their puppet governments. Meanwhile, MEW planned 'the fullest publicity' to exploit the expected German refusal, so the Swiss should be given no undertaking that the matter would remain secret.[20]

Representatives of agencies concerned with humanitarian relief pointed out to MEW the risk that publicity for the schemes might expose hidden Jewish children. A top International Red Cross official, who had heard about the scheme, warned that to draw public attention to any action contemplated to help Jews was 'fatally dangerous' – it would alert Germans set on destroying Jews and lead to the frustration of the intended evacuations. Success, he insisted, required proceeding 'by inconspicuous means and by getting the co-operation of suitable Germans'.[21] Gustav Kullmann, a Swiss citizen, who was Sir Herbert Emerson's deputy, pointed out the danger of proposals made by Foot and by an American official to ensure that selectors chose Jewish children, saying, 'many of the Jewish children in the west are in hiding

[16] FO to UK delegation to the Refugee Conference in Bermuda, no. 23, 25 Apr. 1943, correspondence, 16–25 Apr. 1943 PRO FO 371/36512, W5996/4/49.

[17] Medlicott, *The Economic Blockade*, pp. 280–1, 507 n. 1; Washington to FO, no. 2734, 14 June 1943, PRO FO 837/1215; correspondence, 25 June–16 Sep. 1943, PRO T 160/1271/F18404.

[18] F. E. Harmer, minute, n.d., Playfair, minute, n.d., on Foot to W. Thurnheer, 16 Sep. 1943, PRO T 160/1271/F18404.

[19] Washington to MEW, no. 3736 Arfar, 29 Dec. 1943, PRO FO 837/1215.

[20] MEW to Berne, no. 135, 12 Jan. 1944, PRO T 160/1238/F17602.

[21] Camps, memorandum, 28 Jan. 1944, AJ43/52/255.

and have faked gentile ration cards and documents. Any interference might upset the existing state of things.' In response to these criticisms it was decided that, to avoid identifying orphans or refugees, the selectors would instead be asked to include 'children whose parents are not in a position to give them proper care'.[22] In May 1944 the Swiss confirmed their agreement to accept up to 50,000 children.[23] The Swiss sounded out the Germans about the scheme. No reply was ever received.[24] That was the end of MEW's scheme.

The story of this scheme illustrates what we may term the British 'blockade mentality', a way of thinking which enabled Whitehall to keep its distance from the privations of civilians in occupied Europe. The blockade mentality made it possible to see Jews under Nazism as just another group – albeit a peculiarly unfortunate one – of civilians under enemy control. Those responsible for the blockade probably needed to cultivate such detachment in order to deny civilians under Nazi occupation the necessities of life. A detached attitude towards the sufferings of European civilians probably made it easier for Allied propagandists to feel justified in exploiting such sufferings, whether they took the form of food shortages or of subjection to Nazi atrocities. Such attitudes help to explain the readiness of members of MEW to seize on the Swiss idea of including Jewish children in the evacuation scheme as a way of deflecting Jewish criticism of the blockade and of making the scheme especially unattractive to the Germans.

The blockade mentality reflected an order of priorities tailored to the defeat of Germany. British policy-makers saw little reason to spare European Jews from the Allied food blockade which, if effective, would cause privation to everyone the Germans had to feed. Whether such suffering advanced the war effort is a separate issue. MEW's policy, according to W. N. Medlicott, author of the two-volume official history of the economic blockade, was misguided and inadequately thought out. The ministry, he says, avoided discussing

> its ultimate dilemma: could a food blockade really harm the enemy, except at the cost of widespread starvation. If this occurred, could the British government, after its prompt aid to Greece, refuse help to other areas? If Axis Europe was sufficiently well fed not to need relief, why refuse small relief contributions, and indeed why maintain the blockade at all? The Ministry was partly a victim of its own propaganda, and of the general exaggeration of the potency of the blockade weapon in the First World War.[25]

22 Record of meeting held at MEW on 16 Mar. 1944, AJ43/52/255.
23 MEW to Berne, no. 1840 Arfar, 21 May 1944, PRO T 160/1271/F18404.
24 Foot, draft relief statement, sent to Selborne, 1 Nov. 1944, PRO FO 837/1217; Medlicott, *The Economic Blockade*, p. 275.
25 Medlicott, *The Economic Blockade*, p. 277.

In his *Britain and the Jews of Europe, 1939–1945*, Wasserstein notes the anomalous character of the British policy of giving relief to Greece and he contrasts it with the 'niggardly quantities of food relief' which MEW permitted to be sent to Jews in central and eastern Europe.[26] Yet, relief for Greece is surely significant as an exception to the food blockade generally. The decision to allow supplies for Greece through the blockade was seen in retrospect as misguided since it bestowed benefits on the enemy. The key point being made here about blockade policy is that it hardly distinguished between the deprivation of different groups in consequence of the blockade. The economic warfare authorities were implementing the government's established policy towards humanitarian crises on the mainland. Civilians in enemy-controlled Europe had to endure hunger, Allied bombardment and, in certain cases, Nazi persecution. Ministers repeatedly asserted the principle that Britain could not afford to concern itself with their welfare. Given this overall policy approach of neglecting the welfare of all the populations under Nazi rule, the government would be slow to single out the special plight of Jews, or indeed of any other group, for exceptional treatment, whether over food or other matters.

The British response to the Holocaust up to the end of 1942

The Nazis began the organised mass murder of Jews during the German invasion of the Soviet Union which commenced in late June 1941. The terrifying force and speed of the German advance trapped most Jews living in its path. On the heels of the German front line, men in four new mobile killing units, the *SS* Einsatzgruppen, energetically carried out their task of murdering as many Jews as possible. Other army and police units assisted in the slaughter. The murderers received active support from local populations, especially in the Baltic states and Ukraine. The killing squads rounded up their victims, marched them to open pits and shot them. By the end of October a quarter of a million Jews had been killed in the Baltic states and Belorussia alone. Only a lucky few escaped. The new German civilian administrations forced Jews whom the killing squads had not executed into ghettos established in many of the larger Jewish centres where the Jews were subject to slave labour, starvation and disease. Later the Germans liquidated the ghettos, transporting those Jews left alive to death camps.

[26] Wasserstein, *Britain and Jews*, pp. 354–5.

By 1941 British signals intelligence could decipher enemy messages sent by wireless telegraphy. Once these messages had been interrupted and decoded they were known as decrypts. Batches of these decrypts crossed Churchill's desk each day. Among them were German police messages transmitted in August and September 1941, which reported mass shootings of Jewish civilians, carried out by various German units in several regions of Soviet territory. In red ink, Churchill ringed the figures reporting the numbers of Jews shot, which ranged from scores to thousands.[27] He also noted decrypts of German instructions that, because of the danger of deciphering, reports of executions should no longer be sent by wireless and a further report showing that some German wireless messages were substituting euphemisms such as 'action according to the usages of war' and '"dead" as distinct from "shot"' to send details of executions.[28]

It was not until the following year that the British government concluded that the Hitler regime was carrying out a programme of wholesale murder of European Jewry. Reports of mass killings reached the outside world from various sources in addition to intelligence decrypts – escapees, witnesses, people with access to inside information. From June 1942 onwards, a succession of stories appeared in the press, reporting mass executions in Poland, with hundreds of thousands of Jewish dead and wholesale deportations of Jews to the east. In August 1942 the World Jewish Congress representative in Geneva passed on to the Foreign Office a report suggesting that Germany's leaders were examining a plan to deport to the east and exterminate 'at one blow' all Jews in territory they controlled, thereby resolving the 'Jewish problem' in Europe once and for all.[29]

Some of the detail in this report later turned out to be wrong. The information was also out of date. The murder programme was far beyond the planning stage. Daily massacres of Jewish deportees were being carried out in extermination centres in occupied Poland. Gas vans were first used to murder Jews in early December 1941 in the village of Chelmno in the Warthegau. From early 1942 transports of Jews were murdered in gas chambers at Birkenau, an extension of the Auschwitz concentration camp in Upper Silesia, and murders of Jews in gas chambers commenced in the extermination centres of Belzec and Sobibor in the spring of 1942. In Treblinka the gassing of Jews,

[27] German police messages, 27 Aug. 1941, PRO HW 1/30, 30 Aug. 1941, PRO HW 1/35, 26 Aug. 1941, PRO HW 1/40, 6 Sep. 1941, PRO HW 1/51.

[28] German police messages, 11 Oct. 1941, PRO HW 1/135, 17 Oct. 1941, PRO HW 1/148.

[29] C. Norton to FO containing message from Dr G. Riegner to S. S. Silverman MP, 10 Aug. 1942, PRO FO 371/30917, C7853/61/18.

most of whom came from Warsaw, commenced in late July 1942. About half the estimated total of 5.1 million murders of Jews by the Nazis were committed in the year 1942. It has recently emerged that in 1943 and early 1944, much earlier than had been thought, the Allies received a series of reports of mass extermination at Auschwitz-Birkenau.[30] What the Allies made of this information is another question. Precise figures charting the progress of Nazi extermination policy were lacking, as were complete details of the production line methods of mass murder. But in August 1942 the report from Geneva of the Nazis' murderous intentions towards European Jewry was supplemented by advance information about Nazi deportation plans. The Vichy regime under Laval had stated that it would comply with a German decree ordering the deportation of Jews from unoccupied France to the east. Desperate attempts were made, by Emerson and Anthony de Rothschild of the Central Council for Jewish Refugees among others, to mobilise American diplomatic pressure against such action, but notwithstanding diplomatic protests the wholesale deportations went ahead.[31]

By the time of the deportations from unoccupied France the link between wholesale murders of Jews and the overall intentions of the Nazis had been established. Deportation to the east was understood to be a sentence of death. For example, Cooper, in a memorandum of late August 1942, which was circulated within the Aliens Department, commented that, since the outbreak of war,

> the German Government has been pursuing the policy of sending Jews from all parts of the Reich, and even from occupied countries, to Poland where they are being forced into ghettoes [*sic*], which have been established by the Nazi power, and there starved to death and subjected to mass murder, no doubt with the deliberate intention of exterminating that section of the Jewish race over whom the German Government exercises any control.[32]

On 2 September a rally was held at Caxton Hall in London in protest at Nazi atrocities in Poland and Czechoslovakia. The meeting was organised by the Labour Party and the speakers included the home

[30] Richard Breitman, *Official Secrets: What the Nazis Planned, What the British and Americans Knew* (New York, 1998); Stuart G. Erdheim, 'Could the Allies Have Bombed Auschwitz-Birkenau?', *Holocaust and Genocide Studies* 11, 2 (Fall 1997), 129–70; Gerhard Weinberg, 'The Allies and the Holocaust', in Berenbaum and Peck, *The Holocaust and History*, pp. 480–91; F. H. Hinsley, et al., *British Intelligence in the Second World War*, vol. II, Appendix 5, 'The German Police Cyphers', p. 673.

[31] A. de Rothschild to National Refugee Service, New York, 7 Aug. 1942, Emerson to M. Taylor, 11 Aug. 1942, Taylor to Emerson, 10 Sep. 1942, AJ43/22/123.

[32] Cooper, 'Memorandum on Post-War Problems', 29 Aug. 1942, PRO HO 213/1347, para. 12.

secretary, Herbert Morrison.[33] *The Times*, reporting the meeting, quoted Morrison as saying, 'never before had the human record been so shamed and darkened by the revelation of the unspeakable foulness of which desperate man was capable', and reported that he had pledged that the United Nations would ensure the punishment of those responsible 'for ordering, or executing, the infamous cruelties practised upon the men, women and children of Europe'.[34] Not a word of this committed the government to any effort to prevent the slaughter. Was there a real possibility that Britain would adopt a more humanitarian policy and embark on the rescue of Jews?

The first test of British intentions was a Cabinet discussion in late September of the proposed admission of Jewish refugees from France. Morrison, who initiated the discussion, said that Home Office admissions policy was

> not to admit during the war additional refugees to the United Kingdom unless in some quite rare and exceptional cases it can be shown that the admission of the refugee will be directly advantageous to our war effort.

He assured his colleagues that he was not proposing any policy alteration. He explained that he was seeking approval to make a single exception arising from a proposed scheme put forward by Schiff and backed by a guarantee from the JRC which involved Jewish refugees then in unoccupied France. These refugees, he said, faced danger and suffering as a result of the Vichy government's decision to deport them to Poland. Morrison said he wished to agree to the admission of a limited number of children and elderly people with close relatives in Britain. He envisaged that persons covered by the scheme would be able to obtain visas in Lisbon, if they managed first to escape to Portugal. These visas, Morrison advised, should be the final concession to the lobby for admissions. He claimed that any general departure from the rigidity of existing policy would only encourage fresh appeals. Indeed, he said he planned to refuse the temporary entry of another twenty-eight Jewish children from unoccupied France, who had guarantees for admission to Palestine, because Home Office policy was not to admit persons in transit to Palestine and it would become 'impracticable to draw a line of demarcation' between these and other cases. He also intended to resist all appeals for the admission of adults under the age of sixty.[35]

The Cabinet was in agreement that the current strict admissions policy should be maintained. Ministers gave only partial endorsement to

[33] *Jewish Chronicle*, 11 Sep. 1942, p. 1. [34] *The Times*, 3 Sep. 1942, p. 8.

[35] Morrison, memorandum, 'Admission to the United Kingdom of a Limited Number of Jewish Refugees from Unoccupied France', WP (42)427, 23 Sep. 1942, PRO CAB 66/29; WM 126 (42)5, 21 Sep. 1942, PRO CAB 65/27.

Morrison's proposals, deciding to exclude the admission of the elderly.[36] At Foreign Office insistence, the Cabinet resolved to include Allied children in addition to Jewish children on the basis that extending the scheme thus would avoid the risk of any offence to Allied governments, whose nationals were also suffering, and would avoid discrimination in favour of Jews or Jewish children.[37] The Cabinet initially decreed that only orphan children could be admitted to join close relatives other than parents, but Morrison obtained authority to include children whose parents had been deported, once he explained that

> the children whose position is most pitiful are those who become in effect orphans as the result of the deportation of their parents. The fate of their parents will often be uncertain and as a result of the Cabinet decision it will be necessary to refuse to admit such children unless evidence is forthcoming that both of the parents have perished.[38]

Visas were authorised for 183 children, but the scheme foundered because the Vichy government refused exit permits. Then in November 1942 the Germans occupied the remainder of France and all efforts to rescue Jewish children were forced underground. But later certain children who had been hidden or smuggled out were able to take up British visas in neutral territory.[39]

The government's one-off promise of visas was the first proposal discussed by ministers for saving Jews from the Nazi murder programme in Europe. Thereafter, government spokesmen, following the Cabinet ruling, told campaigners to expect no further concessions.[40] The issue of rescue still hardly figured on the government's agenda. Details of the slaughter of Jews were minuted by officials in the Refugee Department, but did not prompt them to discuss a humanitarian response. These officials' difficulties in confronting the implications of the extermination programme were also evident in their approach to a topic they felt they needed to address – post-war Jewish policy. The Refugee Department launched an interdepartmental discussion of how the victorious Allies

36 WM 130 (42)4, 28 Sep. 1942, PRO CAB 65/27; WP (42)444, 2 Oct. 1942, PRO CAB 66/29; WM 131 (42)9, 5 Oct. 1942, PRO CAB 65/28.

37 Randall, minute, 21 Sep. 1942, PRO FO 371/32680, W12687/4555/48, Randall, Frank Roberts, minutes, 25 Sep. 1942, Randall, minutes, 28 Sep. and 7 Oct. 1942, PRO FO 371/32680, W12853/W13371/4555/48; Morrison, memorandum, cited n. 35.

38 WP (42)444, 2 Oct. 1942, PRO CAB 66/29; Gilbert, *Auschwitz and the Allies*, p. 77, omits subsequent developments.

39 Maxwell to Schiff, 10 May 1944, AJ43/45/216; R. Fellner to E. V. D. Mathews, 4 Dec. 1944, Mathews to Fellner, 1 Jan. 1945, PRO HO 213/615; 'Report to the Governments of the United States and the United Kingdom from their delegates to the Conference on the Refugee Problem held at Bermuda, April 19–29, 1943' (hereafter Bermuda Report), 29 Apr. 1943, PRO FO 371/36725, W6711/6711/48, para. 34.

40 Wasserstein, *Britain and Jews*, pp. 112–14.

should deal with the refugee problem, yet, even in this context, the Department's head, Alec Randall, was unable or unwilling to acknowledge that the destruction of the Jewish presence in Europe made it necessary to abandon outdated policies.[41]

Emerson was more responsive to the plight of the Jews. In mid-December 1942 he took the initiative of impressing on Randall and the US ambassador in London that the issue of how 'practical help can be given in saving refugees in Europe' was a problem the United Nations should address.[42] Emerson said that it was only a matter of time before the German policy to exterminate all Jews of all nationalities extended, for example, to French Jews. Calling at the Foreign Office on 18 December to discuss his memorandum, he predicted that the United Nations declaration vowing ultimate punishment for the perpetrators would intensify the demand for a more forthcoming policy on refugee admissions and that public opinion might become, temporarily at least, more willing to accept the presence of a greater number of aliens. Emerson's proposals included the offer of 10,000 visas to persuade the Swiss not to bar the entry of refugee Jews from France. He also suggested measures to get 3,000 Jews out of Spain, perhaps by means of a refugee camp in North Africa. The steps Emerson proposed were aimed at facilitating escape into neutral territory and helping people already in neutral territory to move on. These measures would, he said, assist no more than a few thousand. He considered that there was no longer a question of dealing with millions of people whom the Nazis might try to unload on other countries.[43]

Emerson had suggested a United Nations conference as a way of furthering a humanitarian response. Randall seized on the idea of a conference, but he envisaged it as a means of deflecting the growing public pressure for action. He planned to involve the Americans, to confine discussion as far as possible to what could be done in the areas freed by the Allied armies and to prevent discussion from 'straying in the various dangerous directions which any refugee discussion is liable to take'.[44] Randall, together with Richard Law, the junior Foreign Office minister, persuaded Emerson that action be deferred until the Amer-

[41] Randall to other departments, 18 Aug. 1942, enclosing memorandum, 'Future of the Refugee Problem', PRO FO 371/32659, W8051/397/48; record of a meeting held at FO on 9 Dec. 1942, to discuss the future of the Refugee Problem, 10 Dec. 1942, PRO T 161/1446/S51823/1.

[42] Emerson to Randall, memorandum by Emerson, 14 Dec. 1942, PRO FO 371/32660, W17084/397/48, and PRO FO 371/32660, W17272/4555/48.

[43] Memorandum by Emerson cited n. 42; copy, Randall to Newsam, 22 Dec. 1942, circulated by Randall to Waley etc., PRO T 161/1446/S51823/1.

[44] Randall, minute, 15 Dec. 1942, PRO FO 371/32660, W17084/397/48.

icans had agreed. Instead, Randall proposed – as 'the next best thing' – promises of programmes to resolve refugee problems after the war.[45]

Widespread uncertainty existed about what direction government policy was likely to take. Law himself was among those who believed it would have to become more generous. On 16 December, the eve of the UN declaration, Law received a deputation from the Council of Christians and Jews on the subject of assistance to Jews in occupied territories. One of the deputation's requests was that the government issue invitations to any Jews who could escape to come to British territory. Law sent his visitors away empty-handed, but concluded

> I was very much impressed by their anger against the home secretary, which quite clearly has not abated, and I feel very doubtful myself whether we shall be able to stand much longer on the very strict line that the Home Office is adopting. It has always seemed to me that the apprehensions of the Home Office have been exaggerated and that it would be very difficult for us to go on confining ourselves to denunciation of the German action while refusing to take any alleviating action ourselves. I did not give the deputation any idea that this was my view.[46]

On 17 December 1942, a joint United Nations declaration made simultaneously in London, Washington and Moscow officially confirmed that the Nazis were engaged in the systematic mass murder of Jewish civilians as part of a policy of extermination of European Jewry. The Commons heard Eden outline the barbaric methods by which the Nazis were carrying out this policy: deportation; working to death; murder through exposure and starvation; and deliberate massacre. The official condemnation of Nazi crimes was not accompanied by any statement of intent to prevent further atrocities or to rescue the victims. The declaration merely promised that the perpetrators would be punished after the war was won. Certain MPs asked about rescue, but Eden deflected them. The House concluded its brief discussion by standing in silence for one minute.[47]

After the declaration, as Emerson had predicted, the British government found itself facing unprecedented pressure to involve itself in rescue. The declaration had alerted the British public to the Nazis' wholesale extermination of European Jewry. Public concern for the victims, once aroused, could not be satisfied by funereal expressions of sympathy. By late December 1942 the problem of how to save the Jews was the focus of exceptional public attention. Hitherto, the government

[45] Randall to Newsam, 22 Dec. 1942, cited n. 43.
[46] Law, minute, 16 Dec. 1942, PRO FO 371/32682, W17401/4555/48.
[47] *Hansard*, House of Commons, vol. 385, cols. 2082–7, 17 Dec. 1942.

had not considered that it needed to address this issue, but the pressure was now too strong to ignore.

The British debate over rescue passed through three discernible phases. The first phase, which started in December 1942, was characterised by intense activity, in a climate of uncertainty about what the government might do. This phase came to an end in mid-1943, following the Bermuda conference, once it became clear that neither the British government nor the Americans proposed to take any substantial action. The second phase was a relative lull: the government was doing hardly anything; the advocates of rescue noted this, but did little to challenge it. The third phase started in early 1944 when rescue campaigners were once again pressing for action. Although the government refused to shift its public stance and the overall thrust of policy remained the same, the government committed itself to certain unpublicised rescue initiatives.

The British government felt equal to dealing with its critics at home and never believed itself to be in danger from them. More worrying was pressure in the United States. The Roosevelt administration was assumed to be vulnerable to Jewish pressure, especially in the run-up to an election. The British government, as we saw with the child evacuation scheme, wished to help the American president by offering material he could use to pacify the Jewish lobby in the United States. The British believed the US government's commitment to saving Jewish lives to be as weak their own and until the end of 1943 this assessment was reasonably accurate. But thereafter the Foreign Office failed to realise the extent to which the substance as well as the appearance of American policy on rescue had changed.

The rescue debate from late December 1942

The day after the 17 December declaration Richard Law considered that it 'had created a new situation in which it might prove impossible for the home secretary to maintain the *non-possumus* attitude which hitherto has come so easily to him'.[48] Law spoke to Peake, the junior Home Office minister, about an estimated 5,000 to 6,000 Jewish refugees in the Iberian peninsula. Having discussed this question with Emerson, Law said he felt that Britain should accept perhaps 2,000 of these people, if current discussions with the Americans about establishing a refugee camp in North Africa failed to result in a practicable scheme.[49] Morrison reacted defensively, telling Maxwell, his top official:

[48] Law to Randall, 18 Dec. 1942, PRO FO 371/32682, W17401/4555/48.
[49] Peake to Maxwell, 18 Dec. 1942, PRO HO 213/1827.

As usual the Foreign Office is good at taking the cheers & also good at passing the real problem to someone else. Mr Peake may not know that the issue has already been discussed some weeks ago by the Cabinet & a decision given in which the Foreign Secy concurred. I had some difficulty in getting that decision as wide as it was. I notice that Mr Law, like Miss Rathbone, holds that the first responsibility must rest on the British.

What I much prefer to this rather dribbling policy is to find a biggish territory where large numbers can go, e.g., Madagascar. Please think on these lines & let us talk about it next week. Meantime the last Cabinet decision holds. Mind the FO doesn't raise in Cabinet while I am away, but don't put the idea into their head. If we start, big numbers will be involved ultimately.[50]

Maxwell quickly disposed of Morrison's notions regarding Madagascar. He argued the case for accepting refugees from Spain and Portugal, saying that the proposal for a refugee camp in North Africa had broken down and that a suggestion that Britain and the Americans each take half of these refugees would be 'difficult to resist', especially as any whose loyalty was in doubt could be detained. Furthermore, their reception would not necessarily involve agreement to their permanent settlement after the war. Maxwell suggested certain preliminary enquiries in connection with such a scheme. He envisaged the entry of 2,000 or 3,000 refugees who might be accommodated in the Isle of Man. He added that, if this scheme were rejected, the Home Office might have to consider a smaller entry scheme Schiff was proposing for children aged up to sixteen who were in camps and prisons in the Iberian peninsula. It would be on the same lines as the facilities previously offered to children in unoccupied France with near relatives already in the UK, and very small numbers of children were likely to be involved. Maxwell said he considered that the Home Office should extend admissions to adults with sons in the forces.[51] Schiff had mentioned that American consuls had now been instructed to offer facilities to proceed to the United States to children in Spain and Portugal, and in some cases to their mothers. Morrison claimed not to follow Schiff's reasoning about the USA. As for responding to the proposals Maxwell was endorsing, he said he 'must keep uncommitted' until the newly set-up secret Cabinet Committee on refugee policy reported; he said the foreign secretary, who chaired the committee, did not propose to convene it until after Christmas.[52]

Schiff had pressed for a humanitarian response:

We hope the United Nations, particularly the United States and Great Britain, will arrive at a policy which will enable Jews to be saved from the horrible

[50] Morrison to Maxwell, 18 Dec. 1942, *ibid.*
[51] Maxwell to Morrison, Schiff to Maxwell, 23 Dec. 1942, *ibid.*
[52] Morrison to Maxwell, 24 Dec. 1942, *ibid.*

massacres which are horrifying the whole civilised world. We daily receive offers of hospitality from non-Jewish quarters, and, in fact, Mr Henry Carter has told me that if any funds have to be raised the churches are very anxious to co-operate in this respect.[53]

Another plea, from the Archbishop of Canterbury to the prime minister, in early January 1943, urged: 'our chief concern is the time factor, our process of consideration takes so long, and the Jews are massacred daily'.[54]

But the new Cabinet Committee was rapidly mobilised in defence of the British policy of inaction.[55] Ministers privately agreed that the direction of policy should not change and they confided to the United States government their intention that the joint Anglo-American policy should be to do as little as possible. In January 1943 Randall's conception of a joint conference as a device to hold off pressure for action was put to the Americans, in terms which made plain the true purpose of the proposed meeting. The British proposed that the two governments should confer in private and said that the proposed conference would be useful even if 'its main result was to elicit full statements of what various governments were doing and the difficulties in the way of doing more'.[56]

In the run-up to the Anglo-American conference, the new Cabinet Committee for the Reception and Accommodation of Refugees met regularly. Initially the committee's name referred to 'Jewish Refugees', but 'Jewish' was soon dropped, to mask the extent to which the matter concerned Jews alone. Randall and his colleagues provided committee members with briefings, support and advice. Members of the Refugee Department, under Randall's direction, took the lead in formulating and defending the government's overall position and when non-governmental representatives submitted proposals for rescue, the officials responded. The role of these officials was thus largely reactive: they deflected pressure and defended inaction. The alleged need not to discriminate was their standard justification for opposing proposals for the rescue of Jews exclusively. But the driving conviction behind the Refugee Department's consistently negative attitude to rescue was that the rescue of Jews was not a British problem.

The government outsmarted its critics by going through the motions of attempting to identify a positive plan of action. Once the impending Anglo-American conference on refugee policy had been announced, it became an excuse for doing nothing. Government spokesmen put off

[53] Schiff to Maxwell, 23 Dec. 1942, *ibid.*

[54] W. Temple to W. Churchill, 8 Jan. 1943, *ibid.*

[55] It was set up on 23 December: WM 172 (42)5, 23 Dec. 1942, PRO CAB 65/28; PRO CAB 95/15 (the Committee's records).

[56] FO to Washington, 12 Jan. 1943, PRO FO 371/36648, W607/49/48.

campaigners by telling them to await the outcome of the discussions at Bermuda. Once the conference was over, the two governments refused to consider any suggestions other than those they had agreed between themselves.

The government's lack of an active humanitarian policy caused growing public concern from late December 1942. It also had its critics within the government. For example, Waley questioned the government's desire to minimise commitments to victims of Nazi persecution in a sharply critical letter to Randall: 'It seems a pity that we should express so much sympathy and desire for reprisals, but refuse to give what help we can in a small way and thereby encourage other countries to do the same.'[57] Waley also emphasised the need to address the question of compensating refugees after the war for assets confiscated in Germany.[58] In the letter to Randall quoted above, he advocated a policy of letting refugees stay in Britain after the war, saying,

> I hope you will not too readily acquiesce in the Home Office view that we ought to refuse to allow permanent settlement after the war to those refugees who are technically in transit, if they wish to stay here rather than to be repatriated. Of course, I express this hope as a human being and not as a Treasury official (or sub-human being).

Another critic of government inactivity, Philip Noel-Baker, had in the past campaigned for a more generous refugee policy but was now, as a junior minister, unable to voice his concern in public. In January 1943 Noel-Baker sent Richard Law a list of practical proposals for help to European Jews by the United Nations and suggested the appointment of a new high commissioner to put them into effect.[59] A month later he privately acknowledged his inability to influence Eden: he still wished that more drastic action be taken.[60]

The public challenge to the government's apparent inaction was led by Eleanor Rathbone, who raised refugee policy repeatedly in Parliament and formed a campaigning organisation, the National Committee for Rescue from Nazi Terror (NCRNT). But, when government representatives pressed Rathbone to moderate her challenges, so as not to endanger their professed efforts for the Jews, she co-operated.[61] Foreign Office officials saw Rathbone as a thorn in their side. In June 1943 a suggestion by Lord Perth of appointing her to an official position on the

57 Waley to Randall, 24 Dec. 1942, PRO T 161/1446/S51823/1.
58 Waley, correspondence with Sir William Malkin and Randall, 23 Dec. 1942–22 Jan. 1943, *ibid.*; correspondence, 4–22 Jan. 1943, PRO FO 371/36694, W1108/124/48.
59 P. Noel-Baker to Law, 8 Jan. 1943, Noel-Baker papers 4/578, Churchill Archives Centre, Cambridge (hereafter Noel-Baker).
60 Noel-Baker to H. Corder, 6 Feb. 1943, *ibid.*
61 Kushner, *Holocaust and Liberal Imagination*, pp. 173–201.

IGC was considered by the Refugee Department. Lady Cheetham commented:

> her sympathy with refugees would find practical expression and she would come up against some of the main difficulties of the problem and realise that a block of visas is no magic carpet which will automatically carry away the persecuted from Nazi occupied Europe.[62]

Alan Walker agreed: 'it seems a good idea to draw the dragon's teeth by taking it into our confidence'.[63] Refugee Department officials were dismissive of Rathbone, for example, referring to her as 'the "perishing" Miss Rathbone' – a waggish allusion to her leaflet, *Rescue the Perishing*.[64]

Rathbone's allies included a group of senior civil servants and their friends who had shown sympathy to Jewish refugees before the war. Alix Kilroy, later Dame Alix Meynell, the first woman principal in the Board of Trade, recalled later that she and her colleagues had stretched to the limit the admission before the war of refugees to set up businesses in the Special Areas. Members of Kilroy's family, together with her close friend and fellow civil servant Evelyn Sharp, later Britain's first woman permanent secretary, undertook responsibility for a boy refugee from Austria. Francis Meynell – later Alix's husband – had guaranteed and accommodated nine pre-war refugees. In war-time, Francis Meynell became a temporary civil servant at the Board of Trade. In early February 1943, inspired by Victor Gollancz's celebrated pamphlet *Let My People Go*, Meynell convened a private meeting of people who were alarmed by the government's policy of inactivity towards Hitler's Jewish victims. His aim was to decide on measures to press upon the government and to agree on how to lobby for their adoption.[65] The participants, apart from Meynell, Kilroy and Sharp, included Gollancz, Rathbone, Dennis Cohen, Alan Sainsbury, Mrs Reginald McKenna, Sydney Bernstein and Tom Driberg MP. The group resolved to campaign publicly for 'a full open-door policy' consistent with the British tradition of asylum, calling on the government to offer a temporary refuge to all Jews who could escape, to set up reception camps under British jurisdiction and to invite other governments to follow suit. They also planned to challenge anti-semitic attitudes. The meeting agreed that a Gallup poll would be commissioned to discover the extent of support for government action.[66] Francis Meynell arranged and helped

62 Cheetham, minute, 17 June 1943, PRO FO 371/36726, W8828/6731/48.
63 Walker, minute, 17 June 1943, *ibid.*
64 Walker, minute, 29 Feb. 1944, PRO FO 371/42727, W2971/16/48.
65 Dame Alix Meynell, *Public Servant, Private Woman: An Autobiography* (London, 1988), pp. 188–9, 201–3; letter from a refugee, 1940, XVII Folder B, Sir Francis Meynell papers, Morison papers, Cambridge University Library (hereafter Meynell).
66 Copy, minutes of meeting on 3 Feb. 1943, Meynell XVII Folder F.

pay for this. The results showed 78 per cent of those polled supported admission. This total was made up of 40 per cent who specified asylum only until refuge elsewhere was available, 28 per cent who supported refuge until the war's end and 10 per cent for an indefinite period.[67] The poll results were widely publicised.[68]

The strength of public feeling in support of rescue attempts was evident from the Foreign Office's incoming correspondence. In January 1943, Randall considered a draft formula for replying to a 'huge number of similar letters' demanding action and offering financial help and hospitality to endangered Jews. These letters came 'from every sort and kind of society and person'. The Foreign Office decided to cease acknowledgement altogether.[69] In mid-February *The Times* printed a letter from leading literary and academic figures, ranging from E. M. Forster to the MP, writer and journalist Harold Nicolson, which deplored the policy of doing nothing 'while a helpless people is assassinated'.[70] During a Lords debate on 23 March 1943, the Archbishop of Canterbury made an especially heartfelt plea for rescue efforts but Lord Cranborne, speaking for the government, rejected the Archbishop's suggestions and rebuked him for wishing to limit rescue proposals to the Jews.[71]

The British and American governments had said enough to warn insiders not to expect much of the forthcoming conference. Thus, in late March 1943, G. G. Kullmann, Emerson's deputy, said that the press campaign in Britain had raised 'unfortunately wild hopes', but, 'I am afraid that the Two Power Conference will have to come down to the very modest problems of assistance and removal of escapees in countries of first asylum.' He said that rescue might be possible through the grant of Palestine immigration certificates to women and young children in the Balkan countries. But Kullmann said that, even if Axis consents were forthcoming, there seemed no prospect of large numbers obtaining refuge in countries outside Europe or of the shipping being available to get them there, and added, 'how could one justify restriction of such rescue measures to the Jews alone when there is untold suffering amongst women and children belonging to the aryan population of some of the occupied territories?'[72]

67 Wasserstein, *Britain and Jews*, p. 131.

68 Meynell to George Macy, 9 Mar. 1943, Meynell XVII Folder F; Francis Meynell's papers do not contain further particulars of the group's activities.

69 Cheetham, minute, 19 Jan. 1943, PRO FO 371/36649 W855/49/48; Randall, minute, 13 Jan. 1943, PRO FO 371/36649, W1034/49/48; correspondence, 20 Jan.–4 Feb. 1943, PRO FO 371/36651, W2139/49/48.

70 *The Times*, 16 Feb. 1943.

71 *Hansard*, House of Lords, vol. 126, cols. 811–62, 23 Mar. 1943.

72 G. G. Kullmann to R. C. Dexter, 25 Mar. 1943, AJ43/8/994.

Emerson had none of Kullmann's squeamishness about action to help Jews alone. In late March he submitted to Randall a memorandum setting out his views on measures for rescue. He considered 'the rescue of limited numbers with the consent or acquiescence' of Axis or Axis-controlled governments 'is practicable, or may become so'. As an example, he cited Britain's agreement that the Jewish Agency for Palestine should arrange the immigration to Palestine of children and women direct from certain Balkan countries, up to the limit of about 33,000 currently allowed by the White Paper. Emerson also raised the possible resumption, should a better chance of success arise, of the previous year's abortive visa offers – totalling 8,000 – by various governments including the British, to get Jewish children out of France. In both these cases, he emphasised, places of asylum were assured, the governments concerned having already committed themselves to the offers. The extension of the same principle to other cases, he said, would depend on obtaining further firm promises of asylum.[73]

Asylum offers could, of course, come only from individual governments. It was logical for Emerson to regard additional firm promises of asylum as a pre-condition of any consensual arrangements to release Jews imprisoned by the Nazis. Wyman has remarked that Emerson's 'idea of "limited numbers" was *very* limited', and that neither he nor the convenors of the Bermuda conference had large-scale action in mind.[74] But to bracket Emerson with the two governments in this way blurs the crucial distinction between them. It was not Emerson who set the limits. He could merely propose; the power to dispose rested with governments. British government spokesmen were systematically ridiculing large-scale rescue proposals. Emerson was taking the practical approach of making recommendations within the limited scope of what the Allies might be prepared to undertake. He acknowledged that offers to take unlimited numbers were out of the question. What he actually said was that suggestions that United Nations governments should offer to take as many victims of persecution as the Axis powers would choose to release would 'in their extreme form' be dismissed, as not conforming to the overriding consideration that rescue measures should not delay victory. Wyman complains here, 'He did not explain why.'[75] But for Emerson to summarise the known governmental objections to offering to take unlimited numbers was surely sufficient. He himself said he endorsed the view that with every extra day of war 'more persons will lose their lives than can be saved by any rescue measures so far

[73] Emerson to Randall, 25 Mar. 1943, enclosing Emerson, Note on Measures for the Rescue of Refugees from Axis Persecution, 24 Mar. 1943, AJ43/37/140.
[74] Wyman, *Abandonment*, p. 112. [75] *Ibid.*

suggested'. No purpose would have been served by Emerson's rehearsing arguments about whether making an unlimited offer could risk delaying victory. He may have suspected that no such offer would have persuaded the Nazis to release Jews, but he could not prove it. In discussing the highly controversial and speculative question of the possible release of captive Jews, Emerson's best chance of influencing governmental decision-makers was to ensure that his proposals took account of their objections and priorities.

Emerson was more assertive about the possible further development of escape into neutral countries. He argued that, even if the Axis powers would not let large numbers out, it was desirable to encourage the maintenance and expansion of existing refuge facilities in four neutral European countries, Spain, Portugal, Switzerland and Sweden. Such measures, he said, could enable more refugees to find their way out of Nazi territory, even through frontiers which were technically closed. Emerson advised that, if these receiving countries were to allow such inflows, what they particularly required, over and above the removal of refugees where possible and help over their maintenance, were assurances from the United Nations that they would not be left with unrepatriable refugees on their hands after the war. He considered it particularly important to support an expanded inflow into Spain by balancing it with a greater outflow of refugees. This, Emerson said, should be achieved by the provision of more asylum opportunities, especially for German and Austrian refugees, who had no government to help them. Extra numbers might need to be accommodated on an emergency basis and for this purpose he proposed establishing an asylum camp, probably in North Africa. Emerson referred briefly to other possibilities of assisting Hitler's victims, through pressure, for example, by the Vatican and the churches, and by the facilitation of remittances through the blockade. Soon afterwards, he raised the further possibility that camps of temporary asylum might be in Allied territory.[76]

It was logical for Emerson to put most emphasis on the immediate need to put resources into expanding current possibilities for saving lives. These possibilities involved escape into neutral territory on the margins of the Nazi empire. As Emerson made clear, such inflows of escapees were to a significant degree dependent on outflows of refugees. He concluded that it was, therefore, crucial to the continuation and expansion of these escape possibilities that governments belonging to the United Nations should make firm offers of asylum, should arrange

[76] Emerson, Note on Measures for Rescue, cited n. 73; Emerson, memorandum, 5 Apr. 1943, sent to Randall, AJ43/37/140.

the removal of refugees from neutral territory where possible and should give assurances to do so after the war.

But the policy-makers within the British government were intent on narrowing the scope of any intended action. The aid they envisaged was effectively limited to refugees in Spain and Switzerland.[77] Nor, Frank Newsam of the Home Office noted, would Jewish refugees from Spain be admitted to either British or US territory, 'since, I imagine, that both countries alike are afraid of being saddled with them indefinitely'; on the other hand, to wait would involve 'interminable delays' and removal to North Africa would commit no one 'either to their next destination or as to their final disposal!'[78] The War Cabinet agreed that the aims of the British delegation to the forthcoming Anglo-American conference on refugees in Bermuda should be to obtain American agreement to three items: the use of North Africa as a haven for refugees from Spain; an approach to United Nations governments to secure an international conference on refugees; and a joint declaration, mainly for the benefit of neutral countries then harbouring refugees, that the United Nations would regard this problem as their responsibility at the end of the war.[79] As for the IGC, British policy makers had never liked it and felt strong reservations about American plans to revive it.

The two governments had decreed that the focus of their conference was to be on 'refugees' rather than 'Jews'. The most important of their reasons for playing down the Jewish aspect of the problem was to discourage pressure to undertake a special effort to save Jews. Any such effort, if successful, would entail a burden neither government would accept – of finding refuge for large numbers of homeless Jews. But the participants knew they were there to discuss Jews, both as potential and as actual refugees, and, except for the purpose of formal or public statements, they made little pretence to the contrary.

The story of the Anglo-American refugee conference, which opened in the seclusion of Bermuda in late April 1943, will be summarised briefly here, in line with the findings of Wasserstein and Wyman. Certain aspects of the discussions will be examined in more detail.[80]

British and American representatives lost little time in confirming that their governments would neither initiate nor support projects of rescue,

77 'Interdepartmental meeting held on 25th March 1943 at the Foreign Office to discuss the Anglo-American conference on refugees', PRO T 161/1446/S51823/1.

78 Newsam, note, 26 Mar. 1943, PRO HO 213/1827.

79 WM 48 (43)7, 5 Apr. 1943, PRO CAB 65/3.

80 This account draws on both the British and American conference minutes; fuller particulars of the proceedings are in Wasserstein, *Britain and Jews*, pp. 183–201, which relies on the British version of the minutes; Wyman, *Abandonment*, pp. 112–20, which relies on the American version.

10 British and American delegates assembled in Bermuda for the Bermuda Refugee Conference in late April 1943. From left to right: George Hall, financial secretary to the Admiralty; Harold W. Dodds, president of Princeton University; Richard Law, minister of state at the Foreign Office and head of the British delegation; Congressman Sol Bloom; Osbert Peake, Home Office under secretary of state.

in the sense of trying to arrange for the release of the Nazis' Jewish captives. Large-scale rescue was rejected as impracticable for the Allies, but it was not considered impossible that the Nazis might offer to release Jews. Indeed, the conference minutes are pervaded by what Wyman calls 'the deep fear the two powers shared that a large exodus of Jews might take place', and this fear helped to determine the restrictions which delegates placed on rescue attempts.[81] British delegates took the lead in articulating the dread of being faced with unwanted Jews and did so in the most explicit terms. Early in the first full session, Richard Law confided that:

> it was thought in London that the most favourable thing that could be done in opening negotiations with Hitler was the receipt of a blank negative to any proposals made by the United Nations – that this clearly was the hope in England.

[81] Wyman, *Abandonment*, p. 114.

He expanded on British fears that Hitler might agree or even offer to release large numbers of Jews, warning:

> if Hitler accepted a proposal to release perhaps millions of unwanted persons, we might find ourselves in a very difficult position. For one thing, Hitler might send a large number of picked agents which we would be forced to take into our own countries. On the other hand, he might say, 'Alright, take a million or two million.' Then because of the shipping problem, we should be made to look exceedingly foolish.[82]

Law did not need to spell out why the latter prospect made his government anxious. If the Allies were offered an opportunity to prevent additional killings of Jews and rejected it, they would face public criticism and might even be accused of complicity in extermination. British objections to making any approach to Hitler to release potential refugees were designed to pre-empt this possibility.[83] Disagreement emerged between the two members of the US delegation present at this discussion, Congressman Sol Bloom, a Jew who represented New York, and Dr Harold Dodds, president of Princeton University, on the question of negotiation: Bloom wished it to be attempted while Dodds advocated a stance of refusing to negotiate with Hitler. Supporting Dodds, an unidentified British delegate said Hitler would not consent to release refugees but would seek to negotiate exchanges and ask for 'things that we could not give'; it was also 'a real problem' to find shipping. The Home Office junior minister Osbert Peake, one of the British delegates, backed up Law's line of argument, speculating that Hitler might offer to release 40 million people (20 or 30 million in the American minutes) who were 'useless mouths' as far as he was concerned. Such an offer, Peake said, would lead to large-scale public pressure to take them, but to attempt this would gravely hinder the war effort; he expressed concern that the British government might be placed in an embarrassing position.[84] The American minutes record Peake's remarks in the following terms:

> To open up negotiations and to have Hitler agree that we can take all we want and have us then to have to say that we cannot take them would place us in an impossible situation. Furthermore, we know that both our governments would never agree to such a recommendation even if this Conference should recommend it to the Intergovernmental Committee.[85]

[82] Morning conference, 20 Apr. 1943, p. 4, Long Mss., Library of Congress, Refugees IGC 1943 (hereafter Long), Box 202, pp. 1–2.

[83] *Ibid.*, pp. 2–4.

[84] Discussion no. 2, 20 Apr., 10.30 am–1 pm, Record of the Discussions at the Bermuda Conference, PRO FO 371/36725, W6785/6711/48, f. 111–12; morning conference, 20 Apr. 1943, p. 4, Long, cited n. 82.

[85] Morning conference, 20 Apr. 1943, p. 4, Long, cited n. 82.

Shortly afterwards Bloom signalled surrender with the remark 'that all he wanted was to somehow not close the door'.[86] But he still requested that the possibility of negotiation be left open.[87]

The delegates agreed to reject all measures proposed for direct aid to Jews under Nazi rule. The final conference report defined 'The Scope of the Problem' as excluding any approaches to Hitler to release Jews. Such approaches, the report stated, envisaged negotiations with Hitler, 'which would be directly contrary to the settled policies of the two Governments concerned and would injure the war effort'; furthermore, such an enquiry 'in equity would have to be extended to all of Hitler's victims who might wish to leave'. The report accordingly recommended, 'That no approach be made to Hitler for the release of potential refugees in Germany or German-occupied territory', but added the qualification that the IGC should bear the question in mind 'in case conditions alter at a later date'.[88] It also excluded, as 'impossible', proposals of exchanging Jews against Nazi internees or prisoners of war or of sending Jews food relief through the blockade.[89]

The delegates now turned to what might be done at the margins. They envisaged limited schemes to assist small numbers of persons who were already out of danger or who might escape to neutral territory in future. Some of these schemes, including certain projects which had already been announced, would be undertaken by the two governments. Other initiatives would be pursued under the auspices of the IGC, which would be revived with an enlarged mandate.

After three days of discussion, Law offered a written summary of the position the conference had reached:

It is clear that any recommendations for direct and immediate action which we can make to our respective governments will be so limited in scope as to bear no relation to the size and urgency of the problem which faces us. It is evident, therefore, that we cannot afford to let the success or failure of the conference be judged by those measures for direct action which we may feel able to recommend. The success of the Bermuda Conference will depend very largely, perhaps almost exclusively, upon the degree of life and authority which can be injected into the Intergovernmental Committee, and upon the speed with which the machinery of the Committee can be set in motion . . .

2. We have been able, in the course of our discussions, to confine the problem to manageable proportions. It is clear that there is nothing that we can recommend and nothing that the Intergovernmental Committee can do which will hold out any possibility of rescue to the millions of potential refugees who exist in German Occupied Europe today. On the other hand there is reason to hope that the Intergovernmental Committee could follow up the work initiated by the

[86] *Ibid.* [87] *Ibid.*, p. 5. [88] Bermuda Report, paras. 8–9, 53.
[89] *Ibid.*, paras. 10–11.

Bermuda Conference and arrange the transfer to other destinations of the many thousands of refugees who have found temporary sanctuary in neutral countries, and that the Committee, by relieving pressure upon those countries, could facilitate the exodus from occupied Europe of many thousands more.[90]

Here Law combined bluntness about what could not be done with avoidance of any commitment by either government to carry out what the conference considered could be done. The delegates had concluded that Jews in the Nazi death trap were beyond the reach of any aid their governments could contemplate. Such humanitarian activities as they envisaged would be directed towards persons who were already refugees or who might escape from occupied to neutral territory. But who would carry these activities out? A revived IGC might provide auspices under which action could be taken. But, as Law did not need to say, only governments could offer asylum, move refugees or give guarantees to neutral governments. The extent to which the two governments were prepared to take these steps was to be a crucial measure of the genuineness of their concern to save Jews.

The inadequacy of the delegates' proposals came under fire when, with no British participants present, the American delegation met with the panel of experts it had brought to Bermuda and explained the conference's key recommendations. One expert, George Backer, who was head of two major Jewish organisations, calculated how few people would be helped and said it was not enough. He argued, 'at least 125,000 have got to be taken out of eastern Europe if this Conference is to yield a result'. The lead in rebuffing Backer's pleas was taken by Senator Scott Lucas, a Democrat from Illinois, who had missed the start of the conference. Lucas, taking up the theme Law and Peake had played on earlier, voiced concern that Hitler might make offers of 'extrusion' of Jews which the Allies would have to decline, and included in his calculations the Jews of Hungary and Italy.[91] In response, Backer offered a glimpse of the reality of the problem, saying that the Polish government-in-exile now estimated that only 10 per cent, or just over 300,000, of Poland's pre-war Jewish population remained alive, but that he would double this to 600,000, 'for the purpose of error on the side of the living'. Wyman considers that on this occasion the American delegation for the first time engaged in a frank debate about the real issues facing the conference. Nonetheless, the debate ended with the crushing of Backer's appeals. The records of this discussion, as of the conference as a whole, convey the powerlessness of any outsider to

[90] Morning conference, 23 Apr. 1943, Long, Box 202, pp. 4–4a.

[91] American delegation meeting, 25 Apr., morning discussion, pp. 54–7, Long, Box 203; Wyman, *Abandonment*, pp. 341–3.

prevent its reaching the outcome – which the two governments had predetermined.

Each delegation was seeking ways of winning the argument with its government's critics. The British side seemed entirely preoccupied in protecting their government from pressure. Reporting to Eden, Law acknowledged that the outcome of the conference 'could never be anything but meagre'. He also asked:

> If neutral shipping is unobtainable, is it really beyond the bounds of possibility that we should find *one* ship? I know all the arguments, but I believe, too, that bread *does* return from the waters and that the story of the Good Samaritan is still valid.[92]

Much later, Law summed up Bermuda as 'a facade for inaction'.[93]

Britain consented reluctantly to the decision made at Bermuda to reactivate the dormant Intergovernmental Committee (IGC). The IGC was to be reorganised and its mandate extended and to acquire new power to receive and spend private and public funds. Its assigned role, while hostilities lasted, was to pursue two modest but worthwhile objectives. The first was to promote resettlement of refugees who were out of immediate danger. The second was to encourage neutral countries, Switzerland and Sweden in particular, to admit potential refugees from enemy territory. But in practice neither objective could be advanced without new commitments to resettle refugees by the governments of the United States and Britain.

The Bermuda delegates were extremely slow over finding destinations for an estimated 6,000–8,000 Jews from central Europe, mostly adult males, whom they felt they should evacuate from Spain.[94] The British delegation advanced reasons that were in part humanitarian in support of such evacuations. They said that clearing Spain was likely to keep open escape routes which the Spanish government might otherwise close. These routes were valued by the British for their own escaping personnel: indeed, in 1944, Randall was to stipulate that routes into Spain should not be developed to help Jews as they might compete with Allied escapers. But what was central to the British recommendation of clearing Spain was the potential impact on public opinion. Spain was seen as a test of Allied resolve. If no action resulted to clear it, British delegates argued, 'public opinion throughout the world would come to the conclusion that the Allies were not making any serious endeavour to deal with the refugee problem'. Clearing the channel into Spain would also test Nazi intentions, since it would

92 Law to Eden, undated, sent from Bermuda, PRO FO 371/36731, W6933/6933/48, circulated as WP (43)191, 3 May 1943, PRO CAB 66/36.

93 Morse, *While Six Million*, p. 63.

94 Bermuda Report, paras. 16–20.

give an opportunity of ascertaining whether the Axis powers would permit any potential refugees in countries now under their control to escape. If they took steps to prevent further emigration, it would be clear to the advocates of relief measures (such as a direct approach to Hitler to release refugees) that their proposals were useless.[95]

This discussion provides further evidence of the extent to which British representatives were preoccupied with fending off the rescue campaigners. It also reveals each delegation's reluctance to commit its own government to expanding the admission of Jews. Each group of delegates was trying to embarrass the government of the other delegation into action, notably over setting up temporary camps in North Africa.

On immigration, the two governments had different systems, but the same objectives. Each clung to the principle of individual assessment of adults for visas. Neither would consider the option of temporary refuge in or near its own territory for adults who had not been individually evaluated. Admission was treated as if it implied permanent residence. Each government wished to go over admissions with a fine-tooth comb. The British said it was to exclude non-war effort admissions. The Americans cited their standard immigration requirements. Each also referred to fears of enemy agents. So, for adults, group visas were not an option. The only category either government would consider for group authorisation was children. Thus different arguments achieved the same result: delay in all cases and the continued exclusion of all but a handful.

Each government's policy for entry to its own territory was thus explicit in excluding humanitarian considerations. The decision to assess admissions according to the current requirements of the receiving country ruled out offers of temporary asylum. Temporary refuge elsewhere – indeed anywhere – might be offered to a limited number who could later go to permanent homes in Palestine – since places were already available under the White Paper, but only to the extent of the unfilled portion of the quota, which then stood at about 34,000.

What of the admission of endangered Jews to the United Kingdom? Actual admissions at this stage of the war were a marginal issue for genuine practical reasons and therefore remained peripheral to the conference. In January 1943 Herbert Morrison had successfully objected to the inclusion in a planned parliamentary statement of a promise that any refugees who succeeded in escaping from German-controlled territory and arrived in the United Kingdom would be admitted. Law agreed: 'It seems a little dangerous' to promise this 'and at the same time to say, as we are doing, that we can't give them visas in

95 British delegation textual proposal, notes of afternoon conference, 21 Apr. 1943, pp. 7–7a, Long, Refugees IGC 1943, Box 203.

order to facilitate their arrival'.[96] Randall agreed with Morrison's advice that accusations that the government's attitude was unsympathetic could be avoided by announcing merely that 'consultations are proceeding with other governments and that no fuller information can be given until those consultations are completed'.[97] In February, Morrison obtained the deletion from a Commons statement of any reference to offers by the government of Palestine to admit 1,000 Jewish children from France, lest it stimulate demands for admissions to the United Kingdom.[98] In the lead-up to Bermuda, the Cabinet Committee noted that it was 'essential to kill the idea that mass immigration to this country and the British Colonies was possible'.[99] Morrison's most generous offer envisaged the entry of a maximum of 2,000 additional refugees, provided they were kept on the Isle of Man as long as he thought necessary. He opposed the entry of 'uncategorised Jews'. Any admissions, he stated, should be part of a United Nations scheme.[100]

The government felt the United Kingdom had admitted as many refugees as it could be expected to receive. To support this stance, a summary of the admissions record prepared for the conference made the numbers look as high as possible and the ban on humanitarian admissions was re-asserted. The current rate of refugee entry was stated to be approximately 800 a month – both authorised and unauthorised – or an annual rate of 10,000.[101] It is unclear how this figure was calculated, but Home Office statistics on refugee admissions show that nearly all were of Allied nationality, suggesting that a mere handful of entrants were Jews, and Maxwell admitted to A. V. Hill MP in mid-April 1943 that the number of Jews who had entered in 1940–2 was 'quite small'.[102] Britain claimed that 'to grant visas more freely would raise false hopes, owing to transport difficulties', and, even if these problems could conceivably be overcome, would add large numbers 'to the population of an already overcrowded island'.[103] At Bermuda, Peake claimed that only 'a vociferous minority' in the United Kingdom wished the government to admit thousands of refugees but that the majority thought 'that quite as many refugees as they could cope with in war

96 Law to Eden, 18 Jan. 1943, PRO FO 371/36650, W1403/49/48.
97 Maxwell to Randall, 18 Jan. 1943, *ibid.*
98 Randall, memorandum, 3 Feb. 1943, *ibid.* The offer also included 200 accompanying adults.
99 JR (43)3rd meeting, 27 Jan. 1943, PRO CAB 95/15.
100 JR (43)1st meeting, 31 Dec. 1942, JR (43)4th meeting, 19 Feb. 1943, JR (43)6th meeting, 1 Apr. 1943, *ibid.*; WM 33 (43)4, 22 Feb. 1943, PRO CAB 65/33.
101 Bermuda Report, paras. 33–5.
102 Copy, Maxwell to A. V. Hill, 16 Apr. 1943, PRO FO 371/36725, W11797/6711/48.
103 Bermuda Report, para. 35.

circumstances had been admitted'.[104] Yet evidence in the government's hands – the Gallup poll findings, the huge volume of letters demanding action – suggests that the opposite may have been nearer the truth.

Echoing the preparations for Evian, the final instructions to Law prior to Bermuda had been that a British offer to accommodate refugees could be made only if the United States made a proposal conditional on similar action by Britain, with an upper limit of 5,000 for the whole British Empire. But as the conference proceedings moved towards their close, criticism prompted reconsideration of this position. In London, Sir David Scott, assistant under secretary of state at the Foreign Office, considered admission of 10,000 to Britain and the empire as the minimum figure to show that the conference had been successful:

> On past form it is very unlikely that HO and DO could be screwed up to such a figure, but it seems ludicrous that this country with a population of nearly 50,000,000 can only absorb 2,000. (It would mean, for instance, on a population basis, no more than 200 for Scotland.) But HO supported by the Ministry of Health and the Security people will be sure to put up a very strong barrage.[105]

Then, delegates telegraphed from Bermuda the news that the American delegation had said it would be helpful if Britain offered to admit several hundred stateless refugees. Any initiative at this juncture required a War Cabinet decision to change the delegation's instructions. At its next meeting, the War Cabinet authorised instructions confirming that Britain would be prepared to make an effort to admit an unspecified number of stateless refugees, provided the United States was prepared to do the same.[106] But all the final conference report offered on future United Kingdom admissions was generalities. It asserted that persons willing and able to render useful service to the war effort experienced little difficulty in securing visas. Beyond this, it contemplated that limited numbers of persons who could not fit into the approved categories could be offered temporary refuge.[107] Following Bermuda, Britain authorised three new categories of entry: parents of persons in the forces; parents of unaccompanied children; and enemy aliens willing to serve in the forces and acceptable to them. These measures had been under consideration before the conference. Their impact was numerically insignificant and the government was slow to implement them.[108] Rathbone pointed out in her leaflet, *Continuing Terror*, that six months later only fifty-two visas had been authorised under all three cate-

[104] Discussion no. 8, 24 Apr. 1943, 10.15 am, PRO FO 371/36725, W6785/6711/48, ff. 77–84.
[105] Scott, memorandum, 25 Apr. 1943, PRO FO 371/36696, W6527/20/48.
[106] WM 59 (43)3, 27 Apr. 1943, PRO CAB 65/34.
[107] Bermuda Report, para. 35.
[108] Dexter to Kullmann, 28 June 1943, AJ43/8/994.

gories.[109] For the rest of the war, the Home Office's position was simple: more Jewish refugees were not wanted. It also steadfastly resisted pressure to offer visas for the United Kingdom as a way of assisting Jews to enter other territory where they would be safe.

By contrast, permanent admissions to Palestine up to the limit allowed under the White Paper required no new commitment as to overall numbers. The British authorities decided to reserve the remaining 29,000 or so certificates for the benefit of children, plus some accompanying adults. A general ban on adults was maintained even though few children were actually able to benefit in the prevailing conditions of persecution and the government knew that there were already facilities for many more children than were able to take advantage of them.[110]

The government's concern to show commitment to action was now largely focused around what could be done for persons destined for Palestine. The colonial secretary, Oliver Stanley, worried that the only practical current proposal to help Jews – the plan to move women and children from occupied Europe to Palestine – would be a 'damp squib'. He wished the government to take 'some fairly drastic step' and argued for the appointment of a 'pushful individual on the spot' – to sort out problems in Turkey.[111] Eden agreed to this. The ambassador in Turkey acquiesced reluctantly, insisting, however, 'in view of Turkish feeling towards Jews, any limited usefulness which appointee might have would be completely prejudiced if he were himself a Jew'.[112] Eden had reservations about Stanley's proposal but said, 'it is most important that we should avoid any reproach that we are not doing all we can to rescue these unfortunate people'.[113]

Eden's remark illustrates the negative character of British policy at this juncture. The object was not to rescue Jews but to avoid the reproach that Britain was not doing all it could to rescue Jews. The priority, therefore, was to reduce public pressure for action and avoid criticism of inaction. Bermuda was seen as a success for British policy. The conference decisions provided a rationale for refusing to act on demands for rescue. They also enabled the government to appear to be trying to ameliorate the position of refugees. This package was enough to keep the rescue campaigners at bay.

The Bermuda delegates had resolved to conceal their detailed

109 NCRNT, *Continuing Terror* (1944), p. 13, copy in PRO FO 371/42751, W2859/83/48.
110 Emerson, Note on Measures for Rescue, cited n. 73.
111 Stanley to Eden, 14 Apr. 1943, PRO CO 733/438/14.
112 Angora to FO, no. 920, 13 May 1943, *ibid.*
113 Eden to Stanley, 20 Apr. 1943, *ibid.*

conclusions from public knowledge, agreeing that the written joint conference report would be kept secret. The War Cabinet, anxious that the forthcoming Commons debate on refugee policy would contain a disproportionate number of speeches 'by members holding extreme views in favour of the free admission of refugees to this country', invited the whips to arrange interventions by members 'who would put a more balanced point of view'.[114] The debate, on 19 May 1943, was timed to coincide with a US Department of State press release. Ministers revealed the two governments' ban on any negotiation with Hitler and confirmed that their plans extended only to aiding refugees. Eden summed up the government's position:

I do not believe it is possible to rescue more then a few until final victory is won . . . I do not believe that until the war is over we can deal with more than the fringe, and it is the fringe with which we have to deal.[115]

Rescue campaigners, realising that the burden of policy towards the Jews of Europe had not altered, expressed their frustration. Following the Commons debate, Bishop Bell of Chichester, in a letter published in the *Manchester Guardian*, wrote, 'It is impossible to conceal one's disappointment at the meagreness of the results of the Bermuda Conference as so far reported.'[116] But the pressure on the government weakened. An intercepted telegram from Rabbi Maurice Perlzweig, a leading British member of the World Jewish Congress, recognised that 'nothing whatever is being done or is even being contemplated for the millions of Jews who still survive in the territories under Hitler's immediate control', but admitted that he was becoming resigned to it.[117] US Assistant Secretary of State Breckinridge Long, who supervised America's restrictive visa policy, shared this intelligence with the British. It was offered as evidence that the line the two governments had taken at Bermuda was gaining acceptance and that less pressure on the issue might be expected from activists like Perlzweig.[118] The government's withholding of hard information, notably the written conference report, obstructed efforts to campaign against British policy. Thus, in late June, a report that Congressman Bloom had pronounced himself satisfied by the outcome of Bermuda was forwarded to Emerson by Schiff, with the comment that he thought it unwise for organisations like

[114] WM 67 (43)5, 10 May 1943, PRO CAB 65/34.
[115] Eden, *Hansard*, House of Commons, vol. 398, col. 1200, 19 May 1943; the debate covers cols. 1117–1204.
[116] G. K. A. Bell, Bishop of Chichester, letter to editor, *Manchester Guardian*, 22 May 1943, p. 4.
[117] M. Perlzweig to A. Easterman, 25 May 1943, papers of the World Jewish Congress (British section), Institue of Jewish Affairs, London.
[118] Long, memorandum, 4 June 1943, Long, Refugees IGC 1943, Box 203.

the NCRNT to engage in agitation until 'something definite' was known about the conference decisions and the action to be taken by the IGC.[119]

What might the prospects of success have been if the Allies had attempted to extract Jews from the Nazis' clutches? It is not possible to say conclusively whether any genuine opportunities might have resulted from a policy which permitted negotiation. Given what is now known of the Hitler regime's dogged pursuit of the systematic murder of Jews between the time the Allies learned of it and Germany's defeat, any chance of success in negotiating the release of substantial numbers appears unimaginable.

But the British and United States governments' insight into Nazi priorities was incomplete. They could not know whether circumstances would arise in which the regime might offer to yield up large numbers of Jewish prisoners. Just in case they should ever be confronted by such an offer, they made strenuous efforts to guard against being obliged to respond to it. They invoked the Allied ban on negotiation with the enemy to justify a position of refusing to negotiate. Their purpose was to eliminate any risk of being saddled with a large-scale exodus of Jews from enemy-controlled Europe. The two governments refused to make substantial new asylum commitments to Jews who had a genuine chance of escaping. The concern to restrict their responsibilities to Jews who might reach safety informed the attitude of Anglo-American policy-makers to every possibility of Jews escaping, whether remote or real, and whether or not it could conceivably lengthen the war. This overriding concern, which pre-dated Bermuda, had the capacity to blight the few constructive plans which emerged from the conference.

The second half of 1943

As a result of the Bermuda conference's decision to revive the IGC, Emerson, as the IGC's director, had been cast in a more prominent role. Since Emerson's selection by the Foreign Office in 1938 as a safe choice for the post, he had not embarrassed the government by pressure to be more generous. He delighted Refugee Department officials in March 1942 by expressing views which echoed their fears that, if Jews believed they could not in future live in most European countries, there would be an uncontrollable post-war exodus.[120] Emerson had even gone so far as to protest to Randall at the 'excessive liberality' of a proposed change of

[119] Schiff to Emerson, 21 June 1943, AJ43/37/140.
[120] Emerson to Taylor, 5 Mar. 1942, *ibid.*

British policy, in the wake of the *Struma* disaster, of allowing illegal immigrants who reached Turkey to proceed to Palestine.[121]

A few months later, Emerson, deeply shocked by the news of the Nazi programme to exterminate the Jews, started to try to galvanise the United Nations into humanitarian action. His attempts to persuade British policy-makers to adopt a more generous approach led to increasing antagonism in his relations with the Foreign Office. After Bermuda, he complained on discovering that his draft proposals had never reached the American delegates. Randall chose to interpret this as wounded *amour-propre*.[122] But Emerson's concern was not for himself. He felt that at Bermuda the two governments had ignored the suggestions and betrayed the hopes of those concerned to save Jews from murder in Europe. This is apparent from his office files and from efforts he made to resurrect the possibility of more extensive activity than that contemplated by either government. Myron Taylor, the American representative on the IGC, was equally dissatisfied. Emerson and Taylor agreed to revive proposals Taylor had submitted in March 1943 during Eden's visit to Washington, setting out steps the US government might take to rescue Jews.[123] They now proposed that both governments should permit refugees to enter some part of their territory as places of temporary safety and make a commitment regarding places of permanent settlement. They should also meet the costs of transport and maintenance. As late as June 1943, Emerson tried to interest the IGC's chairman, Lord Winterton, in this programme, saying he considered Taylor's views 'very sound indeed'. Winterton was flatly dismissive. Emerson decided not to raise the matter with Randall, perhaps aware that it would be pointless.[124] In fact Randall had been forewarned by US State Department officials against Taylor's attempted interventions in refugee policy.[125]

It was difficult for Emerson to achieve anything. He was undermined and obstructed by the officials and ministers to whom he was supposed to turn for support. He took up the tasks allocated to the IGC at Bermuda, but both governments held up progress. In any event, Anglo-American policy severely constricted the scope of what he was allowed to undertake. In August 1943 he admitted to Myron Taylor that the opportunities for action were very limited. He said that the IGC would

121 Emerson to Randall, 8 May 1942, AJ43/22/122.
122 Randall to Hayter, no. 3320, 17 May 1943, PRO FO 371/36725, W6711/6711/48.
123 Taylor to Emerson, 25 May 1943, enclosing note dated 17 Mar. 1943, AJ43/37/140.
124 Emerson to Winterton, 30 June 1943, *ibid.*
125 Randall, minute, 10 May 1943, PRO FO 371/36726, W7147/6731/48.

be able to develop new opportunities as they arose, but he felt its most important role would be to solve post-war problems.[126]

During this period Emerson showed industry and persistence on behalf of Jews trapped in Nazi-controlled territory. He took up the predicaments of individuals, but the scope for saving lives was minimal. He showed sympathy for cases involving claims to British nationality, which – it was believed – could protect Jews in danger of deportation to certain death in the east. First a legal ruling always had to be obtained from the government on the application of arcane technicalities of British nationality law to the facts of each case. Such research was conducted at a leisurely pace and its conclusions were almost invariably negative. In most cases, by the time the legal position was established it was of academic interest, as the people affected had already been deported.

One of these cases concerned the Russian-born wife of a Polish-born refugee from Germany who had entered Britain shortly before the war. He was serving as a private in the British army. His wife was in the Netherlands, facing imminent deportation. She sent him repeated requests for evidence of his British citizenship, to establish that she was a British subject – this, she hoped, might save her. The Home Office reported that the soldier was not yet entitled even to apply, and that, even had he been granted citizenship, his wife would be unable to become a citizen, being in the Netherlands under enemy control and thus unable to complete the declaration wives had been required to make since 1933. The Refugee Department concluded that, since both parties were stateless, it could not ask the Swiss to intervene, but it advised the soldier to approach the Jewish Agency to place his wife's name on a list of persons wishing to immigrate to Palestine. Subsequently, when news came of the wife's deportation from Westerbork to the east, Randall thought it should not be passed on to her husband.[127] Another case, which turned on recondite provisions for the revocation of citizenship, involved the wife and youngest child of a man surnamed Kitchener. Although British-born, in 1918 Kitchener, then aged thirteen and living in Germany, had been lawfully included in the revocation of his father's naturalisation. He later became a tailor and married a German Jewish woman. Although refused a visa to return to Britain as a stateless person in 1937, he succeeded in entering just before the war and was serving in the Pioneer Corps. His wife remained in Germany, apparently unaware that she had not acquired British citizenship. The

[126] Emerson to Taylor, 6 Aug. 1943, AJ43/22/123.

[127] Case of Samuel and Sara Rachel Rotner, 12 Aug. 1943–16 June 1944, AJ43/9/1098; correspondence, 20 Apr.–7 July 1944, PRO FO 371/42776, W6703/616/48.

investigation into this family's national status was launched in April 1943; in August, the Swiss reported that the wife and child had been deported to the east in March 1943.[128]

What had become of the programme planned at Bermuda? The Refugee Department was under pressure to have some progress to show. The Treasury had offered assistance and Waley explored ways of providing finance. He considered the United Kingdom should pay half the IGC budget:

> We are told that Congress would not vote money for refugees unless we put up an equal amount. I think, for the sake of our influence on policy and need to show parliament that we are taking our part we should agree to share expenses equally with the United States Government.[129]

Yet the Treasury was slow over setting up the financial arrangements. The Americans also held up progress. In June 1943 the Foreign Office told the Washington embassy to prod the Americans into action, saying that the current deadlock should be broken without delay,

> if colour is not to be given to the already widespread complaints in this country that neither His Majesty's Government nor the United States Government take the refugee problem seriously . . . refugee enthusiasts here are suggesting that nothing effective has been done, or is even intended. If the provision of a camp in North Africa has, owing to American objections, to be finally abandoned, if the scheme for evacuating Bulgarian Jewish children is wrecked, and if, finally, there is no early meeting of the Intergovernmental Executive with a practical agenda, the bottom falls out of the Bermuda report.[130]

From Washington, William Hayter reassured Randall that, since Bermuda, Backer had been

> quiet and well behaved . . . no public attacks on Bermuda. Lucas and Reams, whom I saw together at a party at the Embassy the other day, were congratulating each other on their cleverness in having shut Backer's mouth. I am not quite sure how they managed it; since they refused to let him into any meeting they can have no hold on him on the grounds that anything he said would be betrayal of inside information. Personally, I regard him as a much-abused man.[131]

Bermuda's secrets were safe for the moment.

What of the assurance to neutrals, promised at Bermuda? A crucial point, which Emerson had spelled out to Randall prior to the conference, was that the assurance had to go beyond saying that refugees

[128] Correspondence, 10 Apr.–31 Aug. 1943, PRO FO 372/3661, T2609/5457/10340/334/378.

[129] Waley to Sir Wilfred Eady, 24 June 1943, Waley to Randall, 1 June 1943, correspondence, 10 May–24 June 1943, PRO T 161/1446/S51823/1.

[130] FO to Washington, nos. 3651, 3652, 2 June 1943, PRO FO 371/36726, W7424/6731/48.

[131] Hayter to Randall, 19 June 1943, PRO FO 371/36726, W9480/6731/48.

would be repatriated after the war. Not all would be repatriable. What neutrals required to expand refuge was a clear commitment to a post-war solution of the refugee problem.[132] Switzerland, the one neutral refuge bordering on Germany, had closed its border with France in August 1942 against Jews fleeing deportation, turning back many thousands. Just before Bermuda, Emerson said Switzerland was 'anxious to obtain assurances that she will be relieved of her burden after the end of hostilities'.[133] Although the United States and Britain did provide funds to maintain refugees in neutral countries during the war, they would not undertake to find permanent homes for refugees admitted by neutral countries bordering on Axis territory. Yet, this issue was incomparably more important to the neutrals than the cost of maintenance or the supply of provisions, as both governments well knew. Indeed, the Bermuda conference report had acknowledged that the future of refugees after the war was 'the aspect of the question which was understood to be of most concern' to neutral governments who had received refugees in the past and might also in future: 'If they could be assured that they would eventually be relieved of this burden by the return of refugees to their homes, it would be a great encouragement to them.' Yet both governments shied away from such assurances. The report signalled as much in its stated plans for a draft declaration. Displaced Allied nationals would get commitments to re-admission, it promised, but all it said regarding persons from enemy territories was that 'it would be necessary to announce the intention of creating conditions in such territories which would enable the refugees to return to them'.[134] After Bermuda, the War Cabinet endorsed the same formula.[135] The two governments' blatant refusal to address the non-repatriability issue greatly diminished the value of the exercise. Thus did the problem of permanent refuge continue to restrict the possibilities of aid to the Jews: prior to the Holocaust the reluctance to accept Jews on a permanent basis had restricted the grant of refuge from persecution; now the same reluctance militated against the provision of temporary refuge from mass murder.

Emerson was unable to make much impact on the question of the declaration to neutrals which had been taken out of his hands as a diplomatic matter and dealt with by the US State Department and the British Foreign Office. The neutrals were still admitting refugees;

[132] Emerson, Note on Measures for Rescue, cited n. 73.

[133] Emerson (in capacity as High Commissioner for Refugees), report, 'International Assistance to Refugees', 19 Apr. 1943, published Aug. 1943 by League of Nations, Geneva, official number: C.19.M.19.1943XII, PRO FO 371/36667, W14316/49/48.

[134] Bermuda Report, para. 24.

[135] WM 67 (43) Annex 5, 10 May 1943, PRO CAB 65/34.

Foreign Office officials interpreted this fact as evidence that there was no urgent need to issue the declaration. By November 1943 the Soviet government had finally agreed to a draft declaration in which Allied nations promised to re-admit their own displaced nationals. The declaration also contained a commitment to a policy of ensuring conditions which would enable displaced persons to return home at the end of the war. But the commitment extended only to repatriable refugees – those able and willing to return to their own countries. Limited thus, it was, as a member of the IGC's Secretariat emphasised, unlikely to satisfy neutrals' apprehensions

> regarding those who are not willing, e.g. some of the German, Austrian and perhaps Polish refugees. It is however understood that the American, British and Soviet governments would not give a more general undertaking.[136]

Kullmann of the IGC confirmed in early 1944 that the main concern of the Swiss was the removal of the non-returnable refugees after the war.[137] Furthermore, without a commitment to resettle unrepatriable refugees, the declaration was worth little to the IGC, which would be responsible for the needs of unrepatriables other than relief.

Further limitations resulted from requests by Allied governments for tighter wording in respect of the return of persons previously given refuge in their territory. The Netherlands government suggested saying that each government would favourably consider return 'in so far as is compatible with the requirements of national security and economy'.[138] Walker commented that the Allied governments' aim was to

> be able to exclude anyone they chose. This will not please Miss Rathbone or her Jewish supporters – nor will it please the Swedes or the Swiss who will suspect that they may be landed with some inconvenient and unassimilable people. Indeed it might be objected that in the form desired by e.g. the French and the Dutch, the declaration will be of little value.[139]

He might have added that if anything dictated British policy on the declaration it was this fear of being 'landed'.[140]

Emerson sought to maintain the appearance of non-discrimination so dear to the Refugee Department. He denied Schiff's request for a closer association for his committee with the IGC, saying he did not wish to give the impression abroad that the IGC existed mainly for the benefit of Jews and that its proceedings were dominated or influenced by Jewish

136 J. G. Sillem to Winterton, 30 Nov. 1943, AJ43/27/212.

137 Kullmann, Report on G. G. Kullmann's visit to Switzerland, Jan.–Feb. 1944, Apr. 1944, PRO FO 371/42745, W6156/26/48.

138 Draft Declaration to Neutrals, n.d., PRO FO 371/36724, W17928/6532/48.

139 Walker, minute, 2 Feb. 1944, FO to Washington, 6 Feb. 1944, *ibid.*

140 See JR (43)26, Note by the Minister of State, 3 Dec. 1944, PRO CAB 95/15, para. 4.

members.[141] He thought it correct for the IGC to assume that, because of the general persecution of the Jews, all Jews in enemy territory came within its mandate, but chose not to reveal this publicly for fear of misunderstandings with Allied governments concerned about their non-Jewish nationals.[142] But Emerson's public compliance with the Foreign Office was accompanied by increasing disillusion. In late 1943 he lost patience with Randall, who was holding up arrangements for the IGC to channel relief funds to remnant groups of Jews in Europe and he eventually decided to bypass Randall altogether.[143]

Emerson was the confidant of governments, civil servants, refugee organisations and individual refugees. His staff was small and he was in a position to move informally and swiftly, should the occasion arise. But by late 1943 he was acutely conscious that the IGC had yet to produce any substantive results.[144]

Eventually, shifts in American policy created new possibilities. In late 1943, rescue agitation in the United States, reinforced by pressure within the American government, exposed the State Department's efforts to suppress information about the implementation of the Nazis' 'Final Solution' and the State Department's policy of ruling out rescue efforts as well as the evasions its officials were using to cover up their actions. The resulting pressure, especially from the secretary of the Treasury, Henry Morgenthau, Junior, and US Treasury officials, led Roosevelt in January 1944 to establish the War Refugee Board (WRB). The new agency's sole purpose was the rescue of Jews. The realisation that what underpinned British opposition to rescue efforts was not economic warfare concerns but political motives, expressed by the Foreign Office as 'the difficulty of disposing of any considerable number of Jews should they be rescued', had horrified the US Treasury group. Its members argued for a different order of priorities, proposing to US Secretary of State Cordell Hull

> that we cut the Gordian Knot *now* by advising the British that we are going to take immediate action to facilitate the escape of Jews from Hitler and *then* discuss what can be done in the way of finding them a more permanent refuge.[145]

Morgenthau told Hull of his opinion that 'due to the attitude of the

[141] Schiff to Emerson, 20 Aug. 1943, Emerson, memorandum, 31 Aug. 1943, AJ43/22/144.
[142] Emerson to Cabot Coville, 24 and 25 Dec. 1943, AJ43/23/222.
[143] Emerson to Randall, 2 Dec. 1943, Emerson to George Hall, 29 Dec. 1943, AJ43/52/255.
[144] Emerson to Taylor, 26 Nov. 1943, AJ43/22/123.
[145] Morgenthau Diaries, Franklin D. Roosevelt Presidential Library, Hyde Park, New York, vol. 688II, pp. 143–6.

British Foreign Office the Jews had been locked up in Europe and were not permitted to escape when there were avenues of escape'.[146] Thus Morgenthau and the officials who were soon to be assigned the key role in promoting rescue within the US government had become deeply suspicious of British intentions.

Developments in rescue policy from early 1944

In Britain, the establishment of the new American agency was watched with envy in the Treasury and apprehension in the Foreign Office. The WRB's planned activities in Europe had implications for foreign exchange and for the blockade. The impression that the US government was preparing to give the WRB twice the proposed operational funds of the IGC for the whole of 1944 led the Treasury's C. H. M. Wilcox to suggest that, if the American administration was for political reasons anxious to help the Jews in Europe, it might help Britain out by providing the foreign exchange needed for the IGC's relief operations.[147] According to a report from Washington to the Foreign Office, John Pehle, the WRB's head, was 'inclined to be impatient with what he regards as previous languid methods in dealing with the problem in London. His great interest is in rescuing Jews of Europe from annihilation.' Pehle himself was described as 'a disinterested and not very well informed enthusiast'.[148] As for Refugee Department officials, they regarded the WRB with resentment from the outset.[149]

Ostensibly, the establishment of this new agency signalled an unprecedented commitment by the US government to rescue. Foreign Office observers were sceptical, preferring to see the WRB as a political publicity stunt. But these officials realised that its establishment ended the formal Anglo-American consensus on a policy of inaction and put the British government under pressure. As one senior member of the Foreign Office noted: 'The creation of this new very high-level body of which the Secretaries of State and of War are members is in itself a not negligible form of pressure.'[150] Would the WRB's arrival on the scene produce any change in British policy?

[146] *Ibid.*, pp. 82–165; Wyman, *Abandonment*, pp. 178–206; Breitman and Kraut, *American Refugee Policy*, pp. 187–8.

[147] Wilcox to H. W. R. Wade, 10 Jan. 1944, PRO T 231/83.

[148] Halifax to FO, no. 686, 10 Feb. 1944, PRO FO 371/42727, W2217/16/48.

[149] Wasserstein, *Britain and Jews*, pp. 323–7; Tony Kushner, 'Rules of the Game: Britain, America and the Holocaust in 1944', *Holocaust and Genocide Studies* 5 (1990), 381–402.

[150] O. E. Sargent to Sir Frederick Bovenschen, 12 Feb. 1944, PRO FO 371/42727, W782/16/48.

At first, the Foreign Office's only concession was presentational, based on the need to appear to be co-operating with the Americans' new approach. Officials accepted that political reasons – the importance of Anglo-American relations and of maintaining British prestige within the alliance – required them to show more support for rescue. For example, as the Refugee Department became increasingly desperate about Britain's continuing failure to establish a token refugee camp in Libya, Walker suggested Syria as a possibility: 'We are under great and increasing pressure from the Americans, not to mention the "perishing" Miss Rathbone. Extra accommodation must be found, if only as "eyewash".'[151] Randall began to worry that Britain might find itself cast in the role of obstructing rescue.[152] Refugee Department officials tended to see the WRB as a rival organisation and tried to cut it down to size. They even obstructed its work. For example, in February 1944 Randall instructed posts abroad to co-operate with the WRB, but undermined these messages with a simultaneous despatch attacking the WRB's credibility and indicating that ambassadors need merely make a show of co-operation. He also displayed a partisan protectiveness towards the IGC, expressing concern that the WRB's claims threatened to supplant or eclipse the IGC and its less spectacular contributions.[153]

The consequences of this competitive attitude were not all negative. The same officials who had energetically opposed rescue now began to feel that Britain's national prestige required support of the IGC to enable it to match the WRB. They also contemplated the possibility that political considerations justified a more active approach on Britain's part. Already, they were asking the Ministry of Economic Warfare not to persist in objecting to proposals for relief to Jews 'in a position of exceptional hardship or danger' to which Allied governments, above all the Americans, attached particular importance.[154] But the impetus to transform the IGC into an effective organisation would have to come from elsewhere.

The WRB's action, taken without consulting Britain, in licensing the remission of $100,000 to the International Red Cross (IRC) to spend on goods for Jews in enemy territory provoked Randall at the beginning of March 1944 into an open display of hostility both to the WRB and to the principle of rescue itself. He defined rescue as:

schemes of secret passage across frontiers into neutral countries and the

[151] Walker, minute, 9 Feb. 1944, PRO FO 371/42727, W2971/16/48.
[152] Randall, minutes, 29 and 31 Jan. 1944, PRO FO 371/42727, W1381/16/48.
[153] Correspondence, 1 Feb.–18 Mar. 1944, PRO FO 371/42727, W1657/16/48; Randall, minute, 3 Mar. 1944, PRO FO 371/42727, W3340/16/48.
[154] Randall to E. H. Bliss, 21 Jan. 1944, PRO FO 371/42771, W701/318/48.

provision of money and goods to persons, principally Jews, in enemy territories, to enable them to bribe Nazi guards, etc. and so escape.

Such schemes, he objected, were 'bound to conflict with our economic warfare policy', but the WRB, under the direction of Pehle, who was 'openly impatient at the meagre results in rescue achieved so far', was determined to push on with them. Randall said that, despite the absence of a concrete WRB programme at that stage, he sought urgent consideration of the question of principle involved:

are HMG, in order to keep step with the United States government's refugee policy, prepared to modify their economic warfare rules and sanction the association of our secret organisations in neutral countries with the similar American organisations for the purpose of bringing large parties of refugees out of enemy territory?[155]

Accordingly, the Cabinet Committee was summoned to discuss the possibility of 'serious differences' with the Americans over refugee policy. In preparation for the meeting, Randall drafted a paper for Eden setting out the 'three disagreeable alternatives' facing the British in reacting to the WRB's licensing activities:

If we object we risk being held up by the War Refugee Board, which is engaged on a publicity campaign, as obstacles to a humanitarian measure which would probably save Jewish lives. If we merely acquiesce, we allow the US Govt to get the credit for a piece of rescue work which critics will say should have been attempted long ago, while if we, too, agree to remit money to the IRC, we may be committed to a relaxation of our financial blockade which may prove of real advantage to the enemy.[156]

Randall already had an indication of how the Ministry of Economic Warfare might react, for in late 1943 E. H. Bliss had said he was inclined to allow exchange transactions for the rescue of Jews from France and Romania, since any financial benefit to the enemy appeared to be minimal and 'the proposal envisages the rescue of a considerable number of Jews at a fairly small cost per head'.[157] Now, in reply to Randall, Bliss played down economic warfare objections to rescue schemes: 'the benefit to the enemy is limited and ceases when rescue is effected', he said, and MEW was 'prepared to look at such schemes on their merits'.[158] The ministry was less keen on schemes involving maintenance of potential refugees in enemy territory pending rescue, but recognised that the WRB might argue that they deserved equally generous treatment.

155 Randall to Bliss and Playfair, 1 Mar. 1944, PRO FO 371/42731, W3199/17/48.
156 JR (44)4, Note by the Secretary of State for Foreign Affairs, 10 Mar. 1944, PRO CAB 95/15.
157 Bliss to Walker, 26 Nov. 1943, PRO FO 371/36747, W16460/15864/48.
158 Bliss to Randall, 3 Mar. 1944, PRO FO 371/42731, W3483/17/48.

At this juncture two crucial developments occurred. The government was asked to back an established rescue scheme just as the IGC finally obtained some funds. Playfair had spent months sorting out the IGC's finances. A protracted wrangle had taken place over whether nations other than Britain and the United States should contribute to IGC administrative expenses. Treasury officials had also battled with Emerson over whether the two governments alone should foot the bill for IGC operational expenses. By late 1943 the IGC still had no funds to spend on actual operations.[159] Since in practice only the British and the Americans would contribute, Playfair said he thought they should pay 'at once, to put some cash in the kitty'.[160] In December, the Treasury completed the financial arrangements to enable the IGC to begin functioning. The two governments accepted Playfair's proposal that to launch its work the IGC should have a capital fund of £1,000,000 for operational expenses, including contingencies. Each would guarantee half this sum. Playfair suggested obtaining contributions from other states, but these would only have the status of voluntary donations. Officials decided that Britain's contribution should, being controversial, undergo the scrutiny of a vote in Parliament.[161] The Commons approved the first instalment on 1 March 1944.[162]

The debate on the IGC grant showed that the WRB's creation had boosted pressure for a British contribution to rescue. Many MPs saw the WRB as a salutary challenge to British inactivity. Its establishment provoked questions about the adequacy of the resources and machinery nearer home. Rathbone offered particularly severe criticisms of the pitifully small resources of the IGC, compared with the vast need for rescue, and called for a new organ of British government to co-operate with the IGC, 'so as to secure the full-time concentration of first-class minds on this question'.[163] Sidney Silverman suggested that the initiative was passing from London to Washington and appealed for rescue efforts.[164] For the government, Law defended the adequacy of the existing governmental machinery in Britain, knowing all too well that its main use had been to deflect demands to save Jews. He sidestepped the central complaint of the government's critics – the lack of commitment to action.[165]

[159] Correspondence, 25 June–27 Oct. 1943, PRO T 161/1446/S51823/1; correspondence, 3–27 Nov. 1943, PRO T 161/1446/S51823/2.
[160] Playfair to Wilcox, 27 Nov. 1943, PRO T 161/1446/S51823/2.
[161] Correspondence, 30 Nov.–17 Dec. 1943, 10–28 Jan. 1944., *ibid.*
[162] *Hansard*, House of Commons, vol. 397, cols. 1458–95, 1 Mar. 1944.
[163] Rathbone, *ibid.*, col. 1471. [164] Silverman, *ibid.*, cols. 1481–3.
[165] Law, *ibid.*, cols. 1490–4.

At least the IGC now had funds. How should they be spent? At this moment an opportunity appeared of contributing to rescue operations in Europe. Emerson asked the government for funds to rescue Jews and some gentiles in Poland. He was proposing a scheme to expand the activities of Saly Mayer, a leading Swiss Jew who was the AJDC representative in Switzerland. Emerson's deputy, Kullmann, had recently returned from Switzerland reporting that Mayer had evolved a system of rescue based on local currency raised on credit inside occupied Europe. These funds were used to maintain and, where possible, bring out, Jews who were underground. The Jews were provided with false identities to enable them to escape into neutral territory. Mayer was operating this system without any written confirmation from the AJDC. Emerson requested further sums, not in the form of cash, but in the form of guarantees to Mayer for his promises to pay in dollars after the war. He also asked that Mayer should be entitled to make such promises in writing. The scheme was operated within enemy territory by the Jewish underground in Poland, apparently under Polish government auspices. Money was spent mainly on assisting escape from concentration camps, subsequent concealment and aiding escape abroad, for example, to Hungary and Romania. A set of false documents apparently cost about $400 and getting a person out of a concentration camp about $500. Non-Jews as well as Jews could benefit from these activities. The small scale of the work could be expanded if greater resources were available and the Polish government would reportedly welcome additional support.[166] Joseph Schwartz of the AJDC visited London and discussed his organisation's needs with Emerson, including an urgent need for more money in France. He suggested that the IGC could act as a conduit for the funds of both the United States and British governments if they agreed to help.[167]

As the blockade authorities were concerned that guarantees regarding Mayer's credit might become negotiable, the minister of economic warfare suggested that Emerson and Kullmann see Playfair, who was responsible for authorising IGC expenditure on operations, to discuss how to overcome this hurdle. They discussed their proposals with Playfair on 9 March 1944. Later that day Playfair, in a lengthy memorandum, advised Waley that he had concluded that the British govern-

[166] Emerson, memorandum, 'Rescue, concealment and preservation of refugees in the occupied and satellite countries of Europe', 1 Mar. 1944, AJ43/52/255; Emerson, two memoranda, 1 Mar. 1944, memorandum, 10 Mar. 1944, PRO FO 371/42745, W3921/26/44; Playfair to Waley, memorandum, 'The IGC and the rescue of Jews in Europe', 9 Mar. 1944, PRO T 161/1446/S51823/2.

[167] IGC memorandum, Visit of Mr Schwartz, 7 Mar. 1944, AJ43/52/255.

ment should back the scheme.[168] He said he had decided that the payments proposed would come within the IGC's mandate and he thought the IGC should fund the scheme's expansion. Playfair emphasised that Britain was under pressure as a result of the setting up of the WRB and that Pehle, the WRB's head, would not be impressed by Foreign Office complaints that the WRB's precipitate action in licensing the remittance of $100,000 to the International Red Cross for the relief of Jews in enemy territory was in breach of the financial blockade. As regards the Foreign Office's approach, Playfair characterised it as

> one of rather frustrated protest backed up by little more than repetition of arguments already used. What I have learned today makes me feel sure that we must adopt a more positive line. In saying this I am rather influenced by the fact that so far the IGC has accomplished little and I think that His Majesty's Government, who have been nothing if not prudent over the matter, may have contributed to this (mea culpa as much as anyone's at my level). Mr Morgenthau, with Mr Pehle's help, may be tactless and he may be doing wrong things from the point of view of the financial blockade, but it remains a fact that we have promised to do our best to help these people in any way consistent with the prosecution of the war (these are actually President Roosevelt's words) and I am by no means sorry to see a little active needling done by energetic men in the United States. Mr Pehle is a nice man and an efficient one. I do not think we must blame him too much if he feels that his first duty is not to Anglo-American co-operation nor to the British conception of a financial blockade but to the Jews in Europe. If we are to get anywhere with him on the blockade points we must first convince him that we are as anxious to help as he is.

Playfair emphasised the record of success of Mayer's credit scheme in saving Jews: 'They are refugees from their home and their identity and I was assured with great warmth that they are nearly all men (and women and children) who, but for this service, would already have been deported and in many cases killed or allowed to die.' The first argument Playfair put forward for giving the government's financial support to the scheme was humanitarian: 'the IGC will at least be doing something in a large way and something which in my submission is infinitely valuable. They are, in effect, buying lives for a not wild expenditure of money.' Secondly, enabling the IGC to back rescue by means of credit would, he claimed, be less damaging to the financial blockade and to Mayer's operations than an inflow of cash. He reported that the cash the WRB had been allowing into occupied Europe was particularly disliked by Mayer, because, if cash payments became frequent, his source of credit would soon dry up. Credit, he advised, could be allowed into enemy territory in much larger sums than cash. Mayer was getting $6,000,000

168 Selborne to Eden, memorandum, 8 Mar. 1944, PRO FO 371/42745, W4320/26/48; Playfair, memorandum, cited n. 166. Subsequent quotations from this source.

a year from the AJDC and seeking a further $14,000,000 and if Britain contributed half this sum this, Playfair said, would be over three times its current contribution to IGC operational expenses. (The exchange rate was then about four US dollars to one pound.) He considered that prompt British action to get a credit scheme agreed with the Americans would forestall unilateral action by the WRB. Bliss of MEW had agreed to find a way of getting round the financial blockade to meet Mayer's requirements, preferably in the form of non-transferable notes, and Playfair therefore thought that the government should immediately agree to give the money to the IGC, subject to the detailed proposals being satisfactory. Playfair added that he believed the Americans would jump at the scheme and that it was important for Britain to put forward constructive suggestions and 'above all, not to allow Morgenthau and Pehle to think that we are lagging behind in order to save a million dollars here or there'. Otherwise, he warned, the Americans would 'simply ignore us and pour money into occupied Europe', destroying both British blockade arrangements and Mayer's organisation in the process. His final point was that 'the whole tone of the recent debate showed that the House would welcome a larger contribution to the IGC'.

The Ministry of Economic Warfare confirmed its support for the credit scheme, provided the credits were non-negotiable, and suggested a joint fund of £2,000,000 to support the credits.[169] On 14 March 1944 the Cabinet Committee, meeting for the first time since late June 1943, approved Eden's proposal that Britain fund the credit scheme through the IGC as Emerson had proposed. Eden presented this course as a better alternative to merely protesting about the WRB's licensing policy. He explained that the scheme entailed the supply of funds 'for bribery of Nazi officials' and subsidies to friendly families for concealing people who could not escape over the frontier. He advised that, with economic warfare objections overcome, the government could avert the political difficulties involved in supporting the scheme, the majority of whose beneficiaries would be Jews, by presenting it as 'at least ostensibly general and not preponderantly Jewish'.[170] The Chancellor of the Exchequer, Sir John Anderson, emphasised the need not to incite the Americans by 'adopting too stiff an attitude' over the WRB's transactions, but rather 'to aim at imposing suitable limits' on them.[171] The committee agreed that Britain would back the scheme.

The next step was to obtain American agreement. The committee

169 Bliss to Walker, 13 Mar. 1944, PRO FO 371/42728, W3866/16/48.

170 JR (44)6, Memorandum by the Secretary of State for Foreign Affairs, 13 Mar. 1944, PRO CAB 95/15.

171 JR (44) 1st meeting, 14 Mar. 1944, PRO CAB 95/15.

had been told that the American ambassador was said to favour the scheme. Bliss of MEW had even suggested that the WRB should agree that refugee operations in enemy or occupied territory should be placed entirely in the hands of the IGC. But when Britain proposed the scheme, offering to contribute £1,500,000 if the Americans would do the same and prefacing the offer with a strong protest about the WRB's licensing activities, the Americans reacted suspiciously.[172] Emerson saw Pehle in Washington to iron out the differences over the work of the WRB and IGC and on his return reported that Morgenthau and WRB officials took the view 'that the Credit Scheme was largely a device to counter their policy regarding licenses, and that the Intergovernmental Committee would be used as an instrument of British policy in this matter'.[173] The Americans had also raised difficulties over finding the necessary funds, claiming that secrecy would be compromised if Congress had to be approached.

Both Emerson and Pehle wanted the tricky question of licensing to be handled separately. They agreed terms for co-operation which involved the two governments in providing an initial joint fund for the IGC of £1,000,000 – one-third of the total the British government had proposed – £900,000 of which was allocated for the purpose of the credit scheme. They also agreed to avoid overlap in their operations. Despite hints in the documents that passed between Emerson and Pehle that the operations of the IGC credit scheme would involve relief more than rescue – the WRB considered rescue to be its particular province – Emerson continued to state the aims of the credit scheme in terms of escape from enemy territory, rescue, preservation and concealment.[174] In practice, the credit scheme contributed to both relief and rescue. The WRB's lukewarm co-operation led the Refugee Department's Ian Henderson to conclude that the WRB 'do not wish the IGC to steal their thunder'.[175] The British concluded that there was no point in fighting the WRB. Emerson warned that Morgenthau showed disproportionate suspicion and bitterness when conflict arose between the two governments, and he advised that it would be

> to the ultimate advantage of the British government, in other matters of far greater importance, if it can accommodate the American government on refugee proposals, where this is possible without the sacrifice of vital principles. The conflict about licenses is a case in point.[176]

[172] FO to Washington, no. 2400, 22 Mar. 1944, JR (44)12, *ibid.*; Bauer, *American Jewry*, pp. 437–41.
[173] Emerson, memorandum, 16 May 1944, JR (44)12, PRO CAB 95/15.
[174] Emerson, memoranda, 16, 17 and 18 May 1944, *ibid.*
[175] Henderson, minute, 27 June 1944, PRO FO 371/42730, W10172/16/48.
[176] Emerson, memorandum, 16 May 1944, JR (44)12, PRO CAB 95/15.

Emerson considered that in practice the sums licensed were unlikely to do much harm and so this issue did not seem big enough to justify British opposition.

The AJDC was to act as the IGC's agent and while in the United States Emerson met AJDC representatives to work out the details for operating the credit scheme, which remained confidential between them.[177] In July 1944, with the scheme finally approved, the AJDC was authorised to incur £225,000 per quarter, of which the British government would contribute half. This was subject to the stipulation that none of the funds were to be used for escape schemes – for example, across the Spanish border – which might compete with British schemes for getting 'various important people' out of occupied Europe.[178] In addition, the Treasury's C. H. M. Wilcox, who had taken these matters over from Playfair, reported that, if the Hungarian regent, Admiral Horthy, responded to pressure to release Jews from Hungary, Emerson would request spare capacity from the credit scheme to supplement the funds of private organisations for paying Hungarian Jews' fares abroad. Emerson also acceded to a request from the AJDC's chairman, Paul Baerwald, to take over existing credit undertakings, to release AJDC funds for rescue work.[179] Thanking him, Baerwald wrote: 'your prompt and generous answer was like manna from heaven'.[180] The Americans made their contribution to the credit scheme but also insisted on continuing to promote money-based operations.[181] Currency did enter occupied Europe through the credit scheme, but indirectly, via Mayer, who was reputedly able to send it to trustworthy recipients, with minimal benefit to the enemy.[182]

By early June 1944, the chief rabbi knew from Emerson that the IGC had agents able to bring help to Jews in occupied Europe and would be able to employ sums provided by Jewish relief agencies for this purpose. He promised to do his utmost to see that British Jewry seized this opportunity.[183] A week later the Jewish organisation confirmed that it had voted a contribution of £5,000.[184]

Officials of the Refugee Department oiled the machinery of the new rescue initiative. Randall had lost the latest battle, but he could still look

177 Baerwald to Emerson, 30 Apr. 1944, AJ43/52/255; correspondence with Randall, 6 June–21 July 1944, PRO T 161/1446/S51823/2; Sjöberg, *Powers*, pp. 155–62.
178 Wilcox to Randall, 21 July 1944, PRO T 161/1446/S51823/2.
179 Emerson to AJDC, 20 July 1944, AJ43/52/255.
180 Baerwald to Emerson, 7 Aug. 1944, *ibid.*
181 Halifax to FO, no. 3420, 24 June 1944, PRO FO 371/42730, W10172/16/48; US government memorandum, 20 June, PRO FO 371/42857, WR41/41/48.
182 Sjöberg, *Powers*, pp. 155–71; JR (44)1st meeting, 14 Mar. 1944, cited n. 171.
183 J. H. Hertz to Emerson, 4 June 1944, AJ43/52/255.
184 Maurice Stephany to Emerson, 15 June 1944, *ibid.*

back on a successful war against the rescue activists. After this, attitudes within the Refugee Department did not seem to become more positive. Morgenthau's comment about the US State Department – that it 'dealt with human lives, at the same bureaucratic tempo and with the same lofty manner [it] might deal with a not very urgent trade delegation' – could equally have been applied to the delays of Randall and his colleagues over carrying out the tasks assigned to them in the implementation of the credit scheme.[185] Randall, who believed that WRB achievements were being exaggerated and that Britain's contribution deserved more recognition in the United States, supplied the Washington embassy with a survey of recent British activities on behalf of refugees.[186] Rescue, from this perspective, was still largely a competition about prestige with the Americans.

As usual, governmental actions to help Jews limped behind those of non-governmental organisations. This was especially so as regards providing the necessary finance. Britain had proposed that each government allocate to the IGC £1,500,000, or $6,000,000, but the Americans had refused to find a sum of this magnitude and the final agreed allocation involved each government in contributing one-third of this sum, the British putting in £500,000, matched by an American allocation of the dollar equivalent, $2,000,000. To the WRB, the US government allocated the smaller sum of $1,150,000 – $603,000 of which the WRB returned at the end of the war. Thus the US government's total allocation of its own funds to both organisations – $3,150,000 – was marginally over half the amount which Britain had suggested each government give to the IGC. By contrast, in 1944 alone the WRB received $20,000,000 from Jewish sources, nearly all from the AJDC.[187] There is no escaping Bauer's conclusion that the WRB 'was an expression of moral and political support by the administration to save Jews with Jewish means'.[188] Much of the WRB's role in rescue activity was the facilitation of the transmission of AJDC funds to agents operating within neutral and enemy-controlled territory. The British government also helped to facilitate the flow into neutral and occupied Europe of the modest funds the two governments gave the IGC, of small sums raised privately by British Jewry as well as very large amounts raised by Jews in the USA, nearly all AJDC funds. Thus, in the context of rescue, the key role of the British and American governments was in providing the

[185] Feingold, *Politics of Rescue*, p. 230.
[186] Michael Wright to Randall, 30 May 1944, Randall to Wright, 21 June 1944, PRO FO 371/42730, W9066/16/48.
[187] US figures are derived from Bauer, *American Jewry*, pp. 400–7.
[188] *Ibid.*, p. 407.

authorisations and international banking facilities for AJDC transactions otherwise prohibited by blockade controls. The extra finance the AJDC could inject into enemy and neutral territory widened the scope of its rescue activities.

The rescue activity itself was designed and managed by the AJDC and its agents, who thought up the schemes, ran the risks and raised most of the money. The British government needed to give AJDC agents a relatively free hand and trust them to spend responsibly. British Treasury officials and their counterparts in the USA granted the necessary authorisations. The British government also agreed to widen the possibilities for the AJDC to switch between credit and cash to achieve the maximum effect.

For some time past, the British Treasury had been authorising similar arrangements to transfer funds into occupied Europe to aid Jews, but on a much smaller scale. R. A. B. Mynors wrote that the Treasury had allowed 'close relatives to send money for expenditure in neutral territory to finance the escape of persons from enemy territory'.[189] It had also licensed the maintenance of stateless and enemy refugees in Spain and was prepared to help in the same way in Switzerland and Sweden, subject to safeguards against diversion of the money at the far end.[190]

Participation in the credit scheme was a minor development within British policy and, while in part a response to public pressure, it was not publicised. The gulf between campaigners and the government remained. Advocates of rescue, re-energised by the WRB's creation, regularly voiced their impatience with government inaction. A typical resolution, from the Standing Conference of Women's Organisations of Croydon and District, urged 'bolder and more comprehensive measures', for 'the rescue of victims of Nazi cruelty'.[191] The NCRNT remained critical, for example, arguing in June 1944 that the 'utilitarian test of usefulness for the war effort applied to refugees seeking admission to this country should be supplemented by a humanitarian test of saving the largest possible number from Nazi persecution'.[192] But the burden of British policy would remain non-humanitarian.

The fear of being saddled with large numbers of homeless Jews as a result of successful rescue operations continued to haunt members of the Refugee Department. They expressed it, for example, in response to the successful intervention by the government of Spain on behalf of

[189] Mynors to Kullmann, 20 Jan. 1943, AJ43/10/818.
[190] Mynors to Kullmann, 7 Aug. 1943, *ibid.*
[191] Hon. secretary to Eden, 1 Feb. 1944, PRO FO 371/42751, W1860/83/48.
[192] NCRNT to Eden, 14 June 1944, PRO FO 371/42730, W9635/16/48.

persons it protected as Spanish nationals. A Spanish intervention saved 367 Sephardic Jews from Salonika from deportation to death camps and the Germans permitted the Jews to depart for Spain. The Spanish government's policy, as stated by its foreign minister, Francisco Gomez Jordana, was to ensure that any groups of Jews holding Spanish citizenship who were rescued by such means should pass though the country 'as light passes through glass, leaving no trace'.[193] Once the Jews reached Spain in mid-February 1944, the Spanish authorities pressed the Allies to remove them and made this a condition for co-operation over Allied projects to evacuate other groups of refugees from Spain.[194] Hoare, now British ambassador in Madrid, reported that the Americans were intending to encourage the Spaniards to continue to use their good offices with the Germans to obtain further releases. He considered Britain should 'swallow this pill' and lend support.[195] Randall had recently agreed to help persuade the governments of Paraguay and Ecuador not to nullify unauthorised passports issued to Jews in enemy-occupied territory.[196] But he now expressed alarm at the prospect of the Germans permitting further escapes of Jews covered by protective documents issued by the Spanish authorities and possibly by Latin American governments, who would then seek to dump the Jews on the Allies. He telegraphed Washington, asking that British concern about 'further similar evacuations' be raised with the Americans.[197] The Washington embassy declined to comply, suggesting that to do so

> would substantiate for the first time an accusation which is frequently made here that our immigration policy in Palestine is responsible in some way for the suffering of the Jews of Europe since the impression would be created that we were discouraging a scheme for getting them out in the grounds that we could not let them into Palestine.[198]

This sharp rebuke was accompanied by demands for positive proposals and clarification. Refugee department officials backtracked, saying that they had been worried about an embarrassing precedent being set, but conceding that Britain would accept responsibility for disposing of the recent arrivals.[199] In this instance Randall and his colleagues had over-estimated what British representatives could risk saying in the current

[193] Cited in Haim Avni, *Spain, the Jews, and Franco* (Philadelphia, 1983), p. 182.
[194] *Ibid.*, pp. 147–56.
[195] Madrid to FO, no. 338, 3 Mar. 1944, PRO FO 371/42764, W3647/177/48.
[196] Correspondence, 17 Feb.–6 Mar. 1944, PRO FO 371/42784, W2621/2621/48; JR (44)16, para. 14, PRO CAB 95/15.
[197] Walker, Randall, minutes, 7 Mar. 1944, FO to Washington, no. 2261, 17 Mar. 1944, PRO FO 371/42764, W3647/177/48.
[198] Halifax to Foreign Office, no. 1465, 23 Mar. 1944, PRO FO 371/42764, W4618/177/48.
[199] Walker, Randall, minutes, FO to Washington, no. 2577, all 27 Mar. 1944, *ibid.*

political climate in Washington. But they had not exaggerated British fears about the disposal of Jews who might escape. The strength of these fears was illustrated again in early July 1944, in the context of British efforts to assess the notorious 'Brand' proposals to evacuate Jews from Hungary in exchange for war materials, when Herbert Morrison told Eden that it was 'essential that we should do nothing at all which involves the risk that the further reception of refugees here might be the ultimate outcome'.[200]

The force of these fears and the limits of the generosity of both the British and US governments' refugee policies are illustrated by their response to the destruction of the Jews of Hungary, the Nazis' last large group of Jewish victims. Only the briefest of summaries is possible here. In March 1944 the Germans occupied Hungary and, two weeks before D-Day, in late May they began deporting the Jews of that country to death camps in Poland, in full sight of the rest of the world. The response of the western powers was little and late. Having finally bowed to pressure to halt the deportations in early July 1944, Admiral Horthy offered to allow Jews from Hungary to depart for Allied territory. Horthy's offer was the signal for weeks of delay and haggling as the British government, before it would concur in a joint declaration with the Americans promising temporary refuge to Jews from Hungary, privately insisted on setting limits to the numbers of Jews for whom it would actually be expected to take responsibility. The British government was once again holding back because of fears of a flood of refugee Jews seeking entry to Palestine. Finally, in mid-August the Allies announced their acceptance of the Horthy offer: if Jews were released from Hungary they would give them temporary refuge. They were never required to honour this undertaking, since the turn of events in Hungary prevented any emigration pursuant to the Horthy offer.[201]

As long as rescue or escape was impossible, relief was crucial and it was inappropriate to make a rigid division between funds for relief and for rescue. The possibility of using spare cash from the credit scheme to help Hungarian Jews escape abroad has already been mentioned.[202] But in August and September 1944 the prospects of getting Jews out of Hungary were unfavourable, so relief was all the more vital. The AJDC reported that credit operations were not possible in Hungary due to the expropriation of Jewish property, and Emerson backed an AJDC request for a variation of the credit scheme to relieve Jews in Hungarian

[200] Morrison to Eden, 1 July 1944, PRO FO 371/42808, WR 170/3/48.
[201] Wasserstein, *Britain and Jews*, pp. 262–7; JR (44)4th meeting, 4 Aug. 1944, PRO CAB 95/15; Kushner, 'Meaning of Auschwitz'.
[202] Wilcox to Randall, 21 July 1944, PRO T 161/1446/S51823/2.

ghettos and concentration camps. The International Red Cross was dispensing relief but could not do so surreptitiously and Emerson said he wished to support secret assistance arranged through Saly Mayer, to 'reach people who could not otherwise be helped'. He sought consent for the AJDC to remit dollars to Switzerland in order to buy Hungarian currency. The WRB already supported the proposal and the IGC had sufficient funds in its US dollar account. The British government agreed, subject to the stipulation that Mayer satisfy himself that the money he used to buy the currency was not used to help the enemy or collaborationists.[203] The IGC managed to alleviate the position of Jews in Hungary.[204] Its work in other enemy-controlled countries in 1944 included giving help in occupied France to children separated from their parents and helping Jews in German-held Yugoslavia.[205]

In November 1944, officials of the World Jewish Congress (WJC) estimated that, since 1941, approximately 5,500,000 Jews had died in continental Europe. The WJC believed that, outside the Soviet Union and Turkey, about 1,160,000 Jews remained alive, not counting concentration camp prisoners. This number comprised Jews in liberated territory and in countries in which the deportations had not been complete.[206]

Increasingly, concern to help the remnants of Jewry surviving in enemy hands was overshadowed by the progress of the armies of liberation. In the latter part of 1944, as the Allies advanced on several fronts, the Treasury agreed to several IGC schemes, many of them proposed by Schwartz, of support for Jews in liberated territory, including Belgium and Romania. Although such schemes involved relief, rather than rescue, Treasury officials managed to overcome the objections to approval and interpret the IGC mandate to permit spending on them. As Wilcox explained, 'we have had to recognise the strong political pressure for doing something to relieve refugees in Europe, and the greatest difficulty up to now has been the fact that nothing could be done without incidentally assisting the enemy'.[207] Authorising short-term relief for distressed Romanian Jews in liberated Romania, R. L. James added that such relief might prevent people leaving their homes and thus becoming 'a more onerous and enduring

203 Wilcox to Mynors, 23 Aug. 1944, *ibid.*; Emerson, memorandum, 4 Sep. 1944, Emerson to H. Bucknell, 14 Sep. 1944, Wilcox to Mason, 15 Sep. 1944, AJ43/52/225.
204 Draft record of proceedings of 8th meeting, 5 Oct. 1944, PRO T 161/1441/S51823/3.
205 Emerson, memorandum, 'Refugee children in France, Belgium and Switzerland', 11 Dec. 1944, record of proceedings of 9th meeting of the Executive Committee 11 am on 21 Dec. 1944, *ibid.*
206 G. Lichtheim and G. Riegner to N. Goldmann, 16 Nov. 1944, AJ43/27/208.
207 Wilcox to J. Winnifrith, 21 Dec. 1944, PRO T 161/1441/S51823/3.

obligation'.[208] More specifically, the Foreign Office feared that, if Romanian Jews left the country in search of better conditions, many would head for Palestine.

Credit schemes, mainly in France, Hungary, Romania and, to a lesser extent, northern Italy, accounted for over half the commitments for operational expenses of IGC schemes for the nine months to 31 March 1945, and other schemes in Belgium and France accounted for most of the remaining funds.[209] By late April 1945 about £400,000 of the total initial budget of £900,000 for the credit scheme had been allocated.[210] Once the war in Europe ended, the British government attempted to limit the commitments of the IGC. The British preferred to maximise the role in relief of the United Nations Relief and Rehabilitation Administration (UNRRA). Hoping to reduce the numbers who would need resettlement, the government argued for a presumption in favour of the repatriability of refugees. In mid-May 1945 the Cabinet Committee took the view that international discussion of the problem was premature and might have the effect of making persons who might have returned to their homes decide that they need not do so, as provision would be made for them. A British policy that the IGC should not help refugees who were repatriable was agreed in July. All these positions were put to the Americans, together with the Treasury point that, if the IGC was to be involved in such new commitments as resettling refugees, or in relief operations, its finances should be reorganised on the basis of full contributions from member states.[211] On these principles the Treasury refused further IGC schemes. The Treasury also refused schemes for Jews in Romania and Hungary on which the AJDC had already spent money in the hope of being recouped by the IGC: officials were prepared to risk the possibility that the refusal would provoke criticism from wealthy Jews who financed the AJDC in the USA.[212] Still, the Treasury did let the IGC assume protection of Spanish Republican refugees in France – the ruling weakened the line, but in this case there was a contribution from the French government.[213]

[208] R. L. James to Winnifrith, 20 Dec. 1944, Mynors to Culpin, 18 Dec. 1944, Mason to Emerson, 1 Jan. 1945, *ibid.*

[209] Schwartz to Emerson, 24 Nov. 1944, Emerson to Mason, Emerson, IGC Office memorandum, 8 Dec. 1944, S. Hughes to Mason, 15 Jan. 1945, *ibid.*

[210] Emerson, memorandum, 27 Apr. 1945, *ibid.*

[211] Correspondence, 30 May–20 Aug. 1945, PRO T 161/1441/S51823/3; CP (45)82, 17 July 1945, PRO CAB 66/67; CM 16 (45)2, 20 July 1945, PRO CAB 65/63.

[212] Winnifrith to Mason, 14 Aug. 1945, *ibid.*; correspondence, 3–13 Sep. 1945, PRO T 161/1441/S51823/4.

[213] Correspondence, 13–21 Sep. 1945, *ibid.*

Since early 1945 Refugee Department officials had perceived Emerson as an opponent and tried to obstruct his activities. He was at odds with these officials on the supposition of repatriability, later declaring it to be 'entirely misplaced' in the case of stateless persons.[214] But the Refugee Department refused to accept either that Jews deprived of German and Austrian nationality by Nazi legislation were stateless or that they could not return home.[215] Emerson also faced antagonism from the Foreign Office and the Treasury over IGC operational expenses. Officials tried to stop Emerson, whom John Winnifrith of the Treasury described as an 'artful customer', from committing Britain to expenditure regarded as inappropriate.[216] The government regarded the distribution of the financial burden of these IGC expenses – it was paying the same amount as the USA – as inequitable. It was not until July 1946, when it secured the Americans' agreement to increase their contribution to 70 per cent, that the British government agreed to the expansion of the IGC's settlement programme. The long-term British objective for resolving such problems over the IGC – the establishment of an organisation under the United Nations – was eventually achieved in June 1947, when the IGC and UNRRA were absorbed in the new International Refugee Organisation (IRO).[217] The IRO was empowered to deal with what had finally been accepted as the only practical solution to dealing with the problem of displaced persons in Europe – resettlement.[218]

In mid-1946 a Treasury official, noting the big reduction in the number of refugees, which had left a large unused balance of IGC funds, observed to a colleague,

> The demand is less than the supply that has been laid on. If there had been no supply the demand might have been even less. Your thesis is strikingly confirmed: no international bodies, no refugees (or virtually none)![219]

And so the same fear which had haunted pre-war policy – that international action increased the scale of the refugee problem – survived into the post-war era.

British policy on rescue

In 1963, Randall, a Catholic convert, wrote a pamphlet, *The Pope, the Jews and the Nazis*, defending Pope Pius XII against recent charges that

214 Mason, memorandum of meeting with Emerson, G. Rendel and others on 16 May, 23 May 1945, PRO T 161/1441/S51823/3; Emerson, memorandum, 13 Dec. 1945, sent to Mackillop, PRO T 161/1441/S51823/5.
215 Mackillop to Emerson, 31 Jan. 1946, PRO T 161/1441/S51823/5.
216 Winnifrith to Mackillop, 19 Mar. 1946, *ibid.*
217 Correspondence, 18 Mar.–9 Apr. 1946, *ibid.*
218 Sjöberg, *Powers*, pp. 208–26.
219 J. D. K. Beighton to Winnifrith, 19 July 1946, PRO T 161/1441/S51823/5.

he had failed to do enough to save the Jews. In the pamphlet, Randall conveys his conviction of the futility of attempting rescue, and says that rescue efforts by governments 'were bound to be puny compared with the horrible reality'.[220] Yet the Allies' inability to avert the vast majority of the murders of Jews the Nazis perpetrated did not render all rescue efforts futile. Indeed, despite hostile officials such as Randall and despite daunting obstacles and objections, it proved possible to initiate worthwhile humanitarian action to save Jews.

There are parallels between the stories of how refugee policy was modified, first in the United States and then in Britain, to include an element of rescue. Both governments came under growing domestic pressure to take humanitarian action. Within the administrations of both countries, Treasury officials played a crucial role in pressing for such action to be initiated and in each case these officials were critical of the record of the government department which had the conduct of refugee policy. But the high drama of the revolution over the conduct of refugee policy in the USA was not repeated in Britain. British policy was altered by means of discussions which took place in the normal restrained and consensual style cultivated in the upper echelons of the government. Yet, notwithstanding this outward appearance of 'business as usual', serious differences existed within Whitehall about how to approach the issue of rescue.

The Foreign Office archives on refugees show British officials adopting attitudes towards advocates of rescue that were defensive and narrowly nationalistic. Such attitudes are particularly evident in the case of Randall, whose stint as head of the Refugee Department lasted from 1942 until he became ill in the summer of 1944.[221] Randall devoted zeal and ingenuity to outmanoeuvring the rescue campaigners. Compared with members of the Foreign Office's Refugee Department, Treasury officials were more sympathetic to the plight of Jews in Europe. Playfair and Waley in particular stand out in expressing humanitarian concern and in identifying ways to save Jewish lives. In December 1942 Waley had been especially critical of the ungenerosity and hypocrisy of British policy. In March 1944 Playfair, who had been impressed by his contacts with Americans working with the WRB, many of whom were US Treasury officials, advocated a more positive line than that hitherto taken by the Foreign Office. Playfair considered American dynamism to be a reproach to British inactivity. He shared Randall's concern to protect the British perception of the blockade against American pressure, but his view of Anglo-American relations was more constructive

220 Randall, *The Pope, the Jews and the Nazis* (London, 1963), p. 13.
221 P. Malin to Randall, 1 Aug. 1944, AJ43/44/M119.

than Randall's view and less competitive. The critical importance for Britain of cultivating the Americans was something Playfair understood: indeed, he was at pains to impress upon other departments the need to give it more priority.[222]

For the British to make confrontational protests to the Americans over WRB rescue activities had been shown to be futile. Indeed, such protests were inconsistent with expressing support for rescue. For, whether the British wished to complain about money going into enemy territory via the WRB or about inconveniently large numbers of Jews coming out of enemy territory and requiring disposal, each of these eventualities, albeit problematic in certain respects, was an inescapable consequence of rescue activity and inseparable from it. Rescue attempts required transfers of value into enemy territory to pay for bribes, documents, travel, food and so on. Furthermore, any Jews who emerged from enemy territory would require maintenance and, while neutrals might offer temporary refuge, the Allies would ultimately face pressure for finding Jews somewhere to go in the longer term. Anglo-American conflicts over the blockade were capable of being resolved. But Britain's continuing reluctance to dispose of Jews meant that the Refugee Department continued to regard rescue measures as a source of problems.

British support for the credit scheme should not be seen as altering the burden of British policy. The introduction of this humanitarian strand into British policy reflected the pressures of the Anglo-American relationship. The hitherto marginal issue of rescue had acquired new importance within the Anglo-American alliance. The British government had finally acquired political motives for playing a part in rescue. The fact that the WRB was attempting to save Jews gave Britain political reasons for making some effort to do so too. As far as the British government was concerned, the newfound political significance of rescue was derived only in part from awareness of the need to appear co-operative towards the WRB. In addition, there was a competitive element, because rescue had become a matter of prestige. British policy-makers believed that backing the credit scheme would enable them to save face and to stop the Americans from reaping all the credit.

But what drove the British government to decide to act in March 1944 was the conclusion that investing in the credit scheme would resolve the conflict which the WRB's transactions produced between the two vital objectives of protecting the financial blockade and keeping Anglo-American relations tranquil. Backing the credit scheme would, albeit at the cost of greater flexibility over the blockade, prevent

[222] Playfair, interview, cited ch. 6, n. 9.

excessive amounts of cash from reaching enemy territory and at the same time remove a source of conflict with the Americans. The Americans' grudging response to the proposal for joint action through the IGC demonstrated their determination to pursue rescue on their own terms. Rescue activists within the American administration preferred to act independently of Britain through the WRB and showed scant regard either for British reservations over the blockade or for British aspirations to share in the glory of saving lives. Britain over several months learned the lesson that, in the context of rescue, the pressures of the Anglo-American relationship dictated, above all, an accommodating response to the activities of the WRB.

The British contribution to rescue in the form of the credit scheme contributed to saving Jewish lives and deserves recognition. But the British contribution through the IGC is little known, compared to the American contribution through the WRB, for several reasons. For one thing, there was no British equivalent of the open confrontations over rescue seen in the United States. This difference partly explains why the internal tension in Whitehall which fostered support for the scheme has been overlooked. Unlike the publicly trumpeted launch of the WRB, the decision to back the credit scheme was kept secret. Secrecy was necessary to safeguard the rescue activity: thus, all Emerson said about the scheme in a report of July 1944 was: 'In another sphere, the Joint Distribution Committee is doing work of very great importance on behalf of the Committee.'[223] Once the need for secrecy was past, certain individuals and organisations chose not to claim credit for their contribution. Others failed to give credit where it was due. For example, the WRB's final report claimed that the IGC's primary concern 'was with rehabilitation and resettlement of refugees, and it had found it difficult for political and other reasons to undertake any relief and rescue operations in enemy territory' – an observation which conveniently ignores the WRB's own objections to the IGC's proposing to operate in enemy territory and which also fails to acknowledge the extensive operations the IGC in fact funded in areas controlled by the enemy.[224] The leading authors on British and American policy have focused on the WRB as the only significant exception to the negative cast of both countries' approach to rescue and they have been unduly dismissive of the IGC's contribution.[225] And, in terms of monetary commitment, the

[223] Report submitted by the director, Sir Herbert Emerson, to Fourth Plenary Session of IGC, 15–17 Aug. 1944, 25 July 1944, AJ43/23, p. 8.

[224] Final summary and report of the executive director, War Refugee Board, 15 Sep. 1945, AJ43/17/387, pp. 8–9.

[225] Wasserstein, *Britain and Jews*, pp. 217–19, claims that the IGC 'never quite shook off the aura of the charity matinee'. The same phrase was used by Richard Law, after

two governments' joint allocation of $4,000,000 to the IGC in 1944 compares favourably with the US government's allocation of $1,150,000 to the WRB.

It was impossible for the British and US governments to undertake large-scale rescue against the will of the enemy. On this, historians agree. Assessment of what was possible is more contentious. The little the Allies actually undertook establishes a baseline of what was possible, because it was done. Support was given to Jews to escape from concentration camps, to hide and to leave enemy territory. The ways in which this was done included providing funds, letting finance through the blockade, offering asylum, encouraging neutrals to admit and protect Jews, and putting pressure on collaborators and satellite governments. Britain undertook all of these at some stage, with beneficial results.

What, then, of the controversial area of what might have been done but was not? Debate continues over British and American responses during the summer and autumn of 1944 to proposals to bomb the railway lines leading to Auschwitz-Birkenau and to bomb the death camp itself. At the time, these proposals were not accepted as having serious rescue potential. Policy-makers' discussions of these proposals offer insights into their attitudes to the Jewish plight. But they do not particularly assist this study, the concern of which is to establish British policy-makers' overall approach to rescue and where they drew the line. This book concentrates, therefore, on British attitudes towards proposals that were agreed to be likely to yield results in the form of saving lives.

In the gulf between what was out of the question and what was actually undertaken there were possibilities that were deliberately neglected. British policy-makers used valid objections to large-scale rescue to hold back from limited actions to save small number of Jews, including actions they had acknowledged to be worth undertaking. The government could have made more effort to remove Jews from neutral countries. The assurances Britain and the Allies gave to neutrals lacked the most significant commitment within their power – to take unrepatriables off their hands after the end of the war – a promise which would not have compromised the war effort. The British government was excessively cautious about offers of asylum. Its failure to do more to

Bermuda, when, advocating giving the IGC two or three full-time paid executives, he said, 'So long as you limit it to one full-time director and a few stuffed-shirts whose function is really little more than that of the patrons of a charity matinee it will command no confidence': Law to Eden, cited n. 92; Wyman, *Abandonment*, pp. 111–12, 137–41.

offer asylum shows policy-makers treating limitations that were self-imposed as irremovable. The position that a welcome could be offered only to Jews who could be allowed to stay in Palestine was maintained because Britain had no intention of being landed with homeless Jews in Britain or anywhere else in the empire. The sole significant exception to this policy, the joint acceptance with the Americans of the Horthy offer in 1944, was belated, grudging, subject to secret qualification on Britain's part and never put to the test. As far as Palestine was concerned, even if the need for Arab goodwill necessitated the maintenance of the White Paper limits, it was possible, as Jewish Agency representatives argued, to show greater flexibility in allocating the places that remained under the quota. Indeed, in February 1944 the government of Palestine suggested some re-allocation to permit more lives to be saved, pointing out, for example, that there were still 20,000 unfilled places 'hypothecated against various schemes of which nothing [is] likely to come', which suggests that a more realistic approach to the calculation of how many places were actually available was overdue.[226] Nor would temporary asylum have breached the quota. Indeed, in April 1944, the Washington embassy told London that it supported Pehle's suggestion that the British government announce that 'until the end of the war in Europe any Jews who managed to escape from Hitler would be allowed at least temporary refuge in Palestine, even after the completion of the quota'.[227] Leaving Palestine aside, a more generous approach to making firm offers of asylum in Britain and the empire for specified numbers or categories of Jews who might escape could have made neutral countries more ready to act as refuges. Lastly, Britain's belated acceptance of the Horthy offer reinforces the argument that something on similar lines could have been done earlier.

How do we assess British fears that unmanageable numbers of Jews would emerge from enemy territory with German permission? However unlikely this may seem now, there was material available in 1943 and 1944 to support such fears. Uncertainty was possible as to the Nazis' determination to murder every last Jew. The Nazi regime's old weapon of expulsion had not necessarily been abandoned altogether. Since the mass murders began there had been two instances of exchanges which freed Jewish prisoners in Nazi hands, the second of these taking place in November 1942. Furthermore, there were cases in which releases of groups of Jews were taking place with German agreement, albeit

[226] Palestine to secretary of state for colonies, no. 269, 24 Feb. 1944, PRO FO 371/42722, W2188/5/48.

[227] C. E. King (British Embassy) to Pehle, 13 Apr. 1944, War Refugee Board records, Franklin D. Roosevelt Presidential Library, Hyde Park, New York, Box 3.

involving small numbers and reflecting special circumstances, such as the success of protective action by non-belligerent governments like Spain. With this background and given British priorities, it is not surprising that Refugee Department officials worried over possibilities that the Germans would force out more Jews.

The task of evaluating the genuineness of British fears of being faced with a flood of Jews is further complicated by the evident determination of British ministers and officials to prevent such a flood from ever taking place. The priority the British gave to this concern made it all too convenient to exaggerate the likelihood and potential scale of such a flood. Indeed, the more menacing such a possibility could be made to appear, the more massive the defences which could be deemed necessary to mount against it. And thus the figures of tens of thousands, even millions of Jews who were in fact already dead or beyond the reach of rescue were mobilised by British government representatives to swell the ranks of the dreaded potential Jewish exodus.

9 Post-war decisions

The post-war British government actively sought immigrants, but not from among Jews. Ministers thought any further Jewish immigration likely to arouse public opposition. Anti-Jewish riots in parts of Britain made such fears seem more substantial. Furthermore, conflict over the future of Palestine and over Jewish immigration to Palestine hardened attitudes towards the plight of homeless Jews. Indeed, the Cabinet Committee on Palestine, which Herbert Morrison chaired, in October 1945 amended the terms of reference of the forthcoming Anglo-American Committee of Enquiry regarding the problems of displaced European Jewry to exclude consideration of possible Jewish immigration into European countries.[1]

The government regarded it as out of the question to allow any substantial new Jewish immigration to the United Kingdom and only small numbers of Jews entered in the post-war period. But sooner or later the position of the Jewish refugees already within Britain would have to be resolved. The story of how politicians and officials dealt with the question of deciding policy towards the existing refugee community is the main subject of this chapter. The record of British post-war immigration policy towards Jews on the continent is a subject falling outside this book's primary concern with British efforts to save Jews from Nazism and does not qualify for detailed treatment here, but the latter part of the chapter briefly considers the circumscribed schemes under which Jewish survivors might apply for entry. We begin, then, with the final phase of the government's dealings with refugees admitted during the Nazi period.

In the arena of political decision-making the role of civil servants is to offer advice, while it is for ministers to take the decisions. Should the government lay down a policy which civil servants consider to be wrong

[1] Committee on Palestine, P(M)(45)2nd meeting, 10 Oct. 1945, PRO CAB 95/14; *Report on the Anglo-American Committee of Enquiry Regarding the Problems of European Jewry and Palestine*, Cmd 6808 (London, 1946).

they must still implement it, but they can advise ministers against policies they believe to be misconceived. The strength of the belief of Home Office civil servants that ministers were wrong to insist that refugees should be required to leave after the end of the war is shown by the effort they put into arguing the case that the only proper course was one of allowing the absorption of refugees who wished to remain. Indeed, the divergence on this issue between the approaches of senior officials and the home secretary led to its becoming a bone of contention between them.

During the war the disposal of refugees was debated, but not resolved. In August 1941 Morrison raised the need for a policy.[2] Officials drafted proposals which suggested a range of possible exceptions to a general policy of repatriation or of pressing German and Austrian refugees to emigrate. They also provided Morrison with figures which put the total number of aliens in Britain at 250,000, including long-established residents, and put non-resident aliens at 110,000, of whom 15,000–20,000 were war refugees who would presumably be repatriated. Morrison responded with the comment, '250,000 aliens is a biggish figure. Pl see the matter is again considered at an appropriate time. I am sure there will be trouble if all possible refugees &c do not go after the war.'[3]

For the next review of the question, Cooper produced a memorandum supporting a policy of absorption. He explained why he was rejecting the possible alternatives: emigration would not revive speedily in the immediate post-war period; compulsory repatriation to Germany of Jewish refugees 'would, humanly speaking, be out of the question', so long as any uncertainty existed about the rights of Jewish and other minorities, and unwilling refugees should not be put under pressure to return. It was now August 1942, and Cooper reinforced his argument by reference to the Nazi policy of exterminating the Jews and its human consequences. What Cooper said about the actions of the Nazis was quoted in the previous chapter (see p. 199); his conclusion about the significance of the annihilation of the Jews for Home Office policy was that parents of refugee children would be dead or untraceable, so the children could not be sent back. He also argued that so long as any natural parents consented, the Home Office should not interfere with arrangements for refugee children to stay permanently with foster-parents.[4]

Morrison was unmoved. He clung to the view that at the end of the war the Home Office should require all refugees to depart, not even

2 H. Morrison to under secretary of state, 2 Aug. 1941, PRO HO 213/1347.
3 Newsam, 'British attitude and policy in relation to refugees and other foreigners after the war', 6 Feb. 1942, Morrison to Peake and Maxwell, 6 Mar. 1942, *ibid.*
4 Cooper, 'Memorandum on Post-War Problems', 29 Aug. 1942, *ibid.*, paras. 12, 13.

excepting those who had voluntarily served in the armed forces, and that those refugees who could not emigrate could be repatriated.[5] To facilitate the enforcement of such a policy, Morrison requested figures on refugees. Maxwell obeyed, but at the same time started to prepare the ground for a more generous approach than that advocated by Morrison, instructing Newsam to include figures showing the difficulty refugees would face in gaining admission to their countries of origin and to give details of those for whom exceptional treatment might be necessary. Maxwell asked rhetorically, 'Can we for example send back . . . a man of 19, who was admitted here as a child aged 14, and has no parents, or whose parents cannot be found, and who may have been adopted more or less by an English family?'[6] Taking into account likely emigration, the Home Office understood that a mere 40,000 Jewish refugees might be expected to apply to settle.[7] But Morrison was implacable, claiming repeatedly that allowing the refugees to remain would lead to outbursts of anti-semitism and public disorder.[8]

Increasingly, Cooper sided with the refugees. In June 1943 he defiantly circulated copies of the memorandum in support of absorption he had produced in August 1942, saying his views had not changed since writing it. Emerson expressed delight that Cooper shared his opinion that compulsory repatriation would not be feasible.[9] After his retirement, Cooper worked for the Central Office for Refugees (COR) and in November 1944 he produced a draft policy on post-war treatment of refugees for COR, reiterating his earlier arguments and proposing an even longer list of candidates for absorption. He used more emotional language than in his Whitehall years, but his proposal to subject refugee agricultural and domestic workers to an employment condition showed that he had not lost the hunger for control.[10] In 1946, at the age of sixty-two, he re-married. His wife, Gertrud Eleanor Isabella Kallmann, was a refugee from Germany.[11]

After Cooper left, Home Office officials still believed that most refugees should be allowed to stay. Officials in other departments agreed.[12] But Morrison was not interested. He refused to announce that

[5] Maxwell to Newsam, 17 Nov. 1942, *ibid.* [6] *Ibid.*

[7] Mathews, note and table, 26 Feb. 1943, I. Haigh to Cooper, 23 Mar. and 18 June 1943, *ibid.*

[8] Kushner, *Persistence of Prejudice*, pp. 152–62.

[9] Emerson to Cooper, 18 June 1943, Cooper to Randall, 11 June 1943, PRO HO 213/1347.

[10] Cooper, COR, 'Proposals in regard to refugees from Nazi Oppression in the United Kingdom after the War', Nov. 1944, RA, XIV/35/109.

[11] Marriage (1946) and death (1948) entries, General Register Office, London.

[12] Correspondence, Aug. 1944–Apr. 1945, PRO HO 213/1009, May–Oct. 1945, PRO HO 213/1008.

aliens of good conduct, even members of the armed forces, need not fear arbitrary expulsion.[13] He ruled that not even successful refugee industrialists, whose potential as exporters the Department of Overseas Trade wished to retain, could be offered formal assurances which might dissuade them from leaving in search of more welcoming surroundings.[14]

Immediately after the end of the European war, Maxwell told Morrison that officials thought the government should speedily announce that it would not force refugees to leave. The arguments were summarised by the most senior official directly concerned with aliens matters, C. D. C. Robinson. He said people admitted for temporary refuge had not been promised they could remain indefinitely, but neither was it true to say they had been told the contrary. He advocated a more positive approach to future policy, citing a mixture of humanitarian and utilitarian reasons. The young, Robinson said, could hardly remember any other country and were substantially Anglicised; the middle-aged had contributed to the war effort and could assist economic development – for example, they might help London maintain its new role as a centre of the fur and diamond trades and they might play a leading role in the toy industry. He emphasised that the elderly had suffered persecution and the liquidation of family and friends: to uproot them again would 'savour of inhumanity'. Robinson estimated that the absorption of perhaps 40,000 refugees would increase the percentage of aliens in the population by a mere 0.1 per cent. Shipping shortages, he pointed out, would make it hard to implement a decision to make refugees leave. He concluded that to keep refugees in continued suspense was unfair and disadvantageous, as the best would go first, and that these considerations outweighed the tactical advantages of deferring a decision. But Morrison was not persuaded. He said that, as Churchill was eliminating Labour ministers from the government, his successor as home secretary should settle this question, adding, 'I am not enthusiastic for the line you have taken.' Morrison told ministerial colleagues not to be influenced by the view that the Jewish refugees

> would be in terror of returning to Germany: It was possible that post-war Germany would abandon anti-Semitism altogether. If the Jews were allowed to remain here they might be an explosive element in the country, especially if the economic situation deteriorated.

[13] Morrison, *Hansard*, House of Commons, vol. 396 cols. 387–8, 20 Jan. 1944.

[14] Lord Woolton, 'Refugee Industrialists', R(I)(44)12, 25 July 1944, Morrison, memorandum, 'Refugee Industrialists', R(I)(44)14, 11 Aug. 1944, minutes of meeting of Reconstruction Committee, Sub-committee on Industrial Problems, 13 Dec. 1944, PRO CAB 124/702.

He said he was

seriously alarmed regarding the possibility of anti-Semitism in this country. If, arising out of the war settlement, territory other than Palestine became available for colonisation by refugees, the best solution would be to send the Jews there.[15]

On this characteristically ungenerous note Morrison ended his period of responsibility for refugee policy. R. G. Somervell, home secretary in the 1945 caretaker government, thought it unwise to offer refugees settlement. He, too, worried about anti-alien agitation. His Cabinet colleagues considered that:

While there was a hard core of refugees who were likely to prove genuinely 'non-repatriable', it was essential that we should not accept any general liability for absorbing permanently the refugees received in this country, many of them on transit visas, in view of conditions in their native countries which no longer held good. Apart from the cost of dispensing relief, the social and general consequences of declaring such refugees non-repatriable would be very serious . . . There was no question of forcing any refugees to return immediately to their parent countries.[16]

Pending a political decision, officials were obliged to deal with cases on an interim basis. In the context of controls on the employment of aliens who sought permission to work at home, Cooper's successor, H. H. C. Prestige, ruled in June 1945, 'nothing shall be done which carries with it an implication or may be used as an argument for permanent residence in this country'.[17] In October 1945, James Chuter Ede, the home secretary in Clement Attlee's new Labour administration, told the secretary of the Refugee Industries Committee that it would be

impossible for me to single out one particular class of alien for preferential treatment and give that class an assurance at a time when I am unable to deal with the problem as a whole. The most I am able to say is that an alien of good character who continues to render valuable services to the community and whose continued residence is deemed by His Majesty's Government to be in the national interest, need not fear that he will be arbitrarily or capriciously expelled.[18]

Ede told Attlee that he wished to deport refugees from Germany and Austria who had proved to be undesirable and planned to enforce deportation orders against a number who had 'become criminals or confirmed prostitutes'. Attlee agreed.[19] Ede stated publicly that he would not deport people if there were grounds for believing that they

15 JR (45)2nd meeting, 16 May 1945, PRO CAB 95/15.

16 CM 16 (45)2, 20 July 1945, PRO CAB 65/53; CP (45)82, 17 July 1945, PRO CAB 66/67.

17 Prestige, memorandum, 'Employment of Aliens: Work at Home', 13 June 1945, PRO HO 213/500.

18 J. Chuter Ede to E. Cove, 3 Oct. 1945, PRO HO 213/879.

19 Ede to Attlee, 29 Oct. 1945, Attlee to Ede, 1 Nov. 1945, PRO HO 213/923.

would be subject to political or religious persecution, but the government interpreted this undertaking as applying only to well-conducted aliens; refugees convicted of crimes were deported.[20]

In early 1946, Lord St Davids came to see the home secretary, seeking help for refugee industrialists in South Wales, who had trouble getting entry permits to travel to the countries of their former residence to build up trade contacts and who found banks reluctant to lend money to persons with only short-term permission to remain. Some had already returned to the continent, finding these restrictions too much of a handicap to their business affairs.[21] Ede replied that he was anxious not to set too precise a period on the residence of foreigners: 'Foreigners, by their very nervousness and by agitation designed to secure reassurance, were likely to stir up anti-alien feeling in this country.' Pointing out that he had taken no action against foreigners who were law-abiding, he suggested that 'it would be much better for those concerned to wait a few months and see how they fared under the naturalisation scheme'.[22]

This scheme was a recent development. Very few refugees had been naturalised in the 1930s. Deferring decisions on naturalisation applications was a way of keeping in reserve the ultimate sanction of deportation. As Sir John Simon later told Hoare, his successor as home secretary, this was the reason why he had 'long resisted official advice at the Home Office just before your time as to the naturalisation of Germans and Italians'.[23] The worries underlying Simon's policy had presumably concerned applicants with Fascist leanings, not refugees, since he ceased being home secretary in May 1937. Indeed, the question of naturalising refugees hardly arose before 1938, as applicants needed to have completed five years' residence. In June 1940 the processing of naturalisation applications had been suspended, a decision which helped the police, who were too busy to make the necessary enquiries. It left 3,500 applications uncleared, including some 1,600 refugee cases.[24] Thereafter, except for resumption of citizenship by British-born women who had lost it through marriage to aliens, naturalisation was granted only in a handful of special cases, where it was required in connection with the war effort. By mid-1943 fewer than fifty such exceptions had been made.[25] Several thousand further applications received from refugees were merely listed. The Home Office rejected pressure to grant

20 HO memorandum, 'Deportation of refugees', n.d., PRO HO 213/920.
21 Lord St Davids, memorandum, 19 Feb. 1946, PRO HO 213/879.
22 RH, minute, 19 Feb. 1946, *ibid.*
23 Simon to Hoare, 27 Feb. 1945, Templewood Papers, XVII/8.
24 D. Seaborne Davies, memorandum, 11 Sep. 1944, PRO HO 213/52.
25 Maxwell to C. B. Yearsley, 31 May 1943, PRO FO 371/36695, W8849/124/48. This author's father was one of the fifty exceptions.

naturalisation to enemy aliens who might be taken prisoner. When an Austrian serving in the Pioneer Corps pressed his case for naturalisation on the basis that it would give the protection of international law should he fall into the hands of the enemy, an official observed 'the consequences feared by this man are hardy likely to be avoided by the parchment protection of a certificate of naturalisation'.[26] The Home Office declined to advise refugees whether they might obtain citizenship after the war.[27]

On 15 November 1945, a Commons announcement on naturalisation by the home secretary finally outlined the categories of refugees still in the United Kingdom who might apply. Priority would be given to certain groups who had earned the nation's gratitude, including refugees with service in the armed forces, as had been expected, and also civilians who had contributed to the war effort or helped the economy. But, since the government could not decide how to define the priority groups, the home secretary directed that the statement should be couched 'in such a manner as to leave us room for subsequent manoeuvre'.[28] As a result individuals could not work out whether they would benefit. The only specific instruction issued was that refugees should not submit applications yet. The machinery and procedure for applicants who thought they had a claim to priority were to be announced at some future date. Furthermore, the backlog of uncleared cases had risen to 10,000 and the processing of applications was expected to be spread over a comparatively lengthy period. How long would it take? In early 1946 the time lag between the submission of an application and its consideration was thought to be two years or more.[29] In July 1948 it emerged that the intervention of other work in the Home Office meant that many orphan refugee children were still awaiting naturalisation, although most of some 800 cases were resolved by early 1949.[30]

Moreover, applicants for naturalisation were required to show the intention to reside in the British dominions or continue in crown service. Home Office officials acknowledged the difficulty of having rules which made 'the alien's intention the criterion without any refer-

[26] C. G. Markbreiter, minute, 17 Sep. 1941, J. Jagger to John Parker MP, 22 Sep. 1941, PRO HO 213/48.

[27] Davies, memorandum, 11 Sep. 1944, cited n. 24.

[28] Maxwell, memorandum, 'Naturalisation policy', 13 Nov. 1945, PRO HO 213/2249; Ede, *Hansard*, House of Commons, vol. 415, cols. 2305–10, 15 Nov. 1945; CP (45)255, 26 Oct. 1945, PRO CAB 129/4; CP (45)263, 30 Oct. 1945, PRO CAB 129/4; Cab 49 (45)2, 6 Nov. 1945, PRO CAB 128/2.

[29] W. Lyon, minute, 5 Feb. 1946, PRO HO 213/798.

[30] G. H. Roberts to J. D. Jamieson, 21 July 1948, HO circular, 11 Jan. 1949, PRO HO 213/22.

ence to his ability to implement it'.[31] Refugees' ability to implement any intention to settle was dependent on immigration policy and this still awaited clarification. Home Office officials thought it unlikely that a large proportion of refugees would be absorbed by naturalisation in the near future.[32] And naturalisation, being a discretionary process, could always be refused. Thus, while refugees found the announcement on naturalisation encouraging, individuals were left with uncertainties, in particular, as to when their immigration status would be resolved. Refugee organisations were soon fencing with the Home Office over whether their financial responsibilities to refugees would cease after naturalisation.[33]

Refugees have tended to regard naturalisation as the milestone which established their settlement in Britain. Indeed, many were naturalised even though they were still subject to immigration conditions at the time they applied for naturalisation. It had been past practice to require an alien whose stay was subject to a specific time condition to obtain cancellation of that condition before he could be regarded as qualified to apply for naturalisation. In early 1946 the Home Office decided that certain groups who were in the United Kingdom on a temporary basis would not be required to leave the country pending naturalisation. Many pre-war refugees benefited from this decision, since the favoured categories included people who had lodged a naturalisation application by November 1940 and those who had completed the statutory qualifications for naturalisation and had a claim to special consideration under the recent policy announcement. More recent arrivals were excluded from this concession, but this affected few Jewish refugees, since most had now been in Britain for at least six and a half years and many for twice as long.[34] But not being under an imminent threat of being forced to leave was still much less than cancellation of immigration conditions. Thus, refugees remained in an immigration limbo, notwithstanding the news that many could apply for naturalisation. The Ministry of Labour considered it risky to offer refugees costly training opportunities which required people to work in Britain after completion of training, since a refugee might be required to leave. The Home Office considered that only exceptionally brilliant refugee children should be exempted from the need to earn their living after reaching the age of sixteen. The Ministry of Education was not allowed to give grants for teacher training

31 Prestige to Gomme, 4 Oct. 1944, PRO HO 213/864.
32 A. W. P., report, 8 Feb. 1946, PRO HO 213/72.
33 Correspondence, Oct. 1946, PRO HO 213/23.
34 Maxwell, circular, 'Prolongation of stay pending naturalisation', 25 Feb. 1946, PRO HO 213/798.

to aliens; the Home Office felt that for it to assist financially in these circumstances would be inconsistent.[35] A policy of allowing the naturalisation of non-orphan refugee minors was agreed only in June 1947. In such cases the Home Office was prepared to give a parent priority if the wait denied the child the benefits of naturalisation. This course was adopted in the case of Gunther Treitel, who had arrived aged eight in March 1939, had since been educated in Britain and was now reading law at Oxford. Treitel's German nationality rendered him ineligible to pursue his wish to join one of the Inns of Court to qualify as a barrister. The Home Office offered to consider an application from Treitel's father in which he would be included.[36]

Was the government ever going to announce a policy on the immigration status of refugees? On assuming office in August 1945 Ede had described the need to decide policy towards refugees in Britain as 'becoming urgent'. Yet he delayed. By mid-1946 the government's position was still that it had no policy on this question.[37] But casework decisions were needed: refugees, impatient to get on with their lives, sought to change their jobs, continue their education and make trips abroad.

By 1945 just 60,000 central and eastern European refugees from Nazism remained on the Home Office's hands. About half were Germans, the rest Austrians, Czechs and Poles.[38] At least another 16,000 had re-emigrated from Britain since 1938, mostly during the war. Others left at the war's end. The Home Office was pleased to see them go. It had little sympathy with the security authorities' misgivings that, once exit permits were no longer required, aliens employed on secret work might depart. The Home Office simply suggested that, to ensure that their knowledge of secret matters was not revealed, departments would have to rely mainly on selecting 'the right type of alien'.[39] A certain amount of unobtrusive administrative control could be exercised by arranging that ex-enemy and stateless aliens should not be issued with certificates of identity in order to travel. But nothing could be done to prevent people already in possession of valid identity documents from leaving.

The toll of the past few years on refugees was increasingly apparent. In March 1946, an outpatient facility – set up to cater for refugees'

35 Robinson to G. N. Flemming, 16 Nov. 1945, PRO HO 213/864.
36 Memoranda, 16 and 26 June 1947, PRO HO 213/45.
37 Ede, minute, 29 Aug. 1945, PRO HO 213/1010; records cited in n. 35; Robinson to G. C. Veysey, 4 May 1946, PRO HO 213/1359.
38 Robinson, memorandum, 30 Mar. 1945, PRO HO 213/1009; HO memorandum, 'Aliens in the United Kingdom', 22 July 1945, PRO HO 213/1010.
39 Correspondence, Oct.–Nov. 1945, PRO HO 213/876.

psychological problems – noted that the number of its patients was increasing, 'owing to the distress caused to the neurotic Refugee by the sad news most of them have received since the end of the war'.[40] A Home Office official later recalled that, 'With the end of hostilities, refugees as a whole were beginning to feel uncertainty for the future, with a consequent incidence of neurotic disturbance and mental breakdown.'[41] But the distressing effect of the uncertainty concerning refugees' immigration status did not motivate the government to remove it speedily.

The Home Office was burdened by the uncomfortable knowledge that its claim to exert continuing control over refugees was of questionable legality. For legal reasons, a succession of measures, largely designed to save clerical labour, had produced the unforeseen result that a very large number of refugees could no longer be subjected to enforceable conditions. As we saw in chapter 4, the Home Office knew by 1944 that many of the conditions it had imposed on aliens within the country, in cases when no such conditions had been imposed at the port, would be legally unenforceable and that any conditions imposed in future would suffer from similar legal defects. Refugees were unaware of the invalidity of the conditions restricting their stay and the Home Office did not enlighten them. As Prestige noted in March 1945, 'we have continued to deal with them as being here on a temporary basis'.[42] Indeed, officials were practised in using bluff to cover difficulties of this nature and had developed formulations which maintained the appearance of the power to exert control without either telling outright lies or revealing the absence of any enforceable limitations. Thus, a letter to an alien visitor whose stay was subject to no valid conditions might use the phrase 'the Secretary of State does not wish to raise objection to the alien's prolonging his stay until a particular date'.[43] Another example of this careful use of language was the description of refugees as being in the country 'on a temporary basis'.

Refugees were kept in ignorance of the legal defects in the immigration conditions governing their cases, but they knew the practical and moral arguments in favour of allowing them to remain in the long term. Many refugees had developed the expectation that permission to settle would ultimately be conceded and some had the confidence to press for

[40] Central Committee for Refugees, report by Mrs Hahn-Warburg, Rehabilitation Department, 15 Mar. 1946, PRO HO 213/987.
[41] R. H. Rumbelow, 3 June 1947, PRO HO 213/972.
[42] Prestige, 'War Refugee Conditions', 5 Mar. 1945, PRO HO 213/795.
[43] HO, 'Memorandum on the subject of the variation by the Secretary of State of conditional landings imposed by the Immigration Officer', 5 Oct. 1946, PRO HO 213/601.

it. Refugees displayed reluctance to submit to any greater restriction and they chafed at existing conditions. Indeed, most refugees felt they had become part of British society. They had stayed throughout the war without needing to approach the Home Office for permission either to remain or to work. Although not intended to make aliens feel secure in any way, the provisions of November 1939 had this effect. These regulations were pragmatic measures, adopted to meet war-time requirements. At a stroke, they effected blanket changes in the immigration status of a large part of the refugee community. The terms of the so-called war refugee condition allowed refugees to remain until a date 'to be specified'; the only restriction on entering employment was a requirement for the permission of the Ministry of Labour and National Service (MOLANS).[44] From the Home Office's point of view, these 1939 provisions had possessed several advantages: they obviated the necessity for regular review of individual cases, they channelled refugee labour power into the war effort and most of the casework burden was transferred to MOLANS.

But the 'war refugee' condition produced its own technical difficulties and created further problems concerning the enforceability of conditions which might be imposed in future. Rather than having people on unenforceable indefinite time conditions, or no time conditions at all, the Home Office wished to impose an enforceable and fixed time condition in all cases. The legality of achieving this through the imposition of a new type of condition on a person already in Britain was, as we have seen, in doubt. To impose new time limits when refugees returned after short visits abroad would have the advantage that their legal validity was unquestioned. This the Home Office decided to do.[45] Accordingly, shortly before the end of the European war, it arranged that the war refugee condition should no longer be given on arrival. Instead, people formerly subject to it would be landed subject either to the word 'visit' being endorsed on their travel document or to a time limit not exceeding one year.[46] Refugee industrialists who made business trips abroad, even to Northern Ireland, found themselves subjected to a twelve-month time limit on their return.[47] Surprised and upset, they besieged the Home Office with anxious queries. Could they get the condition varied? Would going abroad threaten applications for naturalisation? Short periods abroad, so long as continuity of residence was maintained, had

44 SR&O 1939 no. 1659, SR&O 1939 No 1660, 17 Nov. 1939.

45 C. E. Clack, minute, 27 July 1945, PRO HO 213/795.

46 Prestige, 'War Refugee Conditions', 5 Mar. 1945, W. R. Perks to HO Ports, Circular, ' "WR" Conditions', 7 Apr. 1945, Robinson, HO Circular No 233/1945, 'Aliens landed as Visitors', 14 Aug. 1945, PRO HO 213/795.

47 Perks to B1, HO, 21 July 1945, *ibid.*

never detracted from naturalisation applications. But aliens employed by British firms worried about losing their entitlement to work on return from business trips abroad. Refugee businessmen put off visits, even to Northern Ireland, where new industries were badly needed. Of course the Home Office did not explain to refugees the real reason behind the procedural change. It fended off the queries of the Refugee Industries Committee without offering any indication of its likely policy.[48] The Home Office's assurances that its practice was not to prohibit employment but to require that no employment be entered into without MOLANS consent were the merest crumbs of encouragement. Unsurprisingly, industrialists remained nervous. Many felt unable to commit themselves to invest in Britain. The government's failure to offer prompt clarification of immigration prospects cost the country several valuable exporters.

The economic madness of discouraging the commercial activities of refugees in this way was obvious. An official of the Ulster Office based in London questioned the necessity for imposing time conditions on visitors from England and claimed that the practice of constantly re-endorsing refugees' aliens registration certificates was 'having a serious effect on several proposed new industries'.[49] As one Home Office official said, the employment restrictions of the pre-war era had been imposed at a time of serious unemployment, but 'At the present moment the situation is reversed: there is a shortage of workers and not of work and a reversion to the pre-war practice does not seem to be called for.'[50] Indeed, in July 1946 the government decided to accept 100,000 Poles into the workforce. But it was not until November 1946 that the Cabinet's Foreign Labour Committee agreed to the home secretary's suggestion that employment restrictions on pre-war refugees should be lifted. Ministers arrived at this decision in the context of deciding to regularise the position of foreign husbands who had married British women during the war.[51] The Home Office took a further eight months to put this ministerial decision into effect. The new regulations were published only in late July 1947.[52] Even then, refugees were left to find out that they were free to work as and when they next had contact with the authorities. No announcement was made. W. P. Speake explained to the Home Office's press office that the decision to lift employment restrictions was largely due to difficulties of administration. It had been

[48] Correspondence, June–July 1945, HO to Refugee Industries Committee, 29 Nov. 1945, PRO HO 213/796.
[49] J. M. Henderson to A. J. Kelly, 16 July 1945, *ibid.*
[50] J. M. Petersen, minute, 22 Nov. 1945, *ibid.*
[51] FLC (46)6th meeting, extract, 7 Nov. 1946, PRO HO 213/962.
[52] SR&O 1947 no. 1581, SR&O 1947 no. 1582, 23 July 1947, *ibid.*

decided to have no publicity for the new regulations, in the hope that 'a few aliens in their ignorance might continue to do something useful instead of starting up the type of useless business that appeals to so many of them'.[53] Expanding on this theme in a file note, Speake described the new orders as:

symptoms of a relaxation in the powers of the Government to compel aliens to do useful work. They will save work in the Home Office, and the embarrassment of trying to carry out a policy which at this stage is in many cases impractical; but if a lack of publicity may mean that some of the aliens affected by the order will in their ignorance continue to do useful work instead of branching out into the second-hand jewellery business, and that a few of the undesirable ones will fail to get that feeling of being firmly rooted in this country which the public underlining of such orders as these must engender, that will be to our advantage.[54]

By this stage the Home Office had decided that only 'really undesirable' refugees would be deported. This was a reversal of previous policy and was, as Robinson remarked, a development which could not have been foreseen even the previous summer, but he conceded its fairness in the light of plans to hang on to German and Italian prisoners:

At a time when we propose to allow to remain here enemy aliens who actually fought in the opposing teams, provided they are usefully employed and not personally undesirable, we cannot logically send away those who cheered from the touch lines, provided they are similarly qualified.[55]

The general trend was now towards a loosening of Home Office controls. In May 1947 officials noted 'the present relaxed attitude to pre-war refugees'. They also suggested cheerily that not much money would be lost if guarantors were released from their obligations, since the practice of '"dunning" guarantors was largely a bluff, as the guarantees were legally not worth the paper they were written on'.[56] Prestige looked forward to a reduction in the 'rather tiresome work' of employment control, in which the Aliens Department had to act 'nearly always as a cross between a Post Office and a rubber stamp'.[57] It was 'usually unsatisfactory unless the ultimate sanction of deportation is both politically and practically possible (and usually it is neither)'.[58]

While accepting the futility of employment controls, the Home Office wished to keep refugees subject to conditions of landing and still treated them as temporary residents. Refugees returning from abroad were

53 W. P. Speake to G. Griffith, 16 Sep. 1947, PRO HO 213/962.
54 Speake, minute, 11 Sep. 1947, *ibid.*
55 Prestige and Robinson, minutes, 6 and 7 Mar. 1947, PRO HO 213/916.
56 Gen group B1B, HO, to Rumbelow, 31 May 1947, PRO HO 213/972.
57 Prestige, minute, 31 Mar. 1947, PRO HO 213/875.
58 Prestige to Robinson, 11 July 1947, PRO HO 213/875.

made subject to a condition requiring them to leave at some unspecified future date. Circulars implementing the de-restriction of employment stated that, although previous employment conditions were cancelled, refugees were still subject to time conditions and their status was that they were still in the United Kingdom '*on a temporary basis*', unless any time condition had been 'deliberately cancelled'.[59] It was not until December 1948, over fifteen years since the arrival of the first refugees from Germany, that the Home Office finally decided that it was possible to treat pre-war refugees and non-refugees as returning residents, unless they had given up their residence. Aliens admitted as war refugees had to wait a further twelve months, because the Home Office had special reasons for wanting to keep Poles on conditions and considered it inadvisable to treat them differently from other nationalities.[60]

The Home Office had decided in June 1945 that, since refugee doctors and dentists would be needed in the new National Health Service, it would keep their position fluid, pending resolution of general policy on refugees, by retaining the war-time emergency arrangements for their employment. Officials remained reluctant to relinquish controls on doctors and dentists.[61] In August 1947 the Home Office told the police and MOLANS that medical and dental refugees were excluded from the new freedom from employment restrictions set out in recent regulations.[62] Any who raised queries about their position should be referred to the Aliens Department.[63] This was bluff. As Speake explained, the end of employment restrictions left the Home Office without any credible controls on doctors' and dentists' employment, but, since it did not wish to have the government's power to restrict them questioned, the Home Office had not been prepared to draw attention to the issue by a clause excepting them from the new provisions. The plan was to continue the existing controls, in the likelihood that most of these refugees would fail to appreciate that 'the legal sting' had now gone out of the control. For example, foreign doctors had learned to regard consent from the authorities as the ticket to a professional livelihood:

> I doubt whether there is any serious practical objection to their continuing under the same impression. As has been said before, the exercise of this control

[59] HO Circular no. 205/1947, 'Establishment of Aliens in Businesses or Professions', 8 Oct. 1947, PRO HO 213/877.
[60] C. P. J. Ruck, minutes, 18 Dec. 1948, 16 Dec. 1949, PRO HO 213/795.
[61] Memoranda, 8 June 1945, 29 Aug. and 21 Oct. 1946, PRO HO 213/875.
[62] Clark Turner to Prestige, 18 Aug. 1947, V. Horsfall, minute, 27 Aug. 1947, *ibid.*
[63] MOLANS Circular no. 8/64, Employment of Foreigners, 8 Sep. 1947, HO Circular no. 189/1947, 10 Sep. 1947, PRO HO 213/962.

is largely a game of bluff, and at the worst it seems to me we are better placed to play the game with the odd solicitor by pointing to the powers which we say can be put into practice in certain events under Article 11 than we are to tackle heavy attack in the House, as we might have to do if the revoking SRO [a reference to the statutory instrument effecting the change in the controls] appeared to make a target of foreigners belonging to a particular profession.[64]

In fact the powers Speake suggested citing related to the safety of the realm and had no relevance to the issue in question; the Home Office therefore wished to avoid putting to the test the validity of its claim to exercise continued control in these cases. Refugee organisations were told that the special arrangements agreed with the professions for controls on doctors and dentists would remain unaffected and that they should continue to submit applications to the Home Office. Similar qualifications were applied to the right of medical and dental refugees to engage in independent business or professional practice which was conceded to all other refugees in October 1947.[65] Thus, the Home Office clung to controls on refugees in medical and related professions long after they had any legal basis.

The evasions to which the Home Office resorted to prolong its controls demonstrate the government's nervousness over resolving the position of refugees admitted in the past. It is therefore unsurprising that the question of new admissions of Jews was also handled with great caution. Let us now look briefly at British policy on the post-war entry of Jewish refugees and survivors.

In 1945, before the crisis over Palestine hardened attitudes towards Jews, certain schemes for admitting survivors were set up. Small numbers were involved. The schemes were limited to two categories: children and distressed relatives. The schemes were designed as concessions to humanitarian pressure, but took no risks over finance. From 1946 Jewish women were also eligible for entry under a revived permit scheme for domestic service. Obviously, and designedly, all these arrangements minimised the admission of adult males. The many similarities with pre-war admissions policy flowed from the same priorities, namely that the government was opposed to the primary immigration of alien Jews of working age, but would consider admitting certain dependants, in particular children, who would become Anglicised, and it was ready to admit women who were prepared to meet the continuing demand for domestic servants.

64 Speake, minute, 15 Jul. 47, *ibid.*

65 HO Circular no. 205/1947, 'Establishment of Aliens in Businesses or Professions', cited n. 59.

Within a month of the war's end the Home Office agreed to a scheme for the admission from the zones of occupation of up to 1,000 children who had been in concentration camps. The scheme was put forward by Schiff on behalf of his committee and the GEC, which undertook responsibility for non-Jews. Orphan children up to the age of sixteen were eligible. They would stay in hostels. The children's admission would be on a temporary basis: plans for re-emigration included 300 landing permits for Australia; another intended destination was Palestine. Finding candidates for the scheme did not prove easy, since other nations moved more swiftly to take children from concentration camps. But children were found in the Theresienstadt camp and 300 were selected as suitable and arrived in August 1945. Before coming to Britain the children were medically checked in order to weed out any tuberculosis cases, but after arrival a number of children turned out to be suffering from the disease. Anglo-Jewish representatives explained that the United Kingdom lacked facilities to treat tuberculosis and the climate was not conducive to recovery and suggested the use of X-rays to weed out further cases.[66] A delay in the admission of further children was largely due to objections from Jews still in the camps, motivated in part by the increasingly bitter struggle over admissions to Palestine.[67] By the end of October about 450 children had arrived from concentration camps in Germany.[68] Initially the children were admitted on condition that they would emigrate on completion of their training. The Home Office soon varied this to a restriction not to enter employment without consent. The foreign secretary, Ernest Bevin, was anxious to avoid concentrating aliens, especially Jewish refugees, in big towns and suggested steering young people toward agricultural or nursing employment in the countryside. But the minister of labour explained that this was hardly a serious option in the case of the very old, the very young and people who had come to be close to relatives living in towns.[69]

Some 600 child survivors under sixteen, mostly of Polish nationality, who had been found homeless in Germany after the armistice, arrived. A report obtained by the Home Office on the hostel arrangements for these children noted that some had falsified their ages to get out of war-torn Europe.[70] Indeed, the entry of certain 'orphans' was planned in

[66] Memoranda, minutes, June–Nov. 1945, UNRRA Records PAG-4/2.0.6.2:33 (European Region), United Nations Archives, New York.
[67] S. Adler-Rudel to UNRRA Headquarters, Germany, 21 Dec. 1945, *ibid.*
[68] B. Horsfield, minute, 1 Nov. 1945, PRO FO 371/51212, WR3198/1206/48.
[69] G. Isaacs to E. Bevin, 14 Feb. 1946, PRO LAB 8/99.
[70] H. E. Lewington, 'A note on the arrangements for housing and training of Jewish children from Germany', 27 Jan. 1947, PRO HO 45/25197, File 3.

conjunction with their parents on the continent. Rabbi Solomon Schonfeld was involved in bringing Jewish children to the United Kingdom, but the Home Office, with Schiff's approval, rejected his attempt to establish a separate Jewish children's scheme under the auspices of the chief rabbi.[71] Certain recuperative schemes for children from western Europe were set up. Members of the public offering to take orphaned German children into their homes were referred to schemes run by voluntary organisations.[72]

The Home Office worried that any new arrivals who made a perceptible impact on resources would be resented, because of post-war shortages and competition in the labour market. In 1945 it refused most applications for the admission of foreign relatives. However, in response to pressure for admission of camp survivors and others, the government announced a 'distressed persons' scheme in November 1945.[73] This authorised the admission of certain categories of distressed persons with relatives in Britain and was specifically aimed at survivors of concentration camps in Germany and Austria. Most entrants were expected to remain on a long-term basis. They would be subject to an employment restriction. It was decided to favour aged persons who had a special need of filial care and young persons having a special need of a guardian's care. Applicants needed to have a relative in the United Kingdom who was able and willing to guarantee accommodation and maintenance. The government acknowledged that the limited nature of the scheme would lead to refusals in cases where strong compassionate grounds existed. An example of a case which fell foul of the eligibility criteria involved an application by a man who wished to give a home to his niece in Poland aged about nineteen or twenty, the only person of her family to have survived the Holocaust. She had lost her sisters, mother, father and grandparents on both sides in the gas chambers of Auschwitz. The uncle added, 'the irony of it all is that the camp was situated on what was previously their own farmland'.[74] After complaints that after six months only some 220 people had been admitted, a Home Office fact-finding deputation visited the British zones of occupation. It found things working well in Austria, but the system in Germany 'almost unworkable' because of administrative bottlenecks, including postal delays of invitations from the 'host' in Britain to the 'guest' in

[71] Correspondence, 14–20 Aug. 1945, PRO HO 213/781.

[72] Lyon to S. H. Hebblethwaite, 11 Dec. 1945, Mackillop to Mrs H. R. Morgan, 30 Jan. 1946, PRO FO 371/51212, WR3692/3198/1206/48.

[73] Ede, *Hansard*, House of Commons, vol. 415, cols. 1923–5, 13 Nov. 1945.

[74] Sigmund Mehl to Interim Treasury Committee for Polish Questions, 18 Dec. 1945, H. Eggar, marginal notes, 2 Jan. 1946, PRO T 236/1409.

Europe; delays lessened once private postal services with Germany resumed.[75]

On Christmas leave in 1945, after six months at Belsen as head of one of the teams investigating war crimes, a barrister named T. H. Tilling visited his friend, Group Captain Hon. Max Aitken, whose family owned the *Express* newspaper empire. Tilling spoke of his deep concern about the plight of young Jewish men and women stuck at Belsen without prospects. He wished to propose their admission to the United Kingdom as domestic servants. A story and leader in the *Sunday Express* newspaper followed. One of thousands of letters to the paper offering to take the Jews from Belsen was published, alongside a statement that the Home Office had offered to allow these people in. This claim turned out to be incorrect.[76] But the government decided to alleviate the shortage of domestic workers, announcing, in April 1946, the forthcoming revival of the labour permit scheme to recruit female domestic workers from Europe. The scheme was not for refugees as such, but Jews in Europe would be eligible, although German Jews were excluded along with other Germans.[77]

From early 1946 alien fiancées of British servicemen could enter if they produced letters proposing marriage. German and Austrian women were barred from this scheme.[78] By February 1947 wives and children of aliens demobilised from the British forces in the United Kingdom were also eligible for British visas.[79]

Thus, except for the special children's scheme, specific provision for the entry of Jewish survivors was limited to children and relatives of people already in Britain. These schemes did not contemplate new primary immigration of adult Jewish survivors. But individual Jews might still enter if they fitted in with Britain's immigration requirements or if the Home Office was prepared to accept them on an exceptional basis.

In contrast to the elaborate precautions taken over Jewish immigration, the government threw caution to the winds in the case of Britain's European Volunteer Worker (EVW) schemes. From late 1946, some 100,000 men and women EVWs were hastily recruited from displaced persons' camps to work in Britain's understaffed industries and hospitals. The guidelines for selecting EVW candidates explicitly favoured nationals of the former Baltic states, Latvia, Lithuania and Estonia, and,

75 Ede, John Hynd, correspondence, June–July 1946; Distressed Relatives Abroad, report of HO deputation, PRO HO 213/730.
76 T. H. Tilling to Miss Markham, 25 Mar. 1946, PRO HO 213/695.
77 COR Circular no. 180, 4 July 1946, PRO HO 213/696.
78 M. Budny to Eggar, 29 Mar. 1946, PRO T 236/1409.
79 PCD Circular, 11 Feb. 1947, PRO HO 213/745.

with equal explicitness, excluded Jews along with ex-enemy nationals and *Volksdeutsch*. Such screening arrangements as were set up for EVW recruits checked that applicants were healthy and not known to have been involved in criminal activity since the war's end. Otherwise, checks were superficial or non-existent, because the many cases in which recruits were known to have collaborated with the Nazi regime were regarded as a thing of the past. The government saw Britain as a place where displaced persons who might cause political problems on the continent would cause no disruption. EVW workers were soon relieved of time conditions and their employment restrictions were administered by the Ministry of Labour.[80] Over four decades later Britain would launch war crimes legislation, investigations and prosecutions against murder suspects among their ranks.

Why was the government so hasty over recruiting EVWs yet so slow to resolve the position of refugees in Britain? An answer suggested by Beryl Hughes, who was employed in the Home Office at the time, is that the more urgent issue was given priority.[81] This is credible. The EVW schemes neatly solved two pressing problems – Britain's labour shortages and the disposal of politically problematic displaced persons in occupied Europe. The murky past of many recruits was to be overlooked as an irrelevance. Meanwhile, dealing with well-behaved refugee Jews who were now regarded as assimilated could be deferred.

The government was extremely cautious over the post-war settlement and entry of Jews. It let the question of refugees in Britain drift. Since refugees would not seek to embarrass the government publicly, this delay cost the government nothing politically. Delay also spared the government any protests which might meet a formal announcement that refugees could stay, and it facilitated retention of the services of refugees such as doctors and dentists who were subject to employment controls. Accordingly, for several years after the war, the government kept refugees waiting for the signal to resume a normal existence. Meanwhile, the theoretical possibility of deportation hung over them, as the Home Office clung on to control, using bluff to plug gaps in its legal powers. For Britain to admit further Jewish refugees and survivors carried no obvious advantage and several disadvantages. The government did not see immigration to the United Kingdom as part of the long-term solution to the plight of homeless Jewish survivors on the continent. It agreed humanitarian schemes for the temporary admission of children

80 See D. Cesarani, L. London et al., *The Entry of Nazi War Criminals and Collaborators into the United Kingdom, 1945–1950* (London, 1988).

81 Beryl Hughes, interview with the author, 7 Nov. 1988.

and family members which enabled handfuls of survivors to enter, as long as voluntary organisations or relatives bore the running costs. The turnabout in immigration policy generally – the launch of recruitment abroad – did not benefit Jews. On the contrary, selective encouragement of Jewish refugees before the war was replaced by explicit discrimination against Jews in government recruitment of displaced persons. Thus, the immediate post-war years saw a continuation of the self-interested approach Britain had adopted towards persecuted Jews since 1933.

10 Conclusion

A comparison of refugee policy in 1933–48 and in the final two decades of the twentieth century brings into focus changes in the methods British governments have used to keep the persecuted at a distance. We have seen how British officials and volunteers categorised Czech Jews as 'economic refugees' or 'racial refugees': terms the British used to distinguish the Jews from political refugees on the basis that the persecution they faced was motivated by racial and economic motives rather than political animosity. The point of making such a distinction was that it provided a formula for devaluing the Jews' claims to asylum. But the terms did not imply that the Jews were not persecuted or were 'bogus' refugees. Indeed, British representatives' use of such terms had no legal implications, for in the period covered by this book the United Kingdom was free of any legal obligation to grant asylum. The government was, therefore, at liberty to grant or deny refuge as it chose and it could freely acknowledge that Jews were persecuted without compromising its right to exclude them.

The legal position changed as a result of the United Kingdom's ratification of the United Nations Convention on the Status of Refugees of 1951. States which have undertaken to be bound by the convention are obliged not to return asylum seekers to possible persecution if they are refugees. The convention defines refugees as persons who are fleeing persecution 'for reasons of race, religion, nationality, membership of a particular social group or political opinion' and who are outside the country of their nationality.[1] Therefore, today, if the British government acknowledges an individual who has set foot in the United Kingdom to be a 'refugee', that acknowledgment binds it to grant asylum in accordance with the convention.

In recent years the British authorities have found their obligations towards asylum seekers under international law onerous and have become notably reluctant to concede that asylum seekers are refugees

[1] Convention relating to the Status of Refugees, 28 July 1951, and Protocol, 1967.

within the terms of the convention. Instead, the Home Office contends that vast numbers of asylum applicants are 'bogus' refugees, or 'economic migrants': that is, not genuine refugees, but falsely claiming to be persecuted. Furthermore, the question of how promptly applicants make their requests for asylum has become contentious in a way that was unknown in the 1930s. A large proportion of Jewish refugees originally entered as visitors and only later presented themselves as refugees, but the Home Office did not treat this delay as casting doubt on the genuineness of their fears of persecution. Nowadays the British government treats with extra suspicion persons who wait until after entry to apply for asylum and for several years now it has discriminated against such persons in the provision of welfare benefits. Yet many such applicants are subsequently accepted as genuine cases. Indeed, the incentives for genuine applicants to hide the intention to seek asylum have been increased by measures which restrict access to the United Kingdom: during the 1980s and 1990s the British government introduced new visa requirements to exclude asylum seekers from a number of countries, including Sri Lanka, Turkey and the former Yugoslavia; it also brought in laws penalising carriers who bring people to Britain without valid visas or other documents that entrants require.

Action to help people escape persecution abroad would require the British government to be more generous than is required by the letter of its convention obligations, which are owed only to persons who have reached the United Kingdom. But in this period the British government has rarely authorised the entry of would-be refugees who remain in the countries where they are persecuted. In contrast, in the final eighteen months before the outbreak of the Second World War the British government, although it imposed new visa requirements to stem the flow of refugee Jews from Germany, Austria and Czechoslovakia, also chose to authorise tens of thousands of visas for selected Jews, enabling them to emigrate and escape persecution.

The relatively generous face of British policy towards the Jews is more familiar than its self-interested aspects. Indeed, the tendency to focus almost exclusively on the welcome which Britain gave to Jewish refugees still helps to propagate a number of myths: that refugee policy was more humane than it actually was; that Britain put no limits on aid to persecuted Jews; or even that Britain has never turned its back on genuine refugees.

The British government did help and save persecuted Jews, but on its own terms. The United Kingdom was cast in the role of a country of temporary refuge. Refugees received only a qualified welcome. They were guests, kept on their best behaviour for up to fifteen years. Over the same period, perhaps 30,000 re-emigrated, in most cases to the United States. To gain entry to the United Kingdom between 1933 and 1939, refugee Jews needed first to satisfy the government that they had guaranteed financial support. The majority also needed either the capacity to re-emigrate or capital, whether intellectual, industrial or financial; alternatively, women might enter if they were prepared to become domestic servants.

Much of the aid from refugee organisations hinged on factors beyond the control of the individual, such as where Jews came from or why they were persecuted. Anglo-Jewish leaders favoured German Jews over Austrians and declined responsibility for Jews from Czechoslovakia. The activists of the British Committee for Refugees from Czechoslovakia (BCRC) discriminated in favour of political refugees and against those persecuted merely for being Jewish. Bunbury noted the BCRC's reluctance to modify this policy, saying that, after the Germans marched into Bohemia and Moravia,

> Jewish persecution came very prominently into the picture, and the responsibilities of the British Committee were greatly enlarged and to some extent altered. The compulsion to take responsibility for, and to maintain, large numbers of these racial refugees was itself somewhat resented.[2]

The attitude of the BCRC reflected its explicitly political orientation. But it was also a product of a more general lack of sensitivity to the plight of the refugee from racial persecution. Many people had difficulty in assimilating this new type of victim to existing notions of what constituted a refugee. It was widely accepted that the government should offer refuge to individuals persecuted for their political or religious beliefs. But Jews were hounded for what they were, rather than because of anything they did or believed. They were persecuted as members of a group rather than as individuals. These Jews did not automatically elicit the same humanitarian response as persons who fitted the conventional image of the individual political refugee. The prevailing stereotype of the Jew – as the unwanted immigrant against whom Britain needed aliens laws – worked against recognition of the humanitarian plight which led persecuted Jews to seek refuge. Another reason for the categorisation of refugee Jews as immigrants was that, beyond their immediate need for temporary refuge, their ultimate need for permanent settlement was all too apparent.

European Jews needed refuge, family reunification and the freedom to reconstruct a normal existence. Much was done by Britain and other

[2] Bunbury, memorandum, 15 Jan. 1940, PRO HO 294/25.

nations to meet such needs. But in relation to the scale of the problem, these efforts were meagre, a point made by Viscount Samuel in December 1945. As we saw in the introduction, the immediate response to Samuel's complaint was to tell him that Britain had done more than any other country to help the Jews. Indeed, if Britain's overall contribution is compared with that of the USA, it comes out better in terms of percentage of refugees admitted per head of population, and much better in terms of refugees per head of Jewish population. But what do such calculations tell us? Leaving aside the Soviet Union, Britain did more to shelter Jews than any other country except the USA. It did more than might have been expected. Britain was not indifferent to Jewish suffering. But this book's analysis of policy has shown the limits of the aid Britain was prepared to offer.

What of the assumptions on which British policy rested? Surely the sluggish and self-interested character of British policy-making towards persecuted Jews requires some further explanation? Let us, therefore, explore other factors which may have influenced British responses.

Was the widespread anti-semitism in British society responsible for policies toward Jews menaced by Nazism? As we have seen, both the government and Anglo-Jewish leaders limited refugee admissions on the principle that this was essential to avoid stimulating anti-semitism. For example, Chaim Weizmann told a 1936 conference convened by the Council for German Jewry:

> Jews have proved that they are an 'insoluble element' – to use a chemical term – the quantity which can be absorbed in each country proves to be small. The formula reacts quickly, and saturation point is rapidly reached, and the Jewish communities in the respective countries are always full of anxiety lest there will be too many and that anti-semitism may be stimulated.[3]

Weizmann's theme was, of course, that suitable refugees should go to Palestine. So, among Jews, the fear of an anti-semitic reaction to large-scale Jewish immigration was a Zionist argument, as well as an assimilationist watchword.

What of non-Jews? According to certain ministers and officials, the British public was capable of exploding into extreme anti-semitism. Did such conclusions reflect the assumptions of their proponents as much as the reality of popular sentiment? When members of the public wrote in expressing extremist views, Home Office officials treated such effusions dismissively. Yet, their own comments can make uneasy reading. For example, describing a London woman living in the Finchley Road area, who had complained to her MP about the financing of refugees and

[3] Speeches delivered at Anglo-Jewish conference convened by the Council for German Jewry at the Dorchester Hotel, 15 Mar. 1936, CBF, reel 4, file 15.

opposed their naturalisation, the Home Office's W. B. Lyon characterised her as 'anti-alien in outlook and . . . not particularly accurate in her facts or conclusions'. Yet, we may deduce from Lyon's remark that the woman lived 'in a district where alien Jews are thickly congregated and aggressively opulent', that he himself accepted certain negative stereotypes of Jews.[4]

One of the stereotypes most entrenched in British official thinking was of Jews as incorrigibly urban and incapable of settling to agricultural work. Any apparent confirmation of this prejudice was relished, especially if a Jew provided it. For example, in 1946 several unhappy young Jewish refugees wrote from the new Dominican Republic Settlement Association agricultural settlement at Sosua in the Dominican Republic where they had been sent in 1940, but had failed to thrive. Officials in London were not surprised by this outcome, but ruled that the Jews' requests to return to the United Kingdom could not be granted. From Cuidad Trujillo, M. W. Macrae of the British legation sent a report of a conversation with David Stern, head of the Sosua settlement, regarding Jewish settlers' commitment to the project. Stern depicted Jews as preferring a hedonistic urban existence of frequenting night clubs and smoking cigars in cafés to hard agricultural work and Macrae considered that Stern had the qualifications and experience to validate these opinions.[5] Back in the Foreign Office, A. W. H. Wilkinson found the report, 'illuminating . . . the experiences of Sosua are likely to be repeated elsewhere and for the same reasons'.[6]

In Britain, prejudice against Jews was considered unacceptable if it formed an explicit part of a social or political programme. Yet, moderate indulgence in social anti-Jewish prejudice was so widespread as to be unremarkable. Hostile stereotypes of Jews were accepted by law-abiding citizens. For example, R. M. A. Hankey, a Foreign Office official, was ready to show his attachment to the common stereotype of the Jew as profiteer, even in the shadow of the Holocaust. In a minute concerning American proposals to license the transmission of foreign exchange in order to rescue 70,000 Romanian Jews who had been deported to Transnistria, the part of the Soviet Union occupied by Romania, Hankey commented, 'I suspect the real object of the scheme is financial – Jews in Europe getting out into dollars while there is yet time!'[7]

The knowledge that the Nazis were murdering European Jewry did not stem the flow of anti-Jewish remarks. Indeed, the prejudiced

[4] Lyon, minute, 3 Mar. 1944, PRO HO 213/988.
[5] M. W. Macrae to Bevin, 17 Aug. 1946, PRO FO 371/57850, WR2328/533/48.
[6] Wilkinson, minute, 30 Aug. 1946, *ibid.*
[7] Hankey, minute, 30 Dec. 1943, PRO FO 371/36747, W17857/15684/48.

comments discussed above were all made in 1943 or later. But how did the widely diffused anti-Jewish prejudice within the governing classes condition the government's broad approach to Jewish refugee policy? What we can say is that British stereotypes of Jews were significant in marking them out as members of a group that was difficult, even dangerous, to help. Such prejudices helped to cast the image of the Jewish refugee in a problematic mould and thus to strengthen support for policies of restriction.

Huge variations in official attitudes towards Jews and refugees are indicated by police and Home Office reactions in mid-1939 to a Metropolitan Police investigation into alleged corruption among a handful of individuals within the 800-strong staff of the GJAC. Chief Inspector G. Hatherill, who had conducted the police investigation, stated in his report:

> The whole organisation is practically Jewish and at least half of the staff are refugees. Therefore it cannot be expected that these persons are going to consider any rules and regulations in assisting members of their own faith to get out of Germany. That attitude we have heard expressed again and again in the course of this enquiry, and the general belief of Jewry throughout Europe is that if they can only get to England they are safe. Further, that once here the laws in this country are such that it is easy to defy the authorities to send them out again.
>
> Home Office with its policy of sympathetic concern for Jewish refugees has encouraged this belief, and there is no doubt whatever that thousands of these refugees who have come here supposedly for a temporary period have not the slightest intention of ever going elsewhere. In fact it is becoming almost monotonous for police officers to hear refugee Jews boasting, when interviewed regarding allegations of misdeeds on their part, that they cannot be sent out of England.[8]

Hatherill's report was passed up the police hierarchy by a Superintendent Bell who regarded its findings as 'what might be expected considering that the essentials have been left to members of the race concerned who are not of high standing or likely to withstand the chance of exploiting the influx of refugees into this country'.[9] The Metropolitan Police commissioner, Sir Philip Game, acknowledged that there was 'obviously some corruption, how widespread it is difficult to say, but the complete confusion which appears to prevail in the office at Bloomsbury House is the root of the trouble'. Otto Schiff planned to bring in two efficiency experts from Marks and Spencer to overhaul the GJAC but Game still thought 'some supervision by the Home Office

[8] G. Hatherill, report, n.d., 1939, PRO HO 213/1651, p. 59.
[9] Supt. A. Bell to assistant chief commissioner, 10 July 1939, *ibid.*

would be essential sooner or later'.[10] Hatherill had discounted the overhaul proposed by Schiff as:

absolutely hopeless as long as the whole staff remain Jewish with such a large percentage of voluntary workers and refugees. It is notorious of Jews that while brilliant in ideas and business when it comes to actual organisation and executive work there is something lacking. Most of the large Jewish business houses it will be found have Gentiles to run the executive machinery. In fact many prominent Jews have expressed this opinion to me and admitted that the average Jew has not the instinct for the order and discipline necessary in higher routine work.[11]

Home Office officials pounced on these displays of police prejudice. Jenifer Williams wrote: 'The police seem rather anxious lest refugees are getting into this country too easily and through the agency of various undesirable individuals. It may be remarked in passing however that the tone of their report is predominantly anti-Jewish.'[12] Another Home Office member considered the police suggestion 'that a committee of Gentiles should handle the matter takes us perilously near race distinction'.[13]

By this date Home Office officials were inured to criticism from other branches of officialdom for showing too much sympathy for refugee Jews. One does find instances of anti-semitic prejudice within the Aliens Department, notably certain comments made by Speake in 1947.[14] But senior Home Office officials were overwhelmingly sympathetic towards Jews. In this respect they compare favourably with their counterparts in the Foreign Office. Certainly, hostility towards Jews contributed to the lassitude with which Foreign Office officials generally responded to proposals for humanitarian aid to Jews and to the vigour with which they argued against giving such aid.

After the war, and notwithstanding the revelation of the full horrors of Nazi crimes against them, Jews were still perceived as undesirable immigrants. In October 1945, when the disposal of pitifully small numbers of Jewish survivors was under discussion, the Dominions Office decreed that dominion governments were not to be alarmed by the prospect of pressure to take Jews from Europe. Sir John Stephenson, the deputy under secretary, commented:

The Dominions will be very reluctant to accept these intractable and unassimilable settlers and they would certainly take exception to a proposal which in terms suggested them as a possible home for the Jews.[15]

[10] P. Game to Maxwell, 31 July 1939, *ibid.* [11] Hatherill, report, cited n. 8, p. 60.

[12] J. Williams, memorandum, 3 Aug. 1939, PRO HO 213/1651.

[13] HO memorandum, n.d., *ibid.* [14] See ch. 9, n. 54, 64.

[15] J. Stephenson to secretary of state, minutes, 1 and 11 Oct. 1945, Lord Christopher Addison, minute, 7 Oct. 1945, PRO DO 35/1589.

This remark certainly suggests that its author's prejudices against Jews were intractable, but comments such as these, while they offer clues to the thinking behind British policy, do not add up to an explanation of it.

Can a particular individual's acceptance of stereotypes and anti-semitic views tell us how he himself would handle the Jewish refugee issue? We have seen how Sir Horace Rumbold accepted stereotyped prejudices against Jews, but worked to aid Jewish refugees. We have also noted how Chamberlain privately admitted his dislike of Jews, but he redirected British policy in order to expand the temporary admission of refugee Jews for humanitarian reasons. Conversely, Herbert Morrison, who was not overtly anti-semitic, still blamed Jews for many of their misfortunes and argued relentlessly that to keep Jewish refugees in Britain risked causing 'explosions' of anti-semitism. These examples suggest that what determined the responses of British ministers and officials to the Jewish refugee issue was not attitudes to Jews as such, but the degree to which they felt able to adopt a humanitarian stance.

In seeking the basis of British responses to the humanitarian issues involved in helping Jews, let us consider what other factors may have militated against a humanitarian approach. Did the public relations exercises of Evian and Bermuda reflect any wider motivation than self-interest? Was the international consensus over doing little for persecuted Jews based on some political principle? Were any internationally shared assumptions acting as a brake on humanitarian action by governments?

In response to these questions, let us look at the persecution and expulsion of Jews within the broader context of contemporary perceptions of the nation-state. In the inter-war period, as Claudena M. Skran has written, 'The transformation of central and eastern Europe from multi-ethnic empires to nation-states displaced millions of people, primarily members of ethnic minorities, from the new states.'[16] This transformation was the primary cause creating refugees in the period. Indeed, ethnically based refugee movements and large-scale exchanges of population hastened the transformation of countries in the Balkans into nation-states possessing an unprecedented degree of ethnic, cultural and religious homogeneity.[17] The League of Nations' support in the 1920s for this process – which Skran refers to as the 'unmixing of populations' – as a solution to refugee problems helped to give the

[16] Skran, *Refugees*, p. 31. Skran acknowledges indebtedness to the analysis by Aristiole R. Zolberg of the impact of nation-state formation on the production of refugees (pp. 19–20).

[17] *Ibid.*, pp. 47–8 (quote, p. 48).

forcible uprooting of minorities an aura of legitimacy. The popular wisdom of the era was that eliminating ethnically diverse minorities in this way achieved a reduction in political turmoil and thus fostered stability.

Such perceptions of ethnic homogeneity as a legitimate national objective led states to tolerate the expulsion of minorities in the process of nation-state formation in Europe. These attitudes partly explain the failure of the major international actors to react to refugee problems in more than an ad hoc way or to address their root causes. Assumptions that surplus populations could be exported from Europe ran up against selective immigration policies overseas. But the notion that national borders were sounder and more durable if they reflected ethnic divisions was firmly established as one of the assumptions underlying international co-operation. Furthermore, it is within this context of assumptions that Skran locates the aims of Germany under Hitler: 'the Nazis took the goal of creating a homogeneous nation-state to its radical extreme'.[18]

In the inter-war period considerable sympathy was felt with Germany's nationalistic aspirations. Indeed, the 1919 settlement imposed by the victorious Allies at Versailles was widely thought to have been misguided in saddling Germany with new frontiers which left out large ethnic German populations. In 1938 Hitler succeeded in annexing first Austria and then the Sudetenland for Germany. Because these border changes incorporated ethnic Germans within the Reich, they complied with the widely accepted principle of aligning national with ethnic divisions. For this reason the changes themselves were widely accepted, notwithstanding international concern about the methods by which the Nazi regime achieved them. The principle was upheld by Britain and France in the Munich agreement's provisions not only for ceding the Sudetenland but also for associated exchanges of population across the new borders. Thus, the British government was prepared to participate both in redrawing the map of central Europe and in shifting populations across national frontiers in order to place ethnic Germans under German rule and to facilitate the removal of non-Germans. The government also reluctantly allowed itself to be drawn into efforts to mitigate the forced expulsion of Jews from Germany and Austria and, to a lesser extent, the Sudetenland. But it drew the line at endorsing the mass expulsion of the Jewish minority from Czech territory.

Jewish minorities lacked a nation-state to defend their interests. The leaders of the international community were not prepared to embark on

[18] *Ibid.*

such a political step as confronting the German government over human rights abuses against Jews. These statesmen limited the terms on which they would negotiate with Germany over the Jews to improving the conditions of flight. Indeed, as late as 1938 it was generally believed that the Nazis' expulsion of Jews from Germany and Austria created a manageable problem solvable by orderly emigration. The international community was generally resigned to the Jews' permanent expulsion. But its members drew the line at the expulsion of unlimited numbers and the crisis of 1938 led to a new determination to permit only orderly emigration. The nations at Evian, aiming to deter Poland and Romania from expelling their Jewish minorities in a state of destitution, agreed to avoid any co-operation with Germany which would legitimate expulsions.[19] But their alternative approach of attempting through the IGC to arrange the departure of refugees in a humane way without infringing state sovereignty – the only terms on which Germany would negotiate over expulsions from its own territory – came to nothing. Meanwhile the German government continued to force out Jews from all territories under its control. The self-interest of these governments, especially in avoiding responsibility for the disposal of Jews, thus meant that each 'balanced the humanitarian principle against other considerations'.[20]

In Britain, as in other countries of refuge, profound tension existed between a genuine aspiration to adhere to humanitarian principles and self-protectiveness against foreigners whose ethnicity was perceived as alien. British observers found Nazi Germany's goal of homogenising its population much less of an affront than the inhumane methods used to implement it. The British, too, placed a value on homogeneity. Indeed, one reason for British readiness to accept child refugees was because Anglicisation would minimise the extent to which their ethnicity would be perceived as alien. And one of the conclusions the Cabinet Committee on Refugees reached at its last meeting prior to the Bermuda Conference in April 1943 was:

> As regards post-war aspects of the refugee problem, a most important objective to aim at was to return large numbers of refugees to their country of origin. At the same time it would be worth while for the Bermuda Conference to investigate the possibility of allocating some suitable area of large size as a place of settlement for Jewish refugees after the war. In this connection it was pointed out that the Jewish element in the population of Poland was proportionally higher than was healthy.[21]

On this occasion, ministers were expressing their apprehension that a Jewish presence over a certain level constituted a risk to the health of the

[19] *Ibid.*, p. 257. [20] *Ibid.*, p. 273.
[21] JR (43) 6th meeting, 1 Apr. 1943, PRO CAB 95/15.

body politic. Such conceptions of states as most stable when most homogeneous allowed Jewish minorities to be perceived not merely as anomalous, but as being different in a way that spelt danger if their numbers were not restricted.

Refugee policies were influenced by these perceptions of the nation-state and its needs. Indeed, such assumptions may have been as important as specific ideas about Jews in convincing governments that they owed it to themselves to limit the size of their Jewish minorities. At the same time it was highly convenient for statesmen to have an arguable political justification for limiting their governments' generosity to persecuted Jews, even at the risk of consigning them to a cruel fate.

If nation-states were not obliged to save the Jews, who was? As we know, many private individuals felt an obligation to try to help Jews escape, despite the risks involved and the limitations on what they could achieve. Private organisations, especially the Jewish committees, explored and financed the possibilities for refuge and rescue. Such activism paved the way for governments to allow the expanding voluntary movement to take much of the responsibility for giving a lead in financing aid and even in formulating policy, hastening the transformation of the provision of humanitarian aid into the province of specialist organisations rather than of governments. But the British government was still drawn into playing a critical role in assisting refugees. As private organisations ran out of money, the government became involved in overseeing the policy of the BCRC, and later of the Jewish refugee organisation, and in keeping both of these organisations as well as several others financially afloat. The British government, together with the Americans, dominated the Intergovernmental Committee; indeed, it was an expression of their policies. The two governments used the IGC largely as a means to deflect pressure for more governmental aid to the Jews. In 1944 the IGC eventually transcended this role only because the two governments had now agreed to let it embark on a humanitarian programme. It was allowed to dispense assistance to help people escape from the Nazis.

But the power to offer refuge remained a function of state sovereignty. Asylum, refuge, settlement – all were in the gift of governments. And if governments would not offer them, no one else could. How far were governments prepared to go in expanding the prospects of refuge? The Jews were not a pressing problem so long as they remained in the Nazis' clutches. Jews would cause serious international embarrassment only if they escaped and became refugees needing disposal. Jewish refugees were expected to arouse hostility and states were reluctant to accept them as immigrants. The disposal of Jews was thus seen as problematic.

To make offers of refuge would add to the dimensions of the problem. Governments held back, partly because of the underlying prejudices and assumptions considered above, partly because of more immediate concerns. Yet governments did offer refuge, albeit hedged around by limitations whose precise form varied from country to country.

The British government regarded persecuted Jews primarily as a potential refugee problem. The overall policy of the British government was to accept responsibility only for the number of Jews that it believed it could conveniently dispose of. This was how it determined where to draw the line in refugee admissions. It was also the crucial motive for its extreme caution over trying to rescue Jews during the Holocaust, when, once again, the limit on British readiness to offer long-term refuge acted as a constraint on its making temporary refuge available.

The British government repeatedly stated its reluctance to act alone. British representatives would have felt under pressure to do more to expand the prospects of refuge had the United States government shown serious interest in doing so. The Americans' decision at the start of 1944 to initiate unilateral action on rescue took the British by surprise. The British government reacted by seeking to assert some control over the financing of rescue and proposed joint action through backing for the credit scheme via the IGC. The British were surprised once again by the Americans' lukewarm response and their obvious preference for national action through the War Refugee Board. Both governments put a little money of their own into rescue. But going thus far was totally different from expanding the possibilities of refuge for Jews. As regards the expansion of refuge, the one substantial effort made by either government in response to the Holocaust was their belated joint acceptance of the Horthy offer in August 1944, at a time when a number of other states were already taking steps to save the remaining Jews of Hungary. Yet, even at this juncture, the British held back and gave vent to their apprehensions about the disposal of Jews, secretly insisting on limiting their ultimate commitment to find homes for any Jews who might escape the Nazi murderers in Hungary.

Of course, the scope for policy-makers to act on their humanitarian impulses is always limited. The leaders of war-time Britain had to focus on essentials and charity was a luxury. Furthermore, as Emerson noted before the Bermuda conference, with every extra day of war, 'more persons will lose their lives than can be saved by any rescue measures so far suggested'.[22] Britain's great contribution to saving the Jews was its

22 Emerson, Note on Measures for the Rescue of Refugees from Axis Persecution, 24 Mar. 1943, AJ43/37/140.

part in the defeat of Nazi Germany. The reasons for Britain's investment in that defeat had nothing to do with saving the Jews. Its pursuit of that goal is measured by its investment in rescue. This was small. Without lengthening the war, Britain could have attempted more, but not a great deal more, to save lives. The scope for more action than was undertaken has been demonstrated, if by nothing else, by the differences we have seen within the policy community, even during the war, over what measures it might be reasonable to attempt. During the Holocaust, the additional lives saved would have been numerically marginal. It is not possible to assess precisely all the opportunities that were missed. What we can say, however, is that they were missed because, weak though the prospects of saving Jewish lives may have been, the will to pursue such prospects was significantly weaker. This book has sought to explain why that was so. And, while the detailed findings of this book concern British refugee policy as a response to the case of the Jews, it has also shown that the humanitarian crisis affecting the Jews exposed deep tensions within British political culture regarding the proper response of nation-states to the persecution of foreigners abroad – tensions which remain unresolved to this day.

Appendix 1: Biographical notes

Most of the subjects of these notes were ministers or officials of principal or more senior rank within the British government in the period 1933–48. Certain other persons who were prominent in matters concerning refugees during this period are also included. A separate list of holders of the offices of home secretary and permanent under secretary at the Home Office (the civil servant who headed the department) is provided in appendix 2.

These notes highlight aspects of their subjects' lives which are relevant to this study. The details given relate principally to the period 1933–48. In selected cases details are also included of earlier or subsequent careers. Honours conferred before 1933 are incorporated in the subject's name. Honours conferred in 1933 or later are recorded in the body of the entry. References to honours are normally confined to peerages and knighthoods. Repetition of biographical details already provided in footnotes is minimised. Entries in respect of career civil servants begin with the name of the government department in which the person concerned was serving in 1933, or if later, in which he first served.

The following abbreviations are used:

Sec	secretary
US	under secretary
PPS	parliamentary private secretary (backbench member of parliament working for a minister without pay)
Parl US	parliamentary under secretary (junior minister)
Parl Sec	parliamentary secretary (junior minister)
PUS	permanent under secretary (civil servant at head of government department)

ANDERSON, SIR JOHN, 1st Viscount Waverley (1952) (1882–1958): PUS Home Office 1922–32. Governor of Bengal 1932–7. Ind Nat MP 1938–50. Ld Privy Seal 1938–9. Home Sec and Min of Home Security 1939–40. Ld Pres of Council 1940–3; Chancellor of Exchequer 1943–5.

ATTLEE, CLEMENT RICHARD, 1st Earl Attlee (1955)
(1883–1967): Lab MP 1922–50. Leader of Labour Party 1935–55. Ld Privy Seal 1940–2. Sec for Dominions 1942–3. Ld Pres of Council 1943–5. Deputy Prime Minister 1942–5. Prime Minister 1945–51.

BALDWIN, STANLEY, 1st Earl Baldwin (1937)
(1867–1947): Prime Minister 1923–4, 1924–9, 1935–7; Ld Pres of Council 1931–5; Ld Privy Seal 1932–4. Leader of Conservative Party 1923–37.

BENTWICH, NORMAN DE MATTOS
(1883–1971): Attorney-General of Palestine 1921–9. Prof of International Relations, Hebrew Univ of Jerusalem 1932–51. Zionist. Deputy High Commissioner for Refugees 1933–6. Honorary Director and member of Professional Committee, Council for German Jewry (CGJ) 1936. CGJ Director of Emigration and Training 1938. Service in Min of Information and Air Ministry during Second World War.

BEVERIDGE, SIR WILLIAM HENRY, 1st Baron Beveridge (1946)
(1879–1963): Social reformer and economist. Director, London School of Economics 1919–37. Founder, Academic Assistance Council 1933. Master, University College Oxford 1937–44.

BLAND, GEORGE NEVILE MALTBY
(1886–1972): Foreign Office. Brussels, 1930–4; KCVO 1937; Head of Treaty Dept 1935–8; Br Min at The Hague Sep. 1938. Br Min to Netherlands government in London May 1942.

BUNBURY, SIR HENRY NOEL
(1876–1968): Comptroller and Auditor-General of Post Office 1920–37. Authority on control of public expenditure. Administrative work for German Jewish Aid Committee, 1938–9. Director, Czech Refugee Trust Fund 1939.

BUTLER, RICHARD AUSTEN, Lord Butler (1965)
(1902–82): Con MP 1929–65. Parl US India Office 1932–7.
Parl Sec Min of Labour 1937–8. Parl US Foreign Office Feb. 1938–41. President Board of Education 1941–4. Min of Education 1944–5.

CADOGAN, ALEXANDER GEORGE MONTAGU
(1884–1968): Foreign Office. Head, League of Nations Section 1921–33. Br Minister Peking 1934–5. KCMG 1934. Dep US 1936. PUS 1938–46.

CAMPBELL, RONALD HUGH
(1883–1953): Foreign Office. Paris 1929–35. Belgrade 1935–9. KCMG Jan. 1936. Amb at Paris Nov. 1939. London from June 1940. Amb at Lisbon Dec. 1940–5.

CARVELL, JOHN ERIC MACLEAN
(1894–1978): Foreign Office. Port Alegre 1932. New York 1934. Consul-General Munich Apr. 1938. London Aug. 1939. Head, Refugee Section in General Dept 1940. Acting Consul-General, then Consul-General, Algiers 1942. Los Angeles 1945.

CHAMBERLAIN, (ARTHUR) NEVILLE
(1869–1940): Con MP 1929–40. Chancellor of the Exchequer 1931–7. Prime Minister 1937–40. Leader of Conservative Party 1937–40. Ld Pres of Council 1940.

CHURCHILL, WINSTON LEONARD SPENCER
(1874–1965): Lib MP 1904–22. Home Sec 1910–11. Con MP 1924–64. First Ld of Admiralty and member of War Cabinet 1939–40. Prime Minister and Min of Defence 1940–5. Leader of Conservative Party 1940–55. KG 1953.

COOPER, ERNEST NAPIER, OBE
(1883–1948): Home Office: Factory Inspectorate, Inspector Class II 1910. 1918–20 lent to another department. Superintending Inspector (Western and Northern Division), Aliens Branch 1925–31. Seconded for duty as Principal in Aliens Department 1930–1 (move permanent by 1932). Acting Asst Sec by 1939. Chairman, CID Sub-Committee on Control of Aliens in Wartime 1939. Asst Sec by 1940. Ret 1943. Working for Central Office for Refugees 1944. Re-married (widower) Gertrud Kallmann, Apr. 1946.

VISCOUNT CRANBORNE, ROBERT ARTHUR JAMES GASCOYNE-CECIL, 5th Marquess of Salisbury from 1947
(1893–1972): PPS to Eden (q.v.) 1934–5. Parl US Foreign Office 1935–8. Resigned with Eden Feb. 1938. Paymaster-General May 1940. Sec for Dominions Oct. 1940–1. Entered House of Lords Jan. 1941. Sec for Colonies 1942. Ld Privy Seal 1942–3. Sec for Dominions Oct. 1943–5.

CULPIN, EWART G.
(1877–1946): Architect. Labour London County Council member 1937–46. Chairman of the Council 1938–9. Trustee, Czech Refugee Trust Fund 1939.

DELEVIGNE, SIR MALCOLM
(1868–1950): Home Office. Junior clerk 1892. Asst US 1913, Dep US 1922–32. Ret 1932. Trustee, Czech Refugee Trust Fund 1939.

EDEN, (ROBERT) ANTHONY (Sir), 1st Earl of Avon (1957) (1897–1977): Con MP 1923–57. Parl US Foreign Office 1931–3. Ld Privy Seal 1933–5. Min for League of Nations Affairs June 1935. Foreign Sec Dec. 1935–Feb. 1938 (resigned). Sec for Dominions 1939–40. Sec for War May–Dec. 1940. Foreign Sec 1940–5.

EMERSON, SIR HERBERT WILLIAM (1881–1962): Governor of Punjab 1933–8. League High Commissioner for Refugees 1939. Director Intergovernmental Committee on Refugees 1939. Director Central Council for Refugees 1940. Chairman Advisory Council on Aliens 1940.

FISHER, SIR (NORMAN FENWICK) WARREN (1879–1948): Treasury. Permanent Sec, Treasury and Head of Civil Service 1919–39.

GAME, AIR-VICE MARSHALL SIR PHILIP WOOLCOTT (1876–1961): Commissioner, Metropolitan Police 1935–45.

GILMOUR, SIR JOHN (1876–1940): Unionist MP 1910–40. Home Sec Sep. 1932–June 35. Min of Shipping 1939–40.

GUINNESS, WALTER EDWARD, 1st Lord Moyne (1880–1944): Joint Parl US Min of Agriculture 1940–1. Sec for Colonies and Leader of House of Lords Feb. 1941–Feb. 1942. Min in Middle East 1944 (murdered).

HAILEY, WILLIAM MALCOLM, 1st Baron Hailey (1936). (1872–1969): Indian Civil Service 1896–1934. Governor United Provinces 1928–34. Writer on Africa. Employed on missions to African colonies and Belgian Congo 1938–9. Chairman Co-ordinating Committee for Refugees 1938–9.

HALDANE PORTER, (SIR) WILLIAM (1867–1944): Home Office. Inspector under the Aliens Act 1906. Chief Inspector, Aliens Branch 1919–29.

LORD HALIFAX, see WOOD, EDWARD FREDERICK LINDLEY

HANKEY, SIR MAURICE PASCAL ALERS, 1st Baron Hankey (1939) (1977–1963): Sec to Committee of Imperial Defence 1912–38. Sec to Cabinet 1916–38. In War Cabinet as Min without Portfolio Sep. 1939–May 1940. Chancellor of Duchy of Lancaster May 1940–1. Paymaster-General July 1941–2.

HAYTER, WILLIAM GOODENOUGH (1906–1995): Foreign Office. 3rd Sec Vienna 1931. Moscow 1934. 2nd Sec 1935. London 1937. China Oct. 1938. 1st Sec Dec. 1940. Washington 1940. London 1944. Asst US 1948. Br Min at Paris 1949. Amb to USSR 1953–7. KCMG 1953. Dep US 1957–8.

HOARE, SIR SAMUEL JOHN GURNEY, 1st Viscount Templewood (1944)

(1880–1959): Con MP 1910–44. Sec for India 1931–5. Foreign Sec 1935. First Ld of Admiralty 1936–7. Home Sec May 1937–Sep. 1939. Ld Privy Seal and member of War Cabinet 1939–40. Sec for Air 1940. Amb to Spain 1940–4.

HOLDERNESS, SIR ERNEST W. E., Bart

(1890–1968): Home Office. Junior clerk 1913. Private Sec to Parl US 1920. Asst Principal by 1925. Principal by 1927. Asst Sec by 1933. Running Aliens Dept 1933. Seconded to another department 1943.

JEFFES, MAURICE

(1888–1954): Foreign Office, Passport Control Department (PCD). Service with Army in France 1916–19 including Intelligence Corps. Service in unestablished capacity in PCD from 1919. Director PCD July 1938.

KELL, MAJOR-GENERAL SIR VERNON

(1873–1942): MI5. Retired from Imperial Defence Committee 1909. Re-employed War Office, 1909. Head of MI5, 1916–40.

LATHAM, RICHARD THOMAS EDWIN

(d. 1943): Barrister and scholar. Temporary clerk in Foreign Office General Dept Refugee Section 1939–41. War service 1941–3. Killed in action 1943.

LASKI, NEVILLE

(1890–1969): Barrister. President of Board of Deputies of British Jews and Chairman of Joint Foreign Committee, 1933–40.

LEITH-ROSS, SIR FREDERICK WILLIAM

(1887–1968): Treasury. Chief Economic Adviser 1932. Negotiated revised German payments agreement 1938. Director-General Min of Economic Warfare 1939–42. Director-General UNRRA, 1942–6.

MACDONALD, MALCOLM JOHN

(1901–1981): Parl US for Dominions 1931–5. Sec for Colonies June–Nov. 1935. Sec for Dominions Nov. 1935–8. Sec for Colonies May 1938–40. Min of Health May 1940–1. High Commissioner in Canada 1941–6.

MACDONALD, JAMES RAMSAY

(1866–1937): Lab MP 1906–18, 1922–31. National Labour MP 1931–5, 1936–7. Prime Minister 1924, 1929–31, 1931–5. Ld President of Council 1935.

MACKILLOP, DOUGLAS

(1891–1959): Foreign Office. Brussels 1932–6. Moscow 1936–7. Peking 1937. Riga 1938–40. Berne 1940. Head of Refugee Department 1946. Head of Claims Dept 1947.

MAKINS, ROGER MELLOR, Lord Sherfield (1964)
(1904–97): Foreign Office. 3rd Sec Washington 1931. 2nd Sec 1933. Chargé d'affaires Oslo May 1934. London Sep. 1934. League of Nations and Western Dept 1935–8. Asst Adviser on League of Nations Affairs 1937, later Adviser. Central Dept 1939. Acting 1st Sec Sep. 1939. Acting Counsellor Aug. 1940. Head of Central Dept 1941–2. Seconded to Treasury for service with Min Resident in West Africa July 1942. Counsellor 1942. Washington 1945–7. Min Aug. 1945. Asst US 1946. Dep US 1948–52. Amb to US 1953–6. Joint Permanent Sec of Treasury 1956–59. KCMG 1959.

MALCOLM, MAJOR-GENERAL SIR NEILL
(1869–1953): Army. General Officer Commanding in Malaya 1921–4. Ret 1924. High Commissioner for Refugees 1936–8.

MASON, PAUL
(1904–78): Foreign Office. 1st Sec Br Embassy Lisbon 1941. Acting Head, Refugee Dept 1944–5. Acting Counsellor 1945. Head, United Nations Dept 1946. KCMG 1954.

MAXWELL, (SIR) ALEXANDER
(1880–1963): Home Office. Asst US 1924, Dep US 1932. KBE 1936. PUS Home Office 1938–48.

MORRISON, HERBERT STANLEY, Baron Morrison (1959)
(1891–1965): Lab MP 1923–4, 1929–31, 1935–59. Leader London County Council 1934–40. Min of Supply 1940. Home Sec and Min of Home Security Oct. 1940–May 1945. Member of War Cabinet 1942–5. Dep PM 1945–51. Ld Pres of Council and leader of Commons, 1945–51.

LORD MOYNE, 1st Baron, see GUINNESS, WALTER EDWARD

NEWSAM, FRANK AUBREY
(1893–1964): Home Office. Private Sec to Sir John Anderson 1925–8. Principal Private Sec to Home Sec 1928–33. Asst Sec 1933. Principal Officer, South-east Civil Defence Region 1939. Asst US in charge of security 1940. Dep US 1941. KBE 1943. PUS 1948–57.

PARKIN, REGINALD THOMAS
(b. 1882): Foreign Office, Passport Control Department (PCD). Served in First World War. Employed subsequently in the intelligence depts of War Office and Home Office. Asst Director PCD Nov. 1919. Senior Staff Officer 1940. Employed in Foreign Office from Aug. 1941. Ret Feb. 1942.

PEAKE, OSBERT, 1st Viscount Ingleby (1955)
(1897–1966): Con MP 1929–55. Parl US, Home Office 1939–44.

PEDDER, SIR JOHN
(1869–1956): Home Office. Asst Sec 1914. Principal Asst Sec by 1925. Ret 1932.

PHILLIPS, SIR FREDERICK
(1884–1943): Treasury. US 1933. Treasury representation in Washington 1940–3. 2nd Sec July 1942.

PLAYFAIR, EDWARD WILDER
(1909–99): Board of Inland Revenue Secretaries' Office 1931–4. Asst Principal 1933. Treasury 1934–46, 1947–56. PUS War Office 1956–9. Permanent Sec, Min of Defence 1960–1. KCB 1957.

RANDALL, ALEC WALTER GEORGE
(1892–1977): Foreign Office. Sec to Legation to Holy See 1925. Bucharest 1930. 1st Sec (Far Eastern Dept) 1933–5. Copenhagen 1935–8. Acting Counsellor in Foreign Office Oct. 1938. Adviser on League of Nations Affairs 1939. Seconded to Min of Information Dec. 1939. Resumed duty in Foreign Office June 1940. Counsellor Oct. 1940. Head, Refugee Department 1942–4. Br Min Copenhagen June 1945. KCMG 1947.

ROBINSON, COURTENAY DENIS CAREW
(1887–1958): Home Office. Asst Sec 1932. Asst US by 1938. Seconded to Prison Commission as Acting Chairman 1940.

ROTHSCHILD, ANTHONY GUSTAV DE
(1887–1961): Banker. Partner in firm N. M. Rothschild & Sons. Chairman of Central British Fund for German Jewry 1939.

RUMBOLD, SIR HORACE GEORGE MONTAGUE, Bart
(1869–1941): Foreign Office. Br Amb in Berlin 1928–33. Vice-Chairman Palestine Royal Commission, 1936.

SAMUEL, SIR HERBERT LOUIS, 1st Viscount Samuel (1937)
(1870–1963): Lib MP, 1902–18, 1929–35. Parl US Home Office 1905. Chancellor Duchy of Lancaster 1909. Postmaster-General 1910. President Local Govt Board 1914. Postmaster-General 1915. Chancellor Duchy of Lancaster 1915. Home Sec 1916. Resigned 1916. 1st High Commissioner for Palestine 1920–5. Home Sec Aug. 1931–Sep. 1932. Resigned 1932. Chairman Council for German Jewry 1936–9. Chairman Movement for Care of Children from Germany 1938–9. Lib Leader in House of Lords 1944–55.

SCHIFF, OTTO MORRIS, OBE
(1875–1952): Born Frankfurt, Germany. Emigrated to UK. Stockbroker. Voluntary work with refugees during and after First World War. President of Jews' Temporary Shelter from 1922. Founder and Chairman of Jewish Refugees Committee from March 1933. CBE 1939.

SCHONFELD, RABBI SOLOMON
(1912–84): Presiding Rabbi Union of Orthodox Hebrew Congregations and Adath Yisroel Synagogue. Principal Jewish Secondary Schools. Executive Director Chief Rabbi's Religious Emergency Council from 1938.

SCOTT, SIR (ROBERT) RUSSELL
(1877–1960): Home Office. PUS 1932–8.

SIMON, SIR JOHN ALLSEBROOK, 1st Viscount Simon (1940)
(1873–1954): Foreign Sec 1931–5. Home Sec 1935–7. Chancellor of Exchequer 1937–40. Ld Chancellor 1940–5.

SIMPSON, SIR JOHN HOPE
(1868–1961): Authority on refugee problems. Indian Civil Service 1889–1916. Lib MP 1922–4. Vice-President League of Nations Refugee Settlement Commission, Athens 1926–30. Chosen to report on administration of Palestine 1930. Director, National Flood Relief Commission, China 1931–4. Administration of Newfoundland 1934–6. KBE 1937. Author of studies of refugee problem 1938–9.

SNOW, THOMAS MAITLAND
(1890–1997): Foreign Office. Tokyo 1930. Madrid 1934. Br Minister Havana 1935–7, Helsinki 1937. Transferred to Foreign Office 1940. Head of Refugee Section, General Dept of Foreign Office 1941. Br Min Bogota 1941–4, Amb 1944–5. Switzerland 1946–9.

STEVENSON, RALPH CLARMONT SKRINE
(1895–1977): Foreign Office 1933. Acting Counsellor Jan. 1937. Adviser on League of Nations Affairs 1937–8. Barcelona Oct. 1938. Private Sec to Foreign Sec Dec. 1939. Br Min Montevideo Aug. 1941. Amb to Yugoslav Govt in Cairo 1943. KCMG 1946.

STOPFORD, ROBERT JEMMETT
(1895–1978): Banker. Served in First World War, Friends' Ambulance Unit 1914–15, Royal Army Service Corps 1915–19 reaching rank of Lieutenant. Salonika 1915. Palestine and Egypt 1917. Banking 1921–38. Private Sec Chairman of the Indian Statutory Commission 1928–30. Sec to Cons delegation to Indian Round Table Conferences 1930–2. Sec to Joint Cttee of British Short-Term Creditors (Standstill Committee) 1933–8. Temporarily attached to Treasury for negotiations in connection with the Anglo-German Payments Agreement 1938. Member of Runciman Mission to Czechoslovakia 1938. Treasury Liaison Officer for financial and refugee questions with Czech gov Nov. 1938–Aug. 1939. In Second World War Head of Financial Pressure Dept, Min of Economic Warfare Sep. 1939–July 1940, and Financial Counsellor to Washington Embassy July 1940–3. Deputy Director of Civil Affairs

(Economics), later Director of Economics (Civil Affairs), War Office 1943–5. Trieste Boundary Commission and administration of Trieste 1946–9. Vice-Chairman Imperial War Museum 1954–68.

STRANG, WILLIAM, 1st Baron Strang (1954)
(1893–1978): Foreign Office Acting Counsellor Moscow 1930. London Oct. 1933. Adviser on League of Nations Affairs 1936. Head of Central Dept 1937. Acting Asst US Sep. 1939. KCMG Nov. 1943. UK Rep on European Advisory Commission with rank of Ambassador Nov. 1943. PUS 1949–53.

TURK, ERICH (no dates available)
Jewish War Refugees Committee. Hon Sec Jews' Temporary Shelter in 1933. British Committee for Refugees from Czechoslovakia 1938–9. Trustee, Czech Refugee Trust Fund 1939.

TURNOUR, EDWARD, 6TH EARL WINTERTON
(1883–1962): Irish peer (became member of House of Lords when created English peer in 1952). Con MP 1904–51. Chancellor of Duchy of Lancaster 1937–9. March 1938 entered Cabinet as Deputy Sec for Air. Paymaster-General Jan.–Nov. 1939 (no longer in Cabinet). Displaced 1940–5. Represented UK at Evian Conference July 1938. Chairman Intergovernmental Committee on Refugees 1938.

VANSITTART, SIR ROBERT GILBERT, Lord Vansittart (1941)
(1881–1957): Foreign Office. PUS 1930–7. Chief Diplomatic Adviser Jan. 1938–41.

WALEY, (SIR SIGISMUND) DAVID (né SCHLOSS)
(1887–1962): Treasury from 1910. Military service 1916–19. Worked on international finance with Sir Frederick Leith-Ross from 1919. Asst Sec 1924. Princ Asst Sec 1931. Worked on structure of exchange control during Second World War. KCMG 1943. Third Sec 1946–7.

WALKER, EDWARD ALAN
(b. 1894): Foreign Office. 1st Sec 1932. Athens 1934–6. Transferred to Foreign Office July 1936. Stockholm May 1938. Angora (Ankara) May 1939. London May 1941. In Refugee Department 1941–4.

WEIZMANN, CHAIM
(1874–1952): Zionist leader. 1st President of State of Israel 1948.

WHISKARD, SIR GEOFFREY GRANVILLE
(1886–1957): Dominions Office. Asst US and Vice Chairman of Oversea Settlement Department in 1933. PUS Min of Works 1941–3, Town and Country Planning 1943–6.

LORD WINTERTON, 6TH EARL See TURNOUR, EDWARD

WOLFE, HUMBERT
(1886–1940): Min of Labour. Director of Services and Establishments in 1933. Head of Employment and Training 1934. Deputy Sec 1938–40.

WOOD, EDWARD FREDERICK LINDLEY, Baron Irwin
(1881–1959): Succeeded father as Viscount Halifax 1934. Created Earl 1944. Sec for War 1935. Ld Privy Seal and Leader of House of Lords 1935–7. Ld Pres of Council 1937. Foreign Sec Feb. 1938–40. Br Amb to USA 1940–6.

Appendix 2: Home secretaries and Home Office permanent under secretaries, 1906–1950

Secretary of state for the Home Department

Date appointed	
10 Dec. 1905	H. Gladstone
14 Feb. 1910	W. Churchill
23 Oct. 1911	R. McKenna
25 May 1915	Sir J. Simon
10 Jan. 1916	Sir H. Samuel
10 Dec. 1916	Sir G. Cave
10 Jan. 1919	Sir E. Shortt
24 Oct. 1922	W. Bridgeman
22 Jan. 1924	A. Henderson
6 Nov. 1924	Sir W. Joynson-Hicks
7 June 1929	J. Clynes
25 Aug. 1931	Sir H. Samuel
28 Sep. 1932	Sir J. Gilmour
7 June 1935	Sir J. Simon
28 May 1937	Sir S. Hoare
3 Sep. 1939	Sir J. Anderson
3 Oct. 1940	H. Morrison
24 May 1945	Sir D. Somervell
3 Aug. 1945	J. Chuter Ede

Permanent under secretary of the Home Department

1903	Sir M. Chalmers
1908	Sir E. Troup
1922	Sir J. Anderson
1932	Sir R. Scott
1938	Sir A. Maxwell
1948	Sir F. Newsam

Selected bibliography

This bibliography lists unpublished sources consulted, though not necessarily cited. Abbreviations used in the notes to refer to unpublished sources appear in square brackets alongside the full listings given below. Published sources consulted are excluded, but are given full references where they are first cited in the notes.

1 UNPUBLISHED DOCUMENTARY SOURCES

UNITED KINGDOM

1.i *Government papers* (all Public Record Office, Kew)
Record classes consulted (in the notes all citations are given the prefix PRO)

ADMIRALTY
ADM 1 Admiralty and Secretariat Papers, 1660–1976

BOARD OF TRADE
BT 11 Commercial Department: Correspondence and Papers, 1860–1973
BT 56 Chief Industrial Adviser, 1929–32
BT 211 German Division Files, 1944–53

CABINET OFFICE
CAB 15 Committee of Imperial Defence – Co-ordination of Departmental Action Committees, 1911–39
CAB 16 Committee of Imperial Defence, Ad Hoc Sub-Committees, 1905–36
CAB 21 Cabinet Office Registered Files, 1916–60
CAB 23 Cabinet Minutes to 1939, 1916–39
CAB 24 Cabinet Memoranda to 1939, 1915–39
CAB 26 Home Affairs Committee, 1918–39
CAB 27 Committees General Series to 1939, 1915–39
CAB 63 Hankey Papers, 1908–44
CAB 65 Cabinet Minutes 1939–45
CAB 66 Cabinet Memoranda WP and CP Series, 1939–45

CAB 67 Cabinet Memoranda WP (G) Series, 1939–41
CAB 71 Lord President's Committee, 1940–6
CAB 78 Committees, Miscellaneous and General Series, 1941–7
CAB 79 Chiefs of Staff Committee, Minutes of Meetings, 1939–46
CAB 80 Chiefs of Staff Committee (Memoranda), 1939–46
CAB 95 Committees on the Middle East and Africa, 1939–45
CAB 98 Miscellaneous Committees, 1939–47
CAB 104 Supplementary Registered Files, 1923–51
CAB 118 Ministers' Files, 1938–47
CAB 124 Minister of Reconstruction, Lord President of the Council and Minister for Science: Secretariat Files, 1940–65
CAB 128 Cabinet: Minutes (CM and CC series), 1945–74
CAB 129 Cabinet: Memoranda (CP and C series), 1945–67

COLONIAL OFFICE

CO 733 Palestine Original Correspondence, 1921–49

DOMINIONS OFFICE

DO 5 Overseas Settlement Register of Correspondence, 1927–36
DO 35 Dominions Office and Commonwealth Relations Office: Original Correspondence, 1926–61
DO 57 Overseas Settlement Original Correspondence, 1926–36
DO 121 Private Office Papers, 1911–55
DO 175 Commonwealth Relations Office: Migration: Registered File (MIG series), 1954–60

FOREIGN OFFICE

FO 366 Chief Clerk's Department, Archives, 1719–1959
FO 371 Foreign Office – General Correspondence: Political, 1906–57
FO 372 General Correspondence (after 1906) Treaty, 1906–60
FO 404 Confidential Print Central Europe, 1920–47
FO 409 Indexes (Printed Series) to General Correspondence, 1920–51
FO 612 Passport Office: Correspondence, 1815–1974
FO 660 War of 1939 to 1945: Ministers Resident, etc., 1942–5
FO 741 Embassy and Consular Archives Austria: Vienna 1934–47
FO 800 Private Collections: Ministers and Officials: Various, 1824–1960
FO 837 Ministry of Economic Warfare, 1931–51
FO 916 War of 1939 to 1945: Consular (War) Department: Prisoners of War and Internees
FO 919 Archives of Intergovernmental Committee on Refugees, Evian, 1938
FO 1005 Control Commission for Germany: Records Library 1943–59
FO 1052 Control Commission for Germany: Prisoners of War and Displaced Persons Division, 1944–52

HOME OFFICE

HO 45 Home Office Registered Papers, 1839–1971
HO 144 Home Office Registered Papers, Supplementary, 1868–1947

HO 213 Home Office: Aliens Department: General (GEN) Files and Aliens Naturalisation and Nationality (ALN and NTY Symbol Series) Files, 1920–61
HO 214 Internees: Personal Files, 1940–9
HO 215 Internment: General Files, 1940–51
HO 294 Czechoslovak Refugee Trust: Records, 1938–79
HO 326 Home Office – Long Papers, 1897–1963
HO 356 Home Office Establishment Division S.GEN Files, 1908–57

MINISTRY OF LABOUR

LAB 2 Correspondence, 1897–1933
LAB 7 Nominal and Subject Indexes to Correspondence, 1897–1933
LAB 8 Employment, 1909–73
LAB 13 Overseas 1923–67

MINISTRY OF AGRICULTURE, FISHERIES AND FOOD

MAF 47 Labour and Wages Correspondence and Papers, 1900–59

MINISTRY OF HEALTH

MH 55 Ministry of Health: Health Division: Public Health Services, Registered Files (93000 series) and Other Records, 1853–1970
MH 57 Local Government Board and Ministry of Health: Poor Law Department and Successors: Public Assistance, Registered Files and Papers, 1907–70
MH 58 General Health Questions, 1910–12
MH 76 Emergency Medical Services, 1935–70

PRIME MINISTER'S FILES

PREM 1 Prime Minister's Office: Correspondence and Papers, 1916–40
PREM 4 Confidential Papers, 1939–46

TREASURY

T 160 Finance Files, 1887–1948
T 161 Supply Files, 1905–51
T 162 Establishment Files, 1890–1948
T 165 Blue Notes, 1880–1968
T 172 Chancellor of the Exchequer's Office: Miscellaneous Papers, 1792–1960
T 187 Special Areas Loans Advisory Committee, 1937–48
T 188 Leith Ross Papers, 1898–1968
T 199 Establishment Officer's Branch: Files, 1821–1935
T 210 Czechoslovak Financial Claims Office: Files, 1939–47
T 220 Imperial and Foreign Division: Files, 1914–61
T 221 Law and Order Division: Files, 1880–1977
T 231 Treasury: Exchange Control Division: Registered Files (EC and ECA series), 1936–62
T 236 Overseas Finance Division: Files, 1920–66

TREASURY SOLICITOR

TS 26 Treasury Solicitor and HM Procurator General: War Crimes Papers, 1919–46

TS 27 Registered Files: Treasury and Miscellaneous Services, 1843–1971

OTHER

AST 11 Unemployment Assistance Board and Assistance Board: Second World War Assistance, Registered Files, 1914–54

HW 1 Government Code Cypher School: Signals Intelligence passed to the Prime Minister, Messages and Correspondence, 1940–5

PRO 30/69 Ramsay MacDonald Papers, 1793–1937

PRO 30/78 Anglo-American Committee of Enquiry on Palestine, 1945–7

1. ii *Private papers*

Listed by location

Birmingham University Library
Neville Chamberlain [NC]

Board of Deputies of British Jews, London
Committee and Departmental Papers: General papers – Refugees

Bodleian Library, Oxford
Society for the Protection of Science and Learning (including papers of the Academic Assistance Council) [SPSL]

British Library, London
James Chuter Ede

British Library of Political and Economic Science, London
Lord Beveridge
Sir Andrew MacFadyean
Herbert Morrison (Jones/Donoghue papers)
Political and Economic Planning (PEP)

Cambridge University Library
Lord Baldwin
Sir Francis Meynell [Meynell]
Viscount Templewood (Sir Samuel Hoare)

Churchill Archives Centre, Churchill College, Cambridge
Professor Archibald Vivian Hill
Lord Noel-Baker [Noel-Baker]

Imperial War Museum, London
Julian Layton
Robert Stopford

Institute of Jewish Affairs, London
World Jewish Congress (British Section)

Library of the Religious Society of Friends, [SOF] London
Germany Emergency Committee[GEC] Minutes

Liverpool University Library
Eleanor Rathbone

Parkes Library, University of Southampton
Archives of the Council of Christians and Jews
Mrs Leslie Edgar
Cissy B. Rosenfelder
Rabbi Solomon Schonfeld

Rothschild Archive, [RA] London
Anthony de Rothschild
Lionel de Rothschild

Wiener Library, London
Central British Fund for World Jewish Relief (microfilm) [CBF]
Council for German Jewry

UNITED STATES OF AMERICA

1.iii *Government papers*

US National Archives, Washington, DC
Records of the Department of State (Record Group 59), Central Decimal File, File numbers: 548.G1; 740.0011 European War 1939; 740.0016 European War 1939; 840.48 Refugees; 862.4016

1.iv *Private papers*
Listed by location

American Jewish Joint Distribution Committee, New York
Archives of the American Jewish Joint Distribution Committee, 1933–44 [AJDC]

Columbia University, Rare Book and Manuscript Library, New York
Paul Baerwald
James G. McDonald

Franklin D. Roosevelt Presidential Library, Hyde Park, New York
Henry Morgenthau Jnr
Records of the War Refugee Board

Leo Baeck Institute, New York
Margaret Czellitzer

Library of Congress, Manuscripts Division, Washington, DC
Felix Frankfurter
Cordell Hull
Harold L. Ickes
Breckinridge Long [Long]

New York Public Library, Rare Books and Manuscripts Division
Emergency Committee in Aid of Displaced Foreign Scholars

United Nations Archives, New York
UNRRA Records, PAG-4/2.0.6.2. European Region

YIVO Institute of Jewish Research, New York
HIAS (Hebrew Immigrant Aid Society) and HICEM Central Office, New York RG 245.4
HICEM European Office RG 245.5
HICEM Lisbon Office 245.6

FRANCE

1. v *Government papers*
Centre d'accueil et de recherche des Archives Nationales [CARAN], *Paris*
AJ 43 Organisation internationale des réfugiés – 8–23, 29, 36, 37, 40, 44, 45, 46, 50, 52, 630

2 UNPUBLISHED THESES, ETC.

Baldwin, Nicholas, 'Catalogue of the Archive of the Society for the Protection of Science and Learning', Bodleian Library, Oxford (1988) (NR 31126)
Cesarani, David, 'Zionism in England 1919–1939', DPhil. thesis, University of Oxford (1986)
Kushner, Tony, 'British Antisemitism in the Second World War', Ph.D thesis, University of Sheffield (1986)
London, Louise, 'British Immigration Control Procedures and Jewish Refugees, 1933–1942', Ph.D thesis, University of London (1992)
McDonald, Andrew, 'The Formulation of British Public Expenditure Policy 1919–1924', Ph.D thesis, University of Bristol (1988)
O'Halpin, Eunan, 'Sir Warren Fisher, Head of the Civil Service, 1919–1939', Ph.D thesis, University of Cambridge (1982)
Pellew, Jill, 'Administrative Change in the Home Office, 1870–1896', Ph.D thesis, University of London (1976)
Sherman, A. Joshua, 'British Government Policy Towards Refugees from the Third Reich, 1933–1939', DPhil. thesis, University of Oxford (1970)

Shoenberg, David, 'Early Low Temperature Physics in Cambridge', paper given at seminar, 'Chapters in the History of Low Temperature Research in Britain', Royal Institution, London, 26 October 1988 (copy in author's possession)

Stacey, Stephen, 'The Ministry of Health, 1919–1929: Ideas and Practice in a Government Department', DPhil. thesis, University of Oxford (1984)

3 ORAL HISTORY COLLECTIONS

British Library National Sound Archive, London

Recordings: 2047–8 LP 2035b 6–8 Children in Flight; 2716 LP 2716f2 Sir Norman Angell

Columbia University Oral History Collection, New York

Herbert Pell

George Rublee

Imperial War Museum, Department of Sound Records, London

Britain and the Refugee Crisis, 1933–1947

4 INTERVIEWS

Mr Fred Baerwald, 1990, New York

Mrs Nancy Baster, 1993, Clandon, Surrey

Sir Isaiah Berlin, 1989, Oxford

Mrs Hilary Bradshaw, 1988, London

Mr Joseph Bradshaw, 1988, London

Dr Josephine Bruegel, 1988, London

Mrs Catherine Charlton, 1995, Hartford, Cheshire

Mr Albert Cooper, 1989, London

Dr Frank Falk, 1989, London

Mr Ernst Guter, 1989, London

Mrs Jenifer Hart, 1994, Oxford

Mr Sylvain Hayum, 1990, New York

Mrs Susanne Horwell, 1988, London

Mrs Beryl Hughes, 1988, Oxford

Mr Gerald Jackman, 1988, Leeds

Mrs Eva Jones, 1988, London

Mr Rudi Jones, 1988, London

Mr Leo Kahn, 1988, Wembley

Mr Herbert Katzki, 1990, New York

Dr Sullivan Kaufmann, 1987, London

Mr Julian Layton, 1988, London

Mrs Gertrud Levi, 1989, London

Mr Ernst Littauer, 1988, London

Mrs Ilse Meyer, 1988, London

Mrs Ruth Piuck, 1988, London

Sir Edward Playfair, 1997, London
Professor Peter Pulzer, 1987, Oxford
Mrs Susanne Rosenstock, 1989, London
Dr Werner Rosenstock, 1988 and 1989, London
Mr Edmund de Rothschild, 1990, London
Lord Sainsbury, 1989, London
Lord Sherfield, 1990, London
Lady Charlotte Simon, 1985, Oxford
Miss Joan Steibel, 1988, London
Mr Ernst Sterne, 1988, Leeds
Mrs Ruth Sterne, 1988, Leeds
Professor Gunther Treitel, 1987, Oxford
Mrs Sabina Wistrich, 1988, London
Dr Walter Zander, 1989, Croydon

Index

Printed in the United Kingdom
by Lightning Source UK Ltd.
93246